THE TROUBLE WITH HUMAN NATURE

The Trouble with Human Nature brings together biological and cross-cultural evidence to critically examine common preconceptions and challenge popular assumptions about human nature. It sets out to counter genetic and evolutionary myths about human variation and behavior, drawing on both biological and cultural anthropology, as well as from other disciplines including psychology, economics, and sociology.

The chapters address topics such as health and disease, gender and other differences, and violence and conflict. The analysis calls into question the presumed natural foundation for social inequalities and sheds light on both the constraints and possibilities inherent in the human condition.

This book provides students of human diversity and variation, human evolution, and biological anthropology with an excellent resource to better understand human nature. It will also be of interest to those taking courses with a biocultural focus within the fields of social and cultural anthropology, health and medical anthropology, sociology, gender studies, and kinship studies.

Elizabeth D. Whitaker is a biocultural anthropologist specializing in human health, social history, and the relationship between cultural beliefs and scientific thought. She teaches at the Università degli Studi di Bologna, Italy, and has taught anthropology in the United States for a number of years.

THE TROUBLE WITH HUMAN NATURE

Health, Conflict, and Difference in Biocultural Perspective

Elizabeth D. Whitaker

Routledge
Taylor & Francis Group
LONDON AND NEW YORK

First published 2017
by Routledge
2 Park Square, Milton Park, Abingdon, Oxon OX14 4RN

and by Routledge
711 Third Avenue, New York, NY 10017

Routledge is an imprint of the Taylor & Francis Group, an informa business

British Library Cataloguing-in-Publication Data
A catalogue record for this book is available from the British Library

Library of Congress Cataloging-in-Publication Data
A catalog record for this title has been requested

ISBN: 978-1-138-21193-3 (hbk)
ISBN: 978-1-138-21194-0 (pbk)
ISBN: 978-1-315-45173-2 (ebk)

Typeset in Bembo
by Apex CoVantage, LLC
Printed and bound by CPI Group (UK) Ltd, Croydon, CR0 4YY

CONTENTS

PART I
Pathways to the present **1**

1 Envisioning evolution: representations of humanness and causation 3

2 Origin stories: the co-evolution of human anatomy and sociality 23

3 Losses and gains: economic and health transitions since the Neolithic Revolution 47

PART II
Plasticity, identity, and health **73**

4 Thicker than water: blood and milk in human evolution 75

5 Risk and responsibility: power and danger in individualized approaches to preventive health 100

6 Difference as destiny: race, sex, and culture 125

PART III
Sex and gender **147**

7 Choosers and cheaters: the sexual/reproductive conflict hypothesis 149

8 Hoe and plow, pig and cow: work, family, and gender stratification 172

9 Tale of two-spirits: constructing gender and sexuality, aptitudes and inclinations 194

PART IV
Conflict and violence **217**

10 Savage empathy: sources of competitiveness and cooperativeness, greed and generosity 219

11 Why stratify? Inequality and interpersonal violence 242

12 Peace and war: patterns and prevention of violent intergroup conflict 264

Appendix: Life expectancy rate calculations *286*
Index *299*

PART I
Pathways to the present

1

ENVISIONING EVOLUTION

Representations of humanness and causation

Narratives about a dark, self-interested human nature call for a forbidding prehistoric world. Its inhabitants consist of energetic, menacing males who range around in the open while a few idle females huddle in caves looking after a string of babies. Their circumstances are grim: food is scarce in the hot savannah, predators and murderers lurk everywhere, and warfare knocks down those who have not already succumbed to disease, starvation, or violent death. There are no governments, police forces, or prisons to maintain order. Together the people and setting add up to short lives, social stratification, gender inequalities, and relentless violence.

This primordial scenario leads to seemingly self-evident conclusions, such as the idea that humans are born territorial and fearful of strangers, or that groups naturally organize around male relatives and their respective families – ready armies for the all-out warfare. It follows that this in-the-wild humanness has reached us through genes that orchestrate our every movement, but whose controlling role may be clouded by the distorting influence of civilization. In other words, nature and culture are separate things.

Alternatives exist: the noble savage, Adam and Eve before the Fall, the innocence of babes. These images of original goodness suggest that there may be more to human nature than cruel origins and a competitive-individualist nature. Casual observation shows that most behavior within and across societies is prosocial or at least neutral instead of antisocial, and that genetic expression is contingent and complicated. Mutual unconditional love and shared responsibility within families provides an antimodel for the collision-of-wills version of human relationships. "Modern" culture continues to connect humans, nature, and the supernatural through the mystical qualities assigned to power foods, weather events, and restorative travel destinations, in spite of a scientific rationality that allegedly disenchanted the landscape centuries ago. Medical procedures such as blood and organ transfer blur the boundaries separating bodies, digital information storage decenters and collectivizes knowledge, and mounting evidence shows that everything from habits to happiness moves through social networks.

Nonetheless, primitive individualism remains a dominant vision of humanness. It has informed Western government, philosophy, and science for many centuries.[1] Economic theories presume individual responsibility and rational self-interest; political systems promise to subdue natural anarchy. By now, the idea of a genetically determined essence rooted in the faraway past is practically invisible as an indisputable truth rather than a culturally specific idea.

How we think about humanness matters for science, policy, and personal life. The following chapters trace some of the implications in relation to a set of interrelated themes concerning health, human differences, and conflict. This chapter lays the groundwork by identifying dominant ideas about evolution and causation through some of their surface manifestations, and examining the process by which conceptual categories shape perceptions of the world and its meaning.[2]

.....

As a cultural symbol, the gene plays momentous roles: psychic and sage, designer and destroyer. Genes give some people poverty, negativity, or chemical dependency; to others they grant happiness, leadership, or scientific proficiency. The complete gene set is construed as each person's immortal essence, a blueprint or instruction manual that determines everything and is passed on intact from one generation to the next – as if the crossing-over and re-assortment that occur during meiosis did not shuffle genes, scramble chromosomes, and yield genetically unalike half-full sex cells. With its transcendent qualities and its status as the true, unadulterated distillation of individual identity, DNA is contemporary culture's incarnation of the soul.

Although the Human Genome Project has shown otherwise (Commoner 2002), DNA continues to be depicted as an autonomous determining force which neither errs nor lies, unlike the outward actions and phenotypic traits of living things. Scientific and popular reports celebrate the sequencing of one after another organism's genome, as if the truth about them were now being brought to light once and for all. Even the dead must give up their secrets, such as the 15th century English King, Richard III, whose DNA is being sequenced at the University of Leicester.

Visual representations of DNA, customarily described as "maps," imply mastery of a territory. They suggest control over DNA, the chief orchestrator controlling us. In a vision popularized by Richard Dawkins (1976), this everlasting material essence only temporarily resides in individual bodies, which it uses for its own ends. People are just players in Nature's evolutionary drama, our movements the result of subterranean selective pressures and the compulsion to replicate our genes.

The narrative of genetic essentialism lends a grandiosity to DNA's powers that is reminiscent of religious accounts of the divine. The gene gives meaning to misfortune, explains why some individuals are more privileged than others, and holds the truth about human nature. It is no accident that genome sequencing is described as reading the mind of God, revealing God's secrets, and cracking God's code. As then-President Bill Clinton said at a White House event celebrating the sequencing of "the" human genome, "Today we are learning the language in which God created life" (New York Times 2000). Alternatively, knowledge and manipulation of DNA is criticized as "playing God"; to creationists, evolution is a fabrication, a form of trickery, an affront to the sacred.

The attribution of mystical qualities to DNA is apparent in advertising, the media, and everyday conversations that depict the gene as the essence of the individual and the engine of the living world. For instance, Pandora Media's (2016) Music Genome Project© selects playlists for clients based on analysis of their unique music-DNA. The company's official website explains that Pandora means "all gifted" in Greek, and that music from Apollo was one of several gifts the inquisitive maiden received from the gods. The chairman of the company is its "chief evangelist." This set of symbols and meanings suggests that the product delivers not only individualized attention but also edification through a felicitous blend of spiritual redemption, scientific ingenuity, and ancient wisdom.

While all humans' nearly identical DNA could be celebrated as a source of unity, the minute differences tend instead to be amplified in constructions of DNA as the reason for people's appearance and behavior, ancestry and destiny. Genes are credited with giving people special talents and determining their success or failure. Alternatively, genes may be invoked to absolve the individual of responsibility, as in the case of disease or deviant behavior. Either way, genetic essentialism makes learning and social context irrelevant. Nature and nurture, biology and environment, appear to be separate and distinct influences on development.

The idea that genes "for" particular traits ineluctably will reveal themselves sooner or later is buttressed by technological feats such as the high-fidelity storage of information in the form of DNA. Nick Goldman et al. (2013) have translated Shakespeare's sonnets, Dr. Martin Luther King Jr.'s speeches, and other documents from computer to nucleotide code, replicated the DNA strands, and translated the copies back to English. While the work showcases the quality of DNA as an information storage and replication system, it also seconds the prevalent notion that there is no interference between code and message, DNA and trait.

Media coverage disproportionately showcases studies that appear to demonstrate the existence of a "gene for" a particular attribute, and downplays multiple-gene causes and gene-environment interactions. For instance, a study reporting that a particular gene variant is associated with a higher likelihood of depression, provided it is combined with psychosocial stress, is announced with the headline, "Depression Gene Really Exists, New Study Claims" (Pappas 4 January 2011). Alternatively, there is a gene for joy: "'Happiness Gene' Discovered" (Adams 2011).

Even marital faithfulness appears to depend on a gene: "'Fidelity Gene' Found in Voles" (Kettlewell 2004). This story refers to manipulation of genes affecting vasopressin receptors in montane moles, which results in more trust and approach behavior. The voles behave similarly to prairie voles in that they form "monogamous" pair bonds instead of mating "promiscuously." Correlations between men's responses to a survey that included questions about intimate relationships, and the number of vasopressin-receptor gene copies they carry, are taken as proof that the same mechanism explains human marital fidelity: "Monogamy Gene Found in People" (Shetty 2008).

Other genes cause people to be rash and reckless: "Male Impulsivity and Addiction Linked to One Gene" (Pappas 18 November 2011). Yet others make people destined for crime: "Life of Crime Is in The Genes, Study Claims" (*Telegraph* 2012); "Can Your Genes Make You Murder?" (Hagerty 2010). These stories have a concrete impact. Judges and juries have demonstrated more leniency towards violent criminals who carry gene variants associated with a higher frequency of violence, such as a variant of the gene for monoamine oxidase A that, however, correlates with increased violence only if combined with stressful life circumstances (Aspinwall et al. 2012). Evidently, it is assumed that these genes make criminals incapable of exercising free will and moral responsibility and therefore that they should be punished less severely, even though the same logic of hardwiring suggests that these criminals are destined to repeat violent behavior and consequently should be subjected to stricter sentencing.

Political sympathies too would seem to come down to the genes: "Political Beliefs May Be Rooted in Genetics, Study Says" (Castillo 2012), and "Could Your Genes Influence How You Vote?" (Storrs 2012). This idea is based on twin studies, the source of data for many claims about the genetic determination of behavioral and cognitive traits. Researchers compare the scores of fraternal and identical twins on tests or surveys and attribute differences between the two groups' results to an inferred genetic mechanism. Castillo (2012) quotes an expert observer as stating that beliefs about issues including abortion and the death penalty are "strongly rooted in genetics. These are attitudes towards reproduction and survival."

Based on higher levels of agreement between identical than fraternal twins on 28 statements concerning social issues, political scientists John R Hibbing et al. (2013) conclude that political orientation is in the genes. While media reports imply that party affiliation is genetic, they favor the idea of a "political phenotype" or "predisposition" to view issues a particular way. In a study comparing levels of agreement with 28 statements concerning social issues such as taxes, pornography, and unions, they found a 53% genetic component for statements overall versus a 14% genetic component for party affiliation. The authors suggest that people's genetically determined social orientation towards either conservatism or progressivism is the reason why some individuals change party affiliation: they only overcome the environmental influence of being raised in a politically mismatched family after achieving independence in adulthood. The authors add that the growing polarization of gene pools owing to the tendency for people to choose ideologically similar spouses is the reason for the increasingly degraded tone of political debate and campaigning.

These far-reaching conclusions are drawn from modest data which have been generated through questionnaires rather than laboratory studies. The authors admit that most participants in the study did not answer consistently one way or the other across all the questions but rather had a slight bent towards conservative or progressive views. In addition, the level of agreement between fraternal twins was far from zero, while the level of agreement between identical twins was far from complete – as in the 0.46 versus 0.66 correlations for fraternal versus identical twins with respect to school prayer. In their enthusiasm for genetic determination, writers and pundits set aside all such doubts about data quality and interpretation. As a result, life experiences and social contexts appear to be immaterial to beliefs and values, except insofar as they can temporarily muddle the determining influence of the gene.

There is nothing controversial or earth-shattering in the idea that genes play a role in any trait. The trouble arises when rare single-gene diseases are assumed to model how complex behaviors, aptitudes, or thoughts arise. Statistical associations between traits and genetic relatedness or segments of DNA are taken to indicate genetic causation, without the need to demonstrate a biochemical mechanism. One leap leads to another: not only are complex traits reduced to single genes, but they are situated in an evolutionary narrative that reduces complex and variable phenomena into a single storyline and stamps it with the authority of timelessness.

. . . . .

The caveman origin story presents life as nasty and brief until modern times. History books teach that everyone used to die by age 30, or even in their late teens during especially dire times such as the late Roman Empire. College students read that "by 1300, almost every child born in Western Europe faced the probability of extreme hunger at least once or twice during his expected 30 to 35 years" (Bulliet et al. 2005). It appears as if human health has progressively improved from the earliest times to the present. In reality, the Neolithic transition to agriculture some 10,000 years ago brought more disease, violence, and inequality, with a decline in life expectancy.

Whether strategically or unwittingly, life expectancy rates are misrepresented as the typical age at which old people die in a given population. Consequently, today's high life expectancy rates appear to signify that the life span has been extended by 50 or more years and could be stretched out indefinitely: "People Are Living Longer and Healthier: Now What?" (Duke University 2010). The millions of Internet hits generated by the search string "people live longer modern medicine" speak to the assumption that increased life expectancy is a marvelous technical achievement and a reason for hope that immortality drugs are on the horizon. On the other hand, demographic changes are seen as portents of disaster due to the hordes of sickly or, alternatively, indefatigably healthy old people who threaten to burden society to the point of economic collapse: "New Burden of Disease Study Shows a World Living Longer and with More Disability" (Brown 2012); "Can We Afford to Live Longer in Better Health?" (Westerhout and Pellikaan 2005).

At the same time as life is construed as longer because it was short in the past, it has become popular to promote the Paleolithic lifestyle. This is based on the finding that it is extremely rare for present-day hunter-gatherers to suffer from major chronic diseases and disorders including obesity, cancer, and cardiovascular disease. Paleopathological analyses suggest that the same was true of our prehistoric ancestors. Consequently, while the caveman scenario conjures up images of early death from starvation and violence, it can also be associated with an image of physical fitness and good nutrition.

Inactivity together with a diet heavy in simple carbohydrates is unquestionably connected to today's major health problems. As shown in later chapters, an anthropological framework suggests a number of health-promoting practices in line with evolutionary principles and ancestral lifestyles, but they are not the ones behind "Paleo" diets, workouts, and attire marketed as identical to those used by our ancestors for millions of years and therefore adaptive, beneficial, and right. They do not dictate that people should run barefoot or in minimalist footwear, or that it is necessary to eat almost nothing but meat, as prescribed by the Atkins and similar diets, or, alternatively, mainly or only vegetables, as in Paleo-Vegan, Paleo-Vegetarian, and standard vegetarian diets.

These trends draw upon folklore about lusty cavemen who chased after wild animals with spears, or alternative visions of gentle gatherers. In reality, foraging diets contain a mixture of plant and animal foods, and humans have the physiological characteristics of omnivores. Rarely do people run in pursuit of food. Hunting is a recent activity that began after millions of years of scavenging, while cooking is an old one and is practiced by all societies. Significantly, the genome has not remained fixed for the last 10,000 years but instead has changed in important ways, including ones related to novel food sources such as milk from domesticated animals. Finally, an evolutionary perspective shows that diet, exercise, and time outdoors are not the whole story. People also need friends and social integration, which foraging societies promote through egalitarianism and mutual interdependence. In contrast, inequality and social isolation generate chronic stress that causes psychological and physical illness.

In addition to health, genetic-evolutionary reasoning is adaptable to theories of race as the product of biological divergence between a handful of huge groups of people differentiated by interlinked physical and mental traits. Henry Louis Gates (1999) argues that the Upper Nile was the true cradle of civilization; the ancient Nilotic cultures of Southern Egypt and the Sudan the origin of the scientific, philosophical, and material advances of all of the great civilizations of the ancient world and their successors. Leonard Jeffries suggests a deep biological explanation: dark-skinned people are smarter and more inventive than light-skinned people because they have more melanin, which is necessary for nervous system development (Ortiz de Montellano 1993). Geneticist Bruce Lahn recently proposed that two genes taking different evolutionary paths between Europeans and Africans were responsible for the brain power behind the rise of agriculture and the emergence of cities. He and his colleagues later established that the identified gene variants are not related to increased intelligence, but not before the earlier view had spread (Hayden 2013).

Besides the unverifiable assumption that major social transformations and cultural advancements arise because of cognitive changes or differences between populations, these racial interpretations of history are informed by the ethnocentric value judgment that economic and demographic expansion represents progress. Applying these same assumptions to contemporary societies, economists Quamrul Ashraf and Oded Galor (2013) argue that differences in the amount of genetic diversity within populations explain cross-national differences in economic development, measured as per-capita income with respect to the industrial era and population density for earlier times. Like other genetic just-so stories, the argument is based on circular logic – genetic diversity must bring more creativity because creative populations have more genetic diversity.

Ultimate explanations for gender roles and violence center upon ancient reproductive competition among males within groups, and between coalitions of males against each other, that allows violent males to leave more offspring. The proof would seem to lie in chimpanzee coalitional violence, as suggested by the science section of the *Telegraph*: "Apes of War. . .Is It in Our Genes?" (O'Connell 2004). The idea of a biological predisposition to violence resonates in a stratified society which entertains itself with physical and sexual violence, real and imagined, and whose media present crime, warfare, and inequality as chronic afflictions throughout the world. It is no wonder the chimpanzee is the chosen ape for comparisons to humans, rather than more peaceable, less hierarchical species such as bonobos. Anthropologist Napoleon Chagnon's reports on Yanomami violence remain a widely cited substantiation of humankind's natural thirst for blood, in spite of disputed data and the fact that the tribes are not representative of ancestral human foraging societies (see Chapter 10).

The idea that females represent passive resources over which males compete presumes hostile, competitive relationships between the sexes owing to incompatible sexual and reproductive interests. Cooperation would seem to be just a tenuous stand-off that allows couples to propagate their genes. Men are reduced to mating machines who are evolutionarily driven to inseminate as many females as possible while investing as little as they can get away with in intimate relationships and paternal care. This impulse supposedly gives men an inborn attraction to young and therefore more fertile females which makes them fixate on women's physical appearance. In contrast, women are assumed to be utterly dependent on men for provisions, thanks to the unending string of babies that chains them to the cave. Their helplessness supposedly renders women indifferent to looks because what matters to them is wealth: as a result, they naturally seek to snag an older male.

With reference to a brain-imaging study showing 15 male college students' willingness to risk more money in a game of roulette if they were first shown a picture of a woman (Knutson et al. 2008), one of the researchers, finance professor Camelia Kuhnen, is quoted in a newspaper article as saying, "You have a need in an evolutionary sense for both money and women. They trigger the same brain area." A professor not involved in the study adds, "The link between sex and greed goes back hundreds of thousands of years, to men's evolutionary role as provider or resource gatherer to attract women" (Borenstein 2008). Yet, the men made higher bets if shown any pleasurable image, such as chocolate or a winning lottery ticket, than if they saw a frightening image such as a snake, or an uninteresting one such as a stapler. This is to be expected, for priming a human or other animal with pleasurable feelings leads to greater optimism and willingness to take risks, whereas negative emotions such as fear cause a reduction in risk-taking. The argument that men are hardwired to pursue and show off wealth to gain sexual opportunities might be more persuasive if women had been included in the research and had responded differently, but they were left out – both as subjects and as readers, as seen in the comments above.

It follows from the evolutionary scenario above that prehistoric life gave males and females different mental equipment and consequently different social roles. Disparities in the average frequency of all kinds of behavior or test performance are chalked up to the discrete skills needed for hunting versus gathering, provisioning versus nurturing. Men allegedly wound up with athletic, spatial, and leadership skills, whereas women got intuition, communications skills, and multitasking – differences that purportedly have been etched onto sex-specific brain features and connectivity patterns. The idea of separate evolutionary paths for women and men lead authors such as Liza Mundy (2012) to see contemporary masculinity and femininity as alarmingly under threat because men supposedly have no domestic experience and women no work experience, and each is facing new responsibilities for the first time.

These ideas have more to do with cultural beliefs than empirical realities, as seen in the following chapters. Like the other ideas discussed above, they illustrate the versatility of ultimate explanations for human characteristics and behavior, and their grounding in a narrative so dominant and expedient that it escapes scrutiny as a representation. The caveman origin story and its genetic record appear as one with reality.

.....

Final causes offer a sense of order and control in the face of complexity and chaos. In an unequal, unfair, and precarious world, assertions about the fixity of gender, race, and social class differences shut down discussion of causes and remedies. Economists such as Alix Peterson Zwane (2012) ponder whether poverty makes people reason poorly, or if people living in poverty are poor because they lack the right mental equipment. Conservative publications and hate groups reiterate the last century's fears about hordes of inferior people overwhelming the superior races, and the corruption of women by modern society's anti-natalist propaganda and liberal reproductive policies. Writers such as J. Philippe Rushton, Richard Lynn, and *The Bell Curve* authors Richard J. Herrnstein and Charles Murray (1994) argue that alleged racial differences are evident in quantitative data on reproductive potential and intellectual ability.

Genetic essentialism permits the view that privileged people's advantages come from Nature or God, not socioeconomic structures. Historical and politico-economic factors may be set aside if behavioral and intellectual differences are permanent, irremediable, and unevenly distributed between groups. In this view, people whose gender, ethnicity, sexuality, nationality, or socioeconomic class confine them to lower status and a poorer standard of living are differently made. In sum, social inequalities are rendered biological inequalities, meaning that problems such as poverty, crime, and health disparities are inevitable and natural, not contingent and human made.

These same ideas have flourished in other turbulent times. For instance, armed with Darwinian and Lombrosian principles of biological inheritance and behavioral causation, the eugenics movement of the first decades of the 20th century advanced the view that differences between individuals or groups come down to biological factors transmitted in the blood or germplasm. Political leaders and medical experts argued that diseases and faults including poverty, alcoholism, promiscuity, and laziness are transmitted by biological inheritance. Both dictatorships and democracies, including the US and Canada, instituted programs to promote childbearing among favored couples and to restrict the reproductive rights of the poor, mentally ill, and members of socially or ethnically disvalued groups.

The eugenics movement retreated after the Holocaust, which had shown the inhuman ends to which science may be turned. In the decades following the Second World War, Western society struggled with the consequences of racism, sexism, and authoritarianism. Economic recovery and expansion brought increased stability and reduced competition.

Now, at a distance of many decades, science appears detached from past errors. The Nuremberg Code and subsequent ethical rules would seem to have settled the question of medical abuses, and superior scientific knowledge makes current genetics seem distinct from pre-DNA science. Any continuity would seem to be broken, yet earlier eugenicists also believed they were operating according to the highest standards of objective, value-neutral science and for the long-term good of humanity. Ethical questions are as urgent today as ever, but they take a back seat to enthusiasm for new discoveries. As with the computer industry, the current cultural faith in science and technology suspends critical analysis, rendering every innovation unquestionably advantageous.

Media stories of the kind mentioned above trumpet the potential of genetic interventions to bring an end to disease, crime, disability, aging, and even mortality. Science appears poised to clone anyone, including famous historical figures, and to bring back long-extinct animals such as woolly mammoths from bits of DNA. The limits of prenatal testing seem infinite, as if all diseases and defects soon will be avoided through screening, preferably pre-implantation. If that is not enough, useful traits from other species could be inserted into the human genome, as is already being done across species, allowing humankind to truly manufacture babies to order.

The idea that DNA determines everything about human beings implies that the reasons for our troubles are simple and the solutions technological and therefore neutral. Genetic determinism directs research and policy towards understanding and manipulating the molecular constituents of individual bodies rather than analyzing and modifying the politico-economic systems and cultural values of societies. By tracing disease and behavioral defects to genes, it allows us to evade the tangle of complex influences on development and health. In short, by narrowing the focus we forestall the need to address the wider context, especially questions of power and profit.

An individualized, gene-centric view of causation, like the image of the cell as a self-contained molecular universe governed by nuclear DNA, recapitulates the Western view of the individual as an autonomous, bounded, self-determined unit with a mind of her or his own. These cultural values exalt individual agency over civic values and collective responsibility. For genes, cells, and individuals, the realities of existence are a different matter, but the ideal persists all the same. Products create the illusion of individualized attention out of the material of mass production, such as the musical genome mentioned above. Treasured metaphors such as the American dream and the little-red-engine-that-could sustain the belief that individual fortunes depend on effort and merit, even while social mobility declines and inequality and institutionalized unfairness rise. Self-help literature teaches that personal choices and behaviors determine health and mental wellbeing, promoting the image of the individual body/mind as independent and separate from others.

Upholding a determinist, reductionist view of causality benefits individuals and organizations, such as sellers of genetic and biomarker tests to predict disease risks. This industry nourishes the illusion that mapping individual genomes is tantamount to knowing what lies ahead in terms of illness, aging, and years of life – even though the biological as opposed to statistical connection between marker and disease may not be known, while preventive or curative treatments are not necessarily available. The genetic ancestry testing business likewise offers the promise of certainty about future diseases and past glories. Consumers are led to expect that their mailed-in saliva sample will definitively establish their true identity, such as Scandinavian, Native American, or West African in the case of Ancestry (2016), which also promises to "help deliver the richest family stories." Oxford Ancestors (2016) will identify a person's ancestral "clan mother" or, for men, the ancestral "paternal clan." Men from the UK can further determine which ancient tribe of Britain spawned them.

Companies including DNA Diagnostics Center (2016) provide consumers with genetic connections to famous historical figures such as Genghis Kahn. Gene by Gene (2016) offers clients the opportunity to authenticate their origin in esteemed populations such as the Kohanim (Cohanim), the Jewish priestly class thought to derive by direct patrilineal descent from Aaron, who lived 3,000 years ago. Looking forward, parents who desire advanced knowledge of their unborn children's characteristics can purchase probability estimates through the patented "Family Traits Inheritance Calculator" offered by the 23andMe company (2016). The very names of these companies suggest that genetic investigation is the key to self-knowledge: Roots for Real, Gene Tree, Genex Diagnostics.

Like traditional origin myths, the storyline cultivated by these companies involves the *de novo* sprouting of apical ancestors in a specific geographical location. Together with new allegedly race-specific medicines (see Chapter 6), they advance the notion that differences between people are attributable to the existence of a few genetically distinct groups of human beings, after all. The industry feeds on the belief that personality, preferences, abilities, and knowledge spring from genes inherited in blocks which travel as a pack from one generation to the next. The same reasoning explains why women from elite colleges command higher prices for eggs used in assisted reproduction, and why the qualities of sperm donors are described in catalogs for prospective parents to assess. It explains the use of sperm stored before death, or taken from a corpse, to create a child expected to embody its father's essence but destined never to meet him.

The optimism and enthusiasm for reductionism is evident in high levels of public acceptance of genetic screening tests. A survey by the Genetics and Public Policy Center (2007) found that 79% of respondents supported genetic testing for a disease for which no medication or treatment exists; the rate in the case of known treatment was 91%. On the other hand, the same study found that while the majority of respondents expressed trust in physicians, researchers, and spouses with regard to knowledge of their personal genetic information, slightly less than one-half trusted law enforcement, one-fourth trusted health insurance companies, and one-sixth trusted employers. Nonetheless, hospitals, research centers, criminal justice systems, the military, and private businesses avidly collect and store genetic data without waiting for questions of privacy and ethics to be resolved and with virtually no regard for donor access to data.[3] Individuals are encouraged to donate DNA samples for personal benefit and the good of humankind, but other individuals and institutions stand to profit materially, as is evident in the rush to patent genes and other segments of coding and noncoding DNA whose activity may not even be known.

The availability of technology, combined with the association of DNA with objectivity and exactitude, leads to new situations with complex and contradictory dimensions, such as demands for genetic testing of sick family members or deceased relatives who might have carried hazardous genes. In 2011, the CIA, with the help of a local public-health-service physician, ran a free hepatitis B vaccination program in Abbottabad in order to send nurses into Osama bin Laden's compound to obtain blood samples from his children. The purpose was to compare their genes to DNA from his sister, who had died the previous year, and thereby to confirm his whereabouts. The program disregarded the Nuremberg and other codes of medical ethics, and provided concrete reasons for the public to mistrust government and health workers, with potentially very detrimental downstream effects. The incident illustrates the seductiveness of genetic determinism and the ease with which it can lead to disregard for even the most straightforward rules of ethical conduct.

There is every reason to expect that, if given the chance, many parents would choose to manipulate their children's genes not just to avoid impairments or diseases, but also in pursuit of aesthetic or social advantage. Yet, even if single genes or gene combinations caused complex traits independently of other genes and regardless of environmental circumstances, and even if manipulation could achieve the desired result without collateral effects, it is far from clear that the goal of eliminating disabilities is acceptable or desirable from either an ethical or biological standpoint. Moreover, what counts as a disability or disease changes over time and from one culture to the next, as do standards of physical attractiveness as well as praiseworthy personality traits.

Existing medical procedures to promote growth suggest what would happen if people could choose traits based on high social value. In Western society, height correlates with income, especially for men. Parents are motivated to intervene in their children's growth by way of hormonal and surgical treatments. If all parents of shorter children did this and all children reached a height currently associated with economic advantage, the relative difference would disappear. This would push the bar literally higher and higher, at considerable cost in terms both of expenses and diseases associated with taller stature. Paradoxically, surgical and hormonal modifications of the face and body allow individuals who are different to chase capricious cultural ideals and in the process strengthen a social system that disvalues human variability.

Like parents who now choose their child's sex, parents offered genetic treatments with the promise of effects on behavior or cognitive traits would likely be ones most committed to deterministic beliefs about causation.[4] If they could have genes known to affect athletic performance inserted into their offspring's genome, they would be unlikely to allow their child to pursue a passion for poetry instead. If it were possible to order up an architect, parents would not tolerate a child who preferred forestry. This kind of parental tyranny is unlike others because it precludes children's individuality and their right to an open future, both of which arise from the unpredictability of genetic inheritance through sexual reproduction. Moreover, parents could be held accountable for failing to make use of technologies for giving their children special traits or preventing unwanted ones, which would increase social pressure towards conformity and intensify the already existing intolerance of diversity. Evidently, neoeugenics, like earlier forms of genetic determinism, is not simply nature's tool for pursuing the perfectibility of humankind.

. . . . .

To analyze how the ideas about evolution and genetic causation discussed above have come to be taken as commonsense truths about the nature of things, it will be helpful to review the impact of cultural categories on the way the mind organizes information. Shared beliefs influence thought from earliest infancy and affect everything from basic perceptions such as color and sound to abstract engagement in philosophical reasoning. Particularly salient cultural categories such as gender or race can become so thoroughly ingrained that they distort empirical observations and block acceptance of alternative ways of assessing evidence.

The dual nature of culturally bequeathed concepts as tools for thought and pattern recognition, but hindrances to empirical observation and analysis, has been recognized for centuries. In the early 1600s, Francis Bacon (1960) noted how the mind tends to perceive more order and regularity than truly exists. Bacon divided a large set of potential obstacles to scientific reasoning into four "Idols of the Mind." The Idols of the Tribe (Idola Tribus) cause the mind to assign human attributes to nonhuman entities, such as animals, divinities, natural forces – or, for a current example, genes and cells – giving them physical, mental, and motivational characteristics that are not their own. The Idols of the Cave or Den (Idola Specus) cause people to fail to notice the way their cultural beliefs and social identity filter their observations and color their interpretations. The Idols of the Marketplace (Idola Fori) have to do with the constraints imposed by language and constructions of meaning. Those of the Theater (Idola Theatri) concern the confining effect on the mind of blind faith in accepted beliefs and authorities. Each of these is at work in the persistence of caveman-style narratives about humanness.

The reason for the power of the Idols of the Mind is that our species requires culture for survival. Other animals such as newborn horses can stand up and run right away, but humans are born before the brain is fully developed and must continue growing outside the womb. We have to be taught how to live safely in our environment and how to get along with other people in order to learn from them. On the other hand, the mind is not a blank slate. It comes supplied with reactions and tendencies shared with nonhuman primates and other mammals. If a flying object swoops out of the sky, we duck. We are repelled by food that smells or looks spoiled. We demand fairness from others and know how to detect cheating – and perhaps to attempt it when circumstances are favorable. Even tiny babies have inborn social skills and mental models of fairness, along with an understanding of basic mathematical and physical principles.

Beginning at birth, we attend to the people around us. We learn to communicate through the language we hear, and we unconsciously take in our culture's symbolic constructs and categories. As a result, we tend not to question the pathways underlying our thoughts, and they may not even be accessible to our minds. Basic assumptions and categories are absorbed as the standard, which makes the beliefs of others deviations. Our ways appear spontaneous, natural, and right; theirs strange, abnormal, unnatural – in a word, wrong.

The subtle, unconscious processes that lead to this unwitting ethnocentrism begin early and affect the most basic perceptions. As children grow, they learn to attend to the relatively small number of vocalizations their language defines as phonemes, or meaningful sound contrasts. As a result of the winnowing process, the other, nonmeaningful sounds or gestures escape notice. Languages typically have 30–40 phonemes (English included, with about 40), a number that falls within a range from around 15 in Hawaiian to over 100 in some African languages that also use clicking sounds. For instance, "r" and "l" are phonemes in English but not Japanese; "b" and "v" are phonemes in English but not Spanish. Likewise, the number of recognized gesticulations varies widely across languages, from a handful to hundreds. The numbers are not fixed because languages change over time.

Similarly, the way a culture categorizes and names colors restricts the range of tones people identify. Color distinctions that are meaningful to one culture may not be acknowledged by another. For instance, English speakers and semi-nomadic Himba herders in Namibia see different things when presented a ring of 12 green swatches, one of which diverges slightly from the others. When the odd swatch is tinged with more red and less blue, the Himba participants immediately pick it out but the English speakers study the colors at length before attempting an answer. When the odd one is aqua-colored, the English speakers identify it readily but the Himba speakers take more time to venture a guess. These differences in perception correspond to differences in the way the respective languages classify colors.[5]

Culture affects not just what colors we see but also how we see them. In contemporary Euroamerican culture, the color pink is associated with femininity, blue with masculinity. Allegedly these color associations come from sex-based color preferences. As explained in an article in *The Guardian* entitled, "Pink for a Girl and Blue for a Boy – and It's All Down to Evolution," some neuroscientists maintain that girls and women prefer reddish tones because in the faraway past they had to be good at picking out red berries and appetizing leaves against a green background, whereas boys and men prefer blue because it indicates good weather for hunting (Wainwright 2007).

Not only is this a fanciful picture of gender roles in the past, but the gender difference in color preference is not supported by other evidence. Europeans and Americans of both sexes tend to prefer blue. Studies that include non-Western societies indicate that color preferences vary across and within populations, and that there is no universal pattern to explain them – including gender (Taylor et al. 2013). This is because color preferences are acquired by way of affective responses to objects that people associate with positive emotions. Chinese people's preference for red harmonizes with their belief that red brings good luck. American university students end up preferring their school's colors and favoring them to a degree proportional to the strength of their school spirit – such as blues and golds among Berkeley students, reds among Stanford students (Schloss et al. 2011).

If color preferences were inborn, then babies would express them, but infants do not exhibit any such gender difference. Indeed, a study of 12-, 18-, and 24-month-olds showed that both males and females prefer reddish tones, in addition to rounded as opposed to angular forms (Jadva et al. 2010). The color preferences of older children reflect the effects of living in a chromatically divided environment as is typical of wealthy consumer societies, with their arbitrary and capricious gender-and-color associations. A century ago, women's magazines encouraged American and British mothers to dress their boys in the robust, resolute color pink; their girls in gentle, graceful blue (Paoletti 2012). At the outset of the First World War, wounded junior officers taken to Mrs. Freddie Guest's house-turned-hospital in London were kept on the first floor and given blue silk pajamas; senior officers were hosted on the second level and wore pink (MacDonald 1993).

A study comparing languages with and without gendered nouns illustrates the degree to which symbolic associations permeate the objects that surround us (Boroditsky et al. 2003). The research participants were bilingual students who spoke either German or Spanish in addition to English. They were shown pictures of 24 objects which are male in German but female in Spanish, or vice versa, and asked to freely associate three adjectives with each object. The participants' word choices aligned with gender stereotypes: objects the students' native language defined as feminine were described as beautiful, fragile, and delicate, whereas masculine objects were imposing, resilient, and energetic. To Spanish speakers, a bridge, *el ponte,* was "strong," "sturdy," "towering," and "dangerous." To German speakers, the same object, *die Brücke*, was "elegant," "pretty," "fragile," and "peaceful." A key, feminine to Spanish speakers as *la llave*, was "little," "intricate," "golden," and "lovely"; as a masculine object to German speakers, *der Schlüssel* was "heavy," "jagged," "hard," and "useful." Significantly, these associations came through in a study run entirely in English.

In a second experiment, the researchers taught a group of English-only speakers an invented language that included female and male pronouns along with arbitrarily gendered nouns. The students memorized the name and gender of a series of objects such as violins, pens, and forks. They were presented pictures of objects to describe. As in the experiment with bilingual students, the chosen adjectives aligned with cultural beliefs about gender, illustrating the effect of even just a day's training on the way the mind perceives the world.

Learned metaphors even shape the way objects feel to the touch, as shown by an experiment involving two different, seemingly unrelated tasks (Slepian and Ambady 2014). College students were first instructed to learn the contents of a passage by a purported philosopher in which either the present was described as having a more profound effect on the self than the past, or the past was heavy compared to the present. Later, the students were asked to assess the weight, age, and scientific importance of a single book that was presented in one of four forms combining old or new appearance and photograph or actual object. The researchers found that the associations introduced in the first phase of the experiment did not affect perceptions of the book's scientific popularity across the different scenarios, nor did they influence assessments of the book's weight if it was shown in a picture. However, the metaphors had a notable effect on estimates of the book's weight when it was handled. That is, in the guise of a new book, the object was given a greater weight in ounces by the present-is-heavy than past-is-heavy participants. Presented in the form of an old book, the same object's weight was heavier in the estimation of students primed with past-is-heavy than present-is-heavy philosophies. The participants had literally embodied the culturally derived associations introduced in the first phase of the experiment.

Cultural metaphors and symbolic associations also influence what we hear. The Vienna Philharmonic Orchestra is infamous for excluding Asian musicians on account of their presumed lack of the necessary cultural sensibilities, even after they have won a blind audition. Likewise, if women are seen playing "male" instruments such as trumpets, or masculine music such as military marches, listeners believe that they hear an inferior performance. The music is heard differently if candidates are hidden, as Abbie Conant discovered when she auditioned for a position with the Munich Philharmonic Orchestra as first trombonist in 1980. The Orchestra held a blind audition, unusual at the time, to prevent favoritism towards a known candidate. Conant's performance won her the part instantly, but from the moment they saw her the conductor and his orchestra rejected her. They were convinced that women did not have the temperament, the physical or mental strength, or the right hands, lips, and lungs to play the music properly. Over the ensuing decade, Conant was relentlessly subjected to derision, demotion, physical testing, and unfair pay. All the while, outside experts repeatedly praised her performances (McMullen 2006).

This example speaks to the power of cultural categories to channel perceptions and interpretations. In fact, as the US has switched to blind auditions, the proportions of women and men in major orchestras have equalized (Goldin and Rouse 2000). Evidently, seeing a musician is enough to trigger unconscious stereotypes and prevent the brain from hearing the music for what it is.

Gender and ethnicity are such dominant, powerful symbolic categories that they override other aspects of identity, as in the terms "Hispanic actor," "woman doctor," or "black lawyer." The overriding effect of these master categories is clear in a study in which researchers sent thousands of emails to state legislators' offices signed by either Jake Mueller or DeShawn Jackson – names previously tested for carrying white and black ethnic associations (Butler and Broockman 2011). The emails asked for assistance with voter registration and indicated the writer's political affiliation: Republican, Democrat, or neither. The results showed that even where party affiliation matches, white legislators' offices of both parties respond less often to DeShawn whereas minority legislators' offices respond less often to Jake. The fact that party affiliation was included allowed the researchers to rule out preferential treatment based on partisanship. That is, the writers' presumed ethnicity trumps their declared political identity.

Thanks to the overwhelming impact of socially meaningful categories, any observed difference between groups of people belonging to a category, or any conforming behavior on the part of an individual, is automatically attributed to ethnicity, gender, sexual identity, age, and so on – as if no other explanation were possible or need be sought. For example, the belief that women talk more than men fits with assumptions about women's evolved proclivity for communication and socializing, but researchers in the US and Mexico counted an average of 16,000 words a day among both women and men (Mehl et al. 2007). Women's sense of touch is known to be more acute than men's, but fingertip sensitivity is a function of fingertip size. What looks like a sex difference is really a function of the smaller average size of women and their hands relative to men (Peters et al. 2009). Similarly, health disparities between ethnic groups, such as differences in high blood pressure or heart failure rates, are attributed to race instead of racism (see Chapter 6). As we will see, allegedly biologically based differences in academic skills between genders and ethnic groups change drastically over time and can be explained in terms of inequalities in training and the effects of stereotypes on performance.

Euroamerican cultural constructs including gender and ethnicity are embedded in a series of interconnected symbolic dualisms: male/female, clean/unclean, up/down (or top/bottom), right/left, right/wrong, true/false, white/black, reason/emotion (or thought/feeling), strong/weak, hard/soft, active/passive, sun/moon, mind/body, civilization/nature. The fact that some of these opposed qualities have to do with the biophysical properties of bodies in space gives the whole framework the feel of an uncontrived symbolic system, but the oppositions are not natural distinctions or cross-cultural universals. The experiments described above confirm that sensory perception itself is channeled by cultural metaphors.

The first term in each pair of oppositions above has positive, superior connotations relative to the second.[6] Any term from one side raises associations with others on the same side: for example, male is associated with top, right, active, civilization, and mind; female with unclean, weak, nature, and body. The sciences are divided into "hard" physical and natural sciences associated with masculinity and "soft" social sciences associated with femininity. The hard sciences are not all equally hard but range from abstract, "clean" physics to earthy, messy biology. Within biology, the nature-nurture opposition aligns the gene with male-associated attributes, the environment with female-associated ones. That is, the gene is causative, rational, decisive force, whereas the environment is chaotic, contingent, uncertain context.

Thinking in oppositions matches the popular linguistic style by which everyday conversation and public discourse are organized as battles between two sides which only one party can win. This adversarial arrangement forces people to take sides. In debates about genetic and environmental causation, each side is pushed to discredit rather than include the other as a valid influence on development, health, and behavior, even though both know that the question of causality cannot be resolved this way. Biology and culture, or nature and nurture, are always both involved.

. . . . .

The following chapters develop a biocultural framework for examining evidence about human origins and sociocultural variability that challenges dominant metaphors of our caveman origin and its genetic legacies, particularly the alleged human craving for hierarchy, conflict, and lethal violence. The chapters integrate diverse sources of evidence on the social and historical reasons for and biological dimensions of gender inequality, patterns of disease, and violence and crime. They cover a lot of ground in the interest of extracting threads of significance that, woven together, create a synthesis capable of countering entrenched theories of humanness.

The resulting perspective is theoretically promising as well as useful and practical. It suggests reasons and ways to improve human existence through social and gender equality, disease prevention, and peaceful management of conflict. There are implications for the schooling and civic education of children, the organization of the workplace and family life, disease prevention and treatment, and conflict avoidance and dispute resolution. Through a different narrative about human evolution and cross-cultural variability, the analysis opens alternative paths to understanding who we are, how we got here, and what the future holds.

Notes

1 On the history, pervasiveness, and multiple forms of the Western idea of human nature, see Sahlins (2008).
2 In this and the following chapters, endnotes are used for long sections based on one or two sources. Briefer references are indicated with an in-text citation.
3 The Presidential Commission for the Study of Bioethical Issues (2013) reports that across more than 30 publications on genetic databanks from the US and elsewhere, there is no consideration of donor access to data.
4 On ethical issues related to genetic manipulation, see Bowring (2004).
5 On language and color perception, see Roberson et al. (2005). For the color wheel experiment run by Serge Caparos, see Robinson (2011).
6 On symbolic oppositions in relation to gender, see Ortner (1972).

References cited

23andMe, Inc. 2016. 23andme.com. Accessed 15 November 2016.
Adams S. 2011 6 May. "Happiness gene" discovered. *Telegraph*.
Ancestry. 2016. Ancestry.com. Accessed 15 November 2016.
Ashraf Q, Galor O. 2013. The "out of Africa" hypothesis, human genetic diversity, and comparative economic development. *The American Economic Review* 103(1):1–46.
Aspinwall LG, Brown TR, Tabery J. 2012. The double-edged sword: does biomechanism increase or decrease judges' sentencing of psychopaths? *Science* 337(6096):846–849.
Bacon F. 1960[1620]. *The new organon, and related writings*. Anderson F, editor. New York: Liberal Arts Press.
Borenstein S. 2008 7 April. Sex and financial risk linked in the brain. *USA Today*.
Boroditsky L, Schmidt LA, Phillips W. 2003. Sex, syntax, and semantics. In Gentner D, Goldin-Meadow S, editors. *Language in mind: advances in the study of language and thought*. Cambridge, MA: MIT Press. p. 61–79.
Bowring F. 2004. Therapeutic and reproductive cloning: a critique. *Social Science and Medicine* 58(2):401–409.
Brown D. 2012 13 December. New "burden of disease" study shows a world living longer and with more disability. *Washington Post*.
Bulliet RW, Crossley P, Headrick D, Hirsh S, Johnson L. 2005. *The Earth and its peoples: a global history*. Volume I. 3rd ed. Boston: Houghton Mifflin Company.
Butler DM, Broockman DE. 2011. Do politicians racially discriminate against constituents? A field experiment on state legislators. *American Journal of Political Science* 55(3):463–477.
Castillo M. 2012 29 August. Political beliefs may be rooted in genetics, study says. CBS News.
Commoner B. 2002. Unraveling the DNA myth. *Harpers* 304(1821):39-47.
Dawkins R. 1976. *The selfish gene*. New York: Oxford University Press.

DNA Diagnostics Center. 2016. Dnacenter.com. Accessed 15 November 2016.

Duke University. 2010 24 March. People are living longer and healthier: now what? *Science Daily*.

Gates HL. 1999. *Wonders of the African world.* New York: Alfred A. Knopf.

Gene by Gene, Ltd. 2016. Familytreedna.com. Accessed 15 November 2016.

Genetics and Public Policy Center. 2007. http://www.dnapolicy.org/resources/GINAPublic_Opinion_Genetic_Information_Discrimination.pdf. Accessed 12 October 2007.

Goldin C, Rouse C. 2000. Orchestrating impartiality: the impact of "blind" auditions on female musicians. *American Economic Review* 90(4):715–741.

Goldman N, Bertone P, Chen S, Dessimoz C, LeProust EM, Sipos B, Birney E. 2013. Towards practical, high-capacity, low-maintenance information storage in synthesized DNA. *Nature* 494(7435):77-80.

Hagerty BB. 2010 1 July. Can your genes make you murder? Npr.org.

Hayden EC. 2013. Taboo genetics. *Nature* 502(7469):26–28.

Herrnstein RJ, Murray C. 1994. *The bell curve.* New York: Free Press.

Hibbing JR, Smith KB, Alford JR. 2013. *Predisposed: liberals, conservatives, and the biology of political differences.* New York: Routledge.

Jadva V, Hines M, Golombok S. 2010. Infants' preferences for toys, colors, and shapes: sex differences and similarities. *Archives of Sexual Behavior* 39(6):1261–1273.

Kettlewell J. 2004 16 June. "Fidelity gene" found in voles. BBC News.

Knutson B, Wimmer GE, Kuhnen CM, Winkielman P. 2008. Nucleus accumbens activation mediates the influence of reward cues on financial risk taking. *NeuroReport* 19(5):509–513.

MacDonald L. 1993. *The roses of no man's land.* New York: Penguin.

McMullen T. 2006. Corpo-realities: keepin' it real in "music and embodiment" scholarship. *Current Musicology* 82:61–80.

Mehl MR, Vazire S, Ramírez-Esparza N, Slatcher RB, Pennebaker JW. 2007. Are women really more talkative than men? *Science* 317(5834):82.

Mundy L. 2012. *The richer sex: how the new majority of female breadwinners is transforming our culture.* New York: Simon and Schuster.

New York Times. 2000 27 June. Text of the White House statements on the Human Genome Project.

O'Connell S. 2004 7 January. Apes of war. . .Is it in our genes? *Telegraph.*

Ortiz de Montellano B. 1993. Melanin, Afrocentricity, and pseudoscience. *American Journal of Physical Anthropology* 36(17):33–58.

Ortner SB. 1972. Is female to male as nature is to culture? *Feminist Studies* 1(2):5–31.

Oxford Ancestors, Ltd. 2016. OxfordAncestors.com. Accessed 15 November 2016.

Pandora Media, Inc. 2016. https://www.pandora.com/. Accessed 15 November 2016.

Paoletti JB. 2012. *Pink and blue: telling the girls from the boys in America.* Bloomington, IN: Indiana University Press.

Pappas S. 2011 4 January. Depression gene really exists, new study claims. Msnbc.com.

Pappas S. 2011 18 November. Male impulsivity and addiction linked to one gene. Livescience.com.

Peters RM, Hackeman E, Goldreich D. 2009. Diminutive digits discern delicate details: fingertip size and the sex difference in tactile spatial acuity. *The Journal of Neuroscience* 29(50):15756–15761.

Presidential Commission for the Study of Bioethical Issues. 2013. *Anticipate and communicate: ethical management of incidental and secondary findings in the clinical, research, and direct-to-consumer contexts.* Washington, DC: Presidential Commission for the Study of Bioethical Issues.

Roberson D, Davidoff J, Davies IRL, Shapiro LR. 2005. Color categories: evidence for the cultural relativity hypothesis. *Cognitive Psychology* 50(4):378–411.

Robinson S, producer. 2011 8 August. Do you see what I see? [Television series episode]. In *Horizon*. BBC.

Sahlins M. 2008. *The Western illusion of human nature.* Chicago: Prickly Paradigm Press.

Schloss KB, Poggesi RM, Palmer SE. 2011. Effects of university affiliation and "school spirit" on color preferences: Berkeley versus Stanford. *Psychonomic Bulletin and Review* 18(3):498–504.

Shetty P. 2008 1 September. Monogamy gene found in people. *New Scientist* 199(2672):16.

Slepian ML, Ambady N. 2014. Stimulating sensorimotor metaphors: novel metaphors influence sensory judgments. *Cognition* 130(3):309–314.

Storrs C. 2012 27 August. Could your genes influence how you vote? *US News and World Report.*

Taylor C, Clifford A, Franklin A. 2013. Color preferences are not universal. *Journal of Experimental Psychology: General* 142(4):1015–1027.

Telegraph. 2012 26 January. Life of crime is in the genes, study claims.

Wainwright M. 2007 21 August. Pink for a girl and blue for a boy – and it's all down to evolution. *The Guardian.*

Westerhout E, Pellikaan F. 2005. Can we afford to live longer in better health? *ENEPRI Research Reports* No. 10.

Zwane AP. 2012. The implications of scarcity. *Science* 338(6107):617–618.

2

ORIGIN STORIES

The co-evolution of human anatomy and sociality

According to prevailing images of human nature, people inevitably form hierarchies and social inequalities and only recently have learned to impose fairness. Warfare allegedly has been with us from the beginning, when prehistoric men would band together to kill other men and steal their women, and people died at age 20 or 30 because of the violence and lack of medical expertise. The same story holds that women and men have different minds because in the past they needed separate interpersonal and technical skills.

The picture that emerges from an examination of available data on human evolution and cross-cultural variability is surprising in almost every way. It contradicts key cultural assumptions about the bleak origins, history of progressive improvement, and current nature of the human race. This chapter explores the co-evolution of the human life span, infant dependency, shared parenting, brain size, and culture. It lays the groundwork for the analysis of health, difference, and conflict in the rest of the book, and shows that human evolution has shaped who we are today, but not always in the expected ways.

. . . . .

We will begin with foraging societies, given that these were the only kind of human society for all but a small fraction of our species' existence. The following discussion is not meant to imply that contemporary foraging groups or other indigenous peoples represent intact replicas of timeless societies unearthed from beneath the homogenizing sands of civilization. Every society is a unique, dynamic product of historical processes, interactions with other societies, and the intermingling of individual wills. The purpose of the present analysis is to establish a connection between nomadic food collection and certain kinds of behavioral norms and social relationships. The chapter underscores the flexibility of cultural forms, not their fixity. It challenges invented reconstructions of the past which misleadingly counterpose "tradition" and "nature" against "modernity" and "civilization."

During the last half century, anthropologists have studied scores of contemporary foraging populations, also called hunting and gathering societies or hunter-gatherers.[1] These nomadic groups collect food directly from the landscape rather than relying on cultivation, herding, or storage. Their way of life suggests some general features of social and cultural organization that are likely to have prevailed in ancestral societies for the 2.5 million years before the rise of agriculture around 12,000 years before the present (BP).

The geographical zones inhabited by foragers during the last few centuries range from arctic to equatorial. A sample of their locations and names is shown in Figure 2.1. Over the last century, states and private landowners have relentlessly restricted the territory available to foragers and forced them to settle in villages. Already in the 1960s and 1970s, many foraging societies obtained less than half their food by gathering and hunting. Most were in regular contact with nearby farmers for social events, trade, and intermarriage. Archeological evidence suggests that this has been the case for foraging populations ever since the beginnings of agriculture and that, long before then, groups of foragers regularly met up with other groups to trade and socialize. Foraging societies are neither isolated nor unchanging.[2]

Notwithstanding the variability across foraging societies and the sustained contact between foragers and villagers, foraging societies share some distinctive common features that help form a rough picture of preagricultural foraging lifestyles. For example, population density is very low, well below one person per square kilometer. Groups, or bands, are small, averaging about 30–50 people – although they may be as large as 100–150. Economic behavior is governed by the principle of reciprocity; personal possessions are kept to a minimum. Social relationships emphasize cooperation along with respect for individual autonomy. There are no official leaders.

Groups converge periodically for weeks or months, such as during the dry season when there are scarce sources of water. Having relatives and friends in nearby bands allows people to leave their own group if they are not able to get along. The combination of mobility, open access to resources, and food sharing keeps people from using material goods to the disadvantage of others. Consequently there is a relatively high degree of gender and socioeconomic egalitarianism, which is actively defended through criticism of self-aggrandizement.

Almost all foraging populations are nomadic. This is because of the changing availability of food due to depletion and seasonal fluctuations. Territoriality is weak or absent due to nomadism and low population density. Along with networks of friends and relatives across bands, these factors prevent conflict between groups.

A small minority of foraging societies have lived in permanent settlements. They are known as complex or sedentary foraging societies. These are recent, mostly from the last 13,000 years, although possibly the last 25,000 years. They require exceptionally fruitful environments, as along the Northwest Coast of North America and in parts of Europe, Eastern China, Japan, and Australia. Population density is higher than it is for nomads, and there are marked social ranking

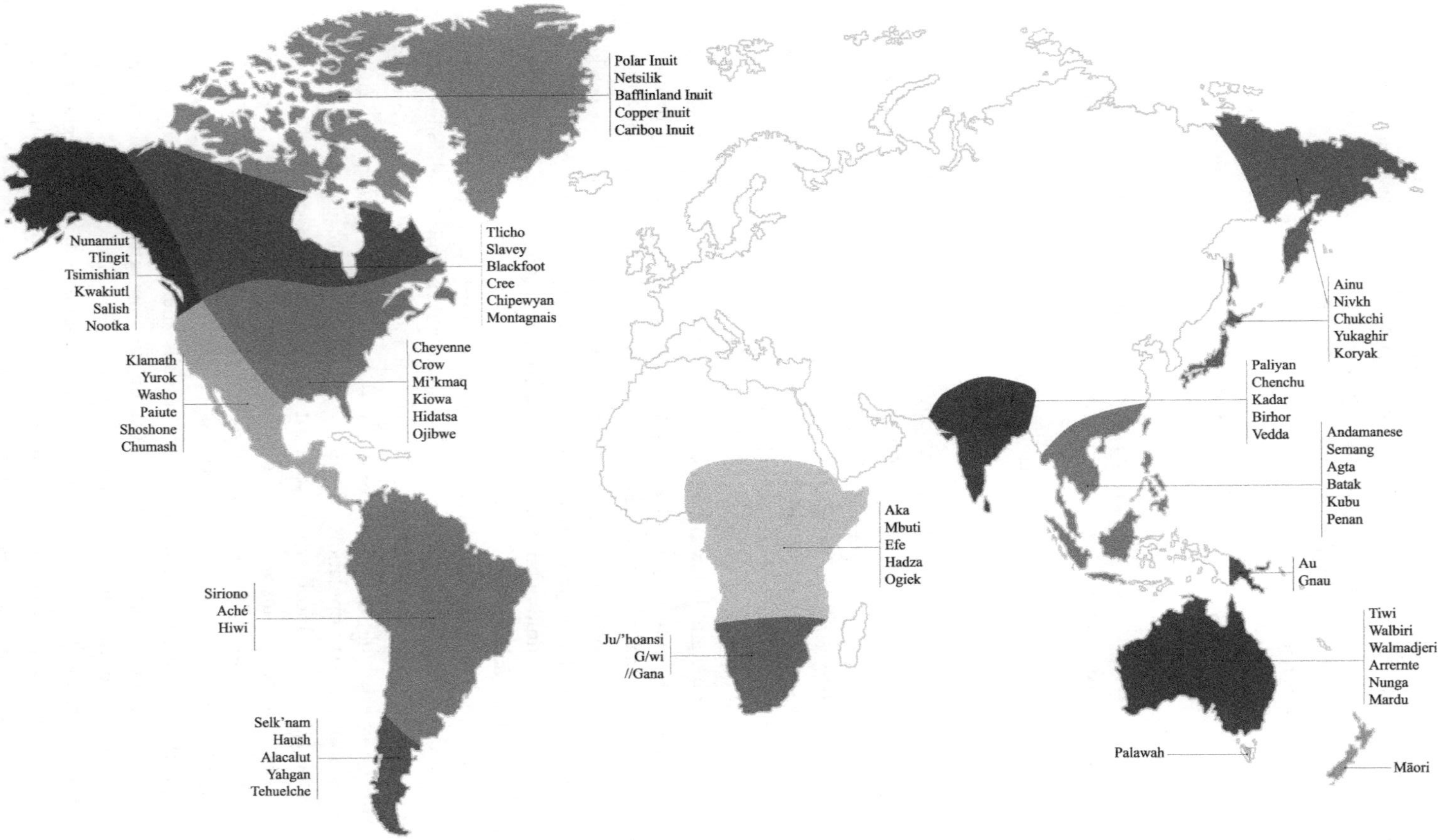

FIGURE 2.1 Approximate geographical distribution of a sample of recent foraging societies.

(© Elisa Sangiorgi, reprinted with permission)

systems including rulers, commoners, and in some cases slaves. In these respects, settled foragers are more similar to agricultural societies than nomadic foragers.

The alternative term to foragers, hunter-gatherers, underscores a cultural tendency to associate human evolution with meat, but the symbolic value of meat does not match its true proportion in the diet. Animal tissues are exceptionally rich in nutritional content, which explains why meat is highly valued throughout the world and why people go to a lot of trouble to get it (Farb and Armelagos 1980). For the same reason and because it connotes masculine strength and risk-taking, scientific and popular narratives about human evolution stress large-game hunting. Humanness itself is attributed to the physical and emotional distance 2-million-year-old tools placed between predator and prey, decoupling aggression from action (Pickering 2013).

However, over the long arc of human evolution, being hunted was a far more defining feature of existence than hunting. For the australopithecine species that preceded the genus *Homo* in the period from about 5–2.5 million years ago (mya, or Ma, for mega-annum), meat was an unlikely part of the diet, as indicated by small teeth suited to chewing and grinding, as opposed to large sharp teeth for holding and tearing. Predators abounded. There were more than 100 species of hyena, many of them far larger than any species left today (one weighed more than 200 kilos); large cats including leopards, saber-toothed tigers, and lions; crocodiles and giant snakes such as pythons and boa constrictors; and huge raptor species including hawks and eagles with talons the size of a human hand. Based on skeletal evidence and analysis of predator anatomy and behavior, Donna Hart and Robert Sussman (2005) argue that these predators routinely hunted australopithecines and nonhuman primates. Noting that all diurnal primate species are organized into stable societies, they conclude that mutual assistance and protection – not hunting or murder – was key to the evolution of human cognitive traits. Indeed, hunting emerged well after the expansion of the hominid brain which resulted from increased ingestion of gathered and scavenged animal matter.

Meat is unpredictable compared to plant foods. Together with the human inability to digest excessive protein in the diet (discussed below), this unreliability is the reason why almost all known foraging populations subsist on a diet that is one-half to two-thirds vegetable matter, as, assuredly, did preagricultural humans. At the extremes, some desert populations obtain less than one-fifth of their calories from animal foods, whereas Northern hunters eat a diet that is almost entirely animal-derived but includes organs and large amounts of fat.

While carrying an infant does not interfere with trapping or hunting with nets (discussed below), it makes hunting with spears or arrows difficult and dangerous. Consequently, the latter type of hunting is usually men's work, although sometimes it is the responsibility of women. Among the aboriginal Tiwi in Australia, women not only hunted but also made their own stone axes until the arrival of steel weapons with the Europeans. In other cases, such as Cagayan Agta in the Philippines, men and women go on extended hunting trips together, and gather plant foods while they are away. Agta men and women engage in the same kinds of hunting. Women carry on hunting even while pregnant. Among Au and Gnau foragers in Papua New Guinea, men hunt in organized groups whereas women kill animals when the opportunity arises during daily foraging. Aka women and men in central Africa take turns hunting and caring for small children.

For many foraging populations, a good portion of the animal protein in the diet comes from insects – grubs, locusts, ants – which, like shellfish, are gathered rather than hunted. Furthermore, plant foods are not mainly easily obtainable berries and fruits, as the Western image of femininity would predict. These foods are relatively scarce and limited to short seasons. The more typical plant foods in the forager diet include starchy roots, protein-rich nuts and seeds, and edible stems and leaves. Gathering can involve both plant and animal foods – eggs, turtles, insects, lizards, fish, and small animals caught in snares or traps. Hunters often gather plant foods while they search for meat. Both gatherers and hunters stay on the lookout for signs of food sources the others may procure later on. In sum, plant foods are not the exclusive purview of women, or animal foods the responsibility of men only. It is common for food procurement activities to overlap. The work is physically demanding, whether it involves plant or animal foods. Women and men both obtain food and share it. No one is provisioned or excluded from access to the environment, although in some cases men supply a majority share of their wives' food during pregnancy and lactation.

Equipment for hunting large animals was developed recently in human evolution.[3] The oldest potential instrument dates to 400,000 BP, the age of the two-meter wooden pointed spear found in Germany. It is likely to have been thrust into small or medium-sized prey rather than launched at a large animal, or used for defense against large predators. Scavenging is suggested by marks left by hand axes and flaked blades on the bones of wild cattle and other large animals in Africa, which appear alongside teeth marks made by carnivorous predator species. The evidence for hunting becomes less equivocal after 75,000–60,000 BP, with the invention of stone or bone tips of the kind found in southern Africa that could be attached to a shaft as a projectile point. Pitch, beeswax, and resins were used to seal and glue implements in the same geographical area by 44,000 BP. Modern humans migrated into Europe bearing projectile points around 45,000 BP.

The spear thrower was invented around 30,000 BP, allowing humans to hunt prey at a distance of tens of meters, and perhaps a hundred meters. There are split-shaft arrows complete with feathers from almost 20,000 years ago, and evidence of poisoned projectile tips from a few thousand years earlier than that. The oldest complete bow specimen dates to 11,000 BP. Bows appear to have been brought to the New World across the Beringia land bridge, but native peoples also used spear throwers. Dogs – useful for hunting – were domesticated from wolves and present in Europe, the Middle East, East Asia, and North America beginning around 15,000 BP. In some areas, they may have been domesticated more than 30,000 BP (Thalmann et al. 2013).

While projectile points made hunting safer and more effective, the timing and spread of the technology was not straightforward. In some areas it appears to have been adopted for a while before being lost or abandoned, as in southern Africa 60,000–45,000 BP. Artifacts suggesting the development of implements in one part of the world do not necessarily mean that the technology was available in other areas. In addition, digging sticks and other implements for procuring plant foods were used alongside ones for hunting, indicating that hunting did not supersede gathering.

Even after hunting became practicable, groups took advantage of opportunities to eat prey killed by other animals or found dead from natural causes, as do contemporary foragers. The Ju/'hoansi (or Ju/wasi, also known as !Kung) of the Kalahari Desert in southern Africa and the Hadza of Tanzania obtain a large part of their meat by chasing off hyenas and other animals from their kills. Likewise, Upper Paleolithic humans in Europe found carcasses of weakened animals such as mammoths which had expired near water or salt sources, and moved camp to take advantage of the food. That they did not hunt the animals is clear from the presence of skulls weighing more than 200 pounds among the bones, which hunters would not have bothered to transport had they killed the animal away from camp.

In addition to scavenging, foragers past and present have relied on net hunting to capture animals. Native American societies including the Blackfoot hunted bison, elk, and bighorn sheep with nets. Mbuti foragers of the Central African Republic, who prize nets above hunting equipment, use nets to scare up smaller forest-dwelling mammals. Net hunting is a collective endeavor involving the entire group: women and men, children and old people. They may travel many kilometers a day. Both men and women carry children and equipment.

The extent of net hunting in the past undoubtedly has been vastly underestimated, as nets are perishable artifacts and until recently archeologists did not look for them. Weaving was believed to be an invention of agricultural societies of the past 12,000 years, and durable artifacts such as spear tips and blades fit the commonsense notion that hunting in prehistory was done with spears or projectiles.

In the 1990s, Olga Soffer and colleagues found evidence of sophisticated weaving techniques in imprints on clay left at several sites in the Czech Republic 25,000 BP (Adovasio et al. 2009). The knots indicate net hunting, as does the preponderance of fox, hare, and bird bones at the sites. These preagricultural humans also made baskets and finely woven cloth. A closer look at many of the durable artifacts from the same sites reveals that they were not made for hunting after all, but were tools such as blades and grinding stones for processing plant foods.

Contrary to the cartoon version of a prehistoric hunter killing 3-ton woolly mammoths with a close-range spear, it is unlikely that hunters worked alone or by endurance running. Massive animals armed with horns and tusks, such as mammoths and elephants, would have been too risky for a lone hunter to approach. Humans have little chance of overcoming prey through speed, although our superior cooling system allows us to outlast certain animals such as kangaroos and small antelope in a long chase. This kind of pursuit – involving a series of chases followed by tracking the animal as it rests under cover until it becomes exhausted – is practicable in a hot, even landscape and sometimes done by foragers in the Kalahari Desert and the Rarámuri of northern Mexico, who cultivate traditional crops and raise livestock. Running after prey is unfeasible in areas with rocky or vertical terrain where four-legged animals have the advantage. It is much more likely that our ancestors cornered animals by working in groups, studying the animals carefully and waiting in opportune places.

In sum, it is safe to say that ancestral humans became effective hunters 50,000–40,000 BP and very capable ones 20,000–10,000 BP. They may have contributed to the disappearance of many animals from Europe, such as lions and saber-tooth tigers, although overharvesting is not typical of foraging societies (see Chapter 3). By 15,000 BP, there were very few large predator species left. Neolithic hunters had the further advantage of metal implements. In the evolutionary scheme of things, hunting is new – not an activity so entrenched that it defines human nature. Moreover, most hunting was nothing like the popular image of a man running across the savannahs or perhaps a forested temperate landscape, spear in hand.

Additional features of the foraging lifestyle will be discussed in detail in later chapters. There we will see how diet, physical activity, outdoor living, and social cohesion relate to life expectancy and infectious, chronic, and degenerative diseases. We will explore how gender egalitarianism results from shared access to resources, bilateral as opposed to patrilineal kinship, and the absence of accumulation and therefore plural marriage. Food sharing, long-term reciprocal exchange relationships, and low relatedness among members of foraging bands mitigate against violent conflict within and between groups. These interconnected patterns are crucial to a biocultural analysis of health, gender, and conflict, but first we will finish filling out a picture of the distant past and how it helped to make us what we are now.

. . . . .

The following sketch outlines the timing of the appearance and disappearance of other species similar to ours, as well as the colonization of different parts of the world. It highlights the anatomical and cultural changes that allowed our species to outlast the others. In particular, we will examine the significance of changes in brain volume for social and family organization.

As shown in Table 2.1, the Ice Age corresponded in time with the Paleolithic (Old Stone) era, during which our ancestors of the genus *Homo* lived only by nomadic foraging (Brace 1995; Jones et al. 1994; Stanford et al. 2011). The Paleolithic began 2.5 mya with the appearance of Oldowan stone tools, which were found in Gona, Ethiopia and distinguish the first *Homo* species from concurrent australopithecine species. In the following pages, we will continue to use this conventional date for marking the divergence, in spite of the recent discovery in Ethiopia of a partial jawbone with teeth from 2.8 mya – much older than the previous earliest *Homo* specimen from 2.4 mya.

The Oldowan cores and flakes had been knapped – struck to break or chip them – indicating an intentional creative process as opposed to the use of unmodified materials as tools. The difference defines humans in terms of culture from the very beginning. That is, our evolution represents the intersection of biology, behavior, and environment. There is no way to distill out a culture-free essence of humanness.

TABLE 2.1 Geological and anthropological time scales in the Quaternary (Fourth) Period of the Cenozoic Era

Geological epoch	*Word origin*	*Years*	*Anthropological era*	*Word origin*	*Phases*	*Years*
Pleistocene Epoch (Great Ice Age)	Greek for "most" and "new"	2.5 million to 12,000 BP	Paleolithic	Greek for "old" and "stone"	Lower Paleolithic	2.5 million to 200,000 BP
					Middle Paleolithic	200,000 to 40,000 BP
					Upper Paleolithic	40,000 to 12,00 BP
Holocene Epoch (Entirely Recent Period, or Alternative Recent Period)	Greek for "whole" and "new"	12,000 BP to present	Mesolithic	Greek for "middle" and "stone"	Mesolithic (Middle Stone Age)	12,000 to 9,000 BP
			Neolithic	Greek for "new" and "stone"	Neolithic (New Stone Age)	9,000 to 3,500 BP

The Neolithic Revolution refers to the transition, beginning 12,000 BP, in which humans switched to cultivating rather than collecting food. The first phase is called the Mesolithic (Middle Stone) age, and refers to a phase of experimentation with plant cultivation and animal domestication along with the collection of wild foods. In the Neolithic (New Stone) age, some populations formed permanent settlements and depended entirely on domesticated plants and animals. For simplicity's sake, we will use the word "Neolithic" for both phases. Metalworking was developed during the Neolithic and eventually marked its end. Beaten copper was used beginning 9,500 BP and smelted bronze beginning around 5,500 BP. Harder and more durable than copper, bronze played a prominent role in the emergence of early civilizations. The end of the Neolithic corresponds with the beginning of the Iron Age around 3,500 BP.

These anthropological periods fall within the Quaternary (Fourth) Period of the Cenozoic Era. The Pleistocene Epoch corresponds with the Great Ice Age, the Holocene with the last 12,000 years. The latter is sometimes called the Anthropocene in recognition of the effects of human activity on the Earth and its climate, although some experts would limit the Anthropocene to the industrial era.

During the Upper Paleolithic, in the last 40,000 years, there were still several different hominid species. The term "hominids" refers to our species plus extinct ones such as the australopithecines, *H. erectus*, and *H. neanderthalensis*. "Hominoids" is a broader term encompassing also the living apes: gorillas, orangutans, chimps, and bonobos.

Four to 7 million years ago, the hominid line diverged from a common ancestor shared with the two now-existing species of chimpanzees (common and bonobo). This split came 1–2 million years after the gorilla line branched off, about 9–10 million years after the orangutan line split away, and about 15 million years after the gibbon line diverged from the common branch. This means that the closest extant nonhuman primate relatives of humans are the two types of chimps, then gorillas, then orangutans, and finally, gibbons (also known as "lesser" apes). This group of species diverged 25–35 mya from ancestors it had in common with the Old World Monkeys. The ancestral species to all of the anthropoids (monkeys, apes, and humans and their ancestors) emerged around 45 mya either in Africa or in Asia with rapid migration to Africa.

These relationships matter because they help us determine the strength of comparisons between humans and various species of nonhuman primate. In addition, they indicate that humans did not evolve from any existing monkey or ape. The common ancestor is no longer walking the Earth.

The earliest confirmed hominid, *Australopithecus anamensis*, dates to 4.2 mya. At least four earlier species lived in the preceding 3 million years. They had a mixture of characteristics shared with apes as well as fully bipedal hominids. These species, which include *Sahelanthropus tchadensis*, *Orrorin tugenensis*, and *Ardipithecus ramidus,* appear to have walked upright although awkwardly, in addition to being able to climb and move about in trees albeit less adroitly than apes.

The australopithecines shared some features with apes, such as similar brain size, shoulder blades, and curved fingers for climbing trees, but they were bipedal. There were many species in addition to *A. anamensis* over the period from 4.5–2.4 mya, such as *A. afarensis* represented by the "Lucy" skeleton. The "robust" *Paranthropus* species had rounder faces and bigger molars, and lived contemporaneously with australopithecine and *Homo* species in Africa during the period from 2.5–1.5 mya. Which species was ancestral to the genus *Homo* remains controversial. Many scholars believe that it was *A. afarensis*, although *A. africanus* is favored by others. Uncertainty also remains about the classification of the first *Homo* skeletal remains, which some experts would place among the australopithecines (McPherron et al. 2010). The distinction is clearer for later specimens, as the *Homo* line developed a progressively larger cranium in relation to body size, but smaller, narrower teeth and more rounded jaws.

Australopithecines spent their days in the grasslands rather than trees. A bundle of traits and adaptations made this possible. Capabilities such as binocular vision and depth perception adapted for life in the trees were crucial for avoiding predators and finding food on the ground as well. Upright posture freed the hands for tools such as sticks and rocks used for digging, defense against predators, cutting and scraping, and possibly chasing predator animals from their kills. Markings on bones found in Ethiopia's Afar Depression suggest stone tool use for processing animal tissues by *A. afarensis* as early as 3.4 mya. The tools had been carried several kilometers, indicating that they were kept on hand to butcher scavenged animals. These discoveries suggest forethought and organization among australopithecines, not just early *Homo* species, and are consistent with observations of chimpanzees using tools.

Other adaptations that benefited early human ancestors include a highly efficient cooling system, which permitted foraging for long hours in a hot environment. Many large mammals such as cats must move about at night to avoid the risk of overheating. Hominids have sweat glands distributed throughout the body, rather than localized in palms, soles, and a few other sites as they are in almost all nonhuman primates. In addition, a smaller hair follicle size gives humans thinner hair covering most of the body, which further promotes evaporative heat loss. The exceptions to reduced hairiness reflect additional adaptations: eyelashes and eyebrows that provide protection for the eyes; head hair that prevents overexposure to the sun and maintains a more constant temperature for the brain; hair in the armpits and genital area that possibly plays a part in pheromonal signaling; and male facial hair that may be the result of sexual selection (Cohn 1998).

Australopithecine species coexisted with the *Homo* branch for a million years. Some species had features of both, such as *Australopithecus sediba,* which lived in South Africa around 2–1.75 mya. Interestingly, *A. sediba*'s brain was small but the impression left by the forebrain on the inner skull indicates a more modern form. This suggests that the brain's structure may have changed before its size increased in our ancestors (Berger et al. 2010). The newly discovered but as yet undated pre-*erectus H. naledi* which also lived in South Africa likewise had a small, globular cranium and mixture of features combining traits of plant-eating tree climbers (large molars, shoulder and digits adapted to climbing) and omnivorous land-dwellers (small front teeth, long legs and short arms, arched feet with all toes aligned, a wrist associated with tool use).

Early *Homo* species from the period between 2.5 and 1 mya include *H. habilis*, *H. rudolfensis*, and *H. ergaster* – the original, African form of *H. erectus* which is credited with inventing the hand ax, and which may have been the first to control fire. *Homo ergaster* emerged in Africa around 1.9 mya, and was present in China and elsewhere in Asia, the Middle East, and Eastern Europe by 1.85–1 mya. *Homo ergaster/Homo erectus* persisted as a species until 500,000 BP and by some estimates until 200,000 or fewer years ago. The different "erectine" species (those with brains under 1,250 cubic centimeters such as *H. antecessor*, *H. mauritanicus*, and *H. soloensis*) are classified together by "lumpers" as *H. erectus* but separately by "splitters."

H. ergaster/erectus, which we will call *H. erectus* from now on, was the ancestor species to many others, including our own. These include *H. antecessor,* which lived in Europe from 1.2 mya to 800,000 BP and has been studied most extensively in northern Spain; *H. heidelbergensis,* which dispersed widely across Africa, Europe, the Middle East, and Asia 600,000–350,000 BP, and possibly until 250,000 BP; and *H. neanderthalensis*, a species that appeared 600,000–400,000 BP and ranged across Africa, Europe, the Middle East, and Asia. Various species of *Homo* reached northern Eurasia and into Great Britain as early as 800,000 BP and returned in a second wave around 300,000 BP. They made fires and built shelters out of rock and wood. The modern form of *H. neanderthalensis* emerged 250,000–200,000 BP, persisted in Europe until around 30,000 BP, and reached as far as northwestern Siberia.

The term "archaic *Homo sapiens*" refers to large-brained species from 500,000–200,000 BP which preceded the anatomically modern *Homo sapiens* that emerged about 200,000 BP in Africa. This species, which gave rise to all the populations on Earth today, was less robust (big boned) than other hominid species, reflecting a greater reliance on culture for survival. Knowledge and social living allowed *H. sapiens* to get by with shorter stature and less bulk and strength. The relationship between brain and body size in our direct ancestors is further proof that culture shapes genes, and behavior shapes anatomy – not just the other way around.

Fully modern humans migrated out of Africa into the Middle East and the Arabian Peninsula 80,000–60,000 BP, although they may have done so as early as 130,000 BP (Armitage et al. 2011). Until recently it seemed that they came from sub-Saharan Africa, but new evidence suggests that groups from eastern and northern regions may have been the ones to migrate (Hublin and McPherron 2012). They soon spread across India and eastward from there. They arrived in East Asia, Europe, and Australia 50,000–40,000 BP.

During the glacial period that kept sea levels low and the Beringia land bridge open between Eurasia and North America, humans with strong genetic links to modern-day East Asians and murkier ties to Northern Europeans colonized the

Western hemisphere. They settled in Beringia for around 8,000 years before moving eastward and then to the south around 15,000 BP. It is widely thought that the original settlers were the Clovis people, named for a site in New Mexico where their distinctive 13,500-year-old fluted stone tips were first discovered. However, non-Clovis sites dated from 15,500–13,000 BP have been found on both coasts of the US and in between, as well as in South America, including the 14,800-year-old Monte Verde site in Chile.

The fact that people used boats to reach islands 10 kilometers off the coast of California 13,000 BP indicates that at least some migrants may have come south by sea rather than overland. Humans had been using boats for many thousands of years by then. It is possible although not likely that migrants reached the Americas by way of the South Pacific 30,000 BP, not much later than humans migrated into Europe. They had already reached Australia in boats or rafts 60,000–40,000 BP.

Modern humans overlapped with other species, and sometimes interbred with them. *H. erectus* may have been in Java between 180,000 and 27,000 BP. Skeletons of the small-bodied species *H. floresiensis* from 38,000–13,000 BP have been found on the Indonesian island of Flores, indicating that hominid species have adapted to isolation similarly to other mammals such as dwarf horses and elephants. *H. denisova* lived in Eurasia as recently as 48,000–30,000 BP, and used some of the same sites as Neanderthals and humans, apparently at the same time. Humans and Neanderthals both were in Asia and the Middle East from 100,000 to 40,000 or 35,000 BP. They came across each other in Europe from 45,000–28,000, and perhaps only 25,000 years ago. Yet another, unnamed species seems to have lived in Siberia 40,000 BP. This is indicated by specimens containing mitochondrial DNA that differs from both Neanderthal and human mitochondrial DNA.

Neanderthals and humans interbred to some degree. Skeletons bearing a mixture of human and Neanderthal traits have been found from periods well after the disappearance of the Neanderthals. Recent DNA analysis indicates interbreeding in Arabia or the Middle East between 100,000–50,000 BP, after both species had migrated out of Africa and before *H. sapiens* moved into Europe (Haak et al. 2010). About 1–4% of the genes of today's Europeans and Asians come from Neanderthals. The Denisovans, which split away from the Neanderthals 500,000 BP, interbred with both Neanderthals and modern humans migrating eastward from Eurasia. This mixing has left small traces of Denisovan DNA in the nuclear DNA of Europeans and Asians, and larger amounts – around 2–4% – in that of native populations of Australia, Papua New Guinea, and Melanesia. All combined, archaic DNA accounts for 2–7% of the modern genome.

Clearly, humans did not evolve only on the African savannahs. Ancestral humans did not typically live in caves, either, for it is rare to find large caves or rock shelters which are not inhospitably damp or cold. Our more distant ancestors had spread around the world's middle latitudes by well over a million years ago, and had diffused vertically to all the latitudes between South Africa and Northern Eurasia by 800,000 BP. Such vastly dissimilar ecological zones demanded different survival strategies, as they do now.

Modern *H. sapiens* colonized new areas by gradual diffusion. While some genetic variations arose that were favorable in specific environments, the maintenance of social and exchange networks over vast distances resulted in continuous contact and mixing. Consequently, although there is biological variability within the species, it does not match up with socially defined races, as shown in Chapter 6.

. . . . .

Hominids colonized much of the Earth thanks to a bundle of behavioral and anatomical changes including a rise in the size and complexity of the brain. These changes were linked to the way our ancestors lived, reproduced, and organized themselves socially. The result was that ancestral humans developed all of the cultural achievements typically attributed to civilization: art, music, technology, religion, and so on.

To begin with the environment, two of the major shifts in hominid evolution corresponded with periods of vast climatic transformation in Africa. The climatic changes were complex. On the one hand, there were cycles of alternating dry and wet periods lasting 10,000–20,000 years; on the other, an overarching drying trend with increasing climatic variability. The result in both periods was an expansion of grasslands and a rise in the number of speciation and extinction events among herbivorous mammal species.

The first climatic shift, between 2.9–2.6 mya, led to the disappearance of *Australopithecus afarensis* and the emergence of the robust *Paranthropus* australopithecine species along with the genus *Homo*. During a second climatic shift, from 1.9–1.6 mya, *Homo erectus* appeared. The more advanced Acheulean stone tools – especially bi-faced flaked hand axes – were developed around this time, and the *Homo* lineage expanded geographically into Asia and Europe.

During the second shift, *Homo erectus* dealt with reduced food resources by expanding its daily range to around 20 kilometers, similar to many modern foragers, and making greater use of tools such as scrapers and sticks. More sophisticated blades and hand axes appeared alongside more human-like hands, permitting further tool development in turn. By 1.4 mya, the third metacarpal bone had a pointy projection where it articulates with the wrist bones, conferring greater stability to the fingers and thumb for a more powerful and precise grip (Ward et al. 2013).

Increased food intake was necessary because of *H. erectus*' greater size relative to the australopithecines and earlier *Homo* species. Larger bodies, including larger brains, require more calories. For instance, human brains use three times more energy than ape brains (25% versus 8% of total energy expended). Brain tissue consumes more than 20 times the energy used by skeletal muscle.

Compared to other large mammals, humans and other primates have a high brain-to-body mass ratio. The australopithecines had a brain about a third the size of ours, similar to modern chimpanzees: about 400–450 cubic centimeters (cc). The brain of *H. habilis* was about 600 cc in volume. The earliest forms of *H. erectus* from 1.9 mya had a brain volume of 550–800 cc, whereas more recent forms from 500,000–200,000 BP reached 1,200 or 1,300 cc. The brain of *Homo sapiens* averages 1,300–1,400 cc, with a larger brain-to-body size ratio compared to *H. erectus*. The Neanderthal brain was bulkier still, at 1,500 cc.

Size alone does not explain the cognitive advantages of modern humans, considering that Neanderthal brains were larger. During the first years of life, human brains develop a more rounded, globular form, with greater expansion of the cerebellum and the parietal and temporal lobes, compared to Neanderthal and nonhuman primate brains. In addition, human brain tissue is packed less densely, allowing for more complex interactions between neurons. Human brains have an especially large neocortex – the rear portion of the cerebral cortex and the most recently evolved brain region. The neocortex is involved in sociality; comparing across species, its size increases with group size.

In sum, a capacious, complex brain allowed our ancestors to handle the cognitive demands of living in larger social groups, which are beneficial for mutual protection and for making a living but engender challenging interpersonal dynamics. Sociality alone does not explain the expansion of the brain, for there are large brains in relatively solitary animals such as orangutans and small brains in highly social mammals such as hyenas. Social living was one of several forces including technical ability and the transmission of knowledge that spurred on and were made possible by changes in the size and complexity of the brain.

The enlargement of the brain was interconnected with other adaptations.[4] Increased body fat and decreased muscle mass partially offset the metabolic cost of large brain size. Upright posture along with more efficient walking and running reduced the portion of energy diverted to muscular movement, leaving more for the brain. The digestive tract shortened, in line with the inverse relationship between brain size and digestive tract length across animal species. Comparing primate species, humans have a digestive tract less than two-thirds the expected length for body size. This reflects the difference between subsisting on tough plant foods requiring more energy to digest, and combining plant foods with calorically dense animal matter such as eggs, insects, and animal meat and organs.

Like carnivores such as felines, humans have a limited ability to convert precursor 18-carbon fatty acids into 20- and 22-carbon fatty acids, and are inefficient at synthesizing precursor amino acids into the amino acid taurine. Both taurine and 20- and 22-carbon fatty acids are found only in animal foods, suggesting that our ancestors consistently ate foods of animal origin. Herbivores must produce these compounds internally, indicating that a mixed diet eliminated the selective pressure to maintain the needed enzymes. Consumption of animal foods gave rise to genetic changes affecting lipid metabolism, neuronal development, and immune function that permit humans to consume significant quantities of animal protein and fat without developing heart disease and other complications. Defects in these genes increase the risk of a broad range of diseases including vascular pathologies (atherosclerosis, stroke), Alzheimer's disease, and multiple sclerosis.

Humans also share metabolic traits with herbivores. For instance, humans must obtain vitamin C from dietary sources, whereas carnivores synthesize it internally. Humans have small mouths and teeth, including teeth with broad surfaces for grinding. They chew their food rather than swallow it whole, and the digestive tract is long relative to that of carnivores. The nitrogen in animal protein limits the amount humans can handle to one-third of calories in the diet. At levels beyond this amount, the liver cannot keep up and nitrogenous waste accumulates as urea that interferes with kidney function and affects blood composition and blood pressure. Chronic overconsumption of protein causes liver enlargement, increased urine production, and bone demineralization. Diarrhea, delirium, and nausea result in weight loss even if the person is able to take in more of the high-protein food. Lean meat does not satisfy hunger. A diet of lean meat is fatal after only a few weeks.

In sum, animal foods were a consistent but not predominant component of the ancestral diet. They played a role in the emergence of a shorter gastrointestinal tract and larger brain size. These changes were connected to a slower rate of aging, as seen below.

Cooking may have contributed to increased brain size by reducing the amount of energy consumed by mastication and digestion. Chimpanzees spend 5 hours a day chewing, whereas humans who eat cooked food chew for an hour or less a day. Heating plants renders the carbohydrate easier to absorb, while cooking meat liquefies the collagen network in animal tissue. Some caloric and nutritional value is lost through cooking given that heat destroys vitamins and melts away fat, but on balance cooking greatly increases the efficiency of eating. The advantage in preparing food with heat is evident in the fact that cooking exists in every society today.

Cooking on the part of *H. erectus* nearly 2 million years ago would explain its large brain and small teeth, jaws, ribcage, and digestive tract (Wrangham 2009). However, the number of archeological sites suggesting cooking is small. At one of these, Wonderwerk Cave in South Africa, there is ash containing plants and animal bone fragments in a stratum from a million years ago, indicating that food was purposely brought to the site to be cooked (Berna et al. 2012).

The evidence for controlled use of fire is stronger at a site occupied by *H. erectus* in Israel 790,000 BP. Reliable evidence of cooking is much more recent still – around 250,000 BP. In sum, cooking may better explain the further increase in brain size in Neanderthals and modern humans relative to *H. erectus*. After 200,000 BP, the faces of these species grew smaller yet, which supports the idea that cooking became customary then since reduced chewing allows for a smaller jaw (Brace 1995).

By keeping predators away, fire allowed our ancestors to sleep on the ground. It might have helped favor anatomical changes away from a body fit for climbing to one adapted to long-distance walking. Campfires also promoted social cohesion. The light extended the amount of time available for social and recreational activities. Campfires and cooking consequently favored social integration, including pair bonding.

Human sociality depended to a large degree on language. Unlike other mammals including nonhuman primates, humans have unpigmented sclerae ("whites of the eyes") and comparatively small colored irises which permit highly efficient and complex nonverbal communication. Spoken language both resulted from and contributed to the increase in brain size and social interaction among our ancestors, and involved genetic changes affecting hearing and speech. Upright posture was the first condition for the emergence of spoken language, for it allows respiration to be controlled independently of locomotion. Around 500,000 BP a set of anatomical changes made it possible for our ancestors to use more precise speech. These include changes in jaw shape and size, as well as the descended larynx which allows humans to push air from the lungs through the windpipe and between the vocal chords primarily into the mouth. Other mammals, along with human newborns, have a larynx positioned behind the tongue rather than below it, which directs most of the air used to produce sound out through the nose.

Hominid skulls from around 400,000 BP have a larger anterior condyloid foramen, the hole in the skull through which the hypoglossal nerve controlling the tongue passes. Given that they are soft tissues, it is impossible to pinpoint the timing of the emergence of brain regions related to language, such as Broca's area involved in speech production, Wernicke's area for processing language, and parts of the prefrontal cortex involved in reasoning and memory. These must have been well established by the time complex symbolic communication involving the separation of sounds from meanings arose in Africa some 160,000–75,000 BP. Our close primate relatives such as chimps produce a similar range of sounds to humans but a smaller corpus of meanings.

Effective communication was certainly developed long before complex language. Similarities in the way that human and dog brains recognize voices and interpret their emotional content indicate that this kind of processing emerged more than 100 mya (Andics et al. 2014). Some kind of speech must have been used by *H. erectus* in order to expand geographically the way it did more than a million years ago, and for *H. sapiens* to do the same in turn. Language facilitates communication within groups and the sharing of knowledge, spouses, and friendship between them.

The agglomeration of groups of hominids contributed to cultural flourishing. The archeological record is particularly rich for periods in which groups were large and geographically concentrated enough for ideas and techniques to spread and build upon each other, such as Africa 100,000 BP and Europe 40,000 BP. There were many artistic and technological innovations during these periods, beyond improvements in tools for procuring and processing food. They were the fruit of a brain that had already developed cognitive abilities roughly the same as ours by 200,000 BP. Even 500,000 years ago, *H. heidelbergensis* made symmetrical hand axes that require symbolic manipulation, or the capacity to plan and imitate a mental image.

Nearly 80,000 years ago, our ancestors in southern Africa slept on mattresses made of grasses and other plants, including laurel leaves to keep the insects away. They made decorative beads, a practice already in use in the Middle East, and extracted, mixed, and stored pigments and liquid paint. Ancestral humans of this period etched patterns onto pieces of ochre, such as the 77,000-year-old specimens found in Blombos Cave, South Africa. Around 60,000 BP, they etched geometric shapes onto ostrich egg shells.

The first rock carvings appeared in Australia 45,000 years ago. During the period from 42,000–14,000 BP in Africa, Asia, Europe, and Australia, humans mined for tints and created artwork on cave walls or rock slabs. They made figurines out of clay, rock, and mammoth tusks, and created jewelry and other decorative objects out of shells, bone, stone, and ostrich eggs. Other objects produced by our Upper Paleolithic ancestors include flutes made from long animal bones as well as etched bones known as "tally sticks" used for notation and to keep track of time, seasons, and geography. The artwork shows high technical skill including perspective and accurate representation of the forms and habits of animals such as horses, rhinoceroses, lions, bison, deer, and boar. In some cases, the figures were half-human, half-animal, such as the "lion man" (lion head, human body) found in Stadel Cave in Germany. In other cases, the creatures were hybrids of two animals apparently in the process of being born, as in Lascaux, France. The images in Altamira Cave in Spain include sculptures of human faces.

Many of these caves are nearly inaccessible, indicating that people did not live there but instead visited to paint and possibly to worship. The artists worked in pairs or groups, given that someone was needed to hold a light source. They taught children, who drew with their fingers in the soft silt that lines caves such as Rouffignac in southwestern France, the youngest ones' tiny hands guided by an adult who lifted them to the higher levels. Expressive and possibly religious activity is further evidenced by sites such as Göbekli Tepe in southeast Turkey, where Stonehenge-sized slabs decorated with sculpted animal figures were left by foragers 11,500–9,500 years ago.

Some of the cave paintings attributed to humans may have been made by Neanderthals, the species that appears to have been the most similar to humans.[5] Neanderthals also may have been the founders of the Châtelperronian culture known for ivory rings and animal teeth found mainly in France. Neanderthals left evidence of cooking, ceremonies, sewing, and jewelry and other decorative objects. Numerous sites suggest that Neanderthals developed burial customs long before modern humans did, although this conventional wisdom is debatable (Sandgathe et al. 2011). While Neanderthals may have imitated human technological and creative arts, and while shifting sedimentary layers create uncertainties about the authorship of artifacts (Higham et al. 2010), some specimens clearly predate the arrival of *Homo sapiens* in Europe, such as 50,000–45,000-year-old shells from Spain that were refashioned into jewelry and storage containers (Zilhão et al. 2010).

Anatomical and behavioral differences contributed to the divergence in the fortunes of humans and Neanderthals. Humans had a lighter skeleton, shorter jaws, and smaller teeth. There were genetic differences related to bone and brain development as well as hair, skin, and sweat glands that probably rendered humans more adaptable to environmental variability. Although Neanderthals in Europe and the Middle East ate a varied diet that included grass seeds, legumes, and fruit, they tended to inhabit cold, hostile environments where there was little vegetation for much of the year and consequently the diet was richer in meat. Their larger chests and lungs, which could absorb two or three times more oxygen – useful for metabolizing animal tissues – were an additional factor that may have rendered Neanderthals less able to thrive in other environments. While Neanderthals eventually developed similar implements to humans, humans used more types of tools made from a greater variety of materials. For some time after contact, Neanderthals continued to use sturdy spears, which can be thrown only a few meters. Finally, Neanderthals lived in smaller and more isolated groups of under a dozen people, leaving them more vulnerable to demographic decline.

In sum, humans were not alone in adapting to their environments culturally and biologically. Other hominids thrived alongside humans until 20,000 or fewer years ago. Yet, some combination of anatomical and cultural features allowed humans to outlast the others. These include reproductive and social behaviors along with a brain that develops largely outside the womb and leaves our species profoundly dependent on culture.

. . . . .

Remarkably, during the period of climatic instability 1.9–1.6 mya, the stress of reduced food availability and increased caloric needs due to larger bodies resulted in more rather than less childbearing among human ancestors. The problem created by the higher energy cost to mothers of shorter interbirth intervals was solved through food sharing, dietary changes, and cooperative childrearing. Increased paternal care may be inferred from the reduction in the size difference between males and females in *Homo* compared to ape species.

Upright posture and large brain size increased the risks associated with childbirth for *Homo* females, making social assistance virtually indispensable.[6] Already some 4 million years ago australopithecine females experienced a unique kind of childbirth compared to other primates, due to the flattened, rigid birth canal associated with upright posture. However, the infant's head was close in size to that of the pelvic opening, as is common for nonhuman primates. The australopithecine infant passed through the birth canal without rotating its head and shoulders, and exited facing the mother rather than facing behind her.

As we have seen, *Homo* had a much larger brain. Between 1 mya and 200,000 BP, the birth canal also expanded and changed shape. In humans, this structure runs side-to-side where the infant's head enters it, but shifts to a front-to-back oval opening at the far end. Given that the infant's head is about the same size and shape as the opening, while its shoulders run perpendicular to the widest part of the cranium, the infant has to make a series of twists in order to move forward.

Mothers must have required assistance during childbirth from the time the new pelvic formation arose, although they may have had help beforehand as well. It is not just that the fit is tight; it is difficult for a mother to assist an infant oriented in the wrong direction when it emerges from the birth canal. Someone else is needed to safely pull the infant without arching its back, and to keep the umbilical cord from entangling its neck. Indeed, with rare exceptions, throughout the world women give birth with the help of one or more assistants. Virtually every society has well established rules about the behavior of mothers and assistants during pregnancy, childbirth, and the post-partum period.

Given the limit on brain size imposed by the pelvis due to upright posture, more brain growth has to take place after birth in humans than other species. Modern human infants are born with a brain one-fourth the size of the adult brain, compared to one-half among the earliest *Homo* species and mammals in general. This renders newborns much more helpless, as they are born neurologically unfinished. They require more and longer care than other animals give to their young. Infants are born with behaviors that elicit social interaction, while adults likewise are psychologically inclined to assist small, helpless creatures.

Also among captive and free-living nonhuman primates it is common for mates and potential mates, siblings, grandfathers and grandmothers, and aunts and uncles to provide care and protection to the young. Adolescent and adult primates carry and protect their young relatives and cuddle, play, and share food with them. Adult tamarins and marmosets call younger animals with a unique sound that signals the location of prized foods they have come upon, such as large insects.

Primatologist Sarah Blaffer Hrdy (2009) points out that "alloparenting" is especially significant in species whose mothers carry babies over long distances, such as humans and langurs. Socioecological factors predict this kind of behavior better than phylogenetic relationships, for our closest relatives such as chimps do less alloparenting. On the other hand, even chimpanzee males, who do not normally provide much care for their own infants, will, like females, adopt related or unrelated infants whose mothers have died (Boesch et al. 2010). They carry their adopted infant around, wait for it to catch up when the group is on the move, and give it food and a safe place to sleep.

Cooperative parenting favored the increase in fertility among human ancestors.[7] Also in nonhuman primates, male care of infants – whether paternal or for gaining mating opportunities – is associated with higher birth rates. Ranging farther for food in order to leave closer sources to the mother is another well-known male contribution to infant care. Grooming and carrying the infant may be even more important. To carry an infant requires about the same energy expenditure as lactation. If someone else takes over, the mother has a more favorable energy balance and can also forage more effectively. Distancing the infant from the breast reduces suckling frequency and speeds the mother's return to a fertile condition. These behavioral changes contribute to reduced interbirth intervals, while improved maternal health through reduced energetic stress is linked to increased child survival. They suggest paternal care and pair bonding, although it could have been other individuals who assisted mothers with child care.

Human mothers breastfeed for a shorter amount of time than expected based on comparisons with nonhuman primates such as chimps and gorillas. Proportions that hold across a range of species, such as the time to reach one-third of adult body weight or the eruption of the first permanent molars, predict that humans should breastfeed infants for 5 or 6 years. That length of time is also the amount needed for the child's immune system to develop fully (Dettwyler 1995). Nevertheless, breastfeeding beyond 5 years is an exception even among hunting and gathering societies, in which babies generally breastfeed for 2–4 years. Earlier weaning points to the importance and reliability of alloparenting. To illustrate, researchers studying Efe foragers in Central Africa counted an average of 14.2 caregivers per infant over the course of an 8-hour day. Even infants only a few months old spent less than half their time with their mothers, and women other than the mother often were the first to breastfeed a newborn (Tronick et al. 1985). Similar customs involving multiple caregivers and milk kinship, by which lifelong bonds are formed between nonrelatives through breastfeeding, are common throughout the world, including many agricultural societies (see Chapter 8).

Changes in men's hormone levels in line with romantic involvement and the birth and care of children further reflect the antiquity and evolutionary importance of paternal care, as shown in Chapter 7. The altered levels of prolactin, testosterone, and other hormones reduce physical aggression and increase trust. On the other hand, the size difference between human males and females reflects an evolutionary history of moderate male-male competition for mates. Across primate species, male-male competition is inversely related to paternal care and is dangerous to infants.

Varying degrees of male-male competition are also linked to sex differences in aging and life span.[8] Life span refers to the average age at death of the longest-living 10% of a population or species. Primate species with no sex difference in size have the most exclusive pair bonding, extensive paternal care, and equality in age-specific mortality rates and life span between females and males. That is, females live longer than males in species such as chimps in which females are the primary caregivers and there is a high degree of male-male competition, whereas males and females have the same life span in monogamous species in which males care for their young and there is limited competition between males – such as gibbons, muriquis or woolly spider monkeys, and New World owl monkeys. Humans fall short of the strictly monogamous end of the spectrum. As shown in the next chapter, there is a difference in mortality risk in favor of females but men's social advantages often overwhelm women's biological advantages.

The long life span of even the earliest *Homo* species allowed grandparents to contribute to the care and protection of the young. Across primate species, those with the longest life spans are the ones with the largest brains and the slowest development of the young. The life spans of our closest primate relatives, the apes, range from 40–60 years both in the wild and in captivity: 40–50 in mountain gorillas; over 50 in common gorillas; 40 to the mid-50s in bonobos and common chimpanzees; and high 50s in orangutans. Life spans of 40 or more years have been recorded for several species of gibbons, spider monkeys, and capuchin monkeys.

In primates, there is a consistent relationship between life span and two variables: body weight and brain size. Using values obtained from our closest relatives, the apes, we can predict a life span for humans of 95 years. The same formula predicts a life span in the low 50s for the australopithecines, and life spans that grew from 60 to nearly 80 years among *Homo* species from 2 million until 250,000 years ago. European *H. erectus* had a life span of around 90 years as long as 100,000 BP; the life span of *H. neanderthalensis* and *H. sapiens* was nearly 95 years by 50,000–40,000 BP. Most individuals may have been unlikely to reach these ages, but there was no biological reason why they could not.

At some point between 1.5 million and 500,000 years ago, reproductive senescence evolved in females and to a lesser degree in males.[9] Males may continue to become fathers even late in life without endangering their own survival, but as females age childbearing becomes riskier to them and their existing children. Accordingly, ovulation ceases for older women but sperm production continues in men, albeit imperfectly. Not surprisingly, maternal grandmothers are the caregivers, aside from mothers, who have the most consistent positive effect on child survival across a large number of societies (Sear and Mace 2008).

In foraging and agricultural societies, old people are recognized as important sources of knowledge and social stability. They have time to engage in teaching, spiritual leadership, and the care of small children, which allows younger adults to collect or produce more food. These roles indicate that old people were essential to the life of the community in the type of society that prevailed for almost all of human evolution, and in many other societies as well. The evolutionary importance of old people and their contributions is congruent with the finding that older people who provide social and emotional support to others enjoy better health and wellbeing than those who do not (Piferi and Lawler 2006).

. . . . .

This chapter has shown that food collection over human evolution does not fit popular assumptions about the ancestral diet, the way animal foods were procured by human ancestors, and the determining role of large-game hunting in the development of tools, social organization, and a large brain in our species. The expansion of the brain was interrelated with dietary changes, increasingly complex social organization, and behavioral innovations such as language, cooking, and symbolic manipulation. Human ancestors formed long-term couples and provided significant paternal and grandparental care that contributed to closer birth spacing and increased child survival. These traits arose long before large-game hunting and any possible gender division of labor.

Groups came into contact with other groups but did not use weapons against each other. Foragers lived longer and healthier lives than Neolithic agriculturalists, whose greater burden of disease was accompanied by endemic warfare and increased interpersonal violence. As seen in the following chapters, food production and permanent settlements profoundly changed the lives of individuals and societies, with lasting effects.

Notes

1 On contemporary foraging societies, see Hill and Hurtado (1996); Howell (1979); Leacock and Lee (1982); Tonkinson (1978).
2 On Paleolithic trade networks, see Bar-Yosef (2002); Headland and Reid (1989); Krause-Kyora et al. (2013).
3 On technological and anatomical changes over hominid evolution, see Hart and Sussman (2005); Jones et al. (1994); Stanford et al. (2011).

4 On diet, brain size, and the rate of aging, see Cordain et al. (2002); Finch and Stanford (2004).
5 On Neanderthals, see Churchill (2014); Henry et al. (2011).
6 On the evolution of childbirth, see Trevathan and Rosenberg (2000).
7 On paternal care, see Gettler (2010); Hewlett (1991, 1992).
8 On primate and hominid life spans and mortality rates, see Bronikowski et al. (2011); Carey (2003); Cutler (1976).
9 On the evolution of grandparenthood, see Judge and Carey (2000); Voland et al. (2005); Weiss (1981).

References cited

Adovasio JM, Soffer O, Page J. 2009. *The invisible sex: uncovering the true roles of women in prehistory*. Walnut Creek, CA: Left Coast Press.

Andics A, Gácsi M, Faragó T, Kis A, Miklósi A. 2014. Voice-sensitive regions in the dog and human brain are revealed by comparative fMRI. *Current Biology* 24(5):574–578.

Armitage SJ, Jasim SA, Marks AE, Parker AG, Usik VI, Uerpmann HP. 2011. The southern route "out of Africa": evidence for an early expansion of modern humans into Arabia. *Science* 331(6016):453–456.

Bar-Yosef O. 2002. The Upper Paleolithic revolution. *Annual Review of Anthropology* 31:363–393.

Berger LR, de Ruiter DJ, Churchill SE, Schmid P, Carlson KJ, Dirks PH, Kibii JM. 2010. Australopithecus sediba: a new species of Homo-like Australopith from South Africa. *Science* 328(5975):195–204.

Berna F, Goldberg P, Horwitz LK, Brink J, Holt S, Bamford M, Chazan M. 2012. Microstratigraphic evidence of in situ fire in the Acheulean strata of Wonderwerk Cave, Northern Cape province, South Africa. *Proceedings of the National Academy of Sciences*. 109(20):e1215–e1220.

Boesch C, Bolé C, Eckhardt N, Boesch H. 2010. Altruism in forest chimpanzees: the case of adoption. *PLoS One* 5(1):e8901.

Brace CL. 1995[1967]. *The stages of human evolution*. 5th ed. Engelwood Cliffs, NJ: Prentice-Hall.

Bronikowski AM, Altmann J, Brockman DK, Cords M, Fedigan LM, Pusey A, Stoinski T, Morris WF, Strier KB, Alberts SC. 2011. Aging in the natural world: comparative data reveal similar mortality patterns across primates. *Science* 331(6022):1325–1328.

Carey JR. 2003. *Longevity: the biology and demography of the life span*. Princeton, NJ: Princeton University Press.

Churchill SE. 2014. *Thin on the ground: Neanderthal biology, archeology, and ecology*. New York: Wiley-Blackwell.

Cohn BA. 1998. The vital role of the skin in human natural history. *International Journal of Dermatology* 37(11):821–824.

Cordain L, Eaton SB, Brand Miller J, Mann N, Hill K. 2002. Original communication. The paradoxical nature of hunter-gatherer diets: meat-based, yet non-atherogenic. *European Journal of Clinical Nutrition* 56(1):S42–S52.

Cutler RG. 1976. Evolution of longevity in primates. *Journal of Human Evolution* 5(2):169–202.

Dettwyler KA. 1995. A time to wean: the hominid blueprint for the natural age of weaning in modern human populations. In Stuart-Macadam P, Dettwyler KA, editors. *Breastfeeding: biocultural perspectives*. New York: Aldine de Gruyter. p. 39–74.

Farb P, Armelagos G. 1980. *Consuming passions: the anthropology of eating*. Boston: Houghton Mifflin Company.

Finch CE, Stanford CB. 2004. Meat-adaptive genes and the evolution of slower aging in humans. *Quarterly Review of Biology* 79(1):3–50.

Gettler LT. 2010. Direct male care and hominin evolution: why male-child interaction is more than a nice social idea. *American Anthropologist* 112(1):7–21.

Haak W, Balanovsky O, Sanchez JJ, Koshel S, Zaporozhchenko V, Adler CJ, Der Sarkissian CS, Brandt G, Schwarz C, Nicklisch N, et al. 2010. Ancient DNA from European early Neolithic farmers reveals their near eastern affinities. *PLoS Biology* 8(11):e1000536.

Hart D, Sussman RW. 2005. *Man the hunted: primates, predators, and human evolution.* New York: Basic Books.

Headland TN, Reid LA. 1989. Hunter-gatherers and their neighbors from prehistory to the present. *Current Anthropology* 30(1):43–66.

Henry AG, Brooks AS, Piperno DR. 2011. Microfossils in calculus demonstrate consumption of plants and cooked foods in Neanderthal diets. *Proceedings of the National Academy of Sciences* 108(2):486–491.

Hewlett BS. 1991. *Intimate fathers: the nature and context of Aka Pygmy paternal infant care.* Ann Arbor: University of Michigan Press.

Hewlett BS, editor. 1992. *Father-child relations: cultural and biosocial contexts.* New York: Aldine de Gruyter.

Higham T, Jacobi R, Julien M, David F, Basell L, Wood R, Davies W, Ramsey CB. 2010. Chronology of the Grotte du Renne (France) and implications for the context of ornaments and human remains within the Châtelperronian. *Proceedings of the National Academy of Sciences* 107(47):20234–20239.

Hill K, Hurtado AM. 1996. *Aché life history: the ecology and demography of a foraging people.* New York: Aldine de Gruyter.

Howell N. 1979. *Demography of the Dobe !Kung.* New York: Academic Press.

Hrdy SB. 2009. *Mothers and others: the evolutionary origins of mutual understanding.* Cambridge, MA: Harvard University Press.

Hublin J, McPherron SP, editors. 2012. *Modern origins: a North African perspective.* New York: Springer Publishing Company.

Jones S, Martin RD, Pilbeam DR, Bunney S, editors. 1994. *The Cambridge encyclopedia of human evolution.* Cambridge: Cambridge University Press.

Judge DS, Carey JR. 2000. Postreproductive life predicted by primate patterns. *The Journals of Gerontology Series A* 55(4): B201–B209.

Krause-Kyora B, Makarewicz C, Evin A, Flink LG, Dobney K, Larson G, Hartz S, Schreiber S, von Carnap-Bornheim C, von Wurmb-Schwark N, et al. 2013. Use of domesticated pigs by Mesolithic hunter-gatherers in northwestern Europe. *Nature Communications* 4(2348). doi: 10.1038/ncomms3348.

Leacock E, Lee R, editors. 1982. *Politics and history in band societies.* Cambridge, UK: Cambridge University Press.

McPherron SP, Alemseged Z, Marean CW, Wynn JG, Reed D, Geraads D, Bobe R, Béarat HA. 2010. Evidence for stone-tool-assisted consumption of animal tissues before 3.39 million years ago at Dikika, Ethiopia. *Nature* 466(7308):857–860.

Pickering TR. 2013. *Rough and tumble: aggression, hunting, and human evolution.* Berkeley: University of California Press.

Piferi RL, Lawler KA. 2006. Social support and ambulatory blood pressure: an examination of both receiving and giving. *International Journal of Psychophysiology* 62(2):328–336.

Sandgathe DM, Dibble HL, Goldberg P, McPherron SP. 2011. The Roc de Marsal Neanderthal child: a reassessment of its status as a deliberate burial. *Journal of Human Evolution* 61(3):243–253.

Sear R, Mace R. 2008. Who keeps children alive? A review of the effects of kin on child survival. *Evolution and Human Behavior* 29(1):1–18.

Stanford C, Allen JS, Antón SC. 2011. *Biological anthropology*. 3rd ed. Upper Saddle River, NJ: Pearson.

Thalmann O, Shapiro B, Cui P, Schuenemann VJ, Sawyer SK, Greenfield DL, Germonpré MB, Sablin MV, López-Giráldez F, Domingo-Roura X, et al. 2013. Complete mitochondrial genomes of ancient canids suggest a European origin of domestic dogs. *Science* 342(6160):871–874.

Tonkinson R. 1978. *The Mardudjara Aborigines: living the dream in Australia's desert*. New York: Holt, Rinehart, and Winston.

Trevathan W, Rosenberg K. 2000. The shoulders follow the head: postcranial constraints on human childbirth. *Journal of Human Evolution* 39(6):583–586.

Tronick EZ, Winn S, Morelli GA. 1985. Multiple caretaking in the context of human evolution: why don't the Efe know the Western prescription for child care? In Reite M, Field T, editors. *The psychobiology of attachment and separation*. New York: Academic Press. p. 293–322.

Voland E, Chasiotis A, Schiefenhövel W. 2005. *Grandmotherhood: the evolutionary significance of the second half of female life*. New Brunswick, NJ: Rutgers University Press.

Ward CV, Tocheri MW, Plavcan JM, Brown FH, Manthi FK. 2013. Early Pleistocene third metacarpal from Kenya and the evolution of modern human-like hand morphology. *Proceedings of the National Academy of Sciences* 111(1):121–124.

Weiss KM. 1981. Evolutionary perspectives on human aging. In Amoss PT, Harrell S, editors. *Other ways of growing old: anthropological perspectives*. Stanford, CA: Stanford University Press. p. 25–58.

Wrangham R. 2009. *Catching fire: how cooking made us human*. New York: Basic Books.

Zilhão J, Angelucci DE, Badal-García E, d'Errico F, Daniel F, Dayet L, Douka K, Higham TF, Martínez-Sánchez MJ, Montes-Bernárdez R, et al. 2010. Symbolic use of marine shells and mineral pigments by Iberian Neanderthals. *Proceedings of the National Academy of Sciences* 107(3):1023–1028.

3

LOSSES AND GAINS

Economic and health transitions since the Neolithic Revolution

The image of carnivorous, self-interested ancestral humans implies that life was miserable and short before modern civilization. Life expectancy rates from times past are taken as proof that human existence has progressively improved since our days in the cave. Since the quantitative increase has been especially dramatic over the last century or two, the narrative of progress attributes an apparent increase in the life span to medical treatments.

However, life span is not the same as life expectancy, and the fall in birth and death rates that began 250 years ago is not the starting point for human demographic history. There was a much earlier transition which resulted in a *rise* in death and birth rates, and a *decline* in life expectancy. The demographic shift was related to the switch from foraging to cultivating food around 12,000 years ago. Far from making life easier, the transition to farming brought less leisure time, a less nutritious and varied diet, more disease, and lower life expectancy. The number of births soared, causing population growth to accelerate in spite of higher mortality. Permanent settlements and stored wealth led to gender and socioeconomic stratification. There was more interpersonal violence. Eventually many societies became embroiled in endemic warfare.

Reduced population health was the baseline for the more recent mortality and fertility transition, which was linked to another major economic transformation, this time involving industrialization and agricultural intensification. It involved a shift from infectious to chronic diseases as the primary causes of death. The second transition occurred first in Europe, then more recently and quickly in other wealthy countries. It is still under way or stalled in impoverished countries. In the last few decades, another health transition has begun, involving an upsurge of new and re-emerging infectious diseases.

This chapter explores changes in health, reproduction, and life expectancy linked to major demographic and epidemiologic transitions. It shows that old age is normal for humans, even if not always common. Since there is a lot riding on the idea that the length of life has done nothing but increase over time, we will begin with an analysis of life expectancy rates.

. . . . .

I once studied all the birth, death, and marriage registers in a northern Italian town covering more than a century beginning in the 1860s (Whitaker 2000). Strikingly, a large number of people died in their 80s and 90s, even in the second half of the 19th century, when life expectancy at birth was half what it is now. One-fifth of the babies died before their first birthday.

Based on life expectancy rates, history books conclude that people lived barely 20 years during the Roman Empire or only 30 years in the Middle Ages, but there were old people then too. The writers of the Old Testament took a normal lifetime of 70–80 years for granted, as in the threescore-and-ten years or, with strength, fourscore years given in Psalm 90:10. The first line of Dante's *Inferno*, written around 1300, places the 35-year-old poet at the midpoint of life ("*Nel mezzo del cammin di nostra vita*"). Table 3.1 lists a tiny sample of historical figures who

TABLE 3.1 Long-lived historical figures from antiquity to the Renaissance

Name	*Birth place*	*Birth and death year*	*Years lived*
King Solomon	Israel/Judah	(-) 1011–932	79
Pythagoras of Samos	Greece	(-) 570–495	75
Siddhartha Gautama	India	(-) 563–483	80
Confucius (Kong Fuzi)	China	(-) 551–479	72
Sophocles	Greece	(-) 496–406	90
Hippocrates of Cos	Greece	(-) 460–377	83
Diogenes of Sinope	Turkey	(-) 412–323	89
Mengzi (Mencius)	China	(-) 371–289	82
Pyrrho of Elis	Greece	(-) 365–275	90
Seleucus I	Macedonia	(-) 358–281	77
Cato the Elder (Marcus Porcius)	Italy	(-) 234–149	85
Juvenal (Decimus Junius Juvenalis)	Italy	60–140	80
Tertullian	Tunisia	160–240	80
Arius	Egypt	250–336	86
Justinian	Macedonia	483–565	83
Saint Columban	Ireland	521–597	76
Pepin of Herstal	Germany	635–714	79
Charlemagne	Belgium	742–814	71
Basil I	Turkey	811–886	75
Eleanor of Aquitaine	France	1122–1204	82
Ibn Khaldun	Tunisia	1332–1406	74
Michelangelo Buonarroti	Italy	1475–1564	88

lived 70 or more years, to illustrate the point that old people have existed throughout the world from the earliest recorded times.[1] Many more historical figures lived 60–70 years, including Ramses II, Thucydides, Aristotle, Cicero, Saint Benedict, Muhammed, and Genghis Khan.

Many rulers reigned for decades, often exceeding the supposed life span of their population. Hammurabi ruled for 42 years, Hatshepsut for 22, King Solomon for 30 or 40, Cyrus the Great for 30, and Emperor Wu for 53. In the Middle Ages, Theodoric ruled for 55 years, Justinian for 38 and Theodora for 21, Frederick II (Stupor Mundi) for 35, and Eleanor of Aquitaine for 50. Greek philosophers and politicians including Plato maintained that only people over age 60 should be considered for political, cultural, and intellectual leadership.

There is nothing new about growing old. Nonhuman primates live to be grandparents, as did early hominid species including australopithecines. Where life expectancy rates are low, the reason is a high rate of loss of infants and small children. Contrariwise, a high life expectancy rate does not signify an expansion in the maximum years of life, but primarily a reduction in infant mortality. Mortality rates in later childhood and adulthood also vary, but the range is much smaller than it is for infant mortality, which is more sensitive to differences in living conditions.

Average life expectancy at birth expresses the number of years left, on average, to the people born in a given year. It is either a projection based on current age-specific death rates, or a synthesis of actual events in the case of cohorts of people whose birth and death years are all known. In contrast, as noted in Chapter 2, life span represents the average number of years lived by the longest-surviving 10% of a population or species. For humans, this is about 95 years, with an upper limit of around 120. Both life expectancy and the human life span refer to populations, as opposed to the lifetime of any single individual.

To illustrate the relationship between infant mortality and life expectancy rates, we will examine three hypothetical scenarios involving three cohorts of 850 people born in a single year in three different centuries. The exercise assumes that there are perfect records for all the people and that the calculations are done after every individual has passed away. The full explanation, with step-by-step calculations of life expectancy rates, is available in the Appendix.

In the first case, living conditions were moderately good and infant mortality rates were fairly low. In the second, conditions had worsened and many babies died. In the last case, conditions had greatly improved and mortality rates were very low for infants and throughout the life course.

The first table presents raw numbers of people grouped together according to the number of years they lived. The most dramatic differences concern the number of deaths in the first year of life: 5% in Cohort A, 27% in Cohort B, and less than 1% in Cohort C.

In all cases, many people lived past age 60: 45% in Cohort A, 27% in B, and 89% in C. Even though life expectancy was only 36 years for Cohort B, more than one-fourth of the population lived more than 60 years.

TABLE 3.2 Number of individuals in Cohorts A, B, and C, by age at death

	Cohort A		*Cohort B*		*Cohort C*	
	n *deaths*	%	n *deaths*	%	n *deaths*	%
0–1 years	42	*4.9*	230	*27.1*	5	*0.6*
1–60 years	428	*50.4*	391	*46.0*	88	*10.4*
60–90 years	328	*38.6*	205	*24.1*	591	*69.5*
Over 90 years	52	*6.1*	24	*2.8*	166	*19.5*
Total	850	*100*	850	*100*	850	*100*

Table 3.3 illustrates the preponderant effect of infant mortality rates on life expectancy rates. Life expectancy rates depend on how many people die each year as a percentage of the total in their age group (age-specific mortality rates). Life expectancy rates represent the average years of life left to the group, whether at birth or some other point in life, such as 5 or 15 years.

TABLE 3.3 Average life expectancy at various ages under three mortality scenarios

	Cohort A	*Cohort B*	*Cohort C*
	Years	*Years*	*Years*
Birth	54.8	36.3	77.7
5 years	53.2	47.6	73.2
15 years	43.9	40.3	63.3
45 years	23.9	21.8	34.8
60 years	16.8	15.4	21.8
75 years	10.7	10.1	11.4
90 years	4.8	4.5	4.9

The differences in life expectancy at birth are dramatic: from 55 to 36 to 78 years. However, the gap narrows considerably at older age levels. At age 15, the numbers are 44, 40, and 63 years. At age 60, they are 17, 15, and 22. By age 75, the average number of years of life remaining is virtually the same at around a decade, and at 90 it is between 4.5 and 5 in all three cases. Historical data such as dates on tombstones likewise show that even where life expectancy at birth is in the teens or 20s, average life expectancy at age 60 is another 12–20 years (Weiss and Wobst 1973). This includes late ancient Roman territories in Europe, Asia, and North Africa. Clearly, even in the worst of times conditions were not as bleak as implied by assumptions about people living only 20 or 30 years.

The three scenarios roughly represent the moderate, high, and low life expectancy rates that have been associated with foraging societies, early agricultural societies, and industrialized societies, respectively. Life expectancy at birth is around 40 for modern-day foraging populations.[2] At age 15, it is about 50 years, similar to the US rate of 47 in the year 1900. Among the Ju/'hoansi of southern Africa, the life expectancy rate at age 15 was 54 years in the 1970s, and 10–20% of the people lived beyond age 60. For Aché foragers in Paraguay, life expectancy at age 15 was 43 years for females, 37 for males around the same time. These values are likely to be lower than they would have been for foragers in the distant past, given that most recently studied foragers have lived in marginal environments.

After the transition to agriculture, life expectancy rates fell to the upper teens and 20s. In Europe, they only reached into the 30s in the mid-18th century in the north, and later in the south. Where living conditions were especially bad, they remained around 20 or lower for much longer. Over the 18th and 19th centuries, rates increased towards 40 years.

By now, life expectancy at birth in Scandinavia, Western Europe, North America, Japan, Singapore, and other developed countries is near or above 80. This is due to low age-specific death rates including infant mortality rates around 0.6%, although these low rates can mask highly uneven mortality risks across subpopulations, as in the US where black babies die at more than twice the rate of white and Hispanic babies. Economically and politically disadvantaged countries have much higher infant mortality rates of around 5%, with maximum values of 10% or higher in countries such as Mali and Afghanistan. Consequently, life expectancy at birth remains lower than in the developed countries – in the 50s and 60s.

. . . . .

We may now turn to the causes and consequences of the three transitions, beginning with the shift towards permanent settlement and the production rather than collection of food. The bleak view of human origins casts this transition in a positive light, as if it replaced deprivation and violence with the leisure, health, and wealth that allowed humans to engage in musical, artistic, philosophical, and scientific endeavors for the first time. Marshall Sahlins (1972) calls this "one of the first distinctly neolithic prejudices." It mistakenly attributes creative and intellectual achievements to recent humans and obscures the fact that the transition brought a decline in health and an increase in work, social stratification, and conflict. The effects were so severe and long-lasting that Jared Diamond (1987) calls agriculture "the worst mistake in the history of the human race."

As seen in the last chapter, Paleolithic humans had sophisticated cognitive abilities at least 50,000–100,000 years ago. Their mobility and egalitarianism precluded the wealth and social stratification necessary for the construction of monuments and other massive permanent structures, but Paleolithic humans left behind other evidence of advanced mental and social skills. The reasons for agriculture had to do with ecological and demographic factors, not changes in the human brain.

The end of the Ice Age around 12,000 years before the present (BP) brought a warming trend that increased the amount of arable land, together with fluctuations in temperature and rainfall that rendered the food supply less predictable.

Population increase, although gradual, may have created local demographic pressure on resources, especially in places where shifting weather patterns caused changes to vegetation or the extinction of large numbers of animals. Some areas appear to have suffered a depletion of game due to improved hunting technology, but analysis of contemporary Amazonian foraging groups together with computer simulations argues against the idea that ancestral humans regularly drained the landscape of game. Traditional amounts of hunting are sustainable even in the case of large-bodied, long-lived mammals with low reproductive rates, as long as cultural beliefs discourage overharvesting and firearms are not available (Shepard et al. 2012).

Humans manipulated the environment for the purpose of increasing the food supply 60,000 BP, long before agriculture.[3] In Papua New Guinea, they cut trees with saws in order to promote the growth of useful plants around 50,000 BP, and introduced animal species into areas with scarce game around 20,000 BP. In Borneo, humans used fire 40,000 years ago to manage the growth of edible plants, and they appear to have used traps to snare pigs.

Beginning 13,000–12,000 years ago, people began to make more intensive use of the resources at hand, including foods that previously had been less attractive. This broad-spectrum revolution brought grinding stones, seed preservation, and the relocation of plants and animals from their original habitats to more productive environments. Rye, wheat, and barley were domesticated in the Near and Middle East between 13,000–11,000 BP, and rice was cultivated in Asia around 12,000 BP. Millet was grown in China 9,000 years ago. By 7,000–5,000 BP, these crops plus sorghum were grown widely in China, India, Southeast Asia, Mesoamerica, and Africa. Squash was cultivated 10,000 BP in the New World, followed by maize, beans, potatoes, and peppers between 9,000–6,000 BP.

The first animals to be domesticated were pigs, sheep, goats, and dogs, followed by cattle. The process began around 11,500–8,000 BP in the Near East, Eurasia, India, and North Africa. At the Hallan Çemi site in Turkey, pig domestication beginning 11,500 BP took place before grain cultivation, indicating that at least some groups kept animals before they began farming. Camels, dromedaries, oxen, and water buffaloes were domesticated between 7,000–4,000 BP for use as draft animals and carriers. Horses and donkeys were domesticated early in this same period and were better adapted for the job. Like humans, they can work for long periods of time because they sweat. These animals were crucial to the spread of early complex civilizations in the Old World. They were extinct in the New World until the Spanish reintroduced them into their original habitats.

The shift to producing rather than gathering food was gradual and involved a mixture of foraging, herding, fishing, and farming – as occurs among many contemporary foraging populations. Some cultivators used the slash-and-burn technique and remained semi-nomadic. Other societies went through phases in which they were settled, followed by a return to mobile foraging. A mixed approach buffered against risk during the long seed selection phase that eventually led to larger grain size. For instance, villagers at El-Hemmeh in Jordan, occupied from about 11,500–8,000 BP, also ate wild roots, tubers, and rushes and other water plants.

Early settlements combined not only subsistence strategies but also the social characteristics of nomadic and settled populations. At Çatalhöyük in Turkey, which was founded around 9,500 BP and inhabited for 2,000 years, up to 8,000 villagers worked the surrounding fields but also collected wild plant and animal foods. Houses were accreted upon one another in a beehive-like structure with openings at the top of each dwelling, the roofs serving as streets. No defensive wall protected the village, although the windowless outer walls of the houses may have served the same purpose. There were no noticeable differences in housing and no public spaces, indicating a lack of socioeconomic stratification. Murals and figurines featured female divinities and suggest worship of a Mother Goddess, while analysis of human remains indicates gender equality in diet and burial customs.

In the Old World, Neolithic agricultural technologies, people, and genes spread generally but not solely in an east-to-west direction from western Asia across Europe, whereas in the New World they moved along a north-south axis. Other flows went from the Middle East into Africa; from West Africa southward; from Korea to Japan; and from Taiwan to the islands of Southeast Asia. Farming had such powerful demographic effects that most people in the world today speak a language deriving from one of a handful of linguistic families present in the geographical areas of Eurasia where agricultural technology was first developed (China and the Near and Middle East).

Of all the possible edible plant and animal species, humans have domesticated only a few, and most were discovered early on. Only 14 of 148 possible large animals (over 45 kg) have been domesticated, while only 150 of at least 30,000 edible plants have been domesticated and about 100 are cultivated commercially (Diamond 2002). Agriculture yields a much higher ratio of calories to unit of land compared to foraging, but the concentration of effort on limited crops reduces food variety. As a result, health tends to worsen, especially in the early stages of economic transition, as seen below.

. . . . .

The better health and longevity of foragers compared to agriculturalists indicates that foragers are not defenseless loners living at the mercy of a capricious environment.[4] Even in marginal ecological areas they have adequate food and make use of a larger range of food sources than agriculturalists. Their food supplies are more stable and predictable given that wild foods are better able to withstand droughts, floods, and pests. Mobility, knowledge of less-desirable food sources that can be accessed in time of need, and social relationships between groups buffer against the risk of shortages.

Paleolithic foragers were tall and physically fit. Those living in the eastern Mediterranean 30,000 years ago were taller than the average American today. Analysis of muscle insertion sites on bones and the size of joint surfaces indicates that preagricultural foragers were stronger than all humans who have followed. Their varied diet supported more bacterial diversity in the mouth, leaving only

2% of teeth damaged by cavities – compared to three-fourths of American and European teeth today (Adler et al. 2013).

On the other hand, preagricultural humans did not enjoy perfect health. Foragers had to deal with seasonal if relatively mild food shortages, infectious diseases, and trauma from accidents and injuries. Foragers suffered from osteoarthritis and other degenerative bone and joint disorders. In later life they developed tooth abscesses from a diet of hard, gritty food. Life expectancy, although higher than for agriculturalists, was lower than it is for most populations today.

Infectious diseases affecting foragers include those transmitted by vectors such as mosquitoes, flies, and fleas, such as yellow fever, typhus, and malaria. Handling wild animals exposes people to zoonotic infections (derived from animal reservoirs) including rabies, anthrax, toxoplasmosis, and brucellosis. Foragers also may come into contact with anaerobic bacteria that live in soil and can be present in wild game, such as those causing gangrene, botulism, and tetanus. These diseases tend to be severe since the rarity of exposure keeps humans from developing immunity.

Although intestinal parasites such as amoebas and worms (hookworm, pinworm) can infect foragers, they probably were rare in the past. Population density was low and foragers moved camp often enough to avoid contact with human wastes. On the other hand, disease-causing microorganisms that live in or on the human body may be maintained even in sparse populations, such as herpes viruses and bacteria including streptococcus, pneumococcus, meningococcus, salmonella, and treponema. These infectious organisms cause relatively mild illness – they neither kill their hosts nor cause them to develop full immunity – unless they manage to enter a different part of the body than usual (as when normally benign skin-dwelling staphylococcus bacteria reach the bones through a deep wound).

The main kind of infectious disease *not* present among foragers is "crowd diseases" which depend on high population density due to the microorganism's short life cycle, including measles, mumps, typhoid fever, smallpox, tuberculosis, and influenza. Infection causes acute sickness, which results either in recovery and immunological resistance or the death of the host. Host resistance is the reason travelers get sick with illnesses that do not bother the local population. It is also why Europeans were able to colonize much of the world by inadvertently or purposely infecting indigenous populations with diseases such as smallpox.

Agriculture and permanent settlements increase the opportunities available to infectious organisms through the concentration of people, food and water stores, domesticated animals, wastes, and the pests they support. With the exception of diseases transmitted through contact with wild game, zoonotic infections flourish due to the mixing of people and domesticated animals. Pigs and ducks carry flu viruses, while cows and other animals harbor variants of human diseases including smallpox, tuberculosis, and measles. Horses and other animals used for work and transportation increase the transmission of soil-borne infections such as tetanus. Old infections spread and give rise to new variants. For instance, human ancestors hosted the relatively mild malaria parasites *Plasmodium vivax* and

P. malariae for at least 50,000 years, and possibly ten times that, whereas the more virulent *P. falciparum* appears to have emerged and spread due to the transition to agriculture.[5] Treponemal bacteria transmitted by nonsexual skin contact – such as *Treponema pallidum endemicum* which causes bejel in arid climates and *T.p. pertenue* which causes yaws in humid zones – have infected humans for 1.5 million years. *T.p. pallidum*, which causes syphilis, emerged long after the Neolithic Revolution, although the timing and presumed New World origin of the disease remain disputed (see Erdal 2006).

Agricultural labor is harder on the bones and joints than foraging, and is less favorable to cardiovascular health. Indoor living in close, dark housing eliminates the germicidal action of sunlight and fresh air. Reduced exposure to sunlight limits vitamin D synthesis, with negative effects on the bones and immune system. The combination of reduced physical activity, indoor living, dietary changes, and inequality fuels a rise in chronic diseases, discussed in later chapters.

The increase in infectious disease is accompanied by and linked to a decline in nutritional quality. This is evident in a 10-centimeter reduction in adult height between Neolithic foragers and agriculturalists. A rise in the strontium-to-calcium ratio in the bones reflects reduced meat consumption, given that strontium comes mainly from plant foods.

The majority of people in agricultural societies subsist – now as in the past – on one or two staples such as rice, wheat, millet, yams, and corn. Cultivation of a single staple food exposes populations to severe famines due to crop loss through pests and climatic events. Food stores can be destroyed, stolen, or unequally distributed. Molds that grow on stored food secrete dangerous toxins such as ergot, the cause of Saint Anthony's Fire, a painful disease prevalent in rye-growing regions of Europe in centuries past; aflatoxin continues to sicken people and stunt children's growth through tainted corn, rice, nuts, and tuberous roots across Africa and parts of Asia today. Staple foods provide energy and stave off hunger, but the protein content is low and the balance of essential amino acids is inferior to eggs or meat. Grains provide scarce quantities of micronutrients such as iron, zinc, and vitamins. In addition, the micronutrients they contain may be poorly absorbed unless combined with other foods. For instance, lime added to corn meal for tortillas makes the niacin more accessible and prevents the potentially fatal nutritional deficiency disease, pellagra, which spread widely among corn-dependent populations of Europe and the US in centuries past. Micronutrient deficiency diseases, anemia, and protein-energy malnutrition are common among populations that obtain most of their calories from a single staple food.

Poor nutrition increases susceptibility to infection and dampens immunological responses to many diseases, including tuberculosis, cholera, various intestinal and respiratory infections, measles, and parasites such as intestinal parasites, schistosomes, and trypanosomes.[6] Contrariwise, infectious diseases interfere with the absorption of nutrients, induce energy-costly metabolic changes needed to mount an immune response, and can reduce food intake and retention through nausea, vomiting, and diarrhea. Growth consequently is impaired in children who are chronically ill. The availability of soft grains and dairy products allows mothers in agricultural societies to breastfeed less often and wean their babies earlier, which reduces infant nutritional status and resistance to disease. For their part, mothers are subjected to increased maternal mortality and nutritional stress through more births spaced closer together and spread over an extended period of years.

Some aspects of village life counterbalance the increase in disease risks. Pigs and vultures clean up wastes, improving hygienic conditions. Cooking helps kill microorganisms, although salmonella can grow on terracotta pots. Trade can improve food variety and availability, although it exposes communities to microorganisms from other places. It may be easier to care for the ill and aged, but, on the other hand, there are more cases of sickness.

.....

The shift to village-based agriculture predictably results in worse health, whether for current or past populations. Contemporary nomadic foragers and herders enjoy better health and nutrition than nearby farming societies or members of their own societies who have moved to permanent settlements, in spite of lower calorie diets and lesser access to schooling and social services.[7] The agricultural population shows higher rates of infant mortality, maternal death in childbirth, childhood malnutrition, and disease and death overall – although rates of particular infectious diseases may be higher among the nomads due to a lack of medical care. Self-reported health and wellbeing also decline. Newly settled people note the loss of interdependent gender roles, the appearance of gender and socioeconomic inequality, and the rise in political power and unequal control over resources. They are aware of being pushed to work far more than before, and for insufficient wages. Religious and spiritual practices and connections to the landscape are disrupted. Drinking and smoking replace socially oriented coping mechanisms. People report feeling more vulnerable to illness and less able to manage sickness. Ambiguous health conditions involving fevers, aches and pains, and fatigue express a generalized distress typical of displaced people everywhere.

Among prehistoric populations, dozens of sites from diverse locations and time periods corroborate these findings.[8] In a minority of cases, there was either no negative effect or an improvement on some measures. In some of these exceptional cases, an earlier deterioration of health was reversed due to increased protein consumption upon the domestication of animals. In other cases, settled societies were able to maintain a high-quality diet through trade and combined cultivation and herding. More rarely, populations may have been able to treat infectious diseases, as in Sudanese Nubia during the period 350–550 CE. In that case, farmers had lower infectious disease rates than foragers. The reason seems to have been tetracycline from Streptomyces bacteria in the soil and fermenting grain used to make beer, which apparently was given intentionally to children as medicine (Nelson et al. 2010).

Far more commonly, health worsened with the transition to agriculture. The following example illustrates the effects of heavy labor, social tensions, and unpredictable, insufficient food supplies. At Dickson's Mounds in Illinois, a thousand skeletons were buried in a dozen mounds from 950–1200 CE. Over this period, the population rose from 2–3 to 25 per square mile as some foragers settled in villages. Agriculturalists and foragers were buried in distinctive positions and separate mounds but were from the same population. The differences in their health consequently were due to differences in ways of life, not genes (Goodman and Armelagos 1985; Martin and Goodman 2002).

The proportion of infants and children with iron-deficiency anemia was twice as high among agriculturalists as foragers. This was manifested as porotic hyperostosis (excessive bone production due to stepped-up red blood cell production) in the cranium – particularly the eye sockets – and other parts of the skeleton. Young women were affected along with infants aged 1–3, in whom the condition reflects diarrheal disease and the use of cereal-based paps, as it does in impoverished countries today. Interruptions in enamel formation on children's teeth provide further information about the timing and severity of nutritional stress. Enamel hypoplasia (under-production) leaves characteristic lesions such as rings. There were more of these marks on the teeth of agriculturalists and they peaked at 2.5 as opposed to 3 years, suggesting increased stress due to earlier weaning. In some individuals there were multiple hypoplasias resulting from annual, probably seasonal nutritional deficits. The leg bones of 5- to 10-year-olds were shorter and thinner, although catch-up growth in adolescence reduced the difference between adults. There was more nutritional deficiency disease, as evidenced by skeletal damage from diseases such as rickets and scurvy.

In addition, infectious disease indicated by periosteal reactions was more frequent and severe among agriculturalists. These lesions in the fibrous outer layer of bone can be caused by both systemic and local infection, and by either inflammation or small hemorrhages resulting from toxins released by bacteria such as staphylococcus or streptococcus. They are most common on the long bones of the arms and legs, where blood circulation is less efficient. More than three-fourths of the agriculturalists' tibias had periosteal reactions, compared to one-fourth among foragers, and the lesions were more severe and appeared at younger ages. They included striped smooth lesions along the bone due to mycobacteria that cause tuberculosis and Hansen's disease (leprosy), as well as similar lesions along with bone deformities due to treponemal bacteria that cause bejel and yaws.

The combined amount of periosteal reactions indicates a lower quality of hygienic and dietary conditions. The lower amount of zinc (which is scarce in corn) in agriculturalists' bones points to the same cause. The skeletons with less zinc had more lesions from infectious disease. Bone damage was more severe in individuals with both periosteal reactions and porotic hyperostosis, further highlighting the connection between nutrition and infection. Women had higher rates of infection than men.

There were almost twice as many cases of arthritis and other degenerative conditions in the joints and spine among adult agriculturalists than foragers. In males there were twice as many fractures of the long bones of the arms and legs. Many of these were located midway across the lower arm bones, indicating self-defense and consequently more social tension and violence, as opposed to falls. Women agriculturalists had a higher frequency of osteoarthritic conditions in the arms and shoulders than males matched for age. Finally, there was a direct relationship between skeletal condition and mortality, for age at death was correlated with signs of disease and nutritional stress. The elevated mortality of agriculturalists translated into a lower life expectancy at birth of 19 years, compared to 26 for foragers. Infant mortality was 22% as opposed to 13%. Life expectancy at age 15 was 18 years for agriculturalists, 23 for foragers.

The presence of nonfood objects (shell necklaces, copper ear decorations) from up to a thousand miles away suggests that the agriculturalists at Dickson's Mounds stepped up production in order to trade for luxury or ceremonial goods. The accumulation of wealth and status objects explains the need for walls around the settlement and suggests that the lower social strata paid the price through food scarcity and hard labor. In addition, the settlement's distance from Cahokia, a city of 30,000, is likely to have contributed to the population's poor health, as is typical for remote villages the world over that give up more of their products to the regional system and receive less protection or economic benefit from the center. The rate of infectious disease at Dickson's Mounds was higher than in another village closer to the city.

Skeletal remains from two sites in Kentucky tell a similar story. Hardin Village was occupied by agriculturalists for about 200 years beginning around 1500. Indian Knoll was a community of village-based foragers inhabited from 950 onwards. The two populations were genetically alike and inhabited similar riverine environments. Among agriculturalists, there was lower life expectancy at all ages; higher infant and childhood mortality, especially between the ages of 1–3 years; more cases of porotic hyperostosis; and more periosteal and other bone lesions indicating infection, especially among children. Tooth decay was frequent among agriculturalists, and appeared as early as age 1, but nonexistent among forager children and rare at other ages. Both groups were stressed, but agriculturalists experienced fewer and harsher episodes of hunger and disease whereas foragers experienced milder seasonal food shortages. Consequently, dental hypoplasias occurred at a similar frequency in both groups but were more severe among farmers. Likewise, although the long bones of farmers had fewer Harris lines, they were less regular. These transverse streaks of calcified material indicate disrupted growth for at least 10 days followed by restored or accelerated growth, and can also indicate protein and mineral deficiencies (Cassidy 1980).

Between 5,000 and 200 years ago, population health worsened further as a result of poor living conditions associated with the social and geographical inequalities that came with the rise of dynastic and imperial civilizations in both the Old and New Worlds (Steckel et al. 2002). Outcomes included reduced height; more bone lesions due to leprosy, tuberculosis, rickets, and scurvy; and more frequent tooth loss and anomalies of enamel formation indicating malnutrition.

Considering the drawbacks of settlement and agriculture, it is perplexing that any population would choose farming over foraging. Whatever the reasons, once the process starts the effects are more certain. Mortality increases, but fertility rises even more, leading to rapid population growth. Overharvesting of wild foods and migration of game away from large settlements contribute to increasing dependence on cultivation. Production allows for accumulation and thereby generates inequalities that create tensions between individuals and groups, increasing psychosocial stress and reducing social cohesion. Trade and taxation fuel the need to produce surplus, transportable products. The strain on the environment generates a constant need for expansion. Eventually people are unable to live any other way, even though they have become more vulnerable to disease, climatic events, and conflict with other territorial groups.

. . . . .

Quantitatively, changes in population health may be assessed through crude birth and death rates, or the number of births and deaths per year per 1,000 people. Fertility rates concern births in relation to women only. The total or completed fertility rate discussed in this chapter is a projection based on age-specific rates covering the childbearing years (births per 1,000 women in each age category per year). It expresses the number of births women can be expected to have over their lifetimes assuming they survive the reproductive period and that current rates remain stable throughout. Table 3.4 provides a schematic representation of the transitions discussed below.

As shown by the table, among nomadic foragers births and deaths hover around 20 per 1,000 people per year – with a very slight surplus of births over deaths. Women have 4–5 births over their lifetimes, but only half of the children reach adulthood. Consequently, population grows very slowly. With agriculture, the burden of infectious disease, insufficient nutrition, bone and joint damage, and injuries from violence increases. Death rates rise along with birth rates. Women have 7–8 children and can have 10 or more thanks to reduced breastfeeding and a widened span of reproductive years (see Chapter 5). Birth rates range from 30–50 per 1,000 people per year. Death rates range from 20–40 or more per 1,000. The difference between births and deaths of 10 or more per 1,000 per year brings very rapid population growth.

This scenario of unbalanced birth and death rates owing to the first transition to agriculture around 12,000 years ago was the backdrop for the second health transition associated with the Industrial Revolution. The European or "classical" form took place in stages. Starting in the north, around 1650 there was a shift from fluctuating mortality due to famines and epidemics to smoother year-to-year mortality rates, with fewer high peaks. Population growth entered an exponential boom phase. Mortality remained high although gradually declining for a century, while fertility levels were more constant and remained consistently greater than mortality. Next, beginning around 1750, mortality rapidly declined. Total mortality rates dropped first, followed by infant mortality after a decade or two as living conditions improved more markedly.

As mortality rates fell, more women survived the childbearing years. Birth rates rose as a result, but the effect was transitory. Thereafter fertility declined roughly in step with mortality, although without closing the gap. Reduced childbearing

TABLE 3.4 Epidemiologic and Demographic Transitions

Time/place	*Annual births/ 1,000 population*	*Annual deaths/ 1,000 population*	*Difference/1,000 population (natural growth)*	*Average life expectancy at birth*
Foragers from Paleolithic to Present	20 to 25	20 to 25	close to 0	30 to 40+
-first transition- *10,000 years ago*	↑ *fertility*	↑ *mortality* ↑ *infectious disease*		
Neolithic to Start of Industrial Revolution in Europe	30 to 50	20 to 40+	10 to 30	below 20 to upper 30s
-second transition- *beginning 1750*	↓ *fertility*	↓ *mortality* ↓ *infectious disease* ↑ *chronic disease*		
Classical Transition, Europe and US 1750–1980; Accelerated Transition, other Developed Countries, 1920–1980	under 10 to 15 (with further decline to current lower limit of 7)	under 10 (with further decline to current lower limit of 2)	close to 0 with variations above and below	upper 70s to lower 80s (with further increase to current upper limit of high 80s)
Contemporary Transition, Less Developed Countries, 1945–present	20 to 45	under 10 to 15	5 to 35	upper 40s to mid 70s
-third transition- *1970–present*		↑ *new infectious diseases;* ↑ *old infectious diseases;* ↑ *drug-resistant strains*		
Worldwide, Probable Effects		stalling or reversal of decline in mortality rates		local reductions in life expectancy rates

further lowered maternal mortality and averted the higher death rates of infants born later than earlier in a series. In the third phase, beginning in the 1940s with the availability of antibiotics, mortality continued to decline, although modestly compared to the previous phase. Fertility also continued to decline, more steeply for a couple of decades and then slowly thereafter, with a temporary reversal during the postwar baby boom. A similar transition occurred in North America as in Europe, although the magnitude of the decline in mortality was smaller given that death rates were lower from the start.

The quantitative change in mortality was accompanied by a qualitative change in the major causes of death, from infectious to chronic diseases. Rates of life expectancy at birth of 20–40 years during the era of famines and epidemics increased to 30–50 as these diminished in frequency and magnitude. Once the major causes of sickness and death shifted to chronic diseases, life expectancy at birth rose above 50 years.

The transition brought death rates below 10 per 1,000 inhabitants per year. Birth rates fell under 20, and in many cases under 10. On average about two children were born to each woman, and almost all survived infancy. As in the case of foragers, birth and death rates equalized or nearly converged. In some countries such as Italy and Spain, birth rates fell further than death rates, resulting in negative natural population growth. Figure 3.1 illustrates the transition in the case of Italy.

In contrast to a gradual transition taking 1–2 centuries, Japan went through a more recent "accelerated" transition over only a few decades in the 20th century. The "contemporary" or "delayed" form occurred over the second half of the 20th century in countries such as Sri Lanka, Chile, and South Korea. It is still under way in many parts of the world, especially in Africa and parts of Asia. The changes include a rapid decline in mortality rates, most of which occurred during the 2–3 decades following the Second World War, variable and slower changes to fertility rates, and variable gains in life expectancy at birth.

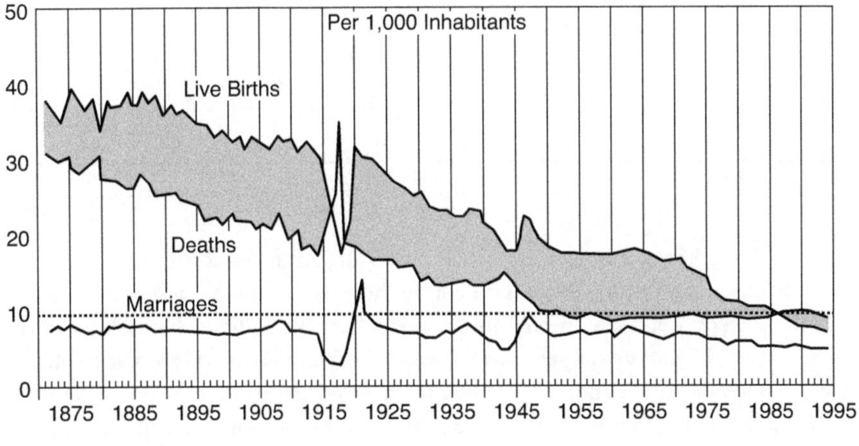

FIGURE 3.1 Live births, deaths, and marriages in Italy, 1872–1994 (Courtesy of Elizabeth D. Whitaker)

Today, death rates fall below 10 in 180 countries, and from 10–15 in 45 countries, with the highest rate in Lesotho. Birth rates fall below 10 in 30 countries, between 10–20 in 111, and at or above 20 in 83 countries, with a maximum of 45 in Niger and Mali. On average women have fewer than 2 children over their lifetimes in 113 countries, from 2–3 in 67, and over 3 in 54, with a maximum of nearly 7 in Niger. The surplus of births over deaths is widest in impoverished countries, generating the kind of rapid population growth typical of Europe in the early stages of its transition.

The major demographic changes outlined above resulted in dramatic increases in world population and population density.[9] From fewer than one million hominids 500,000 years ago, world population increased only to 4 million or fewer by the start of the Neolithic Revolution. By the time of the ancient Mesopotamian and Egyptian civilizations some 5,000 years ago, it had reached the size of one of today's big cities – 12 or 14 million. Within 2,000 years, world population had grown to 50 or more million – similar to the size of France (65 million) or Germany (80 million). As seen in Table 3.5, the rise in numbers has brought a dramatic increase in population density.

TABLE 3.5 World population size and density*

Year	*World population*	*Population density per square mile*	*Population density per square km*
–1,000,000	125,000	0.002	0.001
–300,000	1,000,000	0.017	0.007
–25,000	3,340,000	0.058	0.022
–10,000	4,000,000	0.070	0.027
–1,000	50,000,000	0.870	0.336
1	170,000,000	2.957	1.141
800	220,000,000	3.826	1.477
1400	350,000,000	6.087	2.349
1800	1,000,000,000	17.391	6.711
1950	2,500,000,000	43.478	16.779
2010	6,800,000,000	118.261	45.638

* Based on a total land area of 57.5 million square miles or 149 million square kilometers.

There were about a billion people by 1800. It had taken 2.5 million years to reach that level. Only 123 years passed before there were 2 billion, and only 33 years later there were 3 billion. The number of years between billions then fell to 14 or fewer: 14, 13, 11, and 14, respectively. However the annual rate of growth has been slowing since the 1960s and 1970s, when it exceeded 2%. From the current level of 1% it should fall below 0.5% within 50 years, at which point it will take nearly 200 years for world population to double.

.....

Like the first demographic/epidemiologic transition, the second was rooted in an economic and social transformation involving food production. Agricultural intensification set the stage for the Industrial Revolution starting a century later. As noted above, northern countries began the process a century or two before southern Europe. Between the 17th and 19th centuries, crops brought from the New World such as corn and potatoes were cultivated on a vast scale. New agricultural technology including mechanization and commercial fertilizers, seeds, and other inputs, increased yields.

Inheritance rules played an important part in the timing of agricultural intensification and industrialization. Whereas a single heir system such as England's encouraged permanent emigration of younger siblings, the practice of partible inheritance which divides holdings among a couple's children and is common in southern Europe discourages people from leaving home. In areas with impartible inheritance, industry was not limited by the availability of workers since they would move in search of employment. This is a main reason England was the fastest country to industrialize. In southern Europe, industry tended to locate near labor and favored home and small workshop production. Moreover, large landholdings were better able to produce the agricultural surpluses needed for industrialization (Brennan et al. 1982; Habakkuk 1971).

Mortality rates were higher, fertility rates were lower, and the people were shorter in the crowded, filthy cities than the countryside. Conditions were also bleak for rural families. Their high birth rates generated a steady stream of excess population towards these "population sinks," where the newcomers' lack of exposure to city germs left them vulnerable to infectious diseases. In the countryside, the internationalization of commerce gave rise to local economic crises due to lower prices for foreign products such as corn and wheat. Modern states privatized Church-owned and common lands, closing off peasants' access to wood, pasture, and wild foods. As more land was devoted to growing cash crops, and as taxes rose while prices fell, farmers found themselves with little to eat and virtually no variety in their diet.

Over time, industrialization brought improved economic and health conditions. Expanded transportation and communications networks increased the efficiency and range of food distribution channels. The delocalization of the food supply buffered against crop loss and prevented wide disparities in prices between geographical zones. Initially, the elite classes benefited most, but eventually delocalization led to increased food variety and quality for nearly everyone. Improved hygienic conditions and reduced infectious disease transmission resulted from less crowded and better-ventilated housing, increased personal and general cleanliness, the pasteurization of milk, greater public health surveillance, and the installation of sanitation systems. The draining of marshes and the reclamation of swamplands for farmland eliminated standing water where insect vectors such as mosquitoes reproduce. Organized labor achieved improvements in working conditions and compensation. Attitudes of indifference and fatalism in the face of suffering gave way to personal and political determination with respect to disease control. Fertility declined, which contributed to the decline in mortality through reduced maternal and infant deaths.

Pandemics of infectious disease waned while chronic diseases (cancer, heart disease, hypertension and stroke, and others) became the major causes of morbidity and mortality.

In short, the main causes of the rapid fall in mortality and fertility during the second transition were improvements in nutrition, sanitation, and hygiene, along with behavioral changes. Medical treatments were relatively less important until the late 19th century, although medical care itself has always had a positive – if difficult to capture – effect on outcomes (Kunitz 1983). In any event, the main aggregate change was less sickness rather than improved methods for dealing with it. The vast majority of the transition took place well before there were modern contraceptive methods or medical measures against infectious diseases, aside from early advances such as vaccination against smallpox and tetanus, Salvarsan for syphilis, diphtheria antitoxin, and sterile procedures in surgery and maternal care. For instance, in England and Wales 90% of the decline in mortality from airborne infectious diseases including tuberculosis, measles, pneumonia, and scarlet fever occurred before specific measures were introduced in the 1930s and 1940s, or earlier in the case of measures against diphtheria and smallpox. Only 3% of the decline in tuberculosis mortality between 1848 and 1971 was due to streptomycin (McKeown 1979).

The accelerated and contemporary transitions, in contrast, have occurred in an era of far more effective medical treatments and contraceptive methods. However, whereas Japan's transition was preceded by a slow process of modernization, the contemporary transition in less-wealthy countries has been set against a background of economic insecurity and stagnation. Agricultural intensification and the delocalization of the diet have brought reduced variety in the diet together with increased dependence on low-quality staple foods. Mortality decline primarily has resulted from public health interventions and medical measures such as vaccines, antibiotics, and oral rehydration therapy. Together with persistent economic insecurity, the reduced pace of health improvements after the 1970s contributes to the maintenance of high birth rates in many countries.

. . . . .

The connection between mortality and fertility indicates that health transitions affect women and men differently. We will take a moment to consider what this means, given the social and cultural meanings surrounding the currently higher life expectancy rates for women and the higher number of females in many societies. Even the dry writing of demographic literature suddenly becomes animated when the discussion turns to the greater benefit to women than men of the second demographic transition. Writers decry the "excess" mortality of males, as if diseases cruelly targeted male victims while sparing females. The language is not neutral. It expresses cultural beliefs about the relative value of men and women (Moreau 1982).

The reason for greater historical improvements in death rates for women than men is that women started out at a disadvantage: men enjoyed significantly better living conditions beforehand. The difference was great enough to overwhelm the biological advantage of females that results in higher male mortality rates at all age levels (including during fetal life) across many different animal species (Kalben 2000). For reasons discussed in Chapter 6, in humans at least 1.5 times as many males are conceived as females, but more males than females are spontaneously aborted, born premature, delivered by cesarean section, and lost during the first year of life. The higher rate of loss of male offspring brings the male-to-female sex ratio from 1.05:1 at birth to close to 1:1 by the mid to late 20s, in line with the balanced ratio typical of sexually reproducing species. There are more males than females at ages below about 55 years where living conditions are poor and female mortality relatively high, and at all age levels below 65 years where females are eliminated through sex-selective abortion, infanticide, or neglect. The latter is the case for China and India, whose combined populations of more than 2.6 billion contain more males than females.

At life expectancy levels below 50 years, females have a higher risk than males of dying during childhood and through their reproductive years due to causes such as nutritional deficits, infectious disease, and maternal mortality. Where living conditions are better and more equally shared, male mortality exceeds female mortality due to men's greater risk of accidents and injuries, violence, and many diseases. After reproductive age, women's mortality rates are lower than men's. Today, average life expectancy at birth exceeds 50 years in almost every country, although rates remain at or barely above 50 in Afghanistan and some African countries including Namibia, Swaziland, and Chad.

In brief, for thousands of years after the rise of agriculture, the burden of malnutrition and infectious disease was borne more by females than males. Only in the last 100–200 years have women *not* been at higher risk of death than men for much of their lives. That they outnumber men in some societies today is a reflection of relative equality in living conditions, not a sign that society treats men unfairly. Moreover, as noted below, women's gains have stalled or reversed in recent decades.

Turning now to the fertility transition, it may seem that the fall in birth rates was due to modern contraception, as if it were the only way to control births. Yet, cultural rules about marriage age, divorce, and remarriage influence the timing and number of births in all societies. Other factors include beliefs and practices that influence the frequency of intercourse, the acceptability of contraception and the desirability of large or small families, the feeding of infants, sexual abstinence after childbirth, and the frequency of sexual activity. People's biological capacity to reproduce depends on their state of health and the age of sexual maturation and reproductive senescence, all of which are shaped by local conditions including nutrition and stress. Social and economic factors including inheritance rules and the existence of celibate religious professions also affect fertility rates.

That couples in the Near East and Europe limited family size for thousands of years before modern birth control is evident in criticisms of the withdrawal method in political, and medical, and religious texts including the Old Testament.

In ancient Mesopotamia the upper classes limited births (in part by dedicating some women to priestly roles) in order to avoid dividing landholdings. Commoners were encouraged to have large families to provide laborers and soldiers (Trigger 2003).

In defiance of 18th-century economist Thomas Robert Malthus – who thought it would be wise to cut support for the poor – poverty is associated with large families, not small ones. Improvements in living conditions bring lower mortality and, in turn, shrinking birth rates. Related reasons for declining fertility include changed parental perceptions of the probability of their children's survival, and the emergence of modern states that provide parents some assurance that they will not be left destitute in old age. With rare exceptions, improvements in women's status and economic opportunities bring reduced fertility. The "resource flows" or "wealth flows" hypothesis reliably but not universally predicts that people will have fewer children if they perceive them as drawing from rather than adding to parental wealth.

An historical example from Jane and Peter Schneider's ethnohistorical research in Sicily (1984) will help to illustrate the different forces at play in fertility decision-making. In Sicily, crude death rates declined from 32 to a bit over 9 per 1,000 inhabitants per year between the 1860s and 1960s. Crude birth rates increased from 38.8 in the 1860s to over 40 during the subsequent 2 decades, before declining steadily to 21.1 in the 1960s. The researchers show how the timing of the transition varied across social classes in a part of the island where land was held in large agricultural estates.

As in other parts of Italy and Europe, the land reforms that led to the privatization of feudal, Church, and common lands mainly benefited the elite classes in the second half of the 19th century. They consolidated agricultural land and intensified production, bringing more regular and abundant food supplies to the town along with urban renewal and better hygienic conditions for the wealthy. Women of the landowning, merchant, and professional classes used goat milk to feed their infants, which shortened the intervals between births, while earlier marriages increased the number of childbearing years. Elite families proudly had many children, as did the better-off shop owners and artisans. Rates ranged from 5 or 6 to 8.6, with variation across classes and decades. Peasants had around five or fewer children and lost a higher proportion of them in infancy and early childhood.

In the 1880s and 1890s, the agricultural boom came to an end. Landowners restricted fertility to keep from having to split their holdings upon the marriage of children. The merchant and professional class did the same, now that it needed to educate children in preparation for migration to cities elsewhere in Italy. These classes initially reduced family size largely through illegitimate births among servants. After the First World War, they also had access to mechanical and chemical methods of contraception. The anticlerical, internationally oriented artisan class followed suit during the interwar period, largely by using the withdrawal method. The relative informality and emotional intimacy between artisan couples compared to other social classes favored cooperation with regard to sex and reproduction.

The peasant demographic transition took place last. In the late 19th century, peasants had experienced a rise in population due largely to reduced mortality as a result of the installation of water piping, remittances from family members abroad, and the availability of farm loans. Then, during the first half of the 20th century, these gains in economic wellbeing were reversed, and heightened poverty brought increased birth rates. By necessity peasants eliminated the trousseau as a prerequisite for marriage, resulting in earlier marriages and consequently more childbearing years. Old people told the Schneiders that they just accepted whatever God sent them. Contrary to the resource flows hypothesis, peasants had nothing to gain by having large families, as they could expect no support in old age. During the years of extreme economic hardship in the late 1940s and 1950s, peasant women were driven to abortion to prevent births. Over the following decades, the postwar Italian economic boom brought vastly improved opportunities and living conditions to the peasant class, which eventually joined the others in bringing completed fertility rates to post-transition levels of around two.

This example indicates that birth control is not a simple matter of technology. In fact, as noted earlier, the second demographic transition to low fertility was virtually completed before the Pill became available in the 1960s. Moreover, birth control has not always been the primary responsibility of women, as it has come to be seen in the era of the Pill. Barrier and other contraceptive methods used by men have been available for centuries. Indeed, assumptions about family size as a female concern presume a great deal more agency – or the resources and freedom to know and exercise one's will – than women usually enjoy. A second example from a pair of recent birth-rate reductions further illustrates this point.

Over the last few decades, similar demographic trajectories have resulted from dissimilar causes in China and the Indian state of Kerala.[10] In both places, crude birth rates of around 30 per 1,000 inhabitants fell rapidly over the 1980s to 20 in China and 18 in Kerala. Today, they are 12.5 in China, under 15 in Kerala, and around 20 in India as a whole. In China, the top-down one-child policy passed in 1979 (and reversed in 2016, allowing couples to have two children) was responsible for the decline in births and drove up the rate of female selective abortion and female infanticide. In Kerala, a collaborative approach resulted in vastly reduced fertility and infant mortality rates without the violence against girls that occurs in China along with other parts of India.

Even though Kerala remains an impoverished state in the south of India, the infant mortality rate is about the same as China's at 1.2 per 1,000 live births, and far lower than India's 4.2. Girls do not die at a higher rate than boys, whereas in China infant mortality is the same for girls and boys and in India it is higher for girls – both of which indicate preferential treatment of boys. Moreover, girls are not eliminated before birth, as they are in China and elsewhere in India, where the rates are 115 and 112 male births for every 100 females, respectively, and exceed 130 in some areas.

The comparison between China and Kerala shows that fertility can be reduced through coercion but that the result in a patriarchal society is increased elimination of girls. In Kerala, fertility has responded to improvements in women's status through inexpensive community investment in health care, education, and political efforts focused on women's education and the rejection of early marriage. Results include a much higher female literacy rate compared to India as a whole (82% versus 65%, compared to 96% and 92% among men, respectively). Historical and cross-cultural analysis suggests that further declines will require sustained improvement in living conditions and economic security.

. . . . .

As the second demographic/epidemiologic transition drags out in parts of the world, a third epidemiologic transition is unfolding across the globe. More than 300 new infectious diseases or variants of known diseases have appeared since the mid-20th century. These "emerging" infectious diseases include forms of cholera, yellow fever, tuberculosis, dengue fever, and polio. There are new drug-resistant tuberculosis bacilli, malaria parasites, and bacteria such as *Clostridium difficile* and certain staphylococci and streptococci that circulate in institutions. Some emerging infections have been around at low frequencies for a long time, but appear recent because of a rapid rise in incidence – such as Lyme disease, which seems to have infected the "Ice Man," Oetzi, 5,000 years ago (Kean et al. 2013). Unfamiliar diseases include Legionnaire's, HIV/AIDS, severe acute respiratory syndrome (SARS), Ebola, Nipah virus, and the bunyaviruses such as hantavirus or Rift Valley fever virus. Still other microorganisms have adapted to new vectors, such as the chikungunya virus transmitted not only by the tropical mosquito *Aedes aegypti* but also the Asian tiger mosquito *Aedes albopictus* that thrives in urban areas. Finally, there are zoonotic pathogens such as influenza viruses which circulate among humans and wild and domesticated birds and animals.

Economic and ecological disruptions contribute to the rise and spread of emerging infectious diseases, especially those involving animal reservoirs. Climate change shifts the geographical ranges of animals and insect vectors, opening new opportunities for diseases such as malaria. Drug-resistant microbes arise and thrive where poverty and inequality ensure that treatment remains sporadic and insufficient. They could soon render surgical procedures and hospital stays prohibitively dangerous, and force humankind to find an entirely different approach to medical care.

Emerging infectious diseases join persistent communicable diseases such as malaria and tuberculosis in bringing about stagnation or reversals in population health improvement. In addition, chronic diseases related to Western lifestyles are on the rise. Worldwide, the mortality associated with alcohol abuse, smoking, and obesity is comparable to the devastation wrought by pandemics of infectious disease in centuries past. Political instability, economic constriction, and socioeconomic inequality result in uneven disease exposures and outcomes across and within countries. For instance, in the US, life expectancy rates are lower for low-income whites in the South than the Northeast; Native Americans who live on reservations than Native Americans who live elsewhere; and higher-income people in the South and the Appalachian region than lower-income people in the

Upper Midwest and Northeast. In addition to these geographical differences, life expectancy rates vary by ethnicity, socioeconomic status, and educational level, separately and in combination. The rates are 5 or more years higher for college-educated people than those without a high school diploma, whites compared to blacks, and Asian Americans and Hispanics compared to whites (Ezzati et al. 2008; Olshansky et al. 2012).

At the same time, recently deteriorated living conditions depress life expectancy rates in many countries and subpopulations within countries. In Russia, men's life expectancy fell by 7 years after the breakdown of the Soviet Union. In the US, declines in health since the late 1980s have disproportionately affected women and people without a high school diploma. Life expectancy rates declined for women in 43% of counties but for men in only 3% of counties between 1992 and 2006 (Kindig and Cheng 2013). The new millennium has brought a rise in mortality and a decline in self-reported mental and physical health among non-Hispanic middle-aged white women and men. This reversal is unique among wealthy nations, and is most pronounced among the least educated (Case and Deaton 2015).

Signs of arterial occlusion and metabolic abnormalities once considered typical of older adults have been turning up in children and adolescents, presaging the early appearance of disease. The number of frail and disabled older people is rising, and the health span at the end of life is shrinking rather than expanding (Goldman et al. 2013). Evidently, even in wealthy countries there is still room for improvement, for instance through reductions in psychosocial stress related to economic inequality and insecurity, and increases in physical activity, healthful nutrition, and social cohesion.

While the health span can be expected to respond to these interventions, the life span is another matter. As we have seen, mortality rates among the very old are similar across populations, and the rate of aging is similar across primate species including humans. While there are exceptions to the rule of progressively rising mortality risks at increasing ages, this suggests that broad, unalterable biological causes limit the life span.[11] On the other hand, some medicines which affect metabolic, endocrine, immunological, and cell-regulatory functions provide reason for optimism with respect to preventing cognitive decline, cancer, cardiovascular disease, and other conditions that increase in likelihood with age.[12]

In sum, humankind has made monumental achievements in combined years of life over the last few centuries. Yet, while mortality rates are sensitive to local conditions, the life span is not likely to expand very far. Moreover, there is still a long way to go before everyone on Earth will have the same chances of living into old age.

Notes

1 Spans of years in the text and table are from Bulliet et al. (2005); Trigger (2003).
2 On comparative demographic rates, see CIA (2016); Cohen (1989); Eaton et al. (1988); National Health Mission (2016); Yaukey et al. (2007).

3 On Neolithic and earlier manipulations of the environment, see Cohen (1989); Diamond (2002); Kuijt (2000); Summerhayes et al. (2010); Vigne et al. (2005).
4 Regarding demographic/epidemiologic transitions, see Barrett et al. (1998); Cohen (1989); Kaplan (2000); Kunitz (1984); McKeown (1979); Omran (1971); Schofield et al. (1991); Whitaker (2000).
5 For the argument that *P. falciparum* existed before modern humans migrated out of Africa, see Tanabe et al. (2010).
6 Diseases including typhus and diphtheria are only moderately affected by host nutrition; diseases including malaria, smallpox, and plague are minimally affected. See Livi-Bacci (1991).
7 For contemporary health declines with settlement, see Barkey et al. (2001); Fratkin et al. (1999).
8 For sources, see note 4.
9 Population data in the table and text are from Kremer (1993); Yaukey et al. (2007).
10 This comparison is from Sen (1997), along with Hvistendahl (2011) and sources in note 2.
11 For the exceptional case of medflies, see Carey et al. (1992).
12 Examples include aspirin, the immunosuppressant rapamycin used after organ transplants, and the diabetes drugs acarbose and metformin. See Pollak (2010).

References cited

Adler CJ, Dobney K, Weyrich LS, Kaidonis J, Walker AW, Haak W, Bradshaw CJ, Townsend G, Sołtysiak A, Alt KW, et al. 2013. Sequencing ancient calcified dental plaque shows changes in oral microbiota with dietary shifts of the Neolithic and Industrial Revolutions. *Nature Genetics* 45(4):450–455.

Barkey NL, Campbell BC, Leslie PW. 2001. A comparison of health complaints of settled and nomadic Turkana men. *Medical Anthropology Quarterly* 15(3):391–408.

Barrett R, Kuzawa CW, McDade T, Armelagos GJ. 1998. Emerging and re-emerging infectious diseases: the third epidemiologic transition. *Annual Review of Anthropology* 27:247–271.

Brennan ER, James AV, Morrill WT. 1982. Inheritance, demographic structure, and marriage: a cross-cultural perspective. *Journal of Family History* 7(3):289-298.

Bulliet RW, Crossley P, Headrick D, Hirsh S, Johnson L. 2005. *The Earth and its peoples: a global history*. Volume I. 3rd ed. Boston: Houghton Mifflin Company.

Carey JR, Liedo P, Orozco D, Vaupel JW. 1992. Slowing of mortality rates at older ages in large medfly cohorts. *Science* 258(5081):457–461.

Case A, Deaton A. 2015. Rising morbidity and mortality in midlife among white non-Hispanic Americans in the 21st century. *Proceedings of the National Academy of Sciences* 112(49):15078-15083.

Cassidy CM. 1980. Nutrition and health in agriculturalists and hunter-gatherers: a case study of two prehistoric populations. In Jerome NW, Kandel RF, Pelto GH, editors. *Nutritional anthropology: contemporary approaches to diet and culture*. Pleasantville, NY: Redgrave. p. 117–145.

CIA. 2016. https://www.cia.gov/library/publications/the-world-factbook/. Accessed 17 March 2016.

Cohen MN. 1989. *Health and the rise of civilization*. New Haven: Yale University Press.

Diamond J. 1987. The worst mistake in the human race. *Discover* 8(5):64–66.

Diamond J. 2002. Evolution, consequences, and future of plant and animal domestication. *Nature* 418(6898):700–707.

Eaton SB, Konner M, Shostak M. 1988. Stone agers in the fast lane: chronic degenerative diseases in evolutionary perspective. *The American Journal of Medicine* 84(4):739–749.

Erdal YS. 2006. A pre-Columbian case of congenital syphilis from Anatolia (Nicaea, 13th century AD). *International Journal of Osteoarcheology* 16(1):16–33.

Ezzati M, Friedman AB, Kulkarni SC, Murray CJ. 2008. The reversal of fortunes: trends in county mortality and cross-county mortality disparities in the United States. *PLoS Medicine* 5(4):e66.

Fratkin EM, Roth EA, Nathan MA. 1999. When nomads settle: the effects of commoditization, nutritional change, and formal education on Ariaal and Rendille Pastoralists. *Current Anthropology* 40(5):729–735.

Goldman DP, Cutler D, Rose JW, Michaud PC, Sullivan J, Peneva D, Olshansky SJ. 2013. Substantial health and economic returns from delayed aging may warrant a new focus for medical research. *Health Affairs* 32(10):1698–1705.

Goodman AH, Armelagos GJ. 1985. Disease and death at Dr. Dickson's mounds. *Natural History* 94(9):12–18.

Habakkuk HJ. 1971. *Population growth and economic development since 1750.* New York: Humanities Press.

Hvistendahl M. 2011. *Unnatural selection: choosing boys over girls and the consequences of a world full of men.* New York: PublicAffairs.

Kalben BB. 2000. Why men die younger: causes of mortality differences by sex. *North American Actuarial Journal* 4(4):83–111.

Kaplan D. 2000. The darker side of the "original affluent society." *Journal of Anthropological Research* 56(3):301–324.

Kean WF, Tocchio S, Kean M, Rainsford KD. 2013. The musculoskeletal abnormalities of the Similaun Iceman ("Ötzi"): clues to chronic pain and possible treatments. *Inflammopharmacology* 21(1):11–20.

Kindig DA, Cheng ER. 2013. Even as mortality fell in most US counties, female mortality nonetheless rose in 42.8% of counties from 1992 to 2006. *Health Affairs* 32(3):451–458.

Kremer M. 1993. Population growth and technological change: one million BC to 1990. *Quarterly Journal of Economics* 108(3):681–716.

Kuijt I, editor. 2000. *Life in Neolithic farming communities: social organization, identity, and differentiation.* New York: Kluwer.

Kunitz SJ. 1983. Speculations on the European mortality decline. *The Economic History Review* 36(3):349–364.

Kunitz SJ. 1984. Mortality change in America, 1620–1920. *Human Biology* 56(3):559–582.

Livi-Bacci M. 1991. *Population and nutrition: an essay on European demographic history.* Cambridge: Cambridge University Press.

Martin DL, Goodman AH. 2002. Health conditions before Columbus: paleopathology of native North Americans. *Western Journal of Medicine* 176(1):65–68.

McKeown T. 1979. *The role of medicine: dream, mirage, or nemesis?* Princeton, NJ: Princeton University Press.

Moreau NB. 1982. Excess mortality of males: scientific object or ideological-political tool? *Gender Issues* 2(2):105–111.

National Health Mission, Ministry of Health and Family Welfare, Government of India. http://nrhm.gov.in/nrhm-in-state/state-wise-information/kerala.html. Accessed 17 March 2016.

Nelson ML, Dinardo A, Hochberg J, Armelagos GJ. 2010. Brief communication: mass spectroscopic characterization of tetracycline in the skeletal remains of an ancient population from Sudanese Nubia 350–550 CE. *American Journal of Physical Anthropology* 143(1):151–154.

Olshansky SJ, Antonucci T, Berkman L, Binstock RH, Boersch-Supan A, Cacioppo JT, Carnes BA, Carstensen LL, Fried LP, Goldman DP, et al. 2012. Differences in life expectancy due to race and educational differences are widening, and many may not catch up. *Health Affairs* 31(8):1803–1813.

Omran AR. 1971. The epidemiologic transition: a theory of the epidemiology of population change. *Milbank Memorial Fund Quarterly* 49(4):509–538.

Pollak M. 2010. Metformin and other biguanides in oncology: advancing the research agenda. *Cancer Prevention Research* 3(9):1060–1065.

Sahlins M. 1972. *Stone age economics.* Chicago: Aldine-Atherton.

Schneider J, Schneider P. 1984. Demographic transitions in a Sicilian rural town. *Journal of Family History* 9(3):245–272.

Schofield R, Reher D, Bideau D, editors. 1991. *The decline of mortality in Europe.* Oxford, UK: Clarendon.

Sen A. 1997. Population: delusion and reality. In Lancaster RN, di Leonardo M, editors. *The gender/sexuality reader: culture, history, political economy.* New York: Routledge. p. 89–106.

Shepard GH Jr, Levi T, Neves EG, Peres CA, Yu DW. 2012. Hunting in ancient and modern Amazonia: rethinking sustainability. *American Anthropologist* 114(4):652–667.

Steckel RH, Rose JC, Larsen CS, Walker PL. 2002. Skeletal health in the Western Hemisphere from 4000 BC to the present. *Evolutionary Anthropology: Issues, News, and Reviews* 11(4):142–155.

Summerhayes GR, Leavesley M, Fairbairn A, Mandui H, Field J, Ford A, Fullagar R. 2010. Human adaptation and plant use in Highland New Guinea 49,000 to 44,000 years ago. *Science* 330(6000):78–81.

Tanabe K, Mita T, Jombart T, Eriksson A, Horibe S, Palacpac N, Ranford-Cartwright L, Sawai H, Sakihama N, Ohmae H, et al. 2010. Plasmodium falciparum accompanied the human transition out of Africa. *Current Biology* 20(14):1283–1289.

Trigger BG. 2003. *Understanding early civilizations: a comparative study.* New York: Cambridge University Press.

Vigne J-D, Peters J, Helmer D, editors. 2005. *First steps of animal domestication: new archaeozoological approaches.* Oxford, UK: Oxbow Books.

Weiss KM, Wobst HM. 1973. Demographic models for anthropology. *Memoirs of the Society for American Archeology* 27:i–186.

Whitaker ED. 2000. *Measuring mamma's milk: fascism and the medicalization of maternity in Italy.* Ann Arbor: University of Michigan Press.

Yaukey D, Anderton DL, Lundquist JH. 2007. *Demography: the study of human population.* 3rd ed. Long Grove, Illinois: Waveland Press.

PART II

Plasticity, identity, and health

4

THICKER THAN WATER

Blood and milk in human evolution

It is striking how much people vary in appearance and behavior considering that, genetically, we are all virtually the same. For that matter, humans are nearly identical genetically to other primates and even to far simpler organisms. The unity across individuals and species suggests the importance of noncoding DNA and genetic expression, not just genes, to the form bodies take.

Biological responses to environmental and lifestyle conditions occur over different time scales, from minutes to millennia. Since the Neolithic transition to agriculture, genetic variants have spread in relation to diet, diseases such as malaria, and the colonization of extreme environments. Individuals respond anatomically and functionally to factors such as nutrition, stress, or climatic conditions through plasticity. In addition, some exposures such as early-life stress result in epigenetic marks that influence the way genes are expressed, and that can be transmitted across generations without changing the genes themselves.

This chapter explores interconnections linking genes, environments, and behavior. It shows that major genetic changes have occurred even over the relatively short span of time since humans began to cultivate food and raise livestock. The chapter further highlights the impossibility of separating biology and culture as determinants of human traits, and the fact that the human genome is a work in progress.

. . . . .

While long-lived species such as ours cannot evolve genetically with the speed of bacteria or insects, there have been major changes to the human genome over the last 10,000 years. Rather than negative selection, which eliminates deleterious traits that reduce survival or reproductive success, this chapter focuses on positive selection. Positive selection favors traits that provide a benefit in specific circumstances, and in spite of possible costs. It highlights the biocultural nature of human evolution.

For instance, it is advantageous to be able to digest milk both because of the nutrients and because lactose, or milk sugar, facilitates the absorption of calcium.[1] However, people have not always been able to tolerate lactose in adulthood, and most people in the world today experience symptoms such as gastric distress, diarrhea, and intestinal gas if they drink fresh milk. Yogurt and cheese do not cause problems because the lactose has already been processed. In short, lactose intolerance is the baseline; lactose tolerance, the deviation.

The enzyme lactase, which is produced by cells lining the small intestine, breaks down the lactose in milk. The normal form of the LCT gene makes lactase available for only the first few years of life, after which the amount drops off drastically to one-tenth its original level. People with one of the many alleles of the LCT gene maintain high levels of lactase throughout life. These alleles are named for the location and type of nucleotide substitution that distinguishes it from the standard form, such as -13910C/T in northern Europeans, or -13915T/G in Africans.

As shown schematically by Figure 4.1, genetic variants resulting in lactase persistence are prevalent in populations with a long history of dairying. Low rates of lactose intolerance are found in northern India, northern Europe including the UK, Scandinavia, and parts of Russia and Hungary, and among descendants of these populations in the Americas and elsewhere such as Australia and New Zealand. Low rates are also found among herders in the Middle East and Africa, including Bedouin Arabs, the Tuareg of the Sahara, and the Fulani of the West African Sahel.

Within countries, the percentage of people who can tolerate milk may vary widely across geographical zones and ethnic groups. For example, in northern Italy 60–70% of people can absorb lactose, but in the southern regions the proportions are close to zero. Black Americans of African ancestry have rates intermediate (20–30%) between the low rates of non-dairying African populations (0–10%) and Americans of northern European descent (90%). The rate among Mexican Americans is about 50%, compared to around 25% for rural Mexican populations.

Individual populations such as northern Europeans, northern Chinese, and Middle Eastern nomads tend to carry one or two particular variants of the LCT gene. In contrast, Africa is home to many of them, suggesting that the variants were already present in the ancestral humans who migrated from Africa to southwestern Asia – unless they were brought to the continent by Neolithic agriculturalists much later.

The variants spread in conjunction with the domestication of sheep, goats, cattle, and camels, which was probably due to demographic and environmental stress that reduced the availability of food. Milk residues and other evidence of dairying are present in archeological sites from 9,000 to 7,000 years ago in the Middle East and Western and Eastern Europe, and 6,000 years ago in Britain. The Tell Sabi Abyad site in northern Syria was occupied between 8,900 and 7,300 years ago. An increase in dependence on animals during a two-century-long cold and dry period left its mark in the form of fat molecules on the pottery indicating increased milk consumption and intensified use of animal fibers to make cloth (Evershed et al. 2008).

FIGURE 4.1 Approximate world distribution of dairying traditions and lactose tolerance

(© Elisa Sangiorgi, reprinted with permission)

For northern populations, the lactose in milk compensates for the low calcium content of the soil and vegetation by increasing the mineral's absorption in the gut. These populations have the further disadvantage of scarce sunlight, which, at latitudes above 38 degrees, is insufficient during the winter months to yield an acceptable amount of vitamin D. Vitamin D is a steroid hormone found in fatty fish or synthesized internally through exposure to ultraviolet light. With the exception of northern populations with a marine diet, people obtain only about 10% of their vitamin D from food, even with supplementation as in the US. At latitudes far from the equator, pale skin helps by increasing the absorption of ultraviolet light. Genes for reduced skin pigmentation include very old alleles such as BNC2, inherited from Neanderthals.

Ultraviolet B sunlight converts a precursor molecule (7-dehydrocholesterol) in the skin into vitamin D, which undergoes further biochemical steps in the liver and kidney to reach the active form that regulates calcium levels. Calcium and vitamin D work together to regulate the growth and functioning of the bones, heart, nerves, and immune system. Vitamin D deficiency can lead to seizures and has been implicated in infectious diseases, cancer, heart disease, and autoimmune diseases including type I (insulin-dependent) diabetes and asthma. Without sufficient calcium and vitamin D, cartilage does not mineralize properly in childhood, and the bones warp and break. In adulthood, bones fracture easily. Rickets in children and osteomalacia in adults were common diseases until only a few generations ago, and still occur among dark-skinned people who migrate to northern areas. Indoor lifestyles, the use of sunscreens, and pollution that blocks the sun's rays have generated a resurgence of the disease in recent decades.

Long before vitamin D's discovery in the 1920s, there were cultural adaptations to the problem of scarce sunlight. Throughout Europe, cod liver oil – which is rich in vitamin D – was given to healthy children to promote growth and health, and to patients to favor healing. Tuberculosis patients received both cod liver oil and phototherapy as a standard treatment. In 1848, physicians at the Royal Brompton Hospital in London demonstrated that patients given daily doses of cod liver oil died from the disease at a lower rate than controls (Green 2011).

The evolution of lactose tolerance illustrates the confluence of diet, geography, and genetic variation in human adaptive processes. Cattle likewise have undergone changes over the last 9,000 years in response to life with humans. Genetic variants have brought earlier weaning of calves, which frees their mothers for milking, along with altered sets of milk proteins that suit human tastes. In north-central Europe, high percentages of lactase persistence alleles in people overlap geographically with high frequencies of multiple milk-protein alleles in cattle. In southern Europe and the Near East, both values are relatively low. As an index of selective pressure, the greater genetic diversity in northern cattle speaks to a long history of service to humans (Beja-Pereira et al. 2003).

.....

The transition to agriculture that gave rise to dairying also brought new conditions that favored infectious diseases, as seen in the last chapter.[2] For instance, agriculture brought an unprecedented concentration of people along with pools of standing water where mosquitoes could breed. Malaria had infected humans for many thousands if not millions of years, as indicated by the fact that nonhuman primates also host parasites of the genus *Plasmodium*. Farming and settlements allowed the disease to become endemic.

Like other parasites, plasmodia elude treatment because they spend time inside host cells, undergo life cycle changes that result in constantly shifting surface antigens, and profit from heightened genetic variability by reproducing sexually. Transmission is not easily blocked because the parasite makes use of an insect vector – a few dozen of the hundreds of species of *Anopheles* mosquitoes. Control efforts consequently focus on interfering with the plasmodium's life cycle chemically inside the host, draining standing water, eliminating mosquitoes, and avoiding bites through physical barriers such as window screens and netting. Ancient cultural responses include dietary customs, discussed below, and avoidance of mosquitoes through houses built on stilts, hilltop settlements, beliefs about the noxiousness of swampy areas, and pasturing of animals at higher elevations during the malaria season.

In addition to these responses, people in areas with a long history of malaria – especially the most life-threatening form of the parasite, *Plasmodium falciparum* – carry genetic mutations that alter blood cells in ways that protect against the disease. Figure 4.2 shows the approximate geographical distribution of some of these genetic variants in relation to the malaria zone encompassing the north coast and sub-Saharan regions of Africa, the Mediterranean countries, parts of the Middle East, the Indian subcontinent, and southern and eastern Asia. In some of these areas, such as eastern Asia and southern and central Europe, the disease is no longer endemic thanks to successful mosquito control.

Sickle-cell anemia is a debilitating and potentially fatal disease, but the trait provides a measure of protection against malaria to people who inherit only one copy of the defective gene. They are far more numerous than people who inherit two copies: in West Africa, for instance, 40% versus 4%, respectively. The benefit to carriers outweighs the cost, explaining why the harmful allele persists over time. The term "balanced polymorphism" describes the persistence of deleterious alleles like sickle cell and others mentioned below as a result of heterozygote advantage.

People with sickle-cell trait (only one copy of the defective gene) produce some normal hemoglobin and some hemoglobin S that causes red blood cells to take on a sickled shape. Carriers are just as likely as people without the trait to become infected with *P. falciparum*, but their disease is less severe and less often fatal. Inside the red blood cell, malaria parasites generate free radicals (atoms or groups of atoms with one or more unpaired electrons) that increase oxidative stress, a condition that causes cells to degenerate. Infected cells with normal hemoglobin are destroyed in massive numbers, giving rise to the classic symptoms of fever, headache, and anemia. Cells with hemoglobin S are better able to withstand oxidative stress and therefore tolerate infection better than cells with

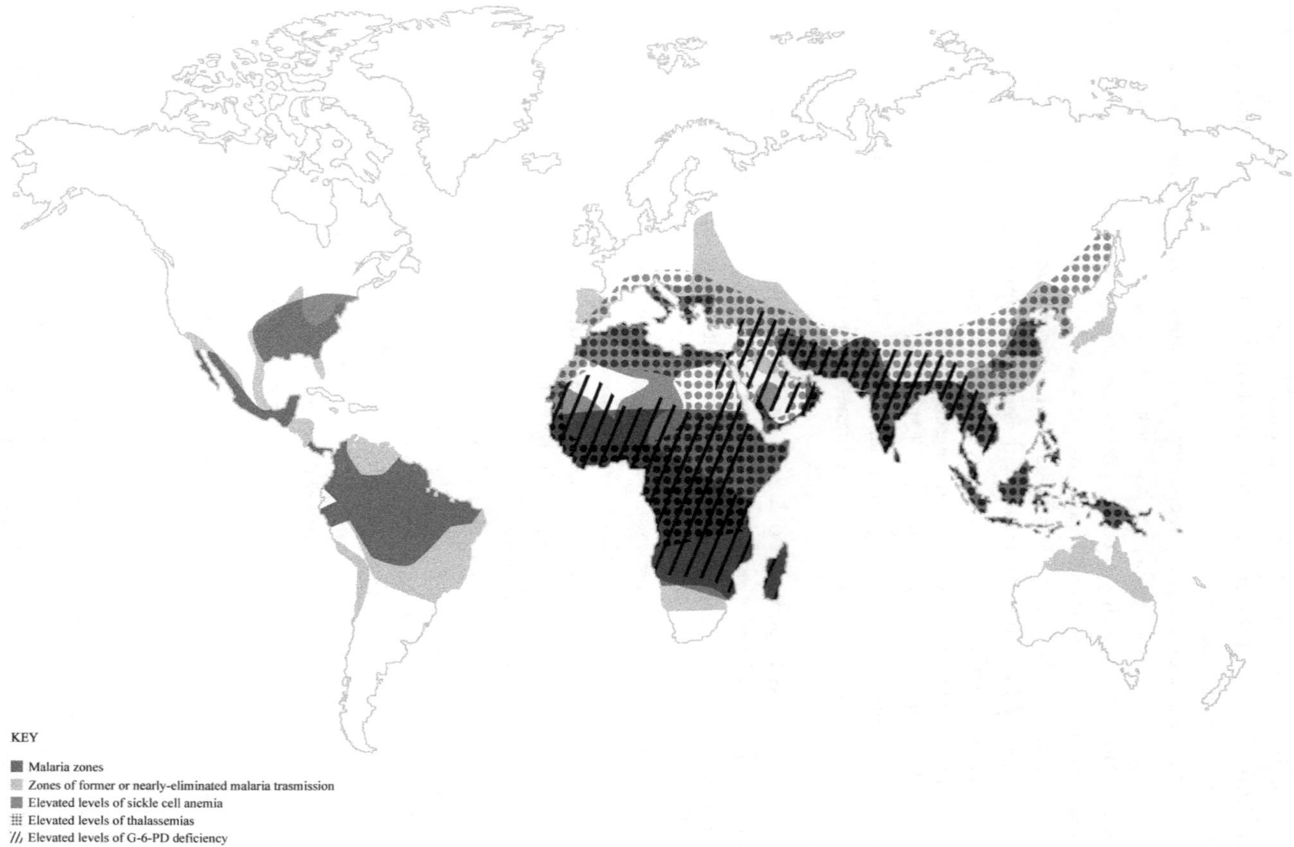

FIGURE 4.2 Approximate world distribution of malaria and malaria-protective genetic traits

(© Elisa Sangiorgi, reprinted with permission)

normal hemoglobin. In addition, cells containing a mixture of normal hemoglobin and hemoglobin S last only 2–3 weeks, as opposed to 4 months in a normal red blood cell. Combined, these two mechanisms reduce the destruction of red blood cells due to illness and the number of parasites available for transmission by mosquitoes. There are fewer parasites and ruined red blood cells in circulation, which reduces blockage of the capillaries and thereby damage to the heart, kidneys, and liver associated with malaria.

By increasing the susceptibility of red blood cells to oxidative stress, thalassemia and G-6-PD deficiency also protect against malaria. Degeneration of infected cells prevents parasite maturation and releases parasites before they are viable. Both forms of thalassemia (alpha and beta) protect against *P. falciparum* and the less virulent *P. vivax*; the alpha form seems to make young children more susceptible to repeated mild infection, although more resistant to serious disease later on. Glucose-6-phosphate-dehydrogenase (G-6-PD) deficiency is almost completely limited to hemizygous males, due to the gene's location on the X chromosome. In rare cases, female carriers may have some cells with an inactivated X chromosome, allowing a defective gene on the other X to be expressed. Any of about 200 alleles causes insufficient production of the G-6-PD enzyme, which neutralizes free radicals in red blood cells. As with thalassemia, the red blood cells are rendered inhospitable to malaria parasites, but this also makes them vulnerable to oxidants from other sources, such as food and medicine. The combined oxidative stress from malaria and ingested oxidants can result in severe and potentially fatal hemolytic crisis. The condition is called favism, after fava or broad beans.

Fava beans and other foods containing oxidant compounds – such as cassava, millet, sorghum, and spices including nutmeg and cloves – are grown and consumed widely in malarial zones. Plants produce these oxidizing compounds – such as vicine, isouramil, and divicine – as a broad-spectrum defense against the insects, microbes, animals, and other plants that threaten them. The wild-growing plant *Artemisia annua* (sweet wormwood or sagewort) has been used for centuries by Chinese herbalists to treat fever and is the source of artemisinin, the chemical analogue of the pharmaceutical anti-malarial agent primaquine. Contrariwise, antioxidant drugs and foods, such as vitamins A and E, reduce the effectiveness of anti-malarial drugs.

Cultural traditions from around the world promote the consumption of oxidant foods during seasons of peak malaria transmission. In Sardinia, the tradition of eating fava beans in raw form maximizes their protective effect, while other customs exclude young males from consuming the beans and thereby minimize the danger posed by inherited anemias. As in the cod liver oil example above, these cultural traditions need not explicitly address a health threat or recognize the mode of action to be effective.

. . . . .

In addition to diet and disease, positive selection occurs in relation to geography. For instance, in addition to plastic responses to the low humidity and low oxygen content at high altitude which occur in all people, some humans have responded with genetic changes.[3] Spontaneous, immediate responses include slowed breathing, which is counterproductive, and a rise in the number of red blood cells and amount of hemoglobin. Prolonged exposure leads to increased lung capacity, with more alveoli. Greater numbers of these tiny involuted sacs in the lungs provide more surface area over which gasses can pass between the air and the blood. Quechua people in the Peruvian Andes and Europeans living at high altitude since childhood develop shorter stature and larger lungs encased in barrel-shaped chests. These anatomical changes are not the result of genes, for they do not appear if the people grow up at lower altitudes.

Cultural adaptations to life at high altitude include special clothing that avoids exposing the limbs to the open air. Frequent tea consumption throughout the day prevents dehydration. Pregnant women come to lower altitude for childbirth. Babies are swaddled in abundant cloth to keep them warm and immobile, which helps conserve energy and moisture.

In addition, there are genetic variants among people living at extremes of altitude that mitigate the effects on the blood and its circulation. Tibetans live at 4,200 meters, where there is only one-third the oxygen present in air at sea level. The air is practically without moisture, and it is very cold at night. For visitors, these conditions cause the blood to thicken and the brain to suffer from lack of oxygen, resulting in dizziness, headache, and droopiness. The increased arterial pressure causes fluid to leak out of the blood vessels and collect in the lungs. In chronic mountain sickness, the blood leaks out of capillaries under the skin and throughout the body, including the gastrointestinal tract, from which it hemorrhages out.

More than 30 variants of genes that affect respiration and circulation help Tibetans deal with the altitude. They include the EPAS1 allele that regulates oxygen sensing and has spread over about 4,000 years to 90% of Tibetans but only a small fraction (about 10%) of Han Chinese living at sea level. Similar genetic responses have not been found among people who inhabit the other highest place in the world, the Andes Mountains. Notwithstanding their anatomical adaptations, Aymara and Quechua people have higher oxygen saturation rates and greater hemoglobin concentration than highland Tibetans, with levels similar to those of acclimatized visitors.

Tibetans breathe at a faster rate and respond better to incremental declines in oxygen concentration through increased respiration, whereas Andeans breathe slowly, as if they just arrived at high altitude. Tibetans' hearts beat faster in response to much smaller declines in oxygen than are needed to induce the same reaction in Quechua and lowland Chinese people. In addition, Tibetans' pulmonary arteries dilate in response to low oxygen, whereas other people's arteries constrict.

Unlike Andeans and acclimatized people everywhere, Tibetans have less hemoglobin and fewer red blood cells than people living at sea level, and this is uncompensated by a difference in blood volume. If Tibetans climb even higher than the plateau, their hemoglobin level rises somewhat but not as much as occurs in other people, apparently because it is more efficient at binding oxygen. The more constant and lower red blood cell count protects against dehydration, while a higher blood flow makes up for the relative deficiency of red blood cells. This minimizes the risk of pulmonary edema because the blood retains a normal thickness. Tibetans do not suffer chronic mountain sickness, whereas Han Chinese and Andean highlanders often do – even after living at high altitude for many years.

In addition, Tibetan babies are born at a sea-level weight in spite of the altitude. Among other adaptations, Tibetan mothers have larger uterine arteries that ensure ample oxygen delivery to the fetus. After birth, Tibetan babies obtain more oxygen from the air on their own than do Han Chinese babies born at the same altitude. Tibetans' normal birthweight at high altitude is striking because worldwide birth-weights decline by an average of 100 grams per 1,000 meters of elevation. Han Chinese women living in Lhasa throughout pregnancy give birth to lower-birth-weight babies as predicted by the altitude, and if they move to lower elevations their babies are born smaller than Han Chinese babies born at sea level. In the Andes, acclimatized mothers give birth to slightly larger babies than unacclimatized mothers at the same altitude, but the effect of altitude remains.

The lack of genetic adaptation among Andeans may be due to the effectiveness of cultural and physiological responses in preventing the potentially fatal effects of high altitude. Alternatively, it could be the result of an insufficient number of generations in the area. The Tibetan plateau undoubtedly has been inhabited much longer than the high Andes, which could not have been settled before 10,000–5,000 years ago. Between nearly 2 million and 500,000 years ago, *Homo erectus* lived in areas bordering the enormous Tibetan plateau; about 50,000 years ago *H. sapiens* lived to the north of it. Ancient trade routes passing by the plateau indicate that it has been explored and settled for many thousands of years and possibly for tens of thousands of years.

As in the case of northern European cattle mentioned above, Tibetan yaks carry genetic variants that allow them to thrive in the environment they share with humans. The various types of cattle from which yaks were bred provided the genetic diversity that gave rise to their large thin-walled pulmonary arteries, capacious lungs, and low levels of hemoglobin. These responses mirror human adaptations to high altitude and point to the interconnectedness of people, animals, and environments.

. . . . .

The genetic changes discussed above are but a few of many human adaptations to environmental and lifestyle conditions.[4] For instance, many Asians have multiple copies of the gene for the digestive enzyme, salivary amylase, which is beneficial where the diet contains starchy roots and tubers. There are genetic variants common in cold regions which give people straight hair that is better for retaining heat, and others in warm climates which yield curly hair that is better for releasing heat. People living in the humid climate of Central China carry gene variants that result in thicker hair and more densely packed sweat glands; indigenous Siberians have ones that help them maintain body temperature in cold conditions through the direct conversion of fat to heat (as opposed to heat production through muscular movement) and reduced heat loss from shivering and blood vessel constriction.

A large category of genetic adaptations helps protect against particular microorganisms that have infected humans for many generations, although usually at some cost.[5] These include balanced polymorphisms similar to the blood cell defects discussed above. Genetic variants that protect against lung and gastrointestinal diseases including tuberculosis, typhoid, and cholera cause cystic fibrosis if inherited from both parents. Nearly all West and Central Africans carry a mutation that results in reduced expression of the Duffy antigen, which acts as a cell-surface receptor for *Plasmodium vivax*. However, the same mutation that protects against *P. vivax* increases susceptibility to *Plasmodium falciparum* because the Duffy antigen is also a receptor for cytokines (regulatory proteins that mediate immune system cell-to-cell communication, such as interleukins and interferons), one of which (the chemokine PF4) destroys malaria parasites inside red blood cells. Other genetic variants that affect cytokines and other components of the immune system have been identified for parasites such as *Plasmodium* and *Cryptosporidium parvum*; bacteria such as salmonella and the mycobacteria that cause tuberculosis and Hansen's disease; fungal organisms such as *Pneumocystis carinii*; and viruses including HIV, influenza, and hepatitis B and C.

Genes in the major histocompatibility complex (MHC), a long stretch of DNA on chromosome 6, affect a variety of immune functions, particularly the production of human leukocyte antigens (HLAs). These HLAs bind small pieces of protein from an intruding organism and present them to the T cells, initiating a cascade of immunological reactions. Antigens on the surface of broken-down body cells, in contrast, are recognized as belonging to the self and are ignored. Every person inherits a unique combination of MHC alleles from their parents except for monozygotic (identical) twins, who are several times more likely to get sick with the same infectious disease, such as tuberculosis or hepatitis B, as dizygotic (non-identical) twins.

A population's history of exposure to infectious diseases leaves traces in the MHC. Differences in MHC genes account for some of the variability in infection rates across populations, such as the lower rates of malaria due to *P. falciparum* among Fulani pastoralists compared to neighboring populations. People in Europe, Asia, and Oceania carry particular HLA alleles inherited from archaic peoples such as Neanderthals and Denisovans 50,000 or more years ago. These alleles account for a disproportionate amount of the 2–7% of archaic genes in the modern genome, highlighting the importance of pathogens as a selective force in human evolution (Abi-Rached et al. 2011).

The MHC is one of the reasons why not everyone gets sick from an infectious disease passing through a group. It prevents epidemic disease if resistant individuals are dispersed throughout the population and susceptible ones are not clustered together. In that case, the disease cannot spread quickly enough to maintain itself in the population. Acquired immunity from immunization or previous exposure has the same effect, which is the reason farmers can induce "herd immunity" by inoculating only a portion of their animals.

In sum, lifestyle and environmental factors including infectious diseases have favored the spread of beneficial genetic variants through positive selection. Like all traits, they have not emerged out of nothing but rather are modifications of already existing systems, and consequently bring costs as well as benefits. For instance, high immune responsiveness from Neanderthal variants is beneficial with respect to infectious organisms but increases the likelihood of allergies and autoimmune disorders. Reduced melanin production increases the absorption of sunlight but also renders the skin more vulnerable to lesions and cancer. As seen below, an evolutionary perspective suggests ways to manage some of these trade-offs and design flaws.

. . . . .

Genetic change is not the only way to adapt. All living things respond morphologically, physiologically, and behaviorally to immediate and prolonged challenges presented by their local environments. Several examples of plasticity have been mentioned already in relation to altitude, such as altered cardiovascular functioning and, with time, large chests and short legs. We see plasticity in action every day. Sunlight induces melanin production and darkens the skin, protecting against sunburn and skin cancer. Endurance exercise changes blood pressure levels and resting heart rates. Cold temperatures endured for weeks due to exposure or lack of indoor heating raise the metabolic rate, whereas warmer temperatures restore it to a lower level.

Growth is far more plastic than it may seem in light of differences in average height across populations.[6] To be sure, genes play a role in adult height. Even if living conditions are uniformly optimal, genetic differences result in variations in stature. On the other hand, genetically identical people grow to different heights depending on circumstances. If monozygotic twins receive different amounts of oxygen and nutrients from the placenta, they are born very different in size. Childhood experiences of disease, stress, and nutrition have the same effect.

Foragers in the Central African forests carry genetic variants that affect pituitary gland activity and contribute to short stature, which is advantageous in warm humid places because the large proportion of surface area to body mass optimizes heat loss through the skin. However, the children reach a taller height if they are raised in nearby villages. This lifestyle effect consistently occurs across populations in response to iodine or other needed nutritional supplements. People from seemingly short populations grow taller if they move to a wealthier country where food is abundant and infectious diseases are relatively rare – although they also quickly come to resemble the new country's population in terms of overweight/obesity. Children of Mayan immigrants to Florida and Los Angeles grow 10 centimeters taller than Mayan children in Guatemala within a single generation. Allegedly short Mapuche children raised in urban areas of Chile grow similarly to children of European ancestry of the same social class, demonstrating that growth depends on living standards, not ethnicity.

Based on data regarding thousands of children under age 6 in Latin America, North America, Africa, Asia, and Europe, the World Health Organization (2006) has published growth standards that no longer make allowances for presumed natural differences between populations. The data show that young children everywhere tend to grow at the same rate provided they are not subjected to neglect, inadequate nutrition, or frequent or prolonged sickness. These factors are much more relevant to growth than is gender or ethnicity.

As noted in Chapter 3, adult height declined drastically after humans began cultivating food, and did not begin to recover until the last couple of centuries. American men were the tallest in the world in 1850, at 5'6" (1.68 meters). Their average height increased over the following generations, but Dutch men, who at 5'4" (1.63 m) were the shortest in Europe in 1850, experienced a more dramatic increase and surpassed them. Dutch men are now two inches taller than US men on average (5'10" versus 5'8" or 1.78 m versus 1.73 m), and, after people from the Dinaric Alps of southeastern Europe, the tallest in the world. The reason for the reversal in rankings between the Netherlands and the US is a more uneven standard of living in the latter. The percentage of low-birthweight babies in the Netherlands is about half the rate in the US, where low-birthweight babies are born twice as often to black as white women, and average height is about an inch lower among lower-class than middle and upper-class adults.

Like growth, reproductive development depends on context. As seen in the next chapter, the average age of puberty and reproductive senescence varies across societies. Moreover, how these changes are experienced varies in relation to living conditions and even the way they are culturally understood. For instance, in Western culture, monthly bleeding is a key symbol of femininity, making it seem logical that menopause is physically harmful and psychologically devastating to women. Hot flushes, night sweats, weak bones, and depression are considered normal and inevitable. However, this view of menopause as a disease state is a recent biomedical construction. A century ago, the phase of life from the mid-40s until about age 60 was considered a delicate transitional period for both men and women. The end of menstruation was just one of many changes, and protected women by preventing pregnancy in older age. Then, over the 20th century, the climacteric came to be seen as a dangerous loss of function that primarily concerned women. The defining symptoms were those described by women who came to their physicians with complaints. By now, these disturbances are attributed to diminishing estrogen secretion and are believed to require medical management.

Yet, many women worldwide do not complain of or even recognize temperature-control symptoms. Very few women report them in Japan, China, Taiwan, Korea, Thailand, the Philippines, and much of Africa. Even in Europe and North America, most women undergo menopause without experiencing serious disturbances (Lock and Kaufert 2001).

The variability in symptom reporting reflects the confluence of cultural expectations with the biological effects of smoking, diet and exercise, hormonal contraception use, and childbearing and breastfeeding history. These complex factors influence estrogen levels and also cast doubt on their presumed causal effects on health. Mayan women in Mexico secrete similarly low levels of estrogen to American women during menopause, but do not report hot flushes or night sweats. Moreover, even though they lose bone mineral density to an even higher degree than American women, Mayan women rarely experience osteoporosis or bone fractures – including women who passed through menopause decades ago (Martin et al. 1993). In other words, estrogen levels do not faithfully predict either perception of symptoms or health outcomes.

In Japan, shoulder stiffness is the most common menopausal symptom. Japanese women are responsible for taking care of older relatives, which can be stressful and physically exhausting. At the same time, their low-fat diet provides plant-derived estrogens through soy products and teas. Older Japanese women rarely smoke, and if they drink coffee or alcohol the amount is small. Their lifestyle includes daily exercise such as walking, riding a bicycle, and carrying things. The combination of psychosocial and lifestyle factors results in different symptoms than in Europe and North America.

The pathological view of menopause includes the assumption that the end of menstruation and childbearing throws women into deep despair. In reality, depression is far more common among women of reproductive age than older women. Moreover, medical management itself can cause depression, which is a side effect of hormone replacement therapy along with bleeding, weight gain, and other threats to psychological wellbeing.

While Western society's emphasis on youth and work as the sources of personal worth undeniably casts aging in a negative light, many people nonetheless experience older age positively as a time for greater involvement in meaningful social, creative, and spiritual activities. Where older people are esteemed, aging brings increased influence and community engagement. For example, among Ju/'hoansi foragers, older women and men are relatively free of responsibility for food procurement and reciprocal gift-giving compared to younger people, which allows them to engage in painful and exhausting trance dancing for purposes of healing others and communicating with the spirit world (Biesele and Howell 1981).

Evidently, human biology means different things in different settings. Plastic responses to culturally shaped environmental circumstances affect the form, function, and subjective experience of the body. Awareness of the localness and responsiveness of human biology can be useful for dealing with health threats and opportunities, as seen below and in the next chapter.

. . . . .

The interrelationships connecting the immune system, infection, and behavior shed additional light on plasticity and suggest techniques for protecting health. The immune system learns to deal with infection through early exposures to microorganisms. In the process, the body is colonized by benign and helpful bacteria. Much of this occurs along the vast surface of the digestive tract which, stretched out, is at least 30 or 35 times the size of the skin. The respiratory system is not far behind. The mucosa lining these areas of interaction with the outside world are a primary focus of the immune system, whose development is shaped early in life through experiences with living and inorganic substances, including dirt.[7]

Along with rodents, insects, birds, and many mammals including primates, humans make a habit of eating dirt. Children everywhere do it, but only some cultures condone it in adults. To Western medicine, eating nonfood items such as dirt is a mental disorder, pica. At first glance, the practice seems to fulfill unmet needs for minerals or grainy particles needed for digestion. A closer look shows that geophagy serves other functions as well, such as detoxification of certain plant foods and stimulation of the immune system.

The first of these is needed because of the foul-tasting defensive chemicals produced by plants, such as tannins and strychnine, which are often concentrated in the shells that protect seeds as they travel through animals' and birds' digestive systems. Parrots in Peru selectively eat very fine clay with low mineral content from particular layers of cliff sides and river banks, which helps them tolerate ingested seeds and unripe fruit (Gilardi et al. 1999). Clay in the stomach binds, or adsorbs, toxic compounds so that they are not absorbed into the bloodstream. The birds' preferred soils are particularly high in kaolin, mica, and smectite – minerals with strong bonding properties. Humans likewise consume kaolin clay in medicines such as kaopectate in order to bind ingested toxins, calm stomach upset, and obtain calcium and other nutrients. Where people eat wild plant foods such as acorn flour, they often detoxify them with a pinch of dirt.

Soil enters everyone's body in small amounts on food, hands, and air currents, but children and pregnant women ingest soil on purpose and in greater amounts. In sub-Saharan Africa, women who live in cities can buy prized soils and clays that women in the countryside can access directly during pregnancy. Some African-American women maintain the tradition in the US. Across cultures, eating dirt is more common where people do not drink milk, suggesting that it plays the same role as milk fat in adsorbing toxins. In addition, soil provides calcium and other minerals. The practice prevents nausea, increases the mother's food intake, and prevents exposure of the fetus to harmful chemicals.

For children, there are additional benefits to geophagy, which plays a significant role in immune system development and functioning. Soil contains microorganisms that interact with the mucosal immune system lining the gastrointestinal and respiratory tracts, stimulating the production of immune system cells and chemical messengers. The interaction helps the mucosal immune system learn to respond appropriately to foreign antigens and to recognize the difference between self and non-self. Immune system functioning is likely boosted by the presence of aluminum salts in the soil – just as aluminum salts potentiate immune responses to vaccines.

After the first birthday, as children's diets increasingly include other foods, there is less milk fat in the diet to adsorb toxins. This is around the same time children begin to eat dirt, which also compensates for the decline in maternal immunities passed through breastmilk. Asthma and allergies are less common in people who were exposed to benign microorganisms in childhood, whether through life in the countryside, vaginal childbirth as opposed to cesarean section, or older siblings and their dirt and mild sicknesses. Excessive cleanliness and avoidance of the outdoors – and therefore not just dirt and dust but also pollen, animals, and sunlight needed for vitamin D synthesis – have contributed to the rapid rise over the past decades in allergies and asthma along with eczema, inflammatory bowel disease, and autoimmune diseases including Type I diabetes. Moreover, contact with dirt appears to promote cognitive functioning and mental wellbeing, an effect familiar to people who enjoy gardening. Experiments with laboratory animals show that exposure to the common soil-dwelling bacterium *Mycobacterium vaccae* (a harmless relative of the mycobacteria that cause tuberculosis and leprosy) favors nerve development and the secretion of mood-influencing neurotransmitters such as serotonin. The animals perform better on tests and show less anxiety than controls.

This is not to say that people should actively breathe in or eat dirt in today's world. Wet dirt and deeper layers of soil contain more bacteria including potentially dangerous ones, which may explain why children prefer surface soils. In addition, much of the Earth's surface has become contaminated with pollutants and organic waste.

At the other extreme, it is counterproductive to attempt to eliminate exposure to microorganisms. Bacteria outnumber the body's own cells by about 10:1 (10 trillion bacteria for 1 trillion cells). Gut bacteria alone come in about 1,000 different species, carrying 100 times the genes of an individual human. Commensal bacteria are themselves hosts to diverse strains of viruses, or bacteriophages. Together, the bacteria, archaea (prokaryotes similar in many respects to bacteria), and mycoses (yeast and molds) constitute a microbiome that, added together, rivals a large organ in size. The microbiome plays a significant role in health and wellbeing through effects on immunity, metabolism, nutrition, and mental functioning. For instance, gut bacteria synthesize vitamins and other chemicals with enzymes humans do not have. They process medicines and keep harmful microbes and parasites at bay. Bacteria help convert food to energy and break down nutrients such as protein and fiber into a more easily absorbed form. By digesting fiber, they generate short-chain fatty acids which stimulate the production of regulatory T cells in the large intestine, suppressing inflammation. Gut bacteria are so important that fecal transplants are given to patients after antibiotic treatment to protect them from further infection, as in institutions where virulent, increasingly resistant bacteria and viruses thrive.

Some bacteria have coexisted with humans for a very long time, such as species of the genus *Helicobacter*, found in the stomachs of many mammals. *H. pylori* protects against allergies and asthma, cancer of the esophagus, and obesity (possibly through its effect on the secretion of ghrelin, a hormone affecting perception of hunger). On the negative side, *H. pylori* is associated with peptic ulcers and stomach cancer. *H. pylori* was widely present in humans everywhere until the antibiotic era and remains common in less developed nations.

Specific bacteria which dominate the infant gut microbiome (*Bifidobacterium longum biovar infantis*) feed on the indigestible oligosaccharides in human breastmilk. These bacteria efficiently remove a food source from harmful competitors, convert these complex carbohydrates into by-products that nourish good bacteria, and provide immunological training to the cells lining the infant's digestive tract. At weaning, other strains of bacteria take over and set up house for the long term, although the composition of the microbiome responds throughout life to dietary intakes of dairy, meat, carbohydrate, saturated versus unsaturated fats, and alcohol.

Both unfavorable species of resident bacteria and reduced species diversity have negative impacts on the host. Particular types of bacteria have been linked to non-alcoholic fatty liver disease, colon cancer, irritable bowel syndrome, inflammatory bowel disease, and behavioral abnormalities including autism spectrum disorders. Obese people tend to host different and less varied bacteria than normal weight individuals. Among the obese, insulin resistance is more common in those with more significantly reduced numbers of bacterial genes. These patterns are congruent with the finding that farm and laboratory animals grow faster and fatter if given low doses of preventive antibiotics, especially if started early in life, which results in fewer bacterial strains and altered functioning in those that remain. Analogously, industrial farming reduces the diversity of the rhizobiome – the collection of microorganisms living around, on, and in plant roots. As a result, the plants lose the nutritional benefits of commensal bacteria along with protection from infection (Rottstock et al. 2014). These findings highlight the evolutionary relationships linking vastly different life forms to each other, the physical world, and human behavior.

. . . . .

The coexistence of humans and microorganisms suggests that infectious diseases are a permanent fact of life. Eradication has rarely been possible and requires auspicious conditions, such as a virus that cannot survive outside humans combined with an effective vaccine, as in the case of smallpox, or a filterable waterborne vector without intermediate hosts, as in the case of the nearly-eradicated nematode *Dracunculus medinensis* that causes guinea worm disease. Otherwise, politico-economic factors render eradication impracticable, even where biological conditions are favorable and technical capability exists, as in the case of measles, viral hepatitis (A and B), and polio (Aylward et al. 2000).

An evolutionary perspective suggests that much could be done by interfering with disease transmission and in the process pushing microbes towards reduced virulence. To help identify strategies, it is helpful to take the microbe's point of view. For instance, vector-borne microorganisms manipulate host behavior to favor their own transmission. Insects bite more often when infected by parasites, such as plasmodia that infiltrate the salivary glands of mosquitoes; *Trypanosoma brucei* which alters the saliva of tsetse flies that carry sleeping sickness; and *Leishmania* parasites that deposit a plug in the sandfly's digestive system. *Toxoplasma gondii* inhibits fear and anxiety in rodents, making them more susceptible to being eaten by cats. Microbes can manipulate the host's immune system, as when bacteria such as staphylococci release chemicals that inhibit the complement system which tags invaders for destruction. Microorganisms also help each other, at the host's expense. Inside host cells, viruses produce protein coats for all the viruses present. Bacteria chemically regulate the pH of their shared environment and release enzymes that break down host tissue, providing food to all the bacteria nearby. Groups of bacteria collectively produce a sticky protective shelter or biofilm that shields them from antibiotics.

Long exposure to infectious organisms has given rise to host defenses such as fever, which makes it harder for microbes to grow and reproduce.[8] The outflow of water in diarrhea expels toxins and bacteria from the gastrointestinal tract. Vomiting removes the stomach contents, while cough and nasal drainage clear bacteria and viruses from the respiratory passages. Storing away circulating iron in the liver keeps it from invading microorganisms which require iron to grow and replicate.

In response, some species of bacteria replicate just as well in the presence of fever as not; others can thrive even where iron is scarce. *Pseudomonas aeruginosa* bacteria that colonize the lungs in pneumonia and cystic fibrosis release iron-binding siderophores that favor growth and replication in all the bacteria around. These interactions suggest a different approach than Western medicine's philosophy of opposites, which leads the body's defensive responses to be routinely counteracted. On the one hand, the low specificity of generalized defensive responses means that they are often activated unnecessarily and consequently may often be suppressed without harm, as in the case of fever, jaundice, or pain (which is useful for inhibiting movement but rarely needed in today's safe environments). In addition, it is essential to intervene in the case of excessive defensive responses such as dehydration from severe diarrhea, seizures from very high fever, fear and anxiety so strong that they distort cognition and behavior, and chronic inflammation – which contributes to many diseases including cancer, heart disease, Alzheimer's.

On the other hand, suppressing a cough can cause pneumonia; suppressing it in the case of pneumonia can be fatal. Stopping diarrhea caused by infection with *Shigella* bacteria prolongs sickness and increases the likelihood of complications. Blocking fever due to many strains of flu virus increases the number of days of sickness and contagiousness, especially in the early stages of infection. Treating anemia with iron supplements favors bacterial growth and carries the risk of iron toxicity.

Host defenses include cultural responses such as disinfectants and medicines, although they may generate counter-responses. Malaria plasmodia have evolved biochemical pumps – similar to those found in cancer cells – which expel medicines out across the cell membrane. Bacteria swap genes conferring antibiotic resistance with bacteria of their own and other species. Antibiotic-resistant bacteria such as strains of *Escherichia coli* and *Streptococcus pneumonia* proliferate in hospitals and other institutions where they are constantly exposed to a bath of medicines. The resistance problem is growing ever more critical thanks to the excessive use of antibiotics in clinical practice along with an explosion in antibiotic household products since the 1990s. Some bacteria have already developed cross-resistance to these products and to antibiotic medicines (Lipsitch and Samore 2002). As a result, new antibiotics must be sought constantly. Fungi growing in caves offer some hope, as does the century-old technique of targeting bacteria with specific bacteriophages, which has been used successfully to treat infected burns and wounds, cholera, typhoid, and many other infections (Ho 2001).

From the microbe's perspective, humans not only put up defenses but also, as vectors, represent opportunities. This knowledge could be used to push microorganisms to lower virulence (deaths as a proportion of cases). Virulence tends to be high if transmission is easy, as occurs where the population has no resistance to the disease or where insect vectors carry it from one person to the next. If transmission is restricted, it pays the microbe to produce less severe sickness. Paul Ewald and colleagues (1988) have shown that not just insects or rodents but also cultural vectors such as unclean rivers or harbors, agricultural workers and equipment, and hospital workers are associated with more virulent disease. Immobilized hosts are easy for insects to bite; sewage released into dirty water carries microbes between people; agricultural workers circulate among infected plants, and health workers among sick patients. For instance, even a normally benign bacterium such as *E. coli* can evolve to a life-threatening form in hospitals, eldercare facilities, and other institutions.

Contrariwise, the balance of disease-causing microorganisms shifts in favor of less-devastating forms where transmission channels are interrupted, as when contaminated water is replaced by safe drinking water. To illustrate, the low-virulence El Tor strain of *Vibrio cholerae* thrives in the algal blooms of warm coastal waters off South America where it infects fish and shellfish and, through them, humans. The bacillus produces much lower levels of toxin compared to classical cholera, resulting in milder sickness, no immunity after recovery, and a contagious period of up to 20 as opposed to 7 days. Across South America, the balance of El Tor strains correlates with the quality of sanitation systems, with predominantly benign forms in Chile where drinking water is no longer a vector, compared to more virulent forms in impoverished parts of Brazil. Similarly, strains of *Plasmodium vivax* and *P. falciparum* cause milder malarial illness in areas where mosquito transmission is low, such as near the edge of the mosquitoes' geographical range, suggesting that effective screens could cause plasmodia to evolve lower virulence.

By the same token, ecological disruption due to climate change and unstable, extreme weather can be expected to increase not only disease transmission but also virulence. Changes in ocean and air currents, snow and ice, air pollution, and land cover alter the distribution of plants and people along with microorganisms, insect and other vectors, and animal reservoirs. Tropical and subtropical countries are especially vulnerable to emerging and re-emerging infectious diseases due to poverty, lack of infrastructure, and low host resistance, as in Europe during the Industrial Revolution. While the primary source of filth in the wealthier countries has shifted from food and water to air, changing the main site for infectious diseases from the gastrointestinal to respiratory system, the poorer countries remain plagued by both.

Finally, control of infectious diseases has implications for the chronic diseases discussed in the next chapter, given that the two categories overlap. Microorganisms with a role in chronic diseases include human papilloma viruses that cause cancers of the cervix, skin, and genitoanal area; the Epstein-Barr virus implicated in Hodgkin's and Burkitt's lymphoma; hepatitis B and C viruses which are associated with liver cancer; and the herpes virus involved in Kaposi's sarcoma. People who carry a variant of the gene for apolipoprotein E, which is involved in lipoprotein metabolism and cardiovascular function, are more susceptible to infection with *Chlamydia pneumoniae*. They also are more susceptible to Alzheimer's disease, stroke, aggressive forms of multiple sclerosis, and atherosclerosis, suggesting that the bacterium rather than the gene may be the cause. Ewald and Cochran (2000) argue that the bacterium may be exploiting a niche created by a deleterious gene that generally affects people in older age and therefore is not under strong selective pressure.

The protozoan *Trypanosoma cruzi* that infects millions of people in South and Central America causes Chagas disease, a chronic infection that can last decades and results in cardiomyopathy and heart failure. There are very few cases in the US, even though it likewise is home to triatomine insects (also called assassin or kissing bugs) that leave infected excrement on food and the skin – from which it may enter a wound or mucous membrane. In addition, there are abundant intermediate animal hosts such as rats, raccoons, opossums, and pets. The difference is that north of the border there are more screens keeping the insects away from people. Besides illustrating an infectious cause for an apparent chronic disease, the distribution of Chagas disease points to the role of cultural and social factors in shaping transmission opportunities for microorganisms.

. . . . .

The discussion above has highlighted plastic and genetic responses to environmental factors, including infectious diseases. We will now take a closer look at the relationship between genes and phenotypic traits by exploring the dynamics of genetic expression. The discussion is relevant also to later chapters on human differences and the intergenerational effects of exposures to harmful conditions, including social inequality.

Genes provide instructions, but they cannot create anything on their own. The materials must already be present in the cell. This is to be expected, as DNA evolved after proteins, not the other way around. Proteins create the chemical energy necessary for linking up molecules into chains such as DNA. Specific enzymes keep DNA from including erroneous nucleotides when it replicates, and recognize and repair errors when they occur. Without these enzymes – as is the case in experimental conditions – the rate of error is many orders of magnitude higher than it is in nature.

The examples discussed throughout this chapter suggest that genetic expression is far more complicated than implied by the mid-20th century discoveries of

Watson, Crick, Wilkins, and Franklin.[9] According to the model they developed, nucleotides are transcribed by RNA in a mirror image, from which 20 possible amino acids – each corresponding to a particular trio of nucleotides – are ordered into a sequence to make up a protein. This chain of events predicts an equal number of proteins to the 20,000–30,000 human genes. However, in 2003 the Human Genome Project (HGP) found that the number of proteins in humans is around 100,000, or 3–5 times the number of genes. The function of the majority of these proteins remains unknown.

Only 1–2% of human DNA codes for proteins. The rest of the three billion base pairs is noncoding DNA within and between genes. Given that humans share about 99% of their genes with mice and many other animals, and that the number of genes does not increase with the complexity of the organism, the differences between species lies in the noncoding DNA together with differences in genetic expression. The RNA transcribed from the noncoding fragments regulates the expression of the protein-coding regions and varies widely from one cell type or stage of development to another. Among human diseases and traits associated with single-base mutations – single-nucleotide polymorphisms, or SNPs – more than half occur in the noncoding regions.

About four-fifths of DNA generates RNA. This means that messenger RNA (mRNA) associated with protein-coding genes is only a small part of the total. Moreover, many thousands of DNA segments code for RNA as an end in itself. There are diverse kinds of RNA, such as extracellular RNA and micro to long RNAs categorized by the number of nucleotides and their source and activity. These RNAs serve a variety of functions inside and outside of cells: they silence DNA sequences, trigger immune responses, and are involved in cell signaling. They prevent mistakes, such as the translation of faulty mRNA into proteins or the movement of rogue DNA fragments (transposons) from one chromosomal location to another.

Contrary to classical genetic theory, mRNA does not faithfully transcribe DNA. It splits the string of information into pieces and may rearrange them in different ways, as has been shown in a number of different cell types including skin, brain, and B lymphocytes. These mRNAs are the product of routine editing processes, not errors. They result in proteins which cannot be predicted from the DNA sequence. A single gene therefore can lead to hundreds and even thousands of proteins. In short, proteins which splice and rejoin RNA end up creating different genetic information than that contained in the DNA.

Like rearranged mRNA segments, genes may be duplicated and put together in new ways within a single organism, depending on developmental stage, cell or tissue type, or environmental conditions. A copied gene may be inserted in a new place, where it may act differently. During cell replication the DNA is frequently altered, resulting in different genomes in different cells and groups of cells – even ones residing in the same organ or tissue such as blood, brain, or skin. While this may be due to differences in the fidelity with which vitally-important genes are copied – leaving others to become altered by mutations, deletions, and duplications – the presence of variations in large numbers of cells suggests that the diversity serves a purpose. Similarly, chromosome number can vary between cells. Some cell types in the heart, liver, and bone marrow regularly contain too few or too many chromosomes. Probable benefits include structural support and bulk, resistance to stress, and tissue regeneration after damage or disease.

Moreover, proteins pass information amongst themselves, independently of DNA. Proteins become active by folding into a specific three-dimensional shape that exposes certain parts of their structure to other molecules, which allows them to influence each other. For instance, the misfolded proteins (prions) in the brains of people and animals with transmissible spongiform encephalopathies (such as Creutzfeldt-Jakob disease or bovine spongiform encephalopathy) cause normal proteins to misfold also, and these go on to infect yet other proteins.

Nuclear DNA interacts with the circular string of DNA in mitochondria, the organelles that were single-celled organisms in their own right before being engulfed by larger cells. Over the last billion years, most of their genes ended up in the nucleus, leaving only 37 in human mitochondrial DNA (mtDNA). Genes in the nucleus code for hundreds of proteins that influence energy production in the mitochondria, while mtDNA also influences the expression of nuclear DNA. Mitochondria play a central role in aging and disease through their role in cell death, chronic inflammation, and neuromuscular functioning.

Classical genetics predicts that embryonic cell differentiation is irreversible. To the contrary, mature cells can be coaxed into reverting to an undifferentiated state – such as skin cells to pluripotent cells. By altering the expression of genes, inserting other genes, and adding extra copies of genes, it is also possible to convert one type of cell directly into another, such as fibroblasts to blood and nerve cells.

In addition to these and more complexities of genetic expression, environmental exposures can result in epigenetic changes to DNA that persist over time without affecting the order of nucleotides or, in other words, the genes themselves.[10] These chemical changes influence whether a gene is expressed or not. Unlike genetic change, epigenetic change is very rapid and responsive to immediate circumstances. It occurs in cells throughout the body and can be transmitted across generations. One of the main pathways, environmentally induced methylation of DNA bases (mainly cytosine), reduces genetic stability and consequently increases mutation rates, and therefore could be a factor in evolution itself.

Methylation involves the attachment of methyl (hydrocarbon) groups to DNA bases. It is a normal regulatory process that results in the suppression or, less commonly, activation of genes. Methylation serves many functions including dampening defective DNA sequences, and inhibiting the second X chromosome in females. Other epigenetic marks include tiny RNAs that bind to DNA and suppress its expression, and the addition to or removal of methyl or other groups such as ubiquitin or acetyl not from DNA bases, but rather, from amino acids in the histones (a type of protein) around which DNA strands coil. These various kinds of marks may arise during development or at any stage in life in response to a wide range of stressors. They may be enduring, as in methylation, or more transient, as in histone acetylation.

Animal studies show that poor maternal care induces methylation at genetic locations related to stress responses mediated by the hippocampus, leading to greater reactivity to stress in adulthood as well as inadequate care of the animal's own offspring. Positive care has the opposite effects. Also in humans, adverse early-life experiences are associated with less favorable mental and physical health throughout life. Children whose mothers experienced severe psychological stress during pregnancy show altered DNA methylation patterns, as do people whose mother or father endured wars and other stressful events during their early childhood. Low socioeconomic status in childhood correlates with DNA methylation at many locations across the adult genome, particularly affecting cell signaling and thereby influencing developmental pathways throughout the brain and body. People who experience severe overnutrition or undernutrition in childhood, especially in the years just before puberty, pass on to their children and grandchildren an elevated risk of metabolic and cardiovascular disease and reduced longevity. Contrariwise, positive social environments result in increased resilience in the face of stress.

While human studies clearly demonstrate intergenerational transfer of epigenetic marks acquired during gestation or through the contents of egg and sperm cells, the evidence for transgenerational transmission involving the DNA in germ cells remains equivocal. In plants and simple laboratory animals, exposure to pesticides or plastics additives, such as the endocrine disruptor bisphenol-A, results in the addition of methyl groups to DNA that persist across multiple generations. In mammals, epigenetic marks tend to be erased at fertilization and when gametes are formed, making transgenerational transmission less likely (Heard and Martienssen 2014).

In any event, the biological effects of socioeconomic inequalities, exposures to toxins and diseases, and other adverse conditions influence genetic expression not only in the individuals concerned but also their descendants. Epigenetic marks cast a different light on the harmful effects of socioeconomic inequalities, which have long been manifested physically in the form of reduced growth and health. However, this is not to say that epigenetic transmission proves Lamarck right with regard to the inheritance of acquired characteristics, given that true transgenerational transmission in humans remains to be demonstrated conclusively. Moreover, epigenetic changes may be reversed in response to new exposures. They demonstrate the flexibility rather than the permanence of biological information storage systems.

Notes

1 On lactose intolerance and lactase persistence alleles, see Ingram et al. (2009); Kretchmer (2000).
2 On malaria, see Etkin (2003); Weatherall (2008).
3 Regarding high altitude, see Beall (2000); Wills (1998).
4 For genetic adaptations to geography, diet, and disease, see Hancock et al. (2010).
5 On genetic factors in infectious disease, see Cooke and Hill (2001); Frank (2002).

6 Regarding growth and height across cultures, see Bogin (2008); Bustos et al. (2001); Jarvis et al. (2012); Murray et al. (2006).
7 On dirt, the microbiome, and allergies, obesity, and other disorders, see Arumugam et al. (2011); Blaser (2005); Callahan (2003); Ewald (1994).
8 On defensive responses and counter-responses, see Ewald (1994); Nesse (2001).
9 On genetic expression, see Keller (2000); Witkowski (2005).
10 Regarding epigenetic marks, see Heim and Binder (2012); Lock (2015); Thayer and Non (2015); Weaver et al. (2004).

References cited

Abi-Rached L, Jobin MJ, Kulkarni S, McWhinnie A, Dalva K, Gragert L, Babrzadeh F, Gharizadeh B, Luo M, Plummer FA, et al. 2011. The shaping of modern human immune systems by multiregional admixture with archaic humans. *Science* 334(6052):89–94.

Arumugam M, Raes J, Pelletier E, Le Paslier D, Yamada T, Mende DR, Fernandes GR, Tap J, Bruls T, Batto J-M, et al. 2011. Enterotypes of the human gut microbiome. *Nature* 473(7346):174–180.

Aylward B, Hennessey KA, Zagaria N, Olivé JM, Cochi S. 2000. When is a disease eradicable? 100 years of lessons learned. *American Journal of Public Health* 90(10):1515–1520.

Beall CM. 2000. Tibetan and Andean patterns of adaptation to high-altitude hypoxia. *Human Biology* 72:201–228.

Beja-Pereira GL, Luikart G, England PR, Bradley DG, Jann OC, Bertorelle G, Chamberlain AT, Nunes TP, Metodiev S, Ferrand N, et al. 2003. Gene-culture coevolution between cattle milk protein genes and human lactase genes. *Nature Genetics* 35(4):311–313.

Biesele M, Howell N. 1981. "The old people give you life": aging among !Kung hunter-gatherers. In Amoss PT, Harrell S, editors. *Other ways of growing old: anthropological perspectives*. Stanford: Stanford University Press. p. 77–98.

Blaser MJ. 2005. An endangered species in the stomach. *Scientific American* 292(2):38–45.

Bogin B. 2008[1999]. *Patterns of human growth*. 2nd ed. Cambridge, UK: Cambridge University Press.

Bustos P, Amigo H, Muños SR, Martorell R. 2001. Growth in indigenous and nonindigenous Chilean schoolchildren from 3 poverty strata. *American Journal of Public Health* 91(10):1645–1649.

Callahan GN. 2003. Eating dirt. *Emerging Infectious Diseases* 9(8):1016–1021.

Cooke GS, Hill AV. 2001. Genetics of susceptibility to human infectious disease. *Nature Reviews: Genetics* 2(12):967–977.

Etkin NL. 2003. The co-evolution of people, plants, and parasites: biological and cultural adaptations to malaria. *Proceedings of the Nutrition Society* 62(2):311–317.

Evershed RP, Payne S, Sherratt AG, Copley MS, Coolidge J, Urem-Kotsu D, Kotsakis K, Özdoğan M, Özdoğan AE, Nieuwenhuyse O, et al. 2008. Earliest date for milk use in the Near East and southeastern Europe linked to cattle herding. *Nature* 455(7212):528–531.

Ewald PW. 1994. *Evolution of infectious disease*. New York: Oxford University Press.

Ewald PW, Cochran GM. 2000. Chlamydia pneumoniae and cardiovascular disease: an evolutionary perspective on infectious causation and antibiotic treatment. *Journal of Infectious Diseases* 181(Supplement 3):S394–S401.

Ewald PW, Sussman JB, Distler MT, Libel C, Chammas WP, Dirita VJ, Salles CA, Vicente AC, Heitmann I, Cabello F. 1988. Evolutionary control of infectious disease: prospects for vectorborne and waterborne pathogens. *Memórias do Instituto Oswaldo Cruz* 93(5):567–576.

Frank SA. 2002. *Immunology and evolution of infectious disease*. Princeton, NJ: Princeton University Press.

Gilardi JD, Duffey SS, Munn CA, Tell LA. 1999. Biochemical functions of geophagy in parrots: detoxification of dietary toxins and cytoprotective effects. *Journal of Chemical Ecology* 25(4):897–922.

Green M. 2011. Cod liver oil and tuberculosis. *British Medical Journal* 343:d7505.

Hancock AM, Witonsky DB, Elher E, Alkorta-Aranburu G, Beall C, Gebremedhin A, Sukernik R, Utermann G, Pritchard J, Coop G, et al. 2010. Human adaptations to diet, subsistence, and ecoregion are due to subtle shifts in allele frequency. *Proceedings of the National Academy of Sciences* 107(Supplement 2):8924–8930.

Heard E, Martienssen RA. 2014. Transgenerational epigenetic inheritance: myths and mechanisms. *Cell* 157(1):95–109.

Heim C, Binder EB. 2012. Current research trends in early life stress and depression: review of human studies on sensitive periods, gene-environment interactions, and epigenetics. *Experimental Neurology* 233(1):102–111.

Ho K. 2001. Bacteriophage therapy for bacterial infections: rekindling a memory from the pre-antibiotics era. *Perspectives in Biology and Medicine* 44(1):1–16.

Ingram CJE, Mulcare A, Itan Y, Thomas MG, Swallow DM. 2009. Lactose digestion and the evolutionary genetics of lactase persistence. *Human Genetics* 124(6):579–591.

Jarvis JP, Scheinfeldt LB, Soi S, Lambert C, Omberg L, Ferwerda B, Froment A, Bodo J-M, Beggs W, Hoffman G, et al. 2012. Patterns of ancestry, signatures of natural selection, and genetic association with stature in Western African Pygmies. *PLoS Genetics* 8(4):e1002641.

Keller EF. 2000. *The century of the gene*. Cambridge, MA: Harvard University Press.

Kretchmer N. 2000[1978]. Genetic variability and lactose tolerance. In Goodman A, Dufour D, Pelto GH, editors. *Nutritional anthropology: biocultural perspectives on food and nutrition*. Mountain View, CA: Mayfield. p. 186–191.

Lipsitch M, Samore MH. 2002. Antimicrobial use and antimicrobial resistance: a population perspective. *Emerging Infectious Diseases* 8(4):347–354.

Lock M. 2015. Comprehending the body in the era of the epigenome. *Current Anthropology* 56(2):151–177.

Lock M, Kaufert P. 2001. Menopause, local biologies, and cultures of aging. *American Journal of Human Biology* 13(4):494–504.

Martin MC, Block JE, Sanchez SD, Arnaud CD. 1993. Menopause without symptoms: the endocrinology of menopause among rural Mayan Indians. *American Journal of Obstetrics and Gynecology* 168(6):1839–1845.

Murray CJ, Kulkarni SC, Michaud C, Tomijima N, Bulzacchelli MT, Iandiorio TJ, Ezzati M. 2006. Eight Americas: investigating mortality disparities across races, counties, and race-counties in the United States. *PLoS Medicine* 3(9):e260.

Nesse RM. 2001. The smoke detector principle: natural selection and the regulation of defensive responses. *Annals of the New York Academy of Sciences* 935(1):75–85.

Rottstock T, Joshi J, Kummer V, Fischer M. 2014. Higher plant diversity promotes higher diversity of fungal pathogens, while it decreases pathogen infection per plant. *Ecology* 95(7):1907–1917.

Thayer ZM, Non AL. 2015. Anthropology meets epigenetics: current and future directions. *American Anthropologist* 117(4):722–735.

Weatherall DJ. 2008. Genetic variation and susceptibility to infection: the red blood cell and malaria. *British Journal of Haematology* 141(3):276–286.

Weaver IC, Cervoni N, Champagne FA, D'Alessio AC, Sharma S, Seckl JR, Dymov S, Szyf M, Meaney MJ. 2004. Epigenetic programming by maternal behavior. *Nature Neuroscience* 7(8):847–854.

Wills C. 1998. *Children of Prometheus: the accelerating pace of human evolution.* Cambridge, MA: Perseus Books.

Witkowski J, editor. 2005. *The inside story: DNA to RNA to protein.* Cold Spring Harbor, NY: Cold Spring Harbor Laboratory Press.

World Health Organization. 2006. *Multicentre growth reference study group, WHO child growth standards.* Geneva: World Health Organization.

5

RISK AND RESPONSIBILITY

Power and danger in individualized approaches to preventive health

The transition to agriculture and permanent settlements predictably brings a decline in health, whether today or in the past. As seen in Chapter 3, the Neolithic transition to food production led to higher mortality and lower life expectancy rates in agricultural compared to foraging societies. The people were shorter and weaker. Along with food shortages and increased infectious disease, inequality and violence escalated. It took many thousands of years for population health to rebound beginning in the 18th and 19th centuries. At that time, nutritional deficiencies and infectious diseases declined dramatically, but new problems arose as a result of factors such as modern diets, inactivity, indoor lifestyles, polluted environments, and psychological distress. As a result, there has been a dramatic rise in chronic degenerative diseases, such as cancer, diabetes, and atherosclerosis, which cannot be explained by the expanded numbers of people living into older age.

This chapter explores the contribution of sedentary lifestyles to chronic disease and the power of behavioral choices to promote health. It also explores the limits of viewing health in terms of individual risks and responsibilities, both behavioral and genetic. Sickness and its outcome depend to a great degree on broad economic, political, and ecological forces that constrain individual choice and subject people to health threats beyond their control. While knowledge of health risks provides opportunities for prevention, it distracts attention away from social causes and brings a burden of increased sickness due to anxiety, stress, and blame.

. . . . .

Many of today's major causes of illness and mortality are either rare or nonexistent among foragers. These include overweight, heart disease, hypertension, cancer, diabetes, hearing loss, orthodontic and dental disorders, nearsightedness, and allergies. Widespread diseases including cancer existed even in ancient times but were confined to the elites, giving them the name, "diseases of civilization" or "diseases of affluence." Their variable frequency points to the impact of ways of life on disease patterns. For instance, every population that shifts to a sedentary lifestyle and Western diet experiences a rapid rise in overweight/obesity and non-insulin-dependent diabetes. In the 1970s and 1980s, rates of prostate and breast cancer were higher among Japanese immigrants to the US than in Japan, and among men and women of the Japanese upper class than other classes (Rose et al. 1986).

Lifestyle factors impinge upon health beginning in gestation and infancy. To illustrate, in sedentary societies girls mature reproductively at an earlier age, allowing them to start childbearing earlier. The number of children women can have over their lifetime increases also because of the availability of soft foods, which reduces the intensity and duration of breastfeeding. These changes not only alter women's long-term disease risks but affect everyone's health through their impact on infant nutrition and growth.[1]

In foraging societies, women begin menstruating at around age 18, compared to 15–17 in less developed countries and historically among peasant and working class girls in Europe, and 12–13 in industrialized societies today. The earlier arrival of menarche is due to changes in exercise, nutritional intake, body composition (a higher proportion of body fat), and exposure to industrial and agricultural chemicals that imitate or interfere with hormones. These same factors push the age at menopause outward to the late 40s and 50s, compared to the early to mid-40s among foragers.

These changes have been accompanied by differences in the number and timing of pregnancies, and the frequency and duration of breastfeeding, which have contributed to the rise in women's reproductive cancers. In foraging societies, babies are born 4–5 years apart thanks largely to several years of breastfeeding. Mothers carry their children and sleep beside them, which allows infants to suckle frequently and throughout the night. Frequent nursing suppresses ovulation and prevents subsequent pregnancy, especially if it includes nighttime feedings. Co-sleeping and nighttime feedings also prevent the Sudden Infant Death Syndrome, which does not exist in foraging and other non-industrialized societies. Reduced breastfeeding, together with an expanded window of time between menarche in the early teens and first birth in the late 20s or 30s, increases women's risk of breast cancer. In the years before a woman's first pregnancy, the high rate of turnover of breast cells leaves the tissue vulnerable to mutations and noxious influences. Pregnancy induces changes to breast tissue that render it more resistant, while breastfeeding provides protection in step with its overall duration – provided it is done intensively and for more than a few months.

While most women in Europe and North America today begin by breastfeeding, few breastfeed exclusively for more than a few months or continue in any fashion for a full year or longer. As a result of limited breastfeeding and few pregnancies, Western women who do not use hormonal contraceptives undergo around 450 ovulations in their lifetimes, rather than about 150. The extra hormonal exposure and tissue damage and repair result in a much higher risk not only of breast cancer but also cancer of the uterus and ovary.

Breastfeeding provides mothers additional health and psychological benefits, including reduced risk of hypertension, heart attack, and non-insulin-dependent diabetes mellitus (NIDDM or adult-onset, Type II diabetes). The insulin resistance that accompanies pregnancy is reversed by breastfeeding, which results in greater insulin sensitivity and glucose control. Like the reduction in cancer risk, the benefits of insulin sensitivity last over the long term and increase in scale with increased duration of breastfeeding. Due to the connection with high glucose, the risk of Alzheimer's disease is lower for women who have breastfed, particularly for long periods of time, and higher for women who have spent a high proportion of time pregnant compared to lactating (Fox et al. 2013).

For children, breastfeeding brings lifelong health benefits largely because it prevents the accelerated growth associated with formula feeding. Childhood nutrition and inactivity can further contribute to rapid growth if excess carbohydrate and insufficient fiber and protein results in insulin resistance and high levels of circulating glucose and insulin. Chronically high blood glucose leads to elevated levels of insulin-like growth factor (IGF), a broad-spectrum promoter of cell division throughout the body and consequently to growth acceleration, higher stature, and earlier puberty. Rapid growth and tall stature are associated with an increased risk of many kinds of cancer, including leukemia, non-Hodgkin lymphoma, malignant melanoma, and cancer of the kidney, colon, and rectum. Soft sugary foods bring high rates of dental caries, as noted in Chapter 3, along with misshapen jaws that crowd the teeth and require orthodontic correction. These problems are uncommon among indigenous populations and rarely affected ancestral humans.

Excessive glucose, insulin, and growth factors contribute to acne, which does not occur among adolescents in foraging and other non-industrialized societies. Similarly, myopia affects less than 2% of foragers and then only mildly. It is rare among older generations of indigenous populations undergoing acculturation, although one-third to one-half of the children are affected, as in all societies with mandatory schooling. Near work, television, and reduced time outdoors – which reduce exposure to natural light and distant views – is only part of the explanation. Much higher rates of myopia among urban than rural schoolchildren, and among urban than rural adults who never attended school, point to the role of Western nutrition. High blood glucose and insulin disrupt the way growth factors interact with their receptors. Dysregulated cell proliferation results in altered structures in the eye, which distort the way images are focused on the retina. In fact, the progression of myopia in children can be reduced by increasing the amount of animal protein in the diet, which tempers blood glucose levels.

At the other end of the life cycle, the foraging lifestyle protects against the common chronic diseases as well as the changes in blood pressure, heart rate, insulin resistance, percent body fat, and bone and muscle condition that Western society takes for granted as inevitable consequences of the aging process. To see why, we will examine how diet, physical activity, time outdoors, and social integration influence population health across the two types of society.

.....

For foragers, there is a tight balance between energy consumed and expended. A high through-put of energy sustains a far greater amount of physical activity and time outdoors. The Western lifestyle destabilizes the balance and reduces the variety of nutritional inputs, creating the conditions for widespread overweight/obesity and chronic diseases including NIDDM, heart disease, hypertension, stroke, osteoarthritis, and many types of cancer.

Like modern-day foragers, Paleolithic humans lived outside, in the elements, which consumes more energy than indoor life with climate control. Their bodies dispersed heat by releasing sweat over relatively hairless skin, an adaptation that reflects the importance of aerobic activity to our ancestors' daily existence. Like contemporary foragers, they had to cover a large land area to gather food through physical effort, such as digging through hard soil to obtain roots or beating small game towards a net.

Foragers average 10 or more kilometers a day while carrying heavy loads including food, firewood, water, and equipment. On top of that, nursing mothers carry children until the age of 2 or 3. Foragers tend to collect food for about 6 hours for one or two days, then stay at camp for one or two days, for an average of 3–4 hours per day. Several times a year they pack up and move camp, carrying everything with them. Like today's cross-training, physical activity varies daily and seasonally in terms of types and intensities of exercise, combines aerobic exercise with strength training, and intersperses days of relative rest between days of heavy activity. This varied activity favors cardiovascular functioning and produces sufficiently high-impact forces to maintain bone mass and density.

Women and men in foraging societies look like endurance athletes, lean and strong. Similarly, the bones of prehistoric foragers resemble those of top athletes today. Compared to agriculturalists, the foragers had stronger bones in every case in which they have been compared. This indicates that the type of exercise foragers practice, with a mixture of endurance and strength activities, is more effective for fitness than long hours of physical labor such as farming or construction work, even if it is backbreaking.

More than two-thirds of the US adult population exceeds a healthy body mass index (BMI, or weight in kilograms divided by height in meters squared), divided about equally between overweight (BMI of 25–30) and obese (BMI of 30 or above). Mexico and parts of Europe have reached the same level, and the rest of Europe is not far behind. Rates of childhood overweight and obesity are higher in Europe than the US, indicating that soon the rates of adult obesity will be equivalent (Cattaneo et al. 2010; Ogden et al. 2012).

The vast majority of people in the industrialized world do not get anywhere near a health-promoting amount of physical activity and time outdoors.[2] About one-fifth of the US adult population practices regular physical activity. At the opposite extreme, about one-fourth is completely inactive. In Europe, southern countries have the lowest rates of physical activity, northern countries the highest: for example, 30% of the population of Portugal exercises enough to benefit health, versus 86% in Finland. Rates of overweight/obesity follow the same north-south gradient, indicating that exercise is the key factor: the "Mediterranean diet" of southern Europe, and of the southernmost regions of southern European countries such as Italy, is associated with more overweight/obesity, not less.

Notwithstanding public health campaigns, rates of obesity and other health indicators continue to worsen. Comparing middle-aged Americans today to a generation ago, 35% as opposed to 50% exercise more than 12 times a month. There is more obesity, hypertension, hypercholesterolemia, disability that precludes work, use of a walker or cane, and functional limitation. Only 13.2% report excellent health, as opposed to 32% in the previous generation (King et al. 2013).

Overweight and obesity lead to altered metabolic and cardiovascular functioning, as indicated by high blood pressure, unfavorable lipid profiles, and impaired glucose metabolism. Obesity increases platelet and fibrin activity and therefore impedes circulation, whereas exercise reduces platelet aggregation and enhances the disintegration of fibrin. Physical activity increases the number of insulin receptors and the effectiveness with which insulin binds glucose. During exercise, glucose moves into the muscles without the need for insulin, but without exercise the muscles need insulin to obtain energy.

Both overweight/obesity and underweight are associated with higher mortality risks than normal weight. In addition, metabolic abnormalities and elevated chronic disease risk occur in some normal-weight individuals, while normal metabolic function and average chronic disease risk affects a similar proportion of obese individuals.[3] These paradoxes are due in part to physical activity, for it is possible to be thin but unfit, and overweight but physically fit. In addition, the distribution of fat makes a difference. Subcutaneous or peripheral fat is less harmful than abdominal fat. That is, waist circumference or the body shape index – which combines BMI and abdominal fat – is more strongly correlated with cardiovascular and other disease risks, along with mortality.

Physical activity correlates with lower all-cause mortality and lower disease and death rates from individual chronic diseases. It not only prevents but provides treatment benefits in the case of metabolic and cardiovascular disorders as well as cancer. Long-term physical activity is associated with a very low likelihood of hypertension. An evolutionary perspective explains why exercising outdoors provides greater fitness and psychological benefits than indoor activity due to the light, air, and additional energy cost of exercise in the elements. In fact, running or walking in a forest or other natural space correlates with a much lower rate of depression and anxiety than doing the same activity in a gym (Mitchell 2013).

In older people, current physical activity and physical strength reduce mortality risk and improve health status, including mobility and motor skills. Exercise also brings a reduction in the frequency and severity of falls, arthritis or rheumatism, and poor quality sleep. It can ameliorate symptoms of depression and reduces cognitive decline. Physical activity helps people deal with the social isolation, role changes, and feelings of being unproductive that can accompany older age. It prolongs independence.

Humans and other animals are rewarded for the physical effort required to procure food with morphine-like endorphins and other neuroactive chemicals released by the hypothalamus and pituitary, but getting started is another matter. Social obstacles include work schedules and employer attitudes that complicate scheduling, especially during the workday. Automobiles and household appliances spare the body the effort of daily tasks. Televisions, computers, and other passive pastimes predominate over more active kinds of leisure activity. Political decisions to invest in roadways and suburban development reflect and further a cultural dependence on cars. In both the US and Europe, short distances that were covered on foot or by bicycle until the latter decades of the 20th century are increasingly made by car. For instance, in urban areas of Europe, one-third of trips by car cover distances under 3 kilometers; one-half under 5 kilometers (World Health Organization Europe 2012). Evidently, everyday physical activity is not valued as exercise, even though it is just as beneficial to health and weight control as structured exercise. In fact, across societies the loss of physical activity for work or transportation tends to drown out any gain in rates of recreational exercise. In one study, bicycling for transportation reduced mortality risk by two-fifths after controlling for health and lifestyle factors, including leisure-time physical activity (Andersen et al. 2002).

Cultural categories that define exercise as structured physical activity involving dedicated spaces and specialized equipment and training can even dampen the positive effect of everyday physical activity. Compared to a control group, hotel housekeeping staff who were primed to think of cleaning as exercise perceived themselves as more physically active after the 4-week experiment and finished with improved measures of blood pressure, body weight, body mass index, body fat, and waist-to-hip ratio (Crum and Langer 2007). Evidently, not just exercise, but how we think about it, affects health and wellbeing.

. . . . .

The challenge for our foremothers and forefathers was to keep weight on, not to lose it.[4] We are drawn to fat, sweets, and salt because these things were in short supply for most of human evolution. It is no accident that most types of dietary fat stimulate genes that promote fat storage, or that fatty foods stimulate the brain's pleasure centers and the dopamine-mediated pathway that increases appetite – although a diet consistently high in fat dampens the response. In experimental animals, fat causes the small intestine to produce endocannabinoids much like the psychoactive component in marijuana.

Our bodies are not prepared to deal with constantly available, abundant, energy-dense food, combined with low energy output. As a result, they tend towards overweight/obesity and consequently to metabolic syndrome, characterized by insulin resistance, elevated fasting blood glucose levels, unfavorable lipid levels (high triglycerides, low high-density lipoprotein), and high blood pressure. Metabolic syndrome in turn is associated with increased risk of NIDDM, cardiovascular disease, and cancer. Both macronutrients – protein, fat, and carbohydrates – and micronutrients such as calcium, sodium, and vitamins play a role in body composition, metabolism, and chronic diseases.

Analysis of modern-day foraging populations suggests that the ancestral diet contained large quantities of leafy plants, roots and tubers, legumes and nuts, and animal and fish products. The diet varied seasonally, and there were more types of food than in agriculturalists' diets. Foragers obtained abundant micronutrients with the exception of sodium, which was eaten in quantities about five times smaller than in modern diets. There was more potassium, calcium, vitamin C, folate, beta-carotene, and B vitamins, and at least as much if not more iron. However, some populations may have consumed deficient amounts of particular micronutrients such as selenium or iodine which vary with soil type.

That humans can ingest defensive plant toxins which are dangerous to insects and other animals, such as caffeine, opiates, nicotine, and cocaine, suggests long exposure. On the other hand, the use of psychoactive substances probably was restricted to ritual specialists as it is in non-Western societies today. The enzymes needed to digest trace amounts of alcohol, as in overripe fruit, are widely distributed across species including other mammals and even fish, although many Asians, especially in southern and eastern China, carry mutations that result in enzyme deficits and make alcohol noxious. Humans did not consume large amounts until they began to distill alcoholic beverages 7,000 years ago, starting with barley beer. Many indigenous societies produce alcoholic drinks for immediate consumption as part of religious or social events. Tobacco was cultivated 5,000 years ago, but was not available to Europeans and Asians until after contact about 500 years ago.

While easy, everyday access of alcohol can lead to abuse that is unmistakably harmful due to liver disease, injuries, and certain cancers and cardiovascular disorders, moderate drinking has significant positive health effects. Moderate, regular alcohol consumption reduces the risk of NIDDM, stroke, and heart disease, a benefit which outweighs the increased risk of cancer. All-cause mortality among moderate drinkers (2–4 drinks per day for men, 1–2 for women) is lower than it is for both abstainers and heavy drinkers. This finding has been demonstrated repeatedly, although there are differences in the magnitude of benefit across populations, and some studies suggest that it comes only from wine as opposed to spirits or beer (Di Castelnuovo et al. 2006).

The variable relationship between alcohol and mortality raises the point that dietary and other exposures can have different effects at different doses.[5] Plants grow faster and thicker when given a miniscule amount of herbicide or heavy metals such as mercury or cadmium. In laboratory animals, low levels of ionizing radiation increase longevity and stimulate growth, reproduction, and resistance to tumor development and infectious diseases. Tiny doses of a carcinogenic substance such as dioxin or saccharine cause less tumor growth in treated rats, not more.

Variable dose-response relationships allow animals to try novel substances without incurring excessive risks. This is how insects, birds, and mammals have discovered the medicinal properties of unpalatable plants. For instance, chimps, bonobos, gorillas, and other primates with digestive problems or nausea eat bitter, non-nutritive plants that relieve their symptoms and empty the gut. Both chimps and people living in sub-Saharan Africa eat the leaves of the bitter *Vernonia amygdalina* bush and chew the hard stalks to release the pith, which contains anti-parasitic and other bioactive substances that are effective against nausea and gastrointestinal sicknesses.

At the same time, excessive doses of beneficial substances and essential vitamins are not necessarily helpful and can be counterproductive. Large doses of vitamins and minerals do not bring any demonstrable advantage with respect to cancer, heart disease, or cognitive decline, and even the presumed relationship between vitamin D supplementation and reduced risk of bone fractures is equivocal. Excessive supplementation can be harmful, especially in the case of fat-soluble vitamins which build up in the body. Excess vitamin E causes osteoporosis, at least in laboratory animals. Vitamins A and E reduce DNA damage due to oxidation, but high doses inactivate the gene for the p53 protein that slows cell replication and induces cell death in cases of catastrophic damage, resulting in more cancer and accelerated tumor growth in the lab and presumably also in at-risk humans such as smokers (Sayin et al. 2014).

In light of the complexities of micronutrient dose-response relationships, the ancestral diet suggests mainly that people should eat a variety of fresh foods that supply adequate nutrients without concentrating the dose of any particular one. Plants grown under stressful conditions are preferable given that they contain more health-promoting substances and less sugar than those which enjoy plentiful water and moderate sunlight and temperature – just as wild and pastured domestic animals produce more nutritious meat than animals raised in barns. In addition, the shift in taste preferences since the Neolithic Revolution to bland, starchy foods should be counteracted by increased consumption of unpalatable but safe foods with sharp and bitter flavors.

. . . . .

Turning now to macronutrients, the proportion of carbohydrates, fat, and protein, and the relationship between the energy they release and the energy the organism uses, are crucial to metabolic functioning and body weight and composition. Surplus energy leads to overweight and obesity and consequently increases the likelihood of chronic diseases. Caloric restriction, on the other hand, benefits the organism through activation of DNA repair enzymes; enhanced immune functioning; improved levels of biomarkers such as circulating triglycerides; and, programmed cell death (apoptosis) which takes damaged and potentially cancerous cells out of circulation. Reduced food intake increases survival time in fruit flies, nematode worms, rodents, and a variety of other laboratory animals. The effect on longevity is less certain in humans and primates, but the reduction in cancer risk is well established.

Comparing ancestral to Western diets, using the US as a typical example, raises three central points: the fat eaten by foragers contains a more healthful balance of fatty acids; the consumption of protein is higher; and, complex carbohydrates predominate over simple sugars.

As noted earlier, the ancestral diet contains no dairy products, which account for 15% of the food energy consumed by Americans. There are either scarce amounts or no grains: no breads or cereals, the base of the current food pyramid and about one-third of food energy consumed. Fruits and other sweets such as honey are available only seasonally and in small quantities, compared to the 20% of daily energy provided by sugar in the US diet – with 4% in the form of candy and white sugar as a sweetener. Water is the only drink, whereas soft drinks and juices account for 8%, and alcoholic beverages for 3%, of Americans' daily calories. Thanks to large quantities of vegetable foods, daily fiber intake among foragers is at least five times higher.

Contrary to the current preference for lean meat, foraging societies especially prize animal fat. Foragers eat fatty internal organs and prefer larger and fattier animals such as deer or elk (with 10–20% fat by weight), to the smallest animals such as rodents (with 2–5% fat by weight). Smaller animals are eaten only during seasons in which they have the most body fat, and foragers throw away lean animals even if they are hungry.

How much fat, protein, and carbohydrate was typical for prehistoric foragers cannot be established with certainty. For instance, coastal populations may have eaten fish and shellfish, but the sea level rose at the end of the Ice Age and covered the evidence, potentially causing the proportion of animal food in their diet to be underestimated. Like ancestral humans, contemporary foragers live in a variety of different environments and consume diverse and changing proportions of animal and plant foods. Today, equipment such as guns and motorized boats and vehicles increases hunting efficiency, although supplies may be lower due to overharvesting. Trade with villagers or European colonists has long influenced the amount of hunting done by foragers, further indicating that practices from a single point in time may not be representative of a lasting pattern.

Available data indicate that animal foods range from about 15% of daily energy intake among desert peoples to 90% or more among Arctic populations. At the lower end of the scale, foragers in southern Africa have access to protein-rich mongongo nuts, allowing them to eat relatively little meat. At the opposite extreme, a nearly all-animal-food diet is possible in the Far North because it consists of fatty meat and organs such as liver, brain, skin, and bone marrow that keep the protein content within acceptable limits and provide micronutrients including vitamins A, C, and D.

On average, by weight 20–50% of the food collected by inland foragers comes from animal sources, with 50–80% from plant sources. The diet of marine (including river and lakeside) communities ranges from 10–50% fish and shellfish, with the remainder coming from plants and some animal foods. For a specific example, by weight two-thirds of the diet (63%) of Ju/'hoansi foragers in southern Africa comes from plants, one-third from meat. The ≠Kade San and the Hadza of Tanzania eat a diet that is 80% plant foods by weight.

With the greater energy density of animal versus plant foods in mind, data from around 60 foraging societies – including highly meat-dependent populations in northern latitudes – suggest that on average our ancestors obtained one-third to one-half their calories from animal foods, and one-half to two-thirds from plant foods. While comparison of the two hundred foraging societies in George Peter

Murdock's *Ethnographic Atlas* (1967) may suggest a reversal of these proportions to almost two-thirds meat and a bit over one-third plants (Cordain et al. 2000), there are strong reasons to doubt a high animal-food proportion. As we have seen, excessive intake of protein makes people sick and can be fatal. In addition, the information in Murdock's database was qualitative in nature and obtained long before ethnographers began to pay attention to plant foods and women's work in the latter decades of the 20th century. Cultural traditions throughout the world place a high value on meat in recognition of its nutritional value and relative scarcity. Foraging societies are no exception, but that does not mean that the people exclusively or even primarily eat meat. Western culture's own distinction between main dishes and side dishes privileges meat even if its caloric contribution to the meal is smaller than that of plant foods.

Based on the 1/3:2/3 meat-to-plant ratio, which is the same in the US today but composed of different amounts of macronutrients, Paleolithic humans ate about twice as much protein as Americans: 20–35% versus 15% of daily caloric intake.[6] There was less fat, just over 20% versus 33%, and the amount of carbohydrate was lower, about 40–45% versus 50%. Using the 2/3:1/3 ratio, for Paleolithic foragers protein intake was 33–35%, fat intake reached 30–60%, and carbohydrate consumption was much lower, at 20–40%. Splitting the difference and assuming a one-half meat, one-half plant diet, results in 20–31% protein, 38–49% fat, and 31% carbohydrate. Taken together, these scenarios share the same protein value of around one-third but vary with respect to fat (20–60%) and carbohydrate (20–45%).

The American Heart Association recommends a diet of 15% protein, less than 30% total fat, and 55–60% carbohydrate. These values fall within the ranges provided by the Food and Nutrition Board of the Institute of Medicine: 10–35% of daily calories from protein; 20–35% fat; and 45–65% carbohydrate. In general, official recommendations favor the low end of the ranges for protein and fat, and the high end of the range for carbohydrate. As seen in Table 5.1, from an evolutionary perspective, current dietary recommendations are set too high for carbohydrates and too low for protein and fat.

TABLE 5.1 Approximate average daily carbohydrate, fat, and protein consumption among foragers compared to US actual and recommended levels

	Foragers	*Foragers*	*Foragers*	*US actual*	*Recommended*	*Recommended*
	1/3 meat 2/3 plant	*2/3 meat 1/3 plant*	*1/2 meat 1/2 plant*	*1/3 meat 2/3 plant*	American Heart Association	Institute of Medicine
Carbohydrate	40–50%	20–40%	31%	50%	55–60%	45–65%
Fat	20–25%	30–60%	38–49%	33%	<30%	20–35%
Protein	20–35%	33–35%	20–31%	15%	15%	10–35%

. . . . .

The proportions of energy derived from different types of macronutrients matter both for body weight and the risk of metabolic syndrome and chronic diseases.

Glucose provides energy to the muscles and especially the brain, which is not able to use fatty acids for fuel. Carbohydrate is the most easily converted source of glucose for energy, followed by fat, and, as a last resort, protein in blood and muscle. Carbohydrate and fat, which are made up of carbon, oxygen, and hydrogen, can be consumed across a wider range of values than protein, which is made up of nitrogen-based amino acids. Protein intakes over one-third of daily calories generate toxic nitrogenous waste (see Chapter 2) and cause calcium and phosphorus imbalances. High-protein diets consequently require abundant intakes of vegetables and fruits to prevent bone demineralization, as is typical of foraging diets.

Besides raising protein consumption closer to the one-third proportion, the evolutionary perspective suggests reducing carbohydrate intake and especially the portion that comes from simple sugars. A century ago, farmers purposely enclosed livestock in pens and fed them cereals to make them grow faster and fatter. Similarly, during the last three decades of the 20th century, as the contribution of carbohydrates to daily calories steadily increased while fat and protein intakes declined among Americans, the rate of obesity more than doubled, from 14.5% to 30.9% (Wright et al. 2004). Where diets have not shifted to increased carbohydrates, as in much of Asia, rates of overweight/obesity, cardiovascular disease, and cancer remain lower.

Compared to carbohydrates, the role of dietary fat with regard to health and body size is more complex. Fat in food such as meat or cheese does not automatically become body fat or fatty deposits on blood vessel walls, and can even prevent these outcomes. Children who drink low-fat milk gain more weight than children who drink whole milk; adults whose diets contain more high-fat dairy products appear to be less susceptible to obesity and cardiovascular disease (Kratz et al. 2013).

As noted earlier, obesity and NIDDM are associated with reduced insulin receptors and consequently high levels of insulin and glucose in the circulation, which, over time, can lead the pancreas to fail. Chronically elevated insulin is associated with high blood pressure, unfavorable lipid levels, and cardiovascular disease. Insulin dysregulation also contributes to cancer through increased production of growth factors. Like normal cells, tumor cells depend on glucose to survive and reproduce. In an environment rich with insulin, growth factors, and glucose, normal cells may become cancerous, and cancer cells may proliferate.

Complex carbohydrates are large molecules containing multiple sugars which have to be broken down to yield energy. This makes them preferable to simple sugars, a category encompassing one-sugar molecules such as glucose, fructose, and galactose, as well as two-sugar molecules such as sucrose or table sugar (glucose and fructose), and lactose or milk sugar (galactose and glucose). Complex carbohydrates contain multiple sugars. They are embedded in cell membranes, as in the glycolipids in red blood cells for which the ABO blood groups are named, and in plant cell walls, the starches in grains, and underground plant foods. Dietary fiber, as in the fibrous husk covering wheat and rice grains, lowers circulating blood glucose. This and other benefits are lost with white flour and rice, from which the husk has been removed, while overcooking simplifies the remaining carbohydrate content.

Consumption of simple carbohydrates causes a spike in insulin levels, with rapid storage of the surplus energy in the form of fat. The brisk fall in insulin levels stimulates feelings of hunger. This effect is especially dramatic with high-fructose corn syrup. Different structures make fructose nearly twice as sweet as glucose even though their chemical formula is the same. While sucrose has equal amounts of glucose and fructose, corn syrup tips the balance towards fructose. In the small intestine, the enzyme sucrase splits sucrose. The glucose passes across the intestinal wall into the bloodstream, but the fructose goes to the liver to be converted into glucose. Excess amounts of fructose pass into the large intestine, where bacteria ferment it and create waste products and digestive symptoms including gas, diarrhea, and bloating. If the liver is suddenly bombarded with fructose, as in a soft drink, it converts the sugar to fat. Some goes into the circulation as triglycerides, which are used to build low-density lipoproteins (LDL) that carry cholesterol, raising the level of "bad" cholesterol in the blood. The rest stays in the liver. Fat in the liver is linked to insulin resistance. In addition, in contrast to glucose, consumption of fructose does not bring feelings of satiety and reward and therefore facilitates overeating (Page et al. 2013).

Turning now to the role of dietary fat in weight gain and health, the analysis above suggests that increasing the proportion of calories from fat would result in less overweight/obesity, not more. However, not all fats are created alike. The proportion of saturated and unsaturated fats affects how cells including neurons function and interact with each other and with chemical messengers, and consequently influences psychological states and cognitive performance, metabolic functions, and cardiovascular disease and cancer risks.

Cholesterol is a fat-based steroid mainly synthesized internally from simpler molecules. It is necessary for fat digestion, vitamin absorption and synthesis, building hormones and cell membranes, and other essential functions. Dietary sources such as meat or dairy products contribute only one-fifth to one-third of the total. The level tends to stay within narrow limits through increased or dampened production based on dietary inputs, but in some cases is poorly regulated. Very elevated blood cholesterol levels are associated with a higher risk of coronary artery disease and heart attack. Very low levels have negative effects on the brain, increasing the risk of aggression and psychiatric distress. In the case of high cholesterol, diet is less effective than medicine for reducing the level.

High-density lipoprotein particles (HDL) and very-high-density lipoproteins (VHDL) transport cholesterol back to the liver, giving them the name "good cholesterol." Low-density lipoprotein particles (LDL) and very low-density lipoproteins (VLDL) carry cholesterol and fatty acids throughout the body where they are needed, including blood vessels where plaques can form, giving them the name "bad cholesterol." Given that HDL removes cholesterol from the circulation whereas LDL keeps it there, the association between cholesterol and heart disease is really a link between heart disease and high LDL and/or low HDL. Significantly, the amount of cholesterol in ancestral and Western diets is similar, but serum cholesterol levels remain low among foragers (low to mid-100s) as a result of exercise and high consumption of protein and fiber. These factors reduce LDL while increasing HDL.

Triglycerides are made up of three fatty acid molecules attached to a glycerol "backbone" of carbon, hydrogen, and oxygen atoms. Saturated fats have only single chemical bonds between the carbon atoms in the fatty acid chain and are the most stable. Unsaturated fatty acids contain one or more weaker double bond between carbon atoms, meaning that they are not fully saturated with hydrogen atoms. Comparing two fatty acids with the same number of carbon atoms, the saturated one releases more energy upon digestion than the unsaturated one. In other words, the forces holding saturated fats together are stronger, which is why their melting point is higher and they remains solid at room temperature. Monounsaturated fats have only one double bond and are more stable than polyunsaturated fats (PUFAs), with multiple double bonds.

Most plant-derived fats are polyunsaturated or monounsaturated, such as PUFAs in walnuts or monounsaturated fats in avocadoes, but animal meat, fat, and dairy products also contain unsaturated fat while plants such as soy and coconut oil contain saturated fat. While unsaturated fat is dispersed in cell membranes throughout the body, the thick fat stores of farm animals contain substantial amounts of saturated fat. In total, farm-raised animals have about five times the fat of wild animals, with a higher proportion of saturated fat and a lower proportion of unsaturated fat. Domestic meat contains two to three times the calories per kilogram as wild meat.

The saturated fat in meat does not exclude it as a healthful food. Even domestic meat contains a substantial amount of monounsaturated oleic acid, the same as in olive oil and a type of fat that raises HDL and lowers LDL. In addition, there is a small amount of the saturated fatty acid, stearic acid, the kind in chocolate, which increases HDL while having little effect on LDL. Another small fraction is polyunsaturated. In all, half or more of the fat in meat is beneficial with respect to cholesterol and the rest is not necessarily harmful in that while it raises LDL it also raises HDL.

For these reasons, the relationship between meat consumption and heart disease remains unclear. Consumption of highly-saturated solid fat, as in meat and cheese, raises serum cholesterol levels. However, moderately high cholesterol levels do not increase the risk of cardiovascular disease. Worldwide, societies in which vegetables and fruits are eaten in large quantities year-round have the lowest rates of heart disease, regardless of increased meat consumption over the last decades in places such as Japan and Mediterranean Europe. On the other hand, high consumption of red and processed meats increases the risk of several types of cancer such as premenopausal breast cancer and gastrointestinal tumors.

Trans-fatty acids are unambiguously detrimental. They are made by adding hydrogen atoms to polyunsaturated vegetable oils and thereby rendering all the carbon-to-carbon bonds single. Trans fats lower HDL and raise LDL, and thereby increase the probability of atherosclerotic buildup in the arteries. Consequently, substitutes for butter (margarine, shortening) are more harmful than butter itself.

Polyunsaturated fats have generally positive effects but, in very high amounts, they appear to promote tumor metastasis and possibly the growth of tumors in the first place. PUFA consumption reduces the risk of a range of diseases, including hypertension, eye diseases, depression, attention-deficit disorder, and amytropic lateral sclerosis (Lou Gehrig's disease). PUFAs dampen prostate tumor growth and improve survival rates. Replacing saturated fats with PUFAs, or PUFAs together with monounsaturated fats, reduces the risk of cardiovascular disease, as does consumption of nuts and whole grain cereals (Astrup et al. 2011).

Most processed foods contain omega-6 fatty acids (named for the position of the first double bond in relation to the methyl-group end of the carbon chain), given their presence in soybean, sunflower, and other vegetable oils. These PUFAs are not particularly advantageous. They are precursors to prostaglandin 2, a necessary molecule found in all cells that, in excess, contributes to inflammation and consequently to asthma, arthritis, and cardiovascular disease. Laboratory animals become obese when fed omega-6 PUFAs, and lean when not.

In contrast, omega-3 fatty acids protect against both weight gain and cardiovascular disease. They increase HDL, lower triglycerides, reduce platelet aggregation, and regulate glucose metabolism. Omega-3 PUFAs are precursors to prostaglandin 3, which has anti-inflammatory effects. These PUFAs are found in small amounts in terrestrial animals, and larger amounts in cold-water fish and algae (and their oils) as well as the blubber of marine animals such as whales and seals. They help explain the extremely low rates of cardiovascular disease, overweight/obesity, metabolic disorders, dental caries, and cancer that prevailed among indigenous populations of the Far North until the mid-20th century. By now, these rates have reached those of the general population except among the oldest generations and those who maintain a traditional lifestyle. Interestingly, genetic variants in Inuit and Yupik peoples result in blood pressure and lipid levels that are lower at equivalent levels of overweight compared to other people. These variants maximize the efficiency of carbohydrate metabolism, reduce oxidative stress caused by a PUFA-rich diet, and boost the activity of enzymes that break down omega-3 and omega-6 PUFAs. They favorably influence insulin, cholesterol, and triglyceride levels, with effects on growth hormones as evidenced by reduced stature and body weight (Fumagalli et al. 2015). The very low frequencies of these variants in other populations argue against excessive consumption of marine foods everywhere, especially if the altered diet is not accompanied by physical activity and exposure to the elements.

All in all, the evidence suggests that it is not advisable for the general population to reduce fat consumption except in the form of saturated and trans fats, whereas limiting simple carbohydrate promotes health. A 20-year study involving 300,000 women found that total dietary fat was not related to stroke or heart disease risk, although trans-fatty acids, saturated fats, and refined grain-based carbohydrates increased risk (Oh et al. 2005). It is especially unhelpful to reduce fat consumption if the balance is made up by carbohydrates, particularly simple sugars, which increases LDL, lowers HDL, and raises triglyceride levels. In older people, high consumption of carbohydrates increases the risk of dementia and cognitive impairment, whereas high consumption of fat and protein reduces risk (R. Roberts et al. 2012).

The demonization of dietary fat even has psychophysical effects that can interfere with metabolism and promote weight gain. Just believing that a food is a sensible, low-fat choice is enough to temper the fall in ghrelin, a gut hormone that stimulates hunger and slows metabolism in case food is not readily available. The exact same food perceived as fattening drops the level of ghrelin several times faster, increasing the metabolic rate and bringing feelings of satiety (Crum et al. 2014).

To sum up, an evolutionary approach suggests an increase in protein consumption – which necessarily entails a moderate increase in fat consumption – and a reduction in the proportion of carbohydrate in the diet, especially simple sugars. The diet should be varied in order to ensure adequate micronutrient intake, not focused on particular items reputed to provide specific health benefits. Very few specific foods have a demonstrated positive effect comparable to the reduction in heart attack risk and stroke associated with pure chocolate. Supplements do not prevent common diseases such as cancer or heart disease and may even increase risk. At the same time, avoiding foods that attain a negative reputation, such as cholesterol in the past or gluten today, needlessly takes away valuable nutrients for all but the small percentage of people with rare medical conditions.

In addition, more time outdoors and exercise for an hour or more every day are needed to counter the overabundance of calories in Western diets. At all ages, physical activity brings lower disease risks and mortality rates, and provides therapeutic benefits across a wide range of diseases. For children, lifestyle change is particularly urgent given the extreme passivity of modern amusements and transportation and the easy access to unsuitable foods, resulting in a global epidemic of overweight/obesity in the very young.

As we will see in Chapter 10, industrialized societies generate chronic disease in other ways besides diet and inactivity. Inequality, displacement, and political and economic instability negatively influence neuroendocrine, immune, and cardiovascular functioning. Psychosocial stress affects body composition and disease risks independently of dietary intakes. Anonymous mass societies do not provide the social support and monitoring typical of nomadic face-to-face societies, which also permit people to easily change residence if they are unhappy or unable to get along. The lack of this combined safety net and safety valve helps explain why anxiety, depression, attention-deficit and related disorders, and distress-dependent health complaints are common features of industrialized societies. There is more crime, violence, and substance abuse. These associations show that health is not a simple matter of individual choices but rather emerges through social processes.

. . . . .

While behavioral choices can reduce disease risks, they are no guarantee against sickness. Moreover, too much attention to them is a health threat in itself. Focusing on personal responsibility blames individuals for sickness, obscures economic and other constraints on their freedom and ability to act in line with their preferences and beliefs, and fails to account for larger forces beyond their control.

Everyone in countries such as the US is exposed to the effects of a competitive, unequal social system; food that is safe and abundant but monotonous and sugary compared to an ancestral diet; a sedentary, machine-dependent lifestyle; and microorganisms and other pests and the chemicals used against them. The environment is tainted with automobile exhausts, industrial and agricultural pollution, consumer products containing mutagenic and hormone-disrupting chemicals, and radiation. No one can control the genes they have inherited or the living conditions their parents experienced and may pass on epigenetically. Individuals have no say over the forces impinging upon their growth during gestation, whether they were breastfed or not, or the health and hygienic circumstances of their childhood. Even the most unambiguous disease-causing behavior, smoking, is not a simple product of free choice.

A perspective that encompasses multiple levels of disease threats contrasts against the Western ideal of autonomous personhood and a medical system grounded in clinical treatment of organs or cells as instances of disease, rather than home-based treatment of people in the fullness of their unique circumstances. Screening for biomarkers and genes takes this reductionism a step further, contributing to a view of health as a matter of risks residing in individuals. While a reductionistic approach has brought and continues to bring enormous benefits to human health, it also has limited scope for addressing broader social conditions and environmental threats. In addition, as shown below, it can increase suffering.

Today's culture of risk construes submission to screening tests and diagnostic procedures as equivalent to taking care of one's health.[7] Even 80-year-olds are expected to go in for tests such as mammography, Pap smears, prostate cancer screening, and colonoscopy – and are judged by a substantial proportion of adults to be irresponsible if they do otherwise (Schwartz et al. 2004). Annual sports physicals are required by schools, camps, and sports programs, even though they do not include procedures that can identify the rare heart defects that have caused sudden deaths in athletes. In obstetrics, routine ultrasound screenings and fetal monitoring remain customary practices, in spite of evidence-based recommendations by panels of neutral experts.

Thousands of genetic tests are available to screen for rare mutations in newborns and children, and for susceptibility genes in the general population, including tests sold directly to consumers. People can have the length of their telomeres assessed as an index of aging and therefore the likelihood of chronic diseases such as Alzheimer's and cardiovascular disease, even though no treatments exist to increase telomere length and even though such treatments would increase the risk of certain malignant cancers. These structures at the end of chromosomes shorten with each cell replication (see Chapter 10). It is not clear whether shorter telomeres are the cause or the consequence of disease, although there is no doubt that they are associated with inactivity, poor diet, stress, smoking, heavy drinking, and overweight/obesity. For men with high cholesterol, longer telomeres are associated with a lower risk of heart disease, but cholesterol-lowering drugs work the same regardless of telomere length (Brouilette et al. 2007).

Early identification is valuable where treatment exists, but even then, it is necessary to evaluate the burden of false-positive results which generate further procedures, costs, and psychological trauma. For instance, screening for abnormal prostate-specific-antigen levels prevents one prostate cancer death for every 1,500 men screened, but 80 men undergo unnecessary surgery (Barratt and Stockler 2009). Changes in thresholds or increased probing for signs of disease can instantly expand the pool of pre-sick individuals requiring additional medical attention. In addition, screening tests themselves involve financial costs and health impacts. The number of computed tomography (CT) scans, which deliver up to 400 times as much radiation as a single chest x-ray and 20,000 times as much as an arm x-ray, has skyrocketed in recent decades. For instance, in the US the annual number of CT scans increased from 3 to 62 million from 1980–2006. This showering of radiation has led to thousands of additional cancer deaths (Brenner and Hall 2007).

Imaging technologies including CT scans, ultrasound, and magnetic resonance imaging (MRI) can lead to the identification of anomalies and diseases that never would have caused the patient any trouble. A large portion of healthy people carry meniscal damage in their knees, compression fractures in their vertebrae, growths in their thyroid glands, and myriad other signs of wear and cellular waywardness. Seeing these things on a scan nearly always sets in motion a process aimed at eliminating them. The same can be expected with regard to new blood tests to detect tumor DNA or abnormal levels of proteins suggesting the presence of cancer, even if the tumor is one that grows so slowly it would never be noticed.

Overdiagnosis may be limited by testing based on known risk factors, and the impact contained by limiting treatment to thresholds above which there are well-established therapeutic benefits. However, there is strong cultural resistance to an evidence-based approach. To illustrate, screening mammography generates an enormous amount of additional mammograms and precautionary surgical procedures, radiation, and pharmaceutical treatment, but the public, along with the American Cancer Society, remains committed to blanket annual screenings beginning at age 40 or younger (Hensley 2015). Current recommendations from panels of neutral experts call for screenings every 2 years for women aged 50–74, with no advice for younger and older women based on insufficient evidence of a net benefit (US Preventive Services Task Force 2016).

In the US, the number of annual early-stage ductal carcinoma in situ (DCIS) diagnoses increased from 112 to 234 cases per 100,000 women over a 30-year period, while the number of late-stage cancer diagnoses declined from 102 to 94 per 100,000. Assuming the baseline cancer burden remained the same, 8 per 100,000 women with early diagnosis out of 122 additional cases detected through screening would have later presented as late-stage cancer, leaving 114 cases of overdiagnosis per 100,000 women per year, or one-third of the annual total. This adds up to over a million cases of overdiagnosis. During those same years, improvements in treatment have had a far greater impact on mortality from breast cancer than has early detection, suggesting that it might be better not to screen for a disease that can be treated adequately upon diagnosis based on clinical symptoms (Bleyer and Welch 2012). In Canada, researchers followed 90,000 women who all received annual physical examinations but were divided into a mammography and control group. After 25 years, the death rate from breast cancer was virtually the same for both, but overdiagnosis occurred in over one-fifth of the cases identified through screening mammography (Miller et al. 2014).

Thanks in part to a successful fear campaign, breast cancer appears to be the paramount women's disease, even though heart disease accounts for more deaths among US women than all forms of cancer combined. In reality, the risk of developing breast cancer is nowhere near 1-in-8, a proportion derived from summing age-specific risks from birth to over 100 years. For instance, the risk of developing breast cancer over the next 10 years is 1.47% at age 40, 3.56% at 60, and 3.04% at 80 (Howlader et al. 2012). Reproductive risk factors along with overweight/obesity and ethnicity make the disease more likely for some women than others, but the primary risk factor is age. Consequently, mass screening is not warranted for rare susceptibility genes such as BRCA1 and BRCA2, which are present in about 5% of women who develop breast or ovarian cancer and 0.33–0.2% of the general population. About 2% of American women have a higher-than-average risk of carrying a mutation and could benefit from genetic testing. These are women with a strong family history of breast and ovarian cancer, not just a single female relative who has had ovarian cancer or breast cancer on one side (see US Preventive Services Task Force 2013).

Complex diseases are unlike rare genetic diseases caused by single-gene mutations which are expressed across all or a very large proportion of the people who carry them. Some high-penetrance genes are dominant and need be inherited from only one parent, as in the case of Huntington's disease or early-onset Alzheimer's. Others are recessive and have high penetrance when inherited from both parents, as in cystic fibrosis, hereditary hemochromatosis, and sickle-cell anemia. These diseases are amenable to gene therapy, which has brought recent successes with respect to diseases including metachromic leukodystrophy, Wiskott-Aldrich syndrome, and severe combined immunodeficiency.

For common chronic diseases the situation is very different. Some 70–90% of cases are due to environmental, social, and behavioral causes, whereas susceptibility genes account for only 2–3%, or in some cases up to 5–10% of cases (Rappaport and Smith 2010). Some susceptibility genes have a clear connection to diseases – such as the BRCA mutations mentioned above, which also increase the risk of pancreatic cancer, or the apolipoprotein E gene variant ApoE4 which increases the risk of vascular and cognitive diseases including late-onset Alzheimer's disease. Yet, penetrance is incomplete, meaning that the disease may or may not develop. Alternatively, not having the gene does not protect against the disease. Moreover, the same genes may have multiple effects. For instance, the genesis and suppression of tumors are both associated with variants of the gene for the Notch 1 transmembrane receptor.

Most people have an equivalent risk of most of the complex diseases regardless of their genes. This has been shown through studies on 54,000 identical twins in five countries, of which one, both, or neither developed each of two dozen diseases including cardiovascular diseases, Types I and II diabetes, dementia, inflammatory bowel disease, and nine types of cancer (N. Roberts et al. 2012). In the case of cancer, very few people carried inherited genetic mutations linked to the disease, while about one-third of people with no susceptibility genes nonetheless developed it. Susceptibility genes were associated with elevated risk for some of the diseases, including Alzheimer's and heart disease in men, but in the former case there is no preventive medical treatment and, in the latter, risk may be more accurately predicted by known factors such as blood pressure, smoking, age, and lipid levels.

In general, the only preventive advice available even where there are identified susceptibility genes is the same given to all patients, such as better nutrition and more physical activity for cancer, mental exercises for Alzheimer's, and anticoagulants for people who have had deep-vein blood clots. Moreover, awareness of genetic susceptibility does not bring greater commitment to lifestyle change, as seen in patients with genetic risks for diabetes or breast and ovarian cancer. People with genetic risks for hypercholesterolemia and nicotine dependence tend to believe that they need a pharmaceutical solution and consequently are *less* likely to follow behavioral advice. Moreover, positive changes may be short-lived, as in the case of smokers with a genetic predisposition to lung cancer. These dismal findings suggest that increased reliance on genetic risk analysis may lead to worse rather than better health outcomes (Grant et al. 2013; Hall et al. 2010).

Cultural concern for health risks and preventive screening creates sickness through the anxiety and stress that result from increased awareness of disease. Hundreds of tests for biomarkers and genetic susceptibilities are offered directly to consumers, leading to more doctor visits (Bloss et al. 2014). While these tests may empower individuals through access to potentially useful medical information, in the case of genetic susceptibilities they inevitably produce uncertainties and uneasiness due to the impossibility of mapping population-based probabilities onto individual futures. To illustrate, if a die is cast many times, it will land with any particular side up one-sixth of the time. Say the side with five dots represents a disease that affects 16.67% of the people who carry a susceptibility gene. For any single individual, the chance of throwing a five is irrelevant, for they only have one life in the balance: either they get the disease or not. It is hardly surprising that people have opted for procedures such as pre-emptive mastectomy and prostate surgery due to apprehensions about cancer. Some physicians likewise prefer a radical course of action in order to settle their own minds (Gifford 1986).

The attachment of any risk, no matter how small, to an identifiable gene presents the further danger of discrimination in insurance and the workplace. There are precedents in the US, such as the response to the discovery of the genetic basis of sickle-cell anemia in the 1950s. Whether or not they had relatives from a part of Africa where the disease was prevalent, black Americans experienced discrimination. Some states imposed mandatory screening. Today, legal protections are unlikely to prevent the misuse of genetic information and would be expensive and difficult to uphold. It is easy to procure a DNA sample from people without their knowledge. Moreover, samples voluntarily given to testing companies, researchers, and medical workers can be traced back to the source, regardless of anonymity procedures. In short, the tools for discrimination against individuals and their relatives are readily available and may be used invisibly.

Even in the absence of worrisome results, routine testing casts permanent doubt on one's status as a healthy person and increases people's psychological dependence on health professionals. In addition, through the nocebo effect, anxiety over a particular threat can bring about the very outcome that is feared.[8] For instance, if research participants are given an innocuous substance presented as an emetic, they vomit. Participants with allergies who are given an innocuous substance presented as an allergen respond with a full-blown allergic reaction. People who believe themselves especially vulnerable to heart attack, but who do not in fact have more risk factors than the general population, die at a higher rate from heart attack. Chinese people born in years believed to make them susceptible to particular types of illnesses do not survive as long as others who come down with the same disease. Men's worry about prostate cancer correlates with abnormal levels of prostate-specific antigen, independently of cancer-related symptoms (Cohen et al. 2003).

Fear of a specific mortal threat can even result in death. Over the last few decades, dozens of healthy Hmong men and a small number of Hmong women refugees in the US have died as a result of the Sudden Unexplained Nocturnal Death Syndrome (SUNDS). Shelley Adler (2011) attributes the syndrome to their fear of the nighttime pressing spirit, *dab tsog*. This local concept describes a universal nightmare phenomenon that involves bodily paralysis during the partially conscious initial phase of REM sleep. Laying on one's back can heighten the resulting anxiety by causing feelings of suffocation, as if something were pressing upon the chest. In the case of SUNDS, the fear appears to cause the brain to send signals to the heart that fatally interfere with its normal contractions.

Adler explains that the displaced Hmong left a context of violence and insecurity in Laos only to face new sources of alarm and apprehension, such as economic stress, social adjustment, and cultural and religious assimilation. They worry that the protective spirits animating the landscape back home may not have crossed the ocean with the ancestor spirits and the nightmare spirit who followed them. Before, a visit from the nighttime pressing spirit would be managed by religious leaders, who prescribed actions to rectify a transgression and ensure that the *dab tsog* would never return. In the US, the spirit continues to visit until finally it presses the life out of a man. Women also have nightmares, but they know that their male relatives are ultimately responsible for fulfilling the family's religious obligations.

Evidently, mind-body effects are powerful enough to bring great and even mortal harm. This suggests that increasing knowledge of health risks can generate additional fear and suffering. Margaret Lock (1998) compares contemporary risk analysis to divination, for, like non-Western spiritual healing, it is an attempt to create a sense of control over uncertainty through analysis of empirical data. Both biomedical and traditional healers explain misfortune and make prophesies about what the future holds. Both enjoy an elevated social position marked by special dress and language, and both predict individual destinies using methods which are considered technologically advanced in their cultural context. Where one might analyze the natural world for signs, such as cracks on animal bones or the arrangement of leaves in a teacup, the other "reads" the genetic code and other biological signs to calculate probabilistic estimates of risk.

In the view of non-Western cultures, the natural world is inhabited by both people and spirits, and sickness stems from malevolent spirits, fate, or failure to fulfill an important social or spiritual obligation. Western culture defines disease as an individual calamity stemming from biological defects or behavioral choices. Individuals are held responsible for managing risks and blamed if they get sick, especially in the case of complex diseases of unspecified origin such as cancer. Cultural beliefs about self-reliance as a virtue leave people to deal with adversity largely on their own. In the case of sickness, people are expected to will themselves to health through optimism and positive thinking.

At the population level, happiness and social integration are associated with lower disease risks and higher recovery rates (Diener and Chan 2011). This does not mean that recovery depends on a positive attitude. Placebo effects rarely can be consciously obtained or nocebo effects averted, although there are some exceptions. For instance, symptoms of irritable bowel syndrome improved more in patients administered pills openly named "placebo" than in untreated patients (Kaptchuk et al. 2010). More commonly, conscious effort does not affect the course of disease. For instance, optimism has no effect on survival in lung cancer patients (Schofield et al. 2004).

Not only can insisting on a happy outlook have little impact on the course of disease, it can worsen patients' suffering where sickness is construed as failed prevention, while a lack of improvement signifies a failure of obedience and effort. Being angry and seeking redress are excluded from the range of legitimate responses to disease. The role of social and environmental exposures and inequalities in access to treatment falls out of sight. In other words, focusing on individuals as the locus of risk distracts attention and resources away from efforts to deal with unambiguous health threats such as addictive substances, sugary drinks, convenience foods, inactivity, psychosocial stress, and pollution. It is no coincidence that the research and public relations efforts of the tobacco, alcohol, food, and gambling industries emphasize an interpretation of poor health as the outcome of individual susceptibilities (Hall et al. 2010).

This chapter has shown that the power of preventive medicine centered on behavior and early detection is offset by the dangers of victim-blaming and avoidance of the need to confront the larger contexts which delimit individual choices, exposures, and outcomes. Searching for warning signs leads to overdiagnosis and increased fear, and creates additional burdens of disease. The allure of genetic interpretations of common chronic diseases promises only to take this tendency further, even though the evidence suggests that awareness of all the risks lurking in individual genomes does not improve preventive behavior and also opens the door to discrimination. In short, risk awareness may be a health hazard in itself.

Notes

1 On breastfeeding and women's health, see Bartick et al. (2013); Whitaker (2006). On dental disease, myopia, acne, and cancer, see Cordain et al. (2002); Eaton et al. (2002a, 2002b); Green et al. (2011).
2 Recommendations tend to call for 20- or 30-minute sessions several times a week, whereas the WHO prescribes an hour of activity on most if not all days. On physical activity levels, recommendations, and impacts on health, see Eaton and Eaton (2003); National Center for Health Statistics (2013); Whitaker (2005); World Health Organization Europe (2012).
3 See Ahima and Lazar (2013), who report these proportions as 8% and 10%, respectively.
4 Regarding dietary intakes and recommendations in the text and table, see Cordain et al. (2000); Eaton et al. (1988); US Department of Agriculture (2016); Wright et al. (2004).
5 On dose-response effects and nutritional supplements, see Gerber et al. (1999).
6 Cordain et al. (2000) estimate that on average about two-thirds of the energy in wild plant foods comes from carbohydrate, one-fifth to one-fourth from fat, and slightly over one-eighth from protein. Butchered animals contain 2–20% fat and almost no carbohydrate, leaving the rest as protein.
7 On overdiagnosis, see Welch et al. (2011).
8 On nocebo effects, see Adler (2011).

References cited

Adler SR. 2011. *Sleep paralysis: night-mares, nocebos, and the mind-body connection.* New Brunswick, NJ: Rutgers University Press.

Ahima RS, Lazar MA. 2013. The health risks of obesity – better metrics imperative. *Science* 341(6148):856–858.

Andersen LB, Schnohr P, Scroll M, Hein HO. 2002. Mortality associated with physical activity in leisure time, at work, in sports, and cycling to work. *Ugeskrift for laeger* 164(11):1501–1506.

Astrup A, Dyerberg J, Elwood P, Hermansen K, Hu FB, Jakobsen MU, Kok FJ, Krauss RM, Lecerf JM, LeGrand P, et al. 2011. The role of reducing intakes of saturated fat in the prevention of cardiovascular disease: where does the evidence stand in 2010? *American Journal of Clinical Nutrition* 93(4):684–688.

Barratt AL, Stockler MR. 2009. Screening for prostate cancer: explaining new trial results and their implications to patients. *Medical Journal of Australia* 191(4):226–229.

Bartick MC, Stuebe AM, Schwarz EB, Luongo C, Reinhold AG, Foster EM. 2013. Cost analysis of maternal disease associated with suboptimal breastfeeding. *Obstetrics & Gynecology* 122(1):111–119.

Bleyer A, Welch HG. 2012. Effect of three decades of screening mammography on breast-cancer incidence. *New England Journal of Medicine* 367(21):1998–2005.

Bloss CS, Schork NJ, Topol EJ. 2014. Direct-to-consumer pharmacogenomic testing is associated with increased physician utilisation. *Journal of Medical Genetics* 51(2):83–89.

Brenner DJ, Hall EJ. 2007. Computed tomography – an increasing source of radiation exposure. *New England Journal of Medicine* 357(22):2277–2284.

Brouilette SW, Moore JS, McMahon AD, Thompson JR, Ford I, Shepherd J, Packard CJ, Samani NJ. 2007. Telomere length, risk of coronary heart disease, and statin treatment in the West of Scotland Primary Prevention Study: a nested case-control study. *The Lancet* 369(9556):107–114.

Cattaneo A, Monasta L, Stamatakis E, Lioret S, Castetbon K, Frenken F, Manios Y, Moschonis G, Savva S, Zaborskis A, et al. 2010. Overweight and obesity in infants and pre-school children in the European Union: a review of existing data. *Obesity Reviews* 11(5):389–398.

Cohen L, Fouladi RT, Babaian RJ, Bhadkamkar VA, Parker PA, Taylor CC, Smith MA, Gritz ER, Basen-Engquist K. 2003. Cancer worry is associated with abnormal prostate-specific antigen levels in men participating in a community screening program. *Cancer Epidemiology, Biomarkers, & Prevention* 12(7):610–617.

Cordain L, Eaton SB, Brand Miller J, Lindeberg S, Jensen C. 2002. An evolutionary analysis of the aetiology and pathogenesis of juvenile-onset myopia. *Acta Ophthalmologica Scandinavica* 80(2):125–135.

Cordain L, Miller JB, Eaton SB, Mann N, Holt SH, Speth JD. 2000. Plant-animal subsistence ratios and macronutrient energy estimations in worldwide hunter-gatherer diets. *American Journal of Clinical Nutrition* 71(3):682–692.

Crum AJ, Corbin WR, Brownell KD, Salovey P. 2014. Mind over milkshakes: mindsets, not just nutrients, determine ghrelin response. *Health Psychology* 30(4):424–429.

Crum AJ, Langer EJ. 2007. Mind-set matters: exercise and the placebo effect. *Psychological Science* 18(2):165–171.

Di Castelnuovo A, Costanzo S, Bagnardi V, Donati MB, Iacoviello L, de Gaetano G. 2006. Alcohol dosing and total mortality in men and women: an updated meta-analysis of 34 prospective studies. *Archives of Internal Medicine* 166(22):2437–2445.

Diener E, Chan MY. 2011. Happy people live longer: subjective well-being contributes to health and longevity. *Applied Psychology* 3(1):1–43.

Eaton SB, Cordain L, Lindeberg S. 2002a. Evolutionary health promotion: a consideration of common counterarguments. *Preventive Medicine* 34(2):119–123.

Eaton SB. 2003. An evolutionary perspective on human physical activity: implications for health. *Comparative Biochemistry and Physiology Part A: Molecular & Integrative Physiology* 136(1):153–159.

Eaton SB, Konner M, Shostak M. 1988. Stone agers in the fast lane: chronic degenerative diseases in evolutionary perspective. *The American Journal of Medicine* 84(4):739–749.

Eaton SB, Strassman BI, Nesse RM, Neel JV, Ewald PW, Williams GC, Weder AB, Lindeberg S, Konner MJ, et al. 2002b. Evolutionary health promotion. *Preventive Medicine* 34(2):109–118.

Fox M, Berzuini C, Knapp LA. 2013. Maternal breastfeeding history and Alzheimer's disease risk. *Journal of Alzheimer's Disease* 37(4):809–821.

Fumagalli M, Moltke I, Grarup N, Racimo F, Bjerregaard P, Jørgensen ME, Korneliussen TS, Gerbault P, Skotte L, Linneberg A, et al. 2015. Greenland Inuit show genetic signatures of diet and climate adaptation. *Science* 349(6254):1343–1347.

Gerber LM, Williams GC, Gray SJ. 1999. The nutrient-toxin dosage continuum in human evolution and modern health. *The Quarterly Review of Biology* 74(3):273–289.

Gifford SM. 1986. The meaning of lumps: a case study in the ambiguities of risk. *Anthropology and Epidemiology* 9:213–246.

Grant RW, O'Brien KE, Waxler JL, Vassy JL, Delahanty LM, Bissett LG, Green RC, Stember KG, Guiducci C, Park ER, et al. 2013. Personalized genetic risk counseling to motivate diabetes prevention: a randomized trial. *Diabetes Care* 36(1):13–19.

Green J, Cairns BJ, Casabonne D, Wright FL, Reeves G, Beral V, for the Million Women Study collaborators. 2011. Height and cancer incidence in the Million Women Study: prospective cohort, and meta-analysis of prospective studies of height and total cancer risk. *The Lancet Oncology* 12(8):785–794.

Hall WD, Mathews R, Morley KI. 2010. Being more realistic about the public health impact of genomic medicine. *PLoS Med* 7(10):e1000347.

Hensley S. 2015 April 25. Poll finds most women believe mammograms should be done annually. www.npr.org.

Howlader N, Noone AM, Krapcho M, Neyman N, Aminou R, Waldron W, Altekruse SF, Kosary CL, Ruhl J, Tatalovich Z, et al., editors. 2012. SEER Cancer Statistics Review, 1975-2009 (Vintage 2009 Populations), National Cancer Institute. Bethesda, MD, http://seer.cancer.gov/csr/1975_2009_pops09/, based on November 2011 SEER data submission, posted to the SEER website, April 2012.

Kaptchuk TJ, Friedlander E, Kelley JM, Sanchez MN, Kokkotou E, Singer JP, Kowalczykowski M, Miller FG, Kirsch I, Lembo AJ. 2010. Placebos without deception: a randomized control trial in irritable bowel syndrome. *PLoS One* 5(12):e15591.

King DE, Matheson E, Chirina S, Shankar A, Broman-Fulks J. 2013. The status of baby boomers' health in the United States: the healthiest generation? *JAMA Internal Medicine* 173(5):385–386.

Kratz M, Baars T, Guyenet S. 2013. The relationship between high-fat dairy consumption and obesity, cardiovascular, and metabolic disease. *European Journal of Nutrition* 52(1):1–24.

Lock M. 1998. Breast cancer: reading the omens. *Anthropology Today* 14(4):7–16.

Miller AB, Wall C, Baines CJ, Sun P, To T, Narod SA. 2014. Twenty five year follow-up for breast cancer incidence and mortality of the Canadian National Breast Screening Study: randomised screening trial. *British Medical Journal* 348:g366.

Mitchell R. 2013. Is physical activity in natural environments better for mental health than physical activity in other environments? *Social Science and Medicine* 91:130–134.

Murdock GP. 1967. *Ethnographic atlas.* Pittsburgh: University of Pittsburgh Press.

National Center for Health Statistics. 2013. Health, United States, 2012. Table 63. Hyattsville, Maryland: US Department of Health and Human Services.

Ogden CL, Carroll MD, Kit BK, Flegal KM. 2012. NCHS Data Brief n. 82, Prevalence of Obesity in the United States 2009–2010. Hyattsville, MD: US Department of Health and Human Services.

Oh K, Hu FB, Manson JE, Stampfer MJ, Willett WC. 2005. Dietary fat intake and risk of coronary heart disease in women: 20 years of follow-up of the Nurses' Health Study. *American Journal of Epidemiology* 161(7):672–679.

Page KA, Chan O, Arora J, Belfort-DeAguiar R, Dzuira J, Roehmholdt B, Cline GW, Naik S, Sinha R, Constable RT, et al. 2013. Effects of fructose vs glucose on regional cerebral blood flow in brain regions involved with appetite and reward pathways. *JAMA* 309(1):63–70.

Rappaport SM, Smith MT. 2010. Environment and disease risks. *Science* 330(6003):460–461.

Roberts NJ, Vogelstein JT, Parmigiani G, Kinzler KW, Vogelstein B, Velculescu VE. 2012. The predictive capacity of personal genome sequencing. *Science Translational Medicine* 4(133):133ra58–133ra58.

Roberts RO, Roberts LA, Geda YE, Cha RH, Pankratz VS, O'Connor HM, Knopman DS, Petersen RC. 2012. Relative intake of macronutrients impacts risk of mild cognitive impairment or dementia. *Journal of Alzheimer's Disease* 32(2):329–339.

Rose DP, Boyar AP, Wynder EL. 1986. International comparisons of mortality rates for cancer of the breast, ovary, prostate, and colon, and per capita food consumption. *Cancer* 58:2363–2371.

Sayin VI, Ibrahim MX, Larsson E, Nilsson JA, Lindahl P, Bergo MO. 2014. Antioxidants accelerate lung cancer progression in mice. *Science Translational Medicine* 6(221):221ra15.

Schofield P, Ball D, Smith JG, Borland R, O'Brien P, Davis S, Olver I, Ryan G, Joseph D. 2004. Optimism and survival in lung carcinoma patients. *Cancer* 100(6):1276–1282.

Schwartz LM, Woloshin S, Fowler FJ Jr, Welch HG. 2004. Enthusiasm for cancer screening in the United States. *JAMA* 291(1):71–78.

US Department of Agriculture. 2016. Dietary reference intakes (DRIs): acceptable macronutrient distribution ranges. http://fnic.nal.usda.gov/sites/fnic.nal.usda.gov/files/uploads/recommended_intakes_individuals.pdf. Accessed 20 April 2016.

US Preventive Services Task Force. 2013. BRCA-related cancer: risk assessment, genetic counseling, and genetic testing. http://www.uspreventiveservicestaskforce.org/Page/Document/RecommendationStatementFinal/brca-related-cancer-risk-assessment-genetic-counseling-and-genetic-testing. Accessed 25 April 2016.

US Preventive Services Task Force. 2016. Breast cancer: screening. http://www.uspreventiveservicestaskforce.org/Page/Document/UpdateSummaryFinal/breast-cancer-screening1?ds=1&s=screening%20mammography. Accessed 25 April 2016.

Welch HG, Schwartz L, Woloshin S. 2011. *Overdiagnosed: making people sick in the pursuit of health.* Boston: Beacon Press.

Whitaker ED. 2005. "The bicycle makes the eyes smile": exercise, aging, and psychophysical well-being in older Italian cyclists. *Medical Anthropology* 24(1):1–43.

Whitaker ED. 2006. Breastfeeding, breast cancer, and the Sudden Infant Death Syndrome in anthropological perspective. In Whitaker ED, editor. *Health and healing in comparative perspective.* Upper Saddle River, NJ: Pearson Prentice Hall. p. 486–496.

World Health Organization Europe. 2012. Action Plan for Implementation of the European Strategy for the Prevention and Control of Noncommunicable Disease 2012–2016. http://www.euro.who.int/__data/assets/pdf_file/0019/170155/e96638.pdf.

Wright JD, Kennedy-Stephenson J, Wang CY, McDowell MA, Johnson CL. 2004. Trends in intake of energy and macronutrients – United States, 1971–2000. *Morbidity and Mortality Weekly Report* 53(4):80–82.

6

DIFFERENCE AS DESTINY

Race, sex, and culture

Biological determinism posits that the same genetic source for superficial differences between people gives rise to separate cognitive abilities. This chapter's discussion of biological variation and brain development shows that humans do not fall neatly into a small number of distinct races or two mutually exclusive sexes, each with its own type of brain. On the other hand, groups of people may use their minds in a distinctive manner consistent with their beliefs, priorities, and ways of life, and in the process literally shape the brain's form and function in its image.

The concept of race conflicts with the way gene frequencies vary continuously across geographical space and therefore fails to characterize the biological variation between populations. Human variation is scientifically meaningful but does not correspond with culturally defined race categories. It does not predict biologically based mental differences between people classified together on the basis of visually observable traits. Similarly, the assumption that mental traits derive from reproductive differences between two distinct sexes does not fit with evidence about sexual differentiation and variability, or the characteristics of human brains. However, hormonal influences – especially during the fetal life of males – contribute to some consistent although culturally variable differences in average behavior between females and males.

This chapter explores what makes humans alike and different. It explores biological variation, brain development, and sex determination. By clarifying the role of biology in human differences, it sets the stage for the analysis of gender and conflict in the second half of the book.

. . . . .

Racial ideologies are built on the assumption that humankind falls into a small number of genetically distinct groups which share physical features and are dissimilar under the surface as well.[1] In the 17th and 18th centuries, scientific racial categories were based on superficial characteristics recorded in drawings comparing white men to "lower" forms of the divine creation. The "savage races" were likened to cavemen or nonhuman primates: they were hairy, with low foreheads and protruding eyebrows and chins. In the 19th century, experts devised instruments for taking physical measurements with which to classify groups according to features that deviated from European men's. Other brain sizes or shapes were thought to prefigure earlier stages of human evolution and therefore indicate a lower degree of civilization, rationality, and intelligence. Scientists such as Cesare Lombroso argued that toes, ears, or skulls of certain dimensions indicated a low level of human progress and therefore a mentally and behaviorally deviant person. Less than a century ago, the scholarly consensus was that women had small, undifferentiated brains with undeveloped frontal lobes, placing them somewhere between a man and a boy, or a European man and a primitive (Gelli 1931).

The cephalic index, attributed to the Swedish anatomist Anders Retzius (1796–1860), was used well into the 20th century to classify people into three types depending on the shape of their heads. Using calibrated instruments, scientists measured the breadth and length of the head from specific, palpable points on the skull.[2] A cephalic or cranial index (breadth over length) over 0.8 denoted brachycephaly (round-headedness); one between 0.75–0.80 mesocephaly (medium head shape); and one below 0.75 dolichocephaly (long-headedness). Dolichocephalic or relatively narrow-headed people were thought to be smarter than brachycephalic rounder-headed people, thanks, it was thought, to the greater development of the frontal regions where cerebral power resided. Dolichocephaly was considered a marker of evolutionary advantage, since Stone Age skulls were predominantly brachycephalic whereas Indoeuropean ones – especially in Scandinavia and northern Europe – were predominantly dolichocephalic.

In the early 20th century, studies led by the German-American anthropologist Franz Boas (1912) called the strict genetic basis of cranium shape into question. Measurements of the heads of thousands of immigrants to the US and their American-born children revealed that, within a single generation, a European subpopulation could sway from dolichocephaly to brachycephaly, or vice versa. The most salient variable was the length of time the mother had been in the US. Clearly, head shape was not a reliable indicator of race if it could change in one generation.

All racial categorizations are arbitrary and dependent upon context. At the time of Boas's study, Bohemians and Sicilians, Slavs and Hungarians, Alpines and Nordics, were considered different peoples with inherently unequal mental and physical characteristics. Now, they all are considered a single Euroamerican "white" race.

Skin color is the paramount racial marker but also the most misleading, even where it can be accurately measured with optical instruments. For one, skin color changes in step with exposure to sunlight and other local conditions, making determinations at any point in time unreliable. For another, pigmentation is one of the very few traits that vary less within populations than between them.

The crucial effect of coloring on survival is evident in the textbook example of pale peppered moths standing out against soot-covered trees and lichen during England's Industrial Revolution. Likewise, in humans, selective pressures have a strong impact on skin, eye, and hair color, along with other superficial characteristics such as facial features.

In addition, while pigmentation affects multiple visible traits, most traits are not transmitted in clusters. In other words, human variation is nonconcordant. Shoe size does not vary together with blood type, or right or left handedness with the color of the eyes. High frequencies of genes for lactase persistence would make a "race" out of pale-skinned Scandinavians as well as dark-skinned nomadic pastoralists in West Africa. Northern Italians would also be in their group, but southern Italians would be in the group of malabsorbers including Native Americans and Chinese people. If people are grouped by genes for blood cell polymorphisms that confer an advantage where malaria is endemic (sickle-cell anemia, thalassemia, G-6-PD deficiency), then Africans in tropical zones but not black South Africans would be in the same race as Mediterranean Europeans and many people in India and Latin America. Black South Africans would be in the same race as Belgians and Scots.

Races or subspecies may arise in species with a short generation length and in cases of reproductive isolation due to behavioral or physical barriers. For instance, birds have divided into subspecies but dogs remain a single species. There have been only 3,000–4,000 generations of modern humans since the migration out of Africa, not enough for sufficient genetic divergence between groups to separate them into races. Moreover, rarely have populations remained geographically isolated or maintained reproductive isolation through strict endogamous marriage (spouses chosen from within a given society).

The fact that Africa is the place inhabited by modern humans longest does not signify uniformity across populations. There are hundreds of ethnolinguistic groups in Africa, all differing genetically to some degree. This fact deserves a pause, considering that current racial categories classify Africans and people of African descent as a single "race."

Virtually all human genetic diversity is present in Africa; the rest of the world's populations carry less. This term refers to the sum total of all variants of the genes in a species' genome. Any group of individuals that leaves the original gene pool carries only a portion of its diversity with them. This "founder effect" probably explains why nearly all Native Americans have type O blood, whereas more than one-half of white Americans have A and/or B antigens embedded in their red blood cell membranes. In addition, over time selective pressure, random mutation, and genetic drift (gradual shifts in the frequency of genes in a given gene pool) can increase the divergence between gene pools. Interbreeding has the opposite effect. The least genetically diverse populations today are those which live on islands or in remote places far from others, such as the indigenous peoples of Australia, New Guinea, and the Far North.

The existence of multiple gene variants or alleles gives rise to genetic variability across humans and groups of humans. Each person can only inherit two alleles, one from each parent, although there may be multiple possibilities – such as A, B, or neither (O) in the case of the ABO blood groups. Variance is a quantitative measure of the difference in allelic frequencies between groups. These frequencies tend to diverge gradually across geographical space along gradients, or clines. Any frequency boundary between groups is necessarily artificial, like the limits defining brachycephaly and dolichocephaly. In general, people are genetically most similar to those living nearest to them, although geography does not account for all genetic variation due to the effects of migration and other factors.

There is a similar amount of genetic variance within populations everywhere, although small populations tend to have slightly less than large ones. In other words, any town, city, or nation contains about the same amount of combined genetic difference between people as any other. That any group of people differs in allelic frequencies from other groups means that the human species could be divided into any number of races. However, the amount of difference between groups is far smaller than the diversity within groups. Analyzing frequency data on red-blood-cell surface antigens, enzymes, and serum proteins, Richard Lewontin (1972) discovered that 94% of the mathematical variance occurred between individuals within races, compared to 6% between races. Since then, researchers have analyzed hundreds of additional genes, with similar results of around 90% within and 10% between. These quantitative assessments further illustrate the poor fit between racial classifications and the realities of human variation.

The 19th-century enthusiasm for classifying traits quantitatively according to scientific race concepts was symptomatic of a broad shift in the way Western culture understood difference. Lennard Davis (2006) explains that before this time, cultural products such as visual art and epic poetry had exalted the ideal, which was associated with the divine and therefore by definition unattainable, leaving humankind unified in its defectiveness. Then, using demographic information collected by modern states to better manage populations, the new science of statistics – which arose hand-in-hand with eugenics and evolutionary biology – produced a quantitative vision of humankind. Not just a measure drawn from a range of values, the average came to be seen as the normal. At the same time, belief in progress required the division of the range into portions that could be ranked along a scale, so that superior values could be given their due and set the bar for improvement. The concept of the "norm" defined everything else as deviant, and the ideal became a personal goal and collective obligation.

Davis describes these changes in the context of cultural perceptions of differences in ability, such as sensory, cognitive, or motor skills. He explains that people with disabilities came to be included in the category of "defectives" along with criminals, the poor, homosexuals, alcoholics, the mentally ill, and members of despised races. As the causes of these conditions were considered hereditary, they all became targets of eugenic policies aimed at eliminating the variability that was once accepted as the human condition, inevitably imperfect.

The following chapters explore the legacy of these ideas in the belief that culturally significant bodily attributes – whether congenital or acquired – speak for all traits, as if membership in a group defined by disability, race, or sex determined everything about a person. The analysis shows how the establishment of a norm or standard automatically casts difference as aberrant, generating aversion, intolerance, and discrimination. While the categories may be accepted as natural, they are culturally and historically variable.[3]

. . . . .

Given that human variation does not suggest particular racial groupings, the categories necessarily are culturally determined. Every US decennial census beginning in 1850 has had a different set of choices. Now, in addition to racial groupings, the census asks for ethnic identity such as "Hispanic" (with four sub-groups). In theory, ethnicity conveys something about language, culture, and history, but in practice the term is used interchangeably with race. Medical literature refers to "Jewish" as an ethnicity rooted in genes that increase the risk of certain diseases. "Caucasian" recalls the elite biological essence of white Europeans and North Americans claimed by 18th-century German anatomist Johann Blumenbach, who designated the Caucasian "race" the original human race, descended from Noah after his ship crashed against Mount Ararat. To Blumenbach, this was the finest race and humanity's default setting; all else was a deviation or degradation (Wolf 2001).

Scientific race concepts permitted US slave owners to force workers to labor in hot, swampy areas under the excuse that Africans were better able to withstand heat stress and resist malaria.[4] Their presumed lower level of civilization allegedly made them stronger but also more sexual and emotional, and therefore more susceptible to hypertension and sexually transmitted infections. These ideas undergirded the infamous Tuskegee study run by the US Public Health Service from 1932–1972, in which some 400 men in Alabama were denied treatment for syphilis in order to illustrate the so-called "natural history" of the disease. The study continued even after penicillin became available, and even though the course of the disease was already well-known. The expectation that black men's response to infection was more basic and true was not supported by the data or any other studies.

These beliefs have left a legacy in current assumptions about the biological basis of differences in susceptibility to high blood pressure, which is greater among darker-skinned people than lighter-skinned people in many locations throughout the world. However, this relationship is due to racism, not race. Researchers in Puerto Rico have shown that, for people culturally classified as black (regardless of actual skin color measured by reflectance spectrophotometry), average blood pressure increases in step with increasing socioeconomic status, whereas it declines among those defined as white or intermediate. In other words, people defined as black are not penalized at low levels of socioeconomic status, whereas at higher levels of socioeconomic status they experience racism-induced psychosocial stress that manifests itself in higher blood pressure (Gravlee et al. 2005).

Given the long history of beliefs about the cardiovascular uniqueness of African Americans, it is not surprising that the first "ethnic drug" approved by the US Food and Drug Administration, BiDil, targets black patients (Sankar and Kahn 2005). Its rationale is an alleged 2:1 difference in death rates from congestive heart failure between black and white Americans. This ratio, reported decades ago, refers to middle-aged patients, who account for 6% of heart failure deaths, but there is virtually no difference in older age. For all age groups combined, the ratio is 1.08:1 and narrowing, reflecting declining inequalities in exposure to health risks and access to medical care. The medicine, which works in all patients regardless of ethnicity, advances the contrary assumption that health disparities derive from fixed biological differences. Through patent protection of the method of administration of two already existing drugs (isosorbide dinitrate and hydralazine), the product costs seven times more than the generic equivalents – now unattainable in the correct proportions – and thereby penalizes an already economically disadvantaged group.

Assumptions about biological differences between racial groups lead health professionals to make instantaneous racial determinations based on patients' appearance. For instance, in the US, patients presenting the same symptoms are more likely to be diagnosed with schizophrenia as opposed to a mood disorder if they are black than white, resulting in differences in treatment (Barnes 2013). Physicians take it for granted that race is clinically relevant and that they should talk to patients about health risks in terms of race, even though they are unsure about the physical characteristics of racial groups, what clinical course of action is warranted by race, or whether race refers to biological ancestry, cultural beliefs, socioeconomic status, or some combination. Physicians adhere to a racial paradigm in the abstract, but are unable to explain how racial-genetic profiles might affect disease processes or responses to medicine, or to verify differences in the way the body works in patients they have treated first hand (Hunt et al. 2013).

While epigenetic marks of the kind discussed in Chapter 4 help to explain the echoing biological effects of social inequality from one generation to the next, any possible genetic difference in how the body works between "races" has not been demonstrated and is unlikely to exist for the reasons outlined above. Nonetheless, the commercial value and political expediency of the race concept contribute to its persistence even in biology and medicine.[5] By organizing studies of genetic susceptibility or resistance to disease in a racial framework, researchers channel data along the lines of chosen racial categories and thereby reaffirm their existence. "Personalized" medicine involves sums of money that are orders of magnitude greater than traditional treatments or preventive measures, fueling the search for gene-frequency differences between groups. However, as noted in the previous chapter, susceptibility genes for common diseases are unlike simple genetic mutations that travel along family lines. Their frequency may be higher in certain populations or risk groups, but belonging to a group does not guarantee the presence of the genes, while having the genes does not necessarily entail disease – both because of incomplete penetrance and because statistical associations may not arise from causal connections.

In anthropological genetics, genetic markers and patterns of epigenetic modifications are used to map migrations and trace historical relationships between populations. Particular mutations in maternally transmitted mitochondrial DNA (mtDNA) and parts of the Y chromosome can be highly indicative because the DNA is replicated without recombination with other DNA, such that mutations pass directly from one generation to the next. However, the existence of a particular variant at high frequencies in two populations does not necessarily indicate a relationship, for it could be the result of similar selective pressures or random genetic processes occurring in unrelated populations. For these and other reasons, the current distribution of gene variants is not a foolproof blueprint of historical relationships.

Commercial genetic ancestry testing downplays or disregards these issues. By comparing a small number of genetic markers to frequency data from reference populations, which themselves are defined through human choices and for which the number of genetic samples is a tiny fraction of the total, the business helps to sustain cultural beliefs about the material reality of race. It holds out the illusory promise of true self-knowledge through genetic ties to a particular territory, population, or historical figure.

Racial categories are by definition static and therefore incompatible with evolutionary theory, which concerns changes in gene frequencies over time and space. Any boundary between groups is necessarily arbitrary given the mixing and migration of people and the non-concordance of genetic traits. All groups are genetically heterogeneous: the individuals in a group vary more amongst themselves than they do as groups compared to other groups. In short, while race may be a socially and commercially valuable concept, it is not useful for thinking about biological difference.

. . . . .

Racial differences in cognition may seem plausible because relatives tend to have similar although not identical intellectual aptitudes, and because of the existence of a few genetic mutations that disrupt complex mental functions and cluster in families. However, mutations that interfere with brain activity are not the same as a "gene for" the behavior or ability in question. For instance, a mutation in the FOXP2 gene causes grave speech impairment in a set of relatives in the UK, but normal speech depends on many other genes, of which several have been identified (Fisher 2006). The orchestration of complex behavior and cognition involves multiple genes whose activity depends on a variety of inputs that can change over time. Moreover, familial traits are not a model for variation between groups – which, as we have seen, differ across thousands of genes inherited separately.

The idea of a few genetically discrete human groups with discontinuous mental abilities is not only implausible on the basis of human variation as described above, but also unreasonable considering that neurons and their chemical and electrical activity hardly differ between species. Cross-cultural and psychological studies conducted over the past century by researchers including Franz Boas (1940), mentioned above, have provided empirical proof that population differences in cognition and perception are the result of cultural influences, not inherited differences in brain anatomy. Cultural contexts shape the kinds of tasks the brain typically faces and the solutions which are considered appropriate, as shown in abundant detail in the following chapters.

Thanks to evolutionary processes described in earlier chapters, including social living and complex communication, about three-quarters of the brain's growth takes place after birth. Moreover, brain remodeling continues throughout life depending on use and training. Babies' brains increase in weight from about 300–400 grams at birth to 900–1,000 grams at 1 year. Over the following year the brain increases by 100–300 grams. By adulthood, it weighs an average of 1,300–1,400 grams. The fact that all this growth occurs after birth indicates the degree to which brain development depends on life experiences and cultural context.

Thanks to the effects of use on brain anatomy and patterns of activity, it is not possible to identify the natural state of any individual brain. The brain pares down areas and functionalities that are superfluous or disused and can shift how and where it processes tasks such as speech or vision in the case of injury, disease, or new needs. In birds, the size of brain regions having to do with singing and spatial relationships depends on behavior, not just the other way around. If marsh tits are prevented from using spatial skills needed for storing and retrieving food, their hippocampus grows at a slower rate than otherwise. At any age, the hippocampus can grow to normal size if the bird is given the opportunity to store and retrieve. Human brains likewise respond plastically to use and disuse, changing their shape and the efficiency with which they accomplish tasks. Taxi drivers develop larger right posterior hippocampi than non-taxi drivers, with a dose-response effect – more years of driving correlates with greater bulk (Maguire et al. 2000).

Daily Zen meditation, which involves intense concentration and conscious management of bodily sensations such as pain, results in thicker areas of the cerebral cortex including the insula which deals with motor control, self-awareness, and various cognitive tasks. It builds up the nearby anterior cingulate cortex which is involved in cognitive and emotional functions, including subjective experience of pain. Here too, more years of training are associated with more brain tissue thickening and more pain tolerance (Grant et al. 2010).

Learning to read, even in adulthood, induces changes to areas involved in speech and vision including the corpus callosum, planum temporale, and parts of the occipital and temporal lobes. Because reading is a new activity for humans, the brain must adapt, diverting functional capacity to novel needs. Activity in a part of the brain that deals with facial recognition (left fusiform gyrus) declines in order to compensate for increased activation of neurons involved in the processing of words, spoken language, and horizontal visual information (Dehaene et al. 2010).

Through training it is even possible to manipulate autonomic functions which are not normally under conscious control. Wearing special glasses that invert visual images results in the ability to read books upside down without the glasses on. Indigenous children in coastal Southeast Asian populations who dive 30–75 feet for pearls and other products of the sea can stay underwater longer thanks to lowered heart rates. Their vision is better as a result of corneal accommodation to water rather than air as the medium through which light hits the eye, and the constriction rather than dilation of their pupils in response to darkness. These children are not biologically different from children elsewhere. Through training, Swedish children have achieved the same proficiency at seeing underwater as Moken sea-gypsy children (Gislén et al. 2006).

Groups of people may use their brains differently, but the reason is not that their brains are differently made. Brain size may vary between populations as a function of differences in height, but brain size does not correlate with cognitive ability (see below). Social and cultural conditions shape the context in which the brain is used and channel its development in particular ways. For instance, broad differences in visual perception have long been noted between people in the West, who tend to examine a visual field in terms of individual objects, and people in the East, who tend to focus on the whole picture and consequently to see objects in relation to one another. Recent research has shown that within China, people in the heavily rice-growing southern regions are more inclined to perceive wholes – in line with the communitarian values associated with rice cultivation – whereas people in the wheat-growing northern regions tend to see scenes in terms of their parts – in line with the more individualistic, analytical orientation encouraged by wheat cultivation (Talhelm et al. 2014).

Stephen Jay Gould (1981) has shown that performance on intelligence tests is a function of the degree of congruence between the social backgrounds and unconscious cultural assumptions of the test makers and test takers. To illustrate, Gould describes intelligence-quotient (IQ) testing of 1.75 million US military recruits before and during the First World War. At the time, statistical analysis revealed an association between IQ and the length of the men's and their forebears' residence in the US. The statistical relationship was attributed to cross-national differences in intelligence, given that the lower-scoring immigrants came from societies considered inferior to the US. Since then, it has become clear that the test measured the similarity between the recruits' cultural background and that of its designer, Robert Yerkes, a white psychologist/primatologist from the Northeast. Ashley Montagu's re-analysis of the data showed that northern whites scored highest, followed by northern blacks, who scored higher than southern whites. The group most distant geographically and culturally from Yerkes, southern blacks, scored lowest.

Intelligence testing not only is culturally constructed but also misleadingly implies that cognitive ability is a fixed, inborn endowment.[6] To the contrary, performance on tests depends on training and is highly sensitive to testing conditions. Scores are much higher if people given an unfamiliar test also receive even a minimum of instruction about what they are expected to do. Classroom learning increases dramatically if students are taught using locally meaningful concepts, as does academic performance if students are taught that intelligence is expandable and depends on learning. The improvement occurs even in poor-performing students typically written off as unintelligent.

In recent decades, the IQ has been replaced by the *g* score, for "general ability." The *g* score is sufficiently predictive of performance across academic domains that it appears to measure intelligence. However, the score does not account for other forms of intelligence or the fact that some students devote their intellectual effort to preparation for jobs that do not depend on academic knowledge. Alternative forms of intelligence include problem-solving skills related to real-world situations or difficult environments such as challenging terrain or harsh urban settings. Intelligence encompasses self-assertion and self-effacement, self-knowledge and humility, and interpersonal ability – including consideration, respect, and benevolence towards others. These various kinds of intelligence are valued to different degrees across populations and subpopulations, leading to differences in the skills taught to children. As seen in Chapter 9, changes in training account for a rapid rise in standardized test scores among US girls and minority students that casts further doubt on biological theories of difference.

. . . . .

Like alleged racial differences in cognitive ability and behavior, gender differences in mental traits are attributed to genes but instead reflect the impact of social and cultural forces on brain development and activity. Not only are male and female brains assumed to vary in line with alleged gender roles in the ancestral environment, but the evolutionary story about male achievements in hunting, exploration, leadership, and technological innovation implies that men's brains are much larger than women's, as if size correlated with computing power. However, it is not clear if a sex difference in brain size really exists, but well established that size does not correlate with function.[7]

In both men and women, the size of the cranium increases roughly although not perfectly in proportion to height. If head size were an index of intelligence, then the argument that men are more intelligent than women would require concluding that tall women are smarter than short men. In any case, individuals with larger brains are not more intelligent than individuals with smaller brains. In fact, larger size may indicate pathology, as in the bulkier brains of autistic than non-autistic children, which are the result mostly of excessive myelination that brings faster signal conduction. Albert Einstein's relatively small brain weighed 1,230 grams, below 1,300–1,400 gram average. Its distinctive shape, visible in photographs of the preserved brain taken in 1955, attests to the effects of a specific pattern of use and disuse.

There seems to be a slight difference in average size between men's and women's brains even for people of the same height, due to longer and bulkier neurons in males as a result of the growth-stimulating effects of testosterone. However, the difference is small enough to remain in doubt. Estimates based on skull size may be inaccurate due to variability in the closeness of fit between the brain and the cranium. If the numbers come from corpses, the age distribution of samples matters because aging brings a decline in brain weight and volume. Infectious diseases and mental disorders such as schizophrenia can decrease the size of the brain. Finally, systematic differences in the treatment of girls and boys in unequal societies could result in different average brain sizes through the effects of malnutrition, disease, and psychosocial stress.

Since overall brain size does not predict intelligence, researchers look for other sex differences by focusing on specific brain structures or activity patterns. This approach reflects the assumptions that form dictates function, and that blood flow and neuronal size, density, and connectivity are intrinsically related to sex. The brain is the presumed source – not the product – of stereotypical gender differences in behavior and cognition. For instance, men's alleged emotional illiteracy is attributed to a smaller limbic cortex; women's purportedly superior verbal skills are chalked up to a larger dorsolateral prefrontal cortex.

As noted above, the way the brain is used or disused, especially during development, leads to anatomical and functional variability across individuals. Training in specific tasks increases the branching of neurons, the number of dendritic connections among them, vascularization, and the production of neurotransmitters. These changes influence the size, shape, and electrical activity of specific brain areas. Consequently, there is a limit to the relevance of data about 20 or 30 brains from one society to the question of species-wide sex differences. Differences between small samples could be the result of chance sampling effects or cultural influences.

By focusing on slight divergences and not exploring similarities, research reports create the impression that male and female brains are more different than alike. To illustrate, a study involving three verbal tests found no sex difference in activated brain regions during the tests that involved letter recognition and semantic categories (Shaywitz et al. 1995). In contrast, in the rhyme test, both hemispheres of 11 of the 19 women were activated, whereas only the left hemisphere was activated in the other 8 women and in all 19 of the men. Even though roughly half of the women's brains behaved the same as the men's in the rhyme test, the researchers conclude that males have an advantage in visuo-spatial tasks that comes from greater brain lateralization due to their thinner corpus callosum. They surmise that this reduced connectivity between hemispheres allows the right hemisphere to devote itself to visuo-spatial tasks instead of being distracted by also handling verbal tasks. Yet, only some of the women's brains used both hemispheres during the test. In addition, there was no relationship between hemisphere involvement and scores on the test. The study speaks more to gender similarities than differences: two of the three tests revealed no difference in brain functioning, and the third yielded a difference in electrical activity that did not correspond to a difference in performance.

Claims about male and female brains are based on single features for which a sex difference in average values has been found. However, even for features with the most difference in average values between females and males, any single value does not predict the individual's sex given that there is a distribution of values for both sexes – as with height and other traits. Whole brains are made up mainly of features that do not differ by sex, plus a mixture of features that are more female-typical and more male-typical. In other words, it is not possible to identify the sex of a person from the morphology or connectivity of their brain. It is rare for any single brain to include only male-typical or only female-typical features.

These points have been demonstrated by Daphna Joel et al. (2015) through analysis of more than 1,400 brains based on MRI scans measuring the volume of specific brain regions (gray matter, or densely packed nerve cell bodies), and the volume of nerve cell fibers that transmit signals throughout the brain (white matter), as well as data from diffusion tensor imaging (DTI) showing the distribution of nerve cell fibers that indicates connectivity between regions. The researchers focused on the 10 traits with the least amount of overlap in the distribution of male and female values – in other words, traits with the largest sex difference. For each trait, they arranged the data points along a scale from male-typical to intermediate to female-typical. Each category represented one-third of the range.

Using these classifications, the researchers assessed the degree to which the brains were internally consistent for the 10 features. They found that most brains were mosaics of features more common in females, features more common in males, and features more common in both females and males. There were many more brains with substantial variability than internal consistency. Across the multiple samples of brains analyzed in the study, one-fifth to more than one-half of brains showed substantial variability in male-end and female-end features, whereas the proportions of brains in which all 10 features fell into one category (female, intermediate, or male) ranged from 0%–5.9%. The tendency to show non-consistent features did not differ between males and females.

The study shows that whole brains do not exist in a female and male form. Brain development is a dynamic, idiosyncratic process. Sexualization of those brain features which vary between females and males occurs independently across different structures.

These anatomical findings match behavioral variability in women and men. That is, individuals show low consistency across gendered characteristics. The authors reaffirm this finding through an analysis of two large data sets. For the seven traits with the greatest gender difference, there was substantial variability in 59% and 70% of individuals. All of the internal consistency occurred in the intermediate range of values, and accounted for 1.8% and 0.1% of individuals, respectively. Finally, the authors analyzed data from a study of highly gender-stereotyped behaviors among US college students, such as playing video games, with high *d* scores falling between 1.00 and 2.02 (see Chapter 9). Even here, analysis of 10 highly gendered activities yielded substantial variability in 55% of individuals and internal consistency in only 1.2%. These findings leave no doubt that anatomical and cognitive traits do not come in separate female and male versions.

. . . . .

The idea that the brain and bodily appearance derive from a single source implies that differences in people's coloring or eye shape indicate something deeper about their minds. However, as noted above, genes are transmitted separately from each other. Genes which are involved in complex mental functions are not the property of a certain race or sex. Moreover, even highly heritable physical characteristics such as head shape arise through dynamic genetic-environmental interactions.

Compared to the plain impossibility that different minds distinguish culturally defined racial groupings, sex differences may appear more plausible as a result of reproductive hormones, if not genetically determined brain structures. As seen in the following three chapters, evolution is credited with giving women and men incompatible sexual and reproductive interests and behavior, disparate productive and social roles, and separate capabilities and intelligence. In order to address these ideas, we will first examine how sex is determined and evaluate the effects of genes on the diminutive Y chromosome which cause males to be exposed to testosterone prenatally. Testosterone makes males larger on average than females, and affects brain development in several ways. As a consequence, males are more likely to behave aggressively than females and to be motivated to seek bodily pleasures.

As seen in Chapter 3, the "stronger" sex is actually weaker biologically and consequently experiences higher mortality rates at all age levels, unless males enjoy disproportionate social advantages.[8] Reasons for male biological disadvantage include polymorphisms and deleterious mutations in mtDNA that have an effect on genetic expression in males. These defects can accumulate given that selective pressure cannot operate through males, although selection on parts of the Y chromosome that influence mitochondria may mitigate the damage. Deleterious genes on the Y which affect only males include ones that influence immune functioning and increase the risk of cardiovascular disease. In addition, females are protected by having two X chromosomes, such that a deleterious allele on one X can be masked by a normal one on the other X. This mechanism explains sex differences in susceptibility to hemophilia, respiratory distress syndromes in children and adults, and some forms of mental retardation, autism, and attention-deficit disorders.

Hormones also contribute to the female mortality advantage. Greater amounts of progesterone in females protect tissues and organs such as the brain from damage and injury, whereas higher testosterone levels in males suppress the immune system. Even the exposure to testosterone experienced by women who give birth to sons has a negative effect on longevity in women, whereas daughters increase the average number of months lived. On the other hand, the role of estrogen remains unclear. The onset of heart disease is about a decade later in women than men, and studies on laboratory animals suggest that estrogen is protective against cardiovascular disease along with neurological diseases such as dementia and Alzheimer's. However, the Women's Health Initiative established not only that hormone replacement therapy raises the risk of uterine and breast cancer, as was expected, but also increases the risk of heart disease and does not prevent osteoporosis.

Evidently, there are significant physical differences between women and men.[9] The problem is not the differences, but the way reproductive development and anatomy is loaded with symbolic meaning derived from cultural beliefs about masculinity and femininity. This cultural content becomes clear through a comparison with other species, for whom maleness and femaleness may not be distinct or permanent attributes. Asexually reproducing microorganisms, algae, and plants do not have sexes at all. Other species alternate between sexual and asexual reproduction, including insects such as aphids and some bees and wasps, and amphibians and reptiles including whiptail and other lizards. There are species with both male and female reproductive organs, including many flowering plants, most snail and slug species, and some fish such as sea bass and wrasses. They produce both female and male gametes, and in some cases such as mangrove killfish they self-fertilize. Species including freshwater snails and nematode worms alternate between sexual and asexual modes depending on the burden of infectious disease. Asexual reproduction is safer and more efficient, but if a more flexible response to environmental conditions is needed it is worth the effort to reproduce sexually.

Even in sexually reproducing species, females sometimes produce viable young without any male contribution. Parthenogenesis routinely occurs in insects and has been observed in some bird, snake, and shark species such as turkeys, cottonmouth snakes, and bamboo sharks. In addition, sex may depend on environmental circumstances and can change over an individual's lifetime. American alligators lay their eggs in nests of plant matter which heats up as it decays: hotter temperatures yield males, cooler ones females, and intermediate ones a mixture. Conditions in the sea anemone or coral environment in which clownfish and wrasses respectively live cause the fish to change sex over their lifetimes.

Sexual and reproductive behavior likewise vary with circumstances. Albatross couples have long been cherished as the picture of marital fidelity, due to collaborative parenting and mating rituals involving elaborate dancing with chest-to-chest and head-to-head contact. However, on some islands in Hawai'i, up to one-third of the pairs consist of two females. The behavior allows females in small colonies with relatively few males and a high degree of immigration to reproduce by mating with an already-mated male. Both females hatch chicks over the years, indicating long-term cooperation. They are not as successful as male-female pairs at hatching an egg, but equally effective at caring for chicks until they fledge (Young et al. 2008). The case illustrates the sensitivity of behavioral systems to ecological and demographic conditions.

The point in all this is that reproductive systems, sex determination, and mating and parenting behavior are variable and flexible. We should be cautious about studying human sex differences under the assumption that they arise directly and uniformly from a simple X/Y base. In reality, humans do not segregate into only two discontinuous sexual categories. A substantial number of people carry a different genetic combination than XX or XY or have an appearance that does not match their genes. Klinefelter syndrome (XXY) affects one in 500–1,000 male births; Turner syndrome (XO) affects one in 2,000–8,000 female births. One in every 1,000 males is born with XYY; one in every 1,000 females is born with XXX (triple X syndrome). Other conditions cause masculinization or feminization opposite to chromosomal sex. People born XX may develop male characteristics, as in congenital adrenal hyperplasia, or people born XY may develop female characteristics, as in 5-alpha-reductase deficiency syndrome or androgen insensitivity syndromes such as Swyer syndrome. These syndromes respectively affect as many as one in every 100 female and 100 male births.

In addition, one in every 4,000 newborns has mosaics of sexual characteristics arising from hormonal anomalies, exposure to exogenous hormones and chemicals that mimic testosterone, and chromosomal errors such as fertilization by two sperm cells or the loss of a sex chromosome by a group of cells early in development. All combined, intersex conditions are present in 1–2 of every 100 births, with variation in rates across societies.

Evidently, maleness and femaleness are not unrelated opposites, in humans or other species. Yet, cultural beliefs insist on a strict binary, imbuing the events of fertilization, sex determination, and development with gender connotations. For instance, the reproductive mismatch described in the next chapter, which is presumed to have placed women and men at odds from the beginning of time, is assumed to begin with their unequal investment in a fixed quantity of large, deteriorating eggs and an unlimited supply of fresh, streamlined sperm cells. This construction harmonizes with cultural images of women as passive and unreliable, and men as purposeful and efficient. However, millions of sperm cells go to waste for every one that fuses with an egg cell, and their quality also declines as men age.

Schoolbooks and scientific literature present fertilization as a romantic drama involving determined, heroic sperm which pursue and eventually vanquish a listless, vulnerable egg. Sperm bearing Y chromosomes are even expected (erroneously) to swim faster than those carrying X chromosomes. Instead of direct, goal-oriented swimming, sperm move randomly and inefficiently, with side-to-side wagging. They do not "penetrate" the egg on their own. Meanwhile, the egg and the woman's reproductive system are expected to be inert, but instead are actively involved in conception.

For centuries, Western scientific beliefs construed the female as derivative of the male, as in the Bible story about Adam's rib. This view takes the male form as the standard, even though the default setting for embryonic development in humans is female. "Default setting" refers to the sex which has two analogous sex chromosomes. The other sex carries two different sex chromosomes and therefore its germ cells determine the sex of the embryo. In birds it is the reverse: males are ZZ, females ZW. Without the W chromosome, a male bird develops.

The concept of a default setting is misleading because, in reality, both X chromosomes are necessary for normal development in females, and both the X and Y chromosome contribute to reproductive and sexual development in males. Female embryos with only one X chromosome tend not to survive, while the 10% which are viable at birth are infertile. In males, genes on the X-chromosome are necessary for the production of sperm cells from spermatogonia in the testes. If the male-specific region on the Y chromosome is missing, an XY embryo develops along the female path; yet, in mice it is possible to create sperm-producing male mice with no Y chromosome by manipulating the expression of genes on the X chromosome – although full reproductive competence requires the Y (Yamauchi et al. 2016). The influence of X chromosome genes on males is evident also in Klinefelter syndrome (XXY), which causes reduced testosterone levels, hypogonadism, and infertility. Men with an extra X chromosome engage in sexual activity more frequently than men with one X. Likewise, male mice with an extra X chromosome are far more sexually active than XY mice; they are quicker to ejaculate and they mount females and ejaculate more often (Bonthius et al. 2012).

Although human embryos look the same for the first 2 months, sexual differentiation begins in the earliest days of development with the precursor cells to eggs and sperm which are bundled in the yolk sac. These cells migrate to the unisex genital ridge, which has two sets of generic ducts leading away from it – one of which will develop later while the other atrophies. If it is not exposed to testosterone beginning the seventh week, the ridge develops into ovaries and the Müllerian ducts become a uterus, vagina, and fallopian tubes. In males, it differentiates into a testis. Cells in the genital ridge secrete hormones that stimulate the development of the scrotum, penis and Wolffian ducts (which give rise to the epididymis, vas deferens, and seminal vesicles), along with estradiol, which crosses the blood-brain barrier into the male brain. In addition to hormonal differentiation, some genes may be expressed differently in male and female brains beginning early in gestation, although studies on mice have identified only a tiny number and their function remains unknown.[10]

Estradiol is one of the principal forms of estrogen and is produced from testosterone through the action of the enzyme, aromatase. Evidently, while classified as "male" and "female," androgens and estrogens are made by male and female bodies alike. They are found in birds, mammals, reptiles, and, in slightly different forms, fish and insects. They are made from precursor molecules such as cholesterol and share the same 4-carbon ring structure common to all steroids. These hormones are synthesized in the adrenal cortex, testes and ovaries, fat cells, breasts, skin, arterial walls, liver, brain, and placenta. The type secreted by particular organs depends on the availability of conversion enzymes. For instance, the ovaries contain high amounts of aromatase and consequently convert testosterone very efficiently into estrogen.

Estrogen, not just testosterone, is needed for penis development during fetal life; lack of estrogen or its receptors results in multiple sexual defects and an inability to produce egg or sperm cells. Testosterone is converted to estrogen before being taken up by neurons. Estrogen helps bring growth of the long bones to a close after puberty; deficiency of the hormone results in elongated limbs in girls and boys. Other examples of shared reproductive anatomy and physiology abound. Female-associated hormones such as oxytocin and prolactin facilitate bonding in both males and females. Also the glands which secrete hormones do not differ by sex. If a castrated male laboratory animal is injected with estrogen, his hypothalamus and pituitary switch to a cyclical rather than continuous pattern of hormone secretion. Human males can produce milk in response to nipple stimulation, starvation, and medical treatment. In sum, female and male are built from the same materials.

. . . . .

With the homology between male and female bodies in mind, we may examine the role of testosterone in the significant and cross-culturally consistent gender difference in violent behavior.[11] Almost all homicides worldwide are committed by men (over 90%), as well as almost all violent crimes in general. Males die at much higher rates than females from accidental and violent causes. They are more likely to commit suicide in most societies, and to choose violent methods such as firearms. However, the magnitude of violence varies considerably across societies, as seen in Chapters 10–12, indicating that the trait is like others in its sensitivity to environmental circumstances.

All people experience a rise in testosterone levels in response to physical activity, school examinations, hostile interpersonal interactions, jockeying for position at work or in social situations, or even just watching or anticipating these events. The scale of the change is the same between women and men, but men's baseline levels are 7–10 times higher than women's. This responsiveness to experience suggests that the hormone does not trigger aggressive behavior. The lack of a relationship between testosterone secretion and aggressive and violent behavior in childhood also argues against a causal relationship. Hormone levels in both sexes remain very low from a few months after birth until puberty, yet boys engage in more aggressive and violent behavior than girls, on average.

On the other hand, male aggressiveness peaks in early adulthood when testosterone levels are high. Intimate partnership and fatherhood bring hormonal changes in men, including reduced testosterone (see Chapter 7), along with a decline in aggressive and violent behavior after about age 30. This pattern can be seen in the age-related rate of homicide committed by men, which rises rapidly in the later teenage years, peaks in the 20s, and declines gradually thereafter. The rate of homicide committed by women remains close to zero throughout the life course. The shape of the curve for males is remarkably uniform across societies, but its magnitude varies dramatically. For example, murder rates are 30 times greater in Chicago than England and Wales (Cronin 1991).

In short, the sex difference in violence is highly consistent across cultures but also highly variable in scale. It stems from the same source as the difference in size: exposure to testosterone beginning in the womb. In male animals generally, testosterone is associated with increased body mass, muscle development, and prominent ornamental features. Human males are born larger than females, and their hormone levels reach a higher peak in the first months after birth, before falling to low childhood levels.

The role of testosterone is clear from studies of female animals exposed to androgens during gestation. They behave more aggressively than other females, although less aggressively than males. Likewise, girls accidentally exposed to androgen-mimicking drugs in utero or born with congenital adrenal hyperplasia tend to engage in more physical play than average, even if they have been treated surgically and hormonally.

Size and aggressiveness are connected to androgens but not necessarily to sex. For instance, female spotted hyenas are more aggressive, larger, and stronger than males. They also have an elongated clitoris about the same size as the males' penis. Pregnant high-ranking females have higher levels of androgens than low-ranking females and give birth to more aggressive cubs. In addition, their vasopressin secretion is similar to the male pattern for other species. While vasopressin facilitates bonding with sexual partners it also promotes aggressive behavior towards individuals of the same sex – females in the case of spotted hyenas. In short, these hormones affect behavior and size irrespective of sex.

Evidence from animal studies indicates that testosterone's main effect on the developing male brain is to increase the size, axonal length, and dendritic density of neurons in the hypothalamus. The hypothalamus is part of the limbic system which deals with emotion, motivation, memory, and sociality and attachment. The limbic system includes the amygdala and septal area, extends to parts of the frontal lobe that deal in emotion, and relays messages to the midbrain that result in muscular movement. Stimulation of or damage to these and other areas including parts of the temporal lobes has specific effects on aggressiveness, rage, and calculated attack. Testosterone seems to increase the reactivity of neurons communicating between the amygdala and the hypothalamus. As a result, both higher baseline levels as well as emotion-induced upsurges may contribute to the rapid transmission of electrical signals involved in aggressive outbursts.

In addition, aggressiveness and impulse control are modulated by neurotransmitters such as serotonin, dopamine, glutamate, and norepinephrine; the enzymes that break them down and prevent their buildup in the brain; and, the density and functionality of receptors for chemical messengers. Relevant genes are located on a variety of chromosomes, including the X chromosome. Deleterious alleles on the X consequently affect males more frequently than females. For instance, the enzyme monoamine oxidase A is needed to degrade neurotransmitters. Women have two copies of the X-chromosome gene and therefore tend to produce sufficient amounts of the enzyme, but men born with defective copies produce less. However, this genetic predisposition to aggressiveness only manifests itself under certain life circumstances, such as alcoholism or childhood experience of abuse and other kinds of severe stress. Men with low levels of the enzyme tend toward social isolation, which in itself contributes to increased aggressiveness. Contrariwise, men with high enzyme levels are less likely to develop antisocial, violent behavior in response to adverse conditions or negative experiences (Hicks et al. 2009).

Aggression involves the same motivation and reward system in the brain that promotes other crucial behaviors such as eating and sex. This system appears to be more active in males than females due in part to higher levels of dopamine. Dopamine is involved in the brain's pleasure system that deals with expectation and desire. Its activity in the brain rises in response to sexual excitement, exercise, drug use, the anticipation of a good meal, and other "appetitive" pursuits. Dopamine increases pleasure and dampens feelings of aversion and displeasure. It also raises tension, which increases the individual's motivation to achieve the desired result and thereby experience calming endorphin-mediated feelings of bliss and fulfillment. In addition, dopamine reinforces the brain's neuronal pathways involved in the activities that lead to accomplishment, and facilitates learning generally. The system allows humans and other animals to become more proficient at important activities such as sex and the pursuit of food, but it malfunctions in the face of addictive substances and nondrug addictions.[12]

Using positron emission tomography, researchers documented higher dopamine levels in the brains of male than female college students (Urban et al. 2010). The dopamine was located in a part of the brain (ventral striatum) that is involved in pleasure and also in addiction formation. The study also found that the men were more highly stimulated by pleasurable feelings than the women, suggesting that extra dopamine renders men more susceptible to alcoholism and other forms of dependency. Alcoholism is nearly twice as common among men as women in the US.

Men's stronger motivation towards pleasure manifests itself in a higher frequency of thoughts about sex as well as other kinds of bodily desire. A recent study found that male college students thought about sex around 18 times a day, compared to 10 times among female students (Fisher et al. 2012). Significantly, males also thought about food and sleep more often than females. The degree of difference was the same for all three variables. That is, there was not a stronger tendency for men to think about sex than to think about food or sleep, relative to women. These results indicate that men are more strongly attracted to bodily pleasures of all kinds, but also that their sexual thoughts – while more frequent than women's – are not nearly as incessant as implied by urban myths such as the once-every-52-seconds statistic.

While hormonal influences make men more invested in bodily pleasure than women, cultural influences also play a role. For men, thinking about sex is not associated with guilt feelings, whereas for women it is fraught with moral overtones – as is thinking about food. That men think more about sex is unremarkable considering the degree to which erotic images directed at men fill the visual landscape and in light of the accessibility and acceptability of pornography. Paradoxically, chronic activation of the motivation-and-reward system without the effort required for courtship – or exercise, in the case of drugs and alcohol – ends up suppressing the secretion of dopamine and alters the level of other neuroactive chemicals, which can impair the dopamine system irrevocably and result in greater susceptibility to further addictions. This means that cultural forces may bring changes to neurons and neurotransmitters that lend themselves to interpretation as inborn sex differences, even though they arise through plasticity.

Motivation towards pleasure, like aggression and violence, is not a discontinuous, all-or-none trait limited to one sex. There is a range of variation across individuals of both sexes, and the degree to which these traits are expressed depends to a great degree on the cultural context. As seen in the following chapters, the same principle applies to skills and abilities popularly considered masculine and feminine, such as map-reading or social competence.

. . . . .

Key ideas tend to fit with what a society wants to believe about the world, and, in turn, to shape perceptions of nature. The flat Earth and heliocentric universe were credible ideas in their time. Today, it is taken for granted that every aspect of the body and mind bears the imprint of one of two chromosomal sexes and one of a handful of genetically singular races. Categories based on reproductive anatomy and physical appearance misleadingly imply the existence of discontinuities and absolute regularities in nature, along with fixed differences in the mental attributes of groups of human beings. This chapter has exposed the unscientific foundation for alleged group-level biological differences which is used to justify bigotry and sustain systems that produce inequalities – and which shapes, in the process, the conditions to which humans respond biologically through plasticity and epigenetic marks. The following chapters examine the implications with respect to gender roles and traits, and the related question of the supposed natural murderousness of humankind.

Notes

1 On human variation, see Brown and Armelagos (2001); Templeton (1998); Tishkoff et al. (2009).
2 Breadth is taken from a spot lying behind the cheekbones, above the supramastoid crest of the temporal bones; length from the depression above the nose between the eyebrows, and the centermost extruding point of the occipital bone at the back of the head.
3 For cross-cultural perspectives on disability, see Ingstad and Whyte (2007).
4 On the history of medical beliefs about African-American health characteristics, see Gamble (1997); Williams (2009).
5 On the commercial value of race in contemporary society, see Roberts (2012).
6 On culture and intelligence testing, see Greenfield (1997); Sternberg (2007).
7 On brain size and function, see Gould (1981); Holloway (1980).
8 Regarding sex differences in disease and mortality rates, see Charchar et al. (2012); Helle et al. (2002); Stein and Wright (2010).
9 On sexual differentiation and reproductive development, see Fausto-Sterling (2000); Mueller et al. (2013).
10 Dewing et al. (2003) have found differential expression in 7 mouse genes and identified 51 candidate genes, out of 12,000 analyzed.
11 Regarding sex differences in violence see Cronin (1991); Konner (2006); Rhee and Waldman (2002).
12 On addiction, see Nestler (2005).

References cited

Barnes A. 2013. Race and schizophrenia diagnoses in four types of hospitals. *Journal of Black Studies* 44(6):665–681.

Boas F. 1912. Changes in bodily form of descendants of immigrants. *American Anthropologist* 14(3):530–562.

Boas F. 1940. *Race, language, and culture.* London: Collier-Macmillan.

Bonthius PJ, Cox KH, Rissman EF. 2012. X-chromosome dosage affects male sexual behaviour. *Hormones and Behavior* 61(4):565–572.

Brown RA, Armelagos GJ. 2001. Apportionment of racial diversity: a review. *Evolutionary Anthropology* 10(1):34–40.

Charchar FJ, Bloomer LD, Barnes TA, Cowley MJ, Nelson CP, Wang Y, Denniff M, Debiec R, Christofidou P, Nankervis S, et al. 2012. Inheritance of coronary artery disease in men: an analysis of the role of the Y chromosome. *The Lancet* 379(9819):915–922.

Cronin H. 1991. *The ant and the peacock: altruism and sexual selection from Darwin to today.* Cambridge: Cambridge University Press.

Davis LJ. 2006. Constructing normalcy: the bell curve, the novel, and the invention of the disabled body in the nineteenth century. In Davis LJ, editor. *The disability studies reader.* 2nd ed. New York: Routledge. p. 3–16.

Dehaene S, Pegado F, Braga LW, Ventura P, Nunes Filho G, Jobert A, Dehaene-Lambertz G, Kolinsky R, Morais J, Cohen L. 2010. How learning to read changes the cortical networks for vision and language. *Science* 330(6009):1359–1364.

Dewing P, Shi T, Horvath S, Vilain E. 2003. Sexually dimorphic gene expression in mouse brain precedes gonadal differentiation. *Molecular Brain Research* 118(1–2):82–90.

Fausto-Sterling A. 2000. The five sexes, revisited. *The Sciences* 40(4):18–23.

Fisher SE. 2006. Tangled webs: tracing the connections between genes and cognition. *Cognition* 101(2):270–297.

Fisher TD, Moore ZT, Pittenger M. 2012. Sex on the brain? An examination of frequency of sexual cognitions as a function of gender, erotophilia, and social desirability. *Journal of Sex Research* 49(1):69–77.

Gamble VN. 1997. Under the shadow of Tuskegee: African Americans and health care. *American Journal of Public Health* 87(11):1773–1778.

Gelli G. 1931. *La guida medica. Ad uso delle donne spose e madri.* Florence: Bemporad.

Gislén A, Warrant EJ, Dacke M, Kröger RHH. 2006. Visual training improves underwater vision in children. *Vision Research* 46(20):3443–3450.

Gould SJ. 1981. *The mismeasure of man.* New York: W.W. Norton.

Grant JA, Courtemanche J, Duerden EG, Duncan GH, Rainville P. 2010. Cortical thickness and pain sensitivity in Zen meditators. *Emotion* 10(1):43–53.

Gravlee CG, Dressler WW, Bernard HR. 2005. Skin color, social classification, and blood pressure in southeastern Puerto Rico. *American Journal of Public Health* 95(12): 2191–2197.

Greenfield PM. 1997. You can't take it with you: why abilities assessments don't cross cultures. *American Psychologist* 52(10):1115–1124.

Helle S, Lummaa V, Jokela J. 2002. Sons reduced maternal longevity in preindustrial humans. *Science* 296(5570):1085.

Hicks BM, DiRago AC, Iacono WG, McGue M. 2009. Gene-environment interplay in internalizing disorders: consistent findings across six environmental risk factors. *Journal of Child Psychology and Psychiatry* 50(10):1309–1317.

Holloway RL. 1980. Within-species brain-body weight variability: a reexamination of the Danish data and other primate species. *American Journal of Physical Anthropology* 53(1):109–121.

Hunt L, Truesdell ND, Kreiner MJ. 2013. Genes, race, and culture in clinical care: racial profiling in the management of chronic illness. *Medical Anthropology Quarterly* 27(2): 253–271.

Ingstad B, Whyte SR, editors. 2007. *Disability in local and global worlds.* Berkeley: University of California Press.

Joel D, Berman Z, Tavor I, Wexler N, Gaber O, Stein Y, Shefi N, Pool J, Urchs S, Margulies DS, et al. 2015. Sex beyond the genitalia: the human brain mosaic. *Proceedings of the National Academy of Sciences* 112(50):15468–15473.

Konner M. 2006. Human nature, ethnic violence, and war. In Fitzduff M, Stout CE, editors. *The psychology of resolving global conflicts.* Volume 1. Westport, CT: Praeger Security International. p. 1–39.

Lewontin RC. 1972. The apportionment of human diversity. *Evolutionary Biology* 6:381–398.

Maguire EA, Gadian DG, Johnsrude IS, Good CD, Ashburner J, Frackowiak RS, Frith CD. 2000. Navigation-related structural change in the hippocampi of taxi drivers. *Proceedings of the National Academy of Sciences* 97(8):4398–4403.

Mueller JL, Skaletsky H, Brown LG, Zaghlul S, Rock S, Graves T, Auger K, Warren WC, Wilson RK, Page DC. 2013. Independent specialization of the human and mouse X chromosomes for the male germ line. *Nature Genetics* 45(9):1083–1087.

Nestler EJ. 2005. Is there a common molecular pathway for addiction? *Nature Neuroscience* 8(11):1445-1449.

Rhee SH, Waldman ID. 2002. Genetic and environmental influences on antisocial behavior: a meta-analysis of twin and adoption studies. *Psychological Bulletin* 128(3):490–529.

Roberts D. 2012. *Fatal invention: how science, politics, and big business re-create race in the twenty-first century*. New York: The New Press.

Sankar P, Kahn JD. 2005. BiDil: race medicine or race marketing? *Health Affairs* W5:455–463.

Shaywitz BA, Shaywitz SE, Pugh KR, Constable RT, Skudlarski P, Fulbright RK, Bronen RA, Fletcher JM, Shankweiler DP, Katz L, et al. 1995. Sex differences in the functional organization of the brain for language. *Nature* 373(6515):607–609.

Stein DG, Wright DW. 2010. Progesterone in the clinical treatment of acute traumatic brain injury. *Expert Opinion on Investigational Drugs* 19(7):847–857.

Sternberg RJ. 2007. Who are the bright children? The cultural context of being and acting intelligent. *Educational Researcher* 36(3):148–155.

Talhelm T, Zhang X, Oishi S, Shimin C, Duan D, Lan X, Kitayama S. 2014. Large-scale psychological differences within China explained by rice versus wheat agriculture. *Science* 344(6184):603–608.

Templeton AR. 1998. Human races: a genetic and evolutionary perspective. *American Anthropologist* 100(3):632–650.

Tishkoff SA, Reed FA, Friedlaender FR, Ehret C, Ranciaro A, Froment A, Hirbo JB, Awomoyi AA, Bodo JM, Doumbo O, et al. 2009. The genetic structure and history of Africans and African Americans. *Science* 324(5930):1035–1044.

Urban NBL, Kegeles LS, Slifstein M, Xu X, Martinez D, Sakr E, Castillo F, Moadel T, O'Malley SS, Krystal JH, et al. 2010. Sex differences in striatal dopamine release in young adults after oral alcohol challenge: a positron emission tomography imaging study with [11 C] raclopride. *Biological Psychiatry* 68(8):689–696.

Williams B. 2009. Deadly inequalities: race, illness, and poverty in Washington, D.C., since 1945. In Kusmer KL, Trotter JW, editors. *African American urban history since World War II*. Chicago: University of Chicago Press. p. 142–159.

Wolf E. 2001[1994]. Perilous ideas: race, culture, people. In E. Wolf, editor. *Pathways of power: building an anthropology of the modern world*. Berkeley: University of California Press. p. 398–412.

Yamauchi Y, Riel JM, Ruthig VA, Ortega EA, Mitchell MJ, Ward MA. 2016. Two genes substitute for the mouse Y chromosome for spermatogenesis and reproduction. *Science* 351(6272):514–516.

Young LC, Zaun BJ, VanderWerf EA. 2008. Successful same-sex pairing in Laysan albatross. *Biology Letters* 4(4):323–325.

PART III

Sex and gender

7

CHOOSERS AND CHEATERS

The sexual/reproductive conflict hypothesis

The evolutionary narrative about contemporary sex differences proposes that women and men have mismatched inclinations and capabilities due to sex-specific selective pressures and divergent contributions to survival and reproduction in the distant past. The idea is built on three main premises. The first is that unequal investments in offspring drive men to seek multiple mates but women prefer to settle with one man, resulting in dissimilar criteria for choosing mates and unique ways of approaching intimate relationships. This idea is related to the second idea that women are utterly dependent on men for provisions and consequently must trade sexual exclusivity for access to resources, whereas men are uninterested in parenting and do their utmost to avoid commitment beyond minimal investment in children they can be sure are their own. The purported underlying reason is that, in the ancestral environment, females were immobilized by having to care for a string of babies born in rapid succession.

Thirdly, women and men are thought to have different social roles and cognitive abilities as a result of the distinct skills needed for survival through hunting and a bit of ancillary gathering. Males allegedly are more intellectual and analytical, females more intuitive and emotional. In this view, gender inequalities in education and the workplace are simply the unavoidable products of a molecular patrimony assembled many thousands of years ago.

The following three chapters expose the inadequacy of final, ultimate explanations rooted in a culturally specific view of human sexuality and gender. We will begin with the idea of opposed sexual and reproductive interests and behavior, after a word about cultural representations of sex and gender.

. . . . .

As noted in the first chapter, culture defines symbolic categories which supply qualities to the objects that fall within them. This was demonstrated through examples such as gendered perceptions of inanimate objects in people who speak languages with gendered nouns. The disjuncture between the commonsense idea that women talk more than men and the actual number of words each utters on a daily basis showed how cultural categories can distort the interpretation of empirical evidence. Similarly, the idea that hunters provide all the food in foraging societies, versus the evidence on plant foods and the contributions of women, illustrates how cultural assumptions are projected onto other cultures and historical periods.

As a result of categorical thinking, the behavior and aptitudes of individual men and women such as multitasking or map-reading appear to derive from the presumed group-wide traits of their sex. As seen in the last chapter, both brains and behavior are mosaics of traits that are more female-typical, more male-typical, and more common in both sexes than one or the other. The following chapters show that observed behavior is not a good measure of biological traits, for it tends to comply with cultural beliefs and expectations. Nonconformity is penalized, resulting in attitudes and aptitudes that appear to validate expected sex differences.

Anthropologist Joan Cassell's (1997) analysis of surgeons in the workplace illustrates the impact of gender expectations on behavior. Cassell finds that outward behavior cannot speak to the existence of sex differences, as she has observed both women and men acting concerned, nurturing, and collaborative, or, alternatively, aloof, uncaring, and hierarchical. It does, however, express cultural rules. In short, women and men surgeons are expected to be unalike in leadership style and interpersonal relationships, and can ill afford *not* to act as if they were intrinsically different.

Cassell observes that in the hospital setting, cross-gendered behavior occurs regularly but is poorly tolerated, whereas affirmations of gender difference are applauded. As a result, in preparation for surgery women surgeons sometimes see to their own garments and gloves, but men never dress without the assistance of a nurse. In everyday conversation, women surgeons are expected to join the nurses in taking an interest in each other's personal lives. Men are prompted to talk about their families but not expected to ask nurses about theirs in return – much less remember details such as children's names and ages.

The way surgeons are perceived by men and women colleagues alike depends on their gender, as shown by different interpretations of the same behavior. Surgeons who display angry, commanding, or exacting behavior are "bitches" if they are women but "strong" professionals if they are men. Insufficiently domineering male surgeons are known as "wimps." Outbursts of whining, complaining, and foul language that nurses call "doctor fits" or "tantrums" are considered ordinary temperamental excesses in men but unacceptable behavior in women. Asking nurses for more than one instrument at a time is considered demanding if the surgeon is a woman, but goes unnoticed in a man. Crankiness in men surgeons brings more solicitous attention from the nurses, but from a woman results in sulking, diffidence, and deliberate sluggishness.

Cassell points out that these different behavioral expectations may be particularly pronounced in a traditionally male-dominated field in which masculine displays are rewarded and encouraged. The staff invests energy in maintaining a sharp distinction between femininity and masculinity. It behooves surgeons to go along, whatever their personality or beliefs, which winds up reinforcing traditional gender expectations.

A second study illustrates how ideas about what constitutes femaleness and maleness are not the same everywhere. Margaret Mead (1935) compared three societies in Papua New Guinea which had highly dissimilar expectations about women and men's attitudes and behavior, in spite of being close together geographically and ethnically. Mead described the Mundugumor, who lived in a densely populated river valley, as brutal, hostile, violent, and competitive. Women handled food production through fishing and agriculture, and preferred these tasks to childrearing. Men concerned themselves with warfare, political affairs, and marriage alliances. Both sexes equally displayed continuous hostility and aggression, and marriage and family relationships were tense. Women and men slept in separate buildings, and men could have several wives. Men viewed women as sinister and unclean, considered sexual contact with women harmful, and hid ceremonial objects from women's view. Women and men both behaved in forceful, uncaring, and possessive ways.

The peaceable Arapesh, who lived in isolated, sparsely populated mountain areas, presented an entirely different picture. Couples lived together, women were not seen as polluting, and there were no taboos on male-female contact. The Arapesh emphasized harmony and gentleness in all forms of social interaction, and both women and men acted in ways Euroamerican culture defined as maternal: nurturing, sensitive, warm, and conscientious of others. Women and men were expected to be similar in temperament and behavior. Their survival in a harsher environment required cooperation. Agricultural work was divided along gender lines, but tasks were not differently valued by gender. The Arapesh were so free of aggressive behavior that they had no established mechanisms for managing conflict.

The last group, the Tchambuli (or Chambri), was settled along the shores of a lake below the mountains where the Arapesh lived. Their gender system was unlike either of the other two. Women managed all of the economic activities: farming, fishing, raising of livestock, marketing, manufacturing. Women and men lived in large group houses segregated by sex, but women were not considered polluting to men and were cooperative with each other. Women were industrious and decisive; they cut their hair short and dressed soberly, with little ornamentation. Men, in contrast, spent their time on artistic expression such as painting and dance, some of which recalled the warfare of previous times. They took care to decorate themselves beautifully, keeping in sight of the women. The men were vain, competed for women's attention, and appeared fragile and insecure. In short, men's temperament fit the Western image of femininity.

These variations call into question the presumed link between biological sex differences and gendered behavior. Other anthropologists have provided further support for Mead's characterizations through work with other populations in New

Guinea, such as the Fore, whose balanced gender system recalls the Arapesh, or the Kukukuku, who are known for taking men's avoidance of women to the extreme of prescribing ritualized sex between adolescent boys and older warriors. On the other hand, Mead's work was flawed in several respects. She depended on translators and other researchers for information due to a hurt ankle and lack of knowledge of local languages. Mead aimed to show that American gender roles were not universal, but at the same time she believed in a small number of inborn personality types. Her intimate relationships with two men of opposite temperament seems to have affected her characterization of the three populations according to a neat typological scheme, even though her own findings – such as fits of rage and interpersonal conflict she witnessed among the Arapesh – suggest overlap between categories (Dobrin and Bashkow 2010). In fact, the Arapesh appear to have conducted warfare before the Australians arrived, according to evidence gathered by other researchers including the second of Mead's three husbands, Reo Fortune, who saw natural tribal murderousness in it. On the other hand, changes in social commitment to warfare supports Mead's argument for the malleability of gender roles and relationships.

Studies such as Cassell's and Mead's illustrate the mutability of both gender traits and cultural beliefs about them. Theories of biological causation, in contrast, propose that gender roles and behavior emerge from a material substrate unique to each sex. That essence is thought to inescapably push the mind along sex-determined paths, one of which leads to separate sexual and reproductive interests, as seen below.

. . . . .

According to conventional scientific wisdom, foraging bands were and are made up of related men and their women and children. In other words, society evolved from a backbone of males who could be sure their children were related to them, and whose genetic relatedness to each other encouraged them to cooperate for mutual benefit. They would join forces to steal territory and females from other patrilineal groups, generating endemic warfare.

These premises are not supported by evidence from contemporary foraging societies. For one, the groups of people living and traveling together are not all relatives, or even predominantly relatives. Only a small number (under 10%) of the people in 32 present-day foraging societies are closely related to others living with them (Hill et al. 2011). Relatives are dispersed across bands, resulting in cross-cutting relationships with birth family members and in-laws in many different bands. The reason for the dispersal of relatives is bilateral kinship organization, the type favored by 59% and 71% of dozens of foraging societies in two ethnographic samples. In addition, couples may live with either the wife's or the husband's band, or they may join a different one entirely – known as matrilocal/virilocal, patrilocal, or neolocal residence, respectively. Matrilocal, neolocal, or mixed residence is practiced by 75% and 90% of foraging societies. In one of the samples, matrilocal residence is four times more common than patrilocal. Patrilineal kin groups of any kind are absent from 72% and 86% of foraging societies in the two samples (Fry 2006).

In contrast to patriarchal agricultural societies, in foraging societies it is common for couples or individuals to change residence from one band to another over time. Women and men both may easily dissolve a marriage and enter another, and both share the same or nearly equivalent sexual rights and responsibilities. Both may take lovers as long as they are discreet about it, although jealousy is not always avoided. Virginity does not have economic value as it does in many agricultural societies, allowing young people of both sexes to engage in sexual relationships before marriage.

These characteristics of foraging societies do not conform to the evolutionistic scenario in which society grew upon a framework of male relationships that ensured female dependence and therefore paternity. The next chapter shows that private property and women's economic dependence are typical of settled agricultural societies with stores of wealth to manage. They are social-historical traits rather than primordial human characteristics.

Human physical dimensions do not support the assumption that men are born to be sexually promiscuous whereas women are made to be chaste and devoted to husband and family. Comparisons across primate species indicate that human females and males share an evolutionary history of one to two additional partners. This means that they are equally impelled by nature to bond with one individual but also to pair with others.

As seen in Chapter 2, males and females of early hominid species formed long-term couples, collaborated in child care, and foraged together. Relatively low male-male aggression is indicated by the small disparity in height between the sexes, which has been stable since the first *Homo* species. Analysis of the *A. afarensis* "Lucy" skeleton indicates that sexual dimorphism in height was similar among the australopithecines as well, contrary to the conventional belief that australopithecine males were twice as large as females (Reno et al. 2003).

Across animal species, female body size depends on the demands of foraging and reproduction, whereas male height and weight are relatively unconstrained.[1] Where males are much larger than females, the cause generally is male-male competition for mating opportunities, whether to exclude each other or to be chosen by females. Male animals may compete either by way of size and strength, or by demonstrating their quality through distinguishing characteristics such as complex bird or frog calls, the long dark mane of male lions, or the showy plumage of some birds – most famously the peacock's unwieldy tail. Costly features indicate better health since the animal is able to devote energy to display that would otherwise be needed for growth and maintenance, including immune responses to infectious disease. Predators and the need to procure food exert downward pressure on these traits, since displays can render the animal more vulnerable and less agile. Where male-male competition involving violent combat is intense, males but not females may be equipped with features such as horns, antlers, and large canines.

Sexual dimorphism in primates ranges widely across species. The females of some primate species are larger than the males, including certain langurs and gibbons, the common marmoset, and potto monkeys. Small-bodied species tend to have little or no difference in size between sexes. Many are monogamous, including certain species of mouse lemur, marmosets, spectral tarsiers, tamarins, and muriquis (woolly spider monkeys). Monogamous pairs are especially common among New World monkeys. Some species, such as pygmy marmosets and saddleback tamarins, are organized in polyandrous relationships in which one reproductively-active female mates with a few males. In both monogamous and polyandrous species, nonmothers including males help care for and carry infants.

Males and females are almost the same size among the "lesser" apes – gibbons and siamangs. These animals live in monogamous pairs with their offspring, but males and females may change mates over their lifetimes. The males stick around in spite of female infertility between births spaced years apart, and provide significant paternal care; male siamangs hold their infants while sleeping. Males and females have equally large canines to defend themselves against rivals of the same sex.

At the opposite end of the scale, large differences in size are typical of larger-bodied species in which males mate with multiple females and restrict lower-ranking males' access to them. These species tend to live on the ground rather than in trees, and to eat fruit as opposed to leaves. Baboon, gorilla, and orangutan males weigh twice as much as females. Baboons live in large mixed groups with intense male-male antagonism, which is typical of terrestrial species. Orangutans eat fruit, which allows a single dominant male to control the territory inhabited by multiple females and their offspring; the females seek out the male only for the purpose of mating. For leaf-eating gorillas, an age-graded male dominance hierarchy excludes all but the largest, top-ranking male from breeding with a group of females; these females also seek out the male when in estrus and initiate all the copulations.

Chimpanzees fall in the middle: female body weight is 75–80% of male body weight in common chimpanzees and bonobos. Height is the same in chimpanzees, but female bonobos are 5–10% shorter than males. Both species live in large mixed-sex groups which include smaller units of mothers and their offspring. In these species both males and females are organized hierarchically and mate with numerous partners. Male hierarchies are more pronounced among chimpanzees, who bargain amongst themselves for priority, although only the top-ranking male can monopolize a female.

The relatively small degree of dimorphism in humans suggests an amount of male-male competition corresponding to males having one to two additional partners beyond the primary mate, as shown in Table 7.1. Women's body weight averages 80–90% of men's, while height averages 88–96% of men's. In terms of body weight, the male-to-female ratio for monogamous monkeys is 1:1, compared to 1.15:1 for humans, 1.25:1 for chimps and 2:1 for gorillas and orangutans.

For humans, height is a more reliable measure than weight, which can vary to a greater degree over the lifetime and across populations due to nutrition, disease, and other factors. Significantly, the amount of sexual dimorphism in height correlates with the average height of populations. That is, taller populations are more

TABLE 7.1 Sexual dimorphism in size in relation to male tendency towards monogamy in primates

	Gorillas Orangutans	*Chimpanzees Bonobos*	*Humans*	*Marmosets Tamarins*
Degree of sexual dimorphism	high	moderate	moderate to low	very low
Scale from low to high male tendency towards monogamy	males mate with multiple females and restrict other males' mating opportunities	males mate with multiple females	males mate with one to a few females	males mate with one female

sexually dimorphic than shorter ones. Populations living in extreme environments, whether arctic or equatorial, tend to be shorter, with males and females of nearly the same height. In temperate mid-latitude climates, populations are generally taller and there is a greater average sex difference in height. Societies with a female-to-male height difference at the low end of the range include the Tolai of New Guinea; those at the high end include the South American Mapuche. The female-to-male height ratio for most societies exceeds 90% (Wolfe and Gray 1982).

The other half of the story is that human females also have an evolutionary history of one to two partners besides the long-term mate, as indicated by the ratio between testes weight and body weight in males. Across species, where females mate with more than one male, males have larger testes which produce more abundant and higher density sperm. Sperm competition also occurs through behavior, such as the chimpanzee strategy of mating last and consequently delivering a higher number of sperm. Human males presented pornographic images as part of an experimental design produce more sperm-dense ejaculate if the pictures include one woman with two men than if they show three women (Kilgallon and Simmons 2005). Separation from a partner has the same effect: the longer the time apart, the greater the number of active sperm released (Shackelford and Goetz 2007).

Sperm competition is intense in species such as chimpanzees and bonobos, in which females mate with a dozen or more males multiple times during estrus. The males have outsized testes as a proportion of body size. In contrast, male gorillas have the same size testes as human males but more than twice the body weight. Male gorillas do not have to worry about their females mating with other gorillas, since groups are stable and relatively isolated from one another.

Testes weight as a proportion of body weight is 0.25–0.27% in chimpanzees and bonobos, 0.08–1.0% in humans and gibbons, 0.05% in orangutans, and 0.03% in gorillas.[2] As shown in Table 7.2, this suggests that female humans have an evolutionary history of coupling with a number of males that falls closer to the one mate seen in gorillas and orangutans, and the many mates typical of species that live in multi-male, multi-female groups such as chimpanzees.

TABLE 7.2 Ratio of testes to body size in relation to female tendency towards monogamy in primates

	Chimpanzees Bonobos	*Humans*	*Marmosets Tamarins*	*Gorillas Orangutans*
Testes-to-body-size ratio	high	moderate	low	very low
Scale from low to high female tendency towards monogamy	females mate with multiple males	females mate with one to a few males	females mate with one male or in some cases a few males	females mate with one male

In sum, human anatomical measurements indicate pair bonding along with multiple, but relatively few, partners. This makes humans similar to birds, bats, beavers, and most other monogamous animal species, among whom lifelong monogamy with strict sexual exclusivity is exceedingly rare. Most couples live in long-term relationships but adultery is common and many people change partners over their lifetimes.

There are reproductive benefits to monogamy combined with a modicum of cheating. For male mammals this is more obvious since they do not lactate and can afford to waste sperm even while devoting resources to the offspring of one principal mate. Female mammals devote more energy to each offspring and are limited in the number they can produce. Still, for females there are gains to be made by copulating with other males on the sly, such as increased opportunities to become pregnant, the possibility of mating with a superior male, and the chance to build beneficial relationships with other males.

A study on women's attraction to the face of a potential mate lends support to the idea that ancestral females had additional partners besides the long-term mate. Research participants watched a computer image of a man's face gradually shift from a more chiseled masculine look to a more feminine aspect, with a less prominent jaw, chin, and cheekbones. Women who were already in a relationship or were seeking a short-term relationship were more likely to stop the progression on a highly masculine-looking image than other women. The researchers conclude that these are the women who benefit from sneaking a copulation that might give them a superior offspring. They choose a more masculine face, with large, prominent features indicating more testosterone. That is, a masculine face signals sufficient biological fitness to overcome the dampening effect of testosterone on the immune system (Little et al. 2002).

The shift in hormone levels with intimate partnership and fatherhood, discussed below, further suggests that such a face signals availability and youth – which is associated with better-quality sperm. In contrast, less chiseled faces indicate greater maturity, trustworthiness, and reliability. Men with gentler features are considered to possess greater warmth, honesty, and integrity. They tend to be more educated, accomplished, and assertive than men with more masculine faces.

They earn more military awards and leadership positions, although studies on public perceptions of politicians show that people tend to judge men with harsher features as more competent (Todorov et al. 2005).

In many societies, men are expected and permitted to cheat on their partners due to an assumed natural dissatisfaction with a single mate, but the information above indicates that it is equally "natural" for women to resist exclusive monogamy. Yet, the value of comparisons with other animals is very limited, given that human concepts such as "monogamy" are a poor fit to animal relationships, while cultural rules determine whether men, women, or both may stray from a single partner, regardless of evolutionary predictions.

.....

As we have seen, testosterone's general effect of stimulating tissue enlargement is the reason for men's larger average size. Exposure to testosterone in males begins in fetal life and has lasting effects on the brain and behavior, especially with respect to violence and motivation towards sex and other bodily pleasures. This section takes a closer look at the relationship between men's behavior and hormone levels in relation to intimate partnership and parenthood.[3]

Baseline hormone secretion and uptake vary across individual men. Higher testosterone activity is associated with extroversion, social dominance, a greater number of lifetime sexual partners, and a stronger tendency towards risk-taking, addictive, and aggressive behavior. On the other hand, low testosterone, as in men with hypogonadism, is associated with mood disorders, aggression, and increased sexual activity.

Testosterone levels vary over the life course. The peak in late adolescence and early adulthood facilitates reproductive development and promotes mating. Among single men, higher testosterone levels correlate with a greater frequency of finding a partner and becoming a father. However, high testosterone brings lower empathy and a higher likelihood of erratic and antisocial behavior, which interferes with intimate relationships and parenting. Accordingly, upon the birth of children men's testosterone secretion falls abruptly to levels far below those of single men. During the andropause in later life, many men experience a further reduction in testosterone which contributes to reduced sexual desire and diminishing bone density and muscle mass – although exercise counteracts these effects through the rise in testosterone described in the last chapter.

Fathers who spend time with their children on a daily basis have significantly lower testosterone levels than fathers who do not. Likewise, fathers who sleep with their babies have lower testosterone levels than men who sleep apart from them. The decline in testosterone secretion is most pronounced with the first child and while children are young. This is significant because high testosterone is most disadvantageous when families are first formed and children are maximally needy and vulnerable. In fact, in fathers, higher levels of the hormone, or higher numbers of androgen receptors, are associated with reduced growth and survival in offspring. Fathers with higher testosterone levels are less active in child care and less attuned to infant needs, as reflected in a lower responsiveness to crying.

Testosterone favors the pursuit of a partner, while other hormones help to strengthen relationships. Childbirth causes a rise in oxytocin and vasopressin in both mothers and fathers. These closely related hormones promote feelings of tenderness and trust, and facilitate social bonding, other-orientation, and nurturing and defense. Both are produced in the hypothalamus and released into the circulation from the posterior pituitary gland. Like cortisol, estrogens and androgens, and other neuromodulators, they amplify or suppress the activity of neurons in the brain, but have different effects elsewhere: oxytocin stimulates uterine contractions during childbirth and the release of milk during lactation; vasopressin (antidiuretic hormone) increases blood vessel constriction and kidney tubule permeability.

Romantic involvement and sexual activity increase oxytocin levels in males and females. In addition, prolactin levels increase in fathers and expectant fathers. Prolactin, the principal hormone involved in milk production, is secreted by the anterior pituitary and has multiple functions throughout the body, including effects on growth, metabolism, and the immune system. Prolactin mediates the feeling of sexual gratification and dampens the dopamine pathway involved in arousal. It favors parenting behavior by promoting nurturing and reducing antagonism and frustration.

The activity of these hormones confirms that pair bonding and paternal care are very old traits for humans. It reflects the importance of intimate relationships to a social species. The hormones secreted in response to mating and the birth of children open the way for the brain to learn new feelings, behaviors, and emotional attachments by weakening prior neural connections, fixed mental routines, and self-orientation. These effects occur in males and females alike and contribute to positive pair bonding and infant care behavior in the next generation of males and females, whereas a thwarted hormonal or behavioral response favors opposite outcomes.

Women and men also share biochemical pathways involved in sexual motivation and gratification, although there are some differences. As noted in the last chapter, on average women are less distracted by sexual desire. Their interest in sex varies cyclically, with an increase during the fertile phase of the menstrual cycle. For a number of anatomical and psychological reasons, women may not reach orgasm as consistently as men. Yet, none of this suggests that women and men have a completely different sexual-reproductive scope that leads them to look for different things in a mate.

The idea that men naturally desire youth in women as an indicator of fertility potential, whereas women fancy age in men as a proxy for wealth and rank, rests upon a very shaky empirical foundation. Its cornerstone is David Buss's (1989) analysis of surveys from 37 countries. This is an impressive number, but the samples were neither random nor representative, and Buss and his colleagues combined surveys using ranked and rated factors. Some samples were exceedingly small, such as 55 people in Iran, 101 in Italy, and 247 in India. Respondents from the US and West Germany alone made up one-fourth of the total: 2,574 out of 10,047. Beyond these problems of data quality and analysis, by focusing only on qualities in a desired partner, the study failed to account for differences between people's ideal mate and the one they end up with.

While the data reveal a shared predominant preference for values and personality traits, Buss focuses upon minor gender differences that support the evolutionistic hypothesis. The factors that interest him fall much lower on the list of valued traits: economic prospects and slightly higher age chosen by female respondents, and attractiveness and chastity desired by males. It is not until the 13th of 14 pages, in the section on "qualifications and limitations," that Buss concedes that both sexes "ranked the characteristics 'kind-understanding' and 'intelligent' higher than earning power and attractiveness in all samples, suggesting that species-typical mate preferences may be more potent than sex-linked preferences."

Notwithstanding his own finding that convergent preferences far outweigh divergent ones, Buss and others have continued to argue that women and men seek fundamentally different things in a partner. Given that actual choices do not lend much support to the idea, evolutionary psychologists look for unconscious expressions of women's deepest desires in places such as fiction. Heather Schell (2011) shows that, in the early 1990s, romance novels became a source of data just as the novelists brought in a wave of alpha male heroes popularized by evolutionary psychology. At that time, the industry was tightly controlled and writers were held to a uniform template. They had fallen under the scrutiny of feminist critics, and had responded that their stories were about female empowerment. Accordingly, new plots revolved around a dominant male over whose aversion to commitment the novel's heroine eventually triumphed. Evolutionary psychologists saw this spate of novels as an expression of subterranean female psychological needs and preferences rooted in the eternal reproductive conflict. Within a decade, the alpha male hero had disappeared from the novels, thanks to relaxed industry standards, greater autonomy for writers, and the limits of a fixed and formulaic character, but it was too late: by then, he had jumped to widely cited articles as a timeless personification of permanent, inborn gender differences.

The evolutionistic narrative about women's longing for a provider leads to the conclusion that men, but not women, crave status competition. It is taken for granted that women simply gravitate towards the most successful men, and that men who are flashier with their wealth or more willing to take financial risks desire and gain more sexual opportunities. Men's "hardwiring" for associating sex with money was the point of the roulette study described in the first chapter. Its distorting effect on research can be seen further in a study led by David Gal (2012) which aimed to establish whether the brain has a single motivation-and-reward system that activates salivation in response to nonfood items, but ended up focusing on men's combined aspirations for wealth and women.

The study had two parts, each involving priming two groups of college students with a writing exercise before showing them pictures of either an attractive item or a plain piece office equipment. Cotton rolls in the students' mouths were weighed before and after the intervention to assess saliva production. In the first experiment, which included women, students were asked to write either about a situation in which they had felt either powerful or powerless. Only in the group primed to feel powerless did seeing an image of money increase the amount of salivation. The experiment demonstrated that if a person is primed to actively desire something that connotes power, then money triggers a physiological response.

The second experiment included only male students. One group was primed by seeing pictures of women and writing about dating one of them, while the other was primed to think about going to the barbershop. Salivation increased on seeing a picture of a car in the group primed with a mating goal, but not the barbershop group. The results showed that seeing a car evokes desire when a man is primed to think about dating. While this is not a surprising outcome for students in a consumer society, in which cars are central to personal identity and courtship, it was interpreted as proof that for men's brains, women and wealth are linked. Moreover, the study makes it appear as if reward circuits in the brain were the product of masculine interests, and endorses prevailing gender ideologies in a very effective, naturalizing way.

Cars and money are not analogous to resources in the ancestral environment, which, as we have seen, were not monopolized by males. Moreover, socially acceptable acquisitiveness and showiness is culturally specific behavior. In nomadic face-to-face societies in which humility and sharing avert status competition, men who venture to act the way favored by consumer culture are shunned. It is only in agricultural and industrial societies that personal wealth is permitted to be accumulated and used strategically. In these societies, both men and women engage in conspicuous consumption to impress each other as well as people of their own gender. Immediate social factors readily explain the behavior, making it unnecessary to seek ultimate explanations based on a hypothesized past in which females and males pursued opposite goals.

. . . . .

There are other complications for theories of separate sexual/reproductive interests. One is that people regularly and intentionally sever the connection between sex and reproduction. Another is that human sexuality does not exist in a state of nature anywhere, for every society imposes rules for acceptable behavior.

Many animals engage in sexual activity that serves non-reproductive ends such as pleasure, social competition as well as cooperation, and interpersonal bonding. Bonobos are known for everyday sexual behavior that offers no possibility of conception, such as the females' genital to genital (G-G) rubbing and the males' penile "sword play." These activities serve important social functions. Sex calms the animals down when they come upon fruit trees in the wild or at feeding time in captive populations – situations that could cause friction and frenzied eating. Females who join a new group reduce the level of tension and form social relationships through sexual interactions with females and, secondarily, males. In the wild, estrus lasts 15 days – far longer than 6 for chimpanzees. Female sexual swelling never disappears completely, the inverse of human continuous but concealed sexual receptivity. Like humans, bonobo females mate with males even when conception is unlikely or out of the question, including during pregnancy.[4]

While sexual activity has social dimensions and increases intimacy between individuals in humans and other primate species, humans are unique for purposely interfering with reproduction. That is, humans obstruct the evolutionary mechanisms that purportedly determine sexual behavior. Throughout the world, men do not act upon their supposed Darwinian imperative to inseminate as many females as possible, and probably never did. Most men do not have babies all their lives, not even in foraging societies where they do not have to worry about their bank accounts. Women likewise rarely maximize reproduction. Family size in all societies is shaped by individual choices and social norms affecting variables such as marriage age and nursing frequency. Couples may determine family size in advance, rather than having it decided for them by maximal reproduction combined with high infant mortality. Births are also manipulated through technology that overcomes infertility and preterm delivery, and that allows parents to select embryos on the basis of sex and other characteristics.

Social and cultural systems shape sexual and reproductive behavior in additional ways that defy evolutionary expectations. The choice of a partner can be so constrained that individual preferences are virtually irrelevant. Patriarchal societies in which girls are married at a young age eliminate female choice altogether, as does arranged marriage in general. In many societies, couples who marry outside their class or caste are ostracized and perhaps disinherited. Marriages across such lines are the exception, not the rule, contrary to what one would expect if men chose wives on the basis of youth and looks rather than social and economic status.

Other customs and systems direct behavior towards opposite ends than maximizing reproductive success, such as permanent celibacy among monks and nuns. The inheritance of property by firstborn sons can cause a significant portion of the population to be excluded from marriage and parenthood. In patriarchal systems, young women may be assigned to permanent housekeeping for a widowed or unmarried male relative. Where there are multiple sex/gender categories, as discussed in the following chapters, people may choose partners with whom it is socially or biologically impossible to procreate. Personal choices, social structures, and gender inequalities shape whether or not people have children, independently of genetics.

The standard evolutionary explanation for foregone reproduction is that people who never have children nonetheless favor their own genes' transmission by investing in the children of their relatives. They make sacrifices for other people's children in proportion to the amount of shared genes – favoring a sibling over a niece, for example. Similarly, small family size is explained as a strategy that maximizes reproductive success through greater investment in each child, whose increased likelihood of survival increases the probability of offspring in the next generation. The problem is that such open-ended models push the calculation of reproductive success indefinitely outwards and into the future, and therefore have limited explanatory power with regard to social customs or individual behavior.

Sociocultural systems also structure sexual behavior, calling into question women's allegedly natural sexual probity. Where there is a high level of gender inequality, female virginity tends to be imposed until marriage and chastity prescribed afterward, but men's philandering is acceptable and even expected regardless of marital status. These rules lead to differences in behavior and beliefs that may appear to support the evolutionistic hypothesis. However, women and men have similar sexual views and experience in societies with relatively little gender inequality. The similarity extends to behavior before and during intimate encounters. Where women are economically independent, both women and men initiate playful physical engagement, including roughhousing, and consider themselves physical equals who are equally invested in the pursuit of sexual pleasure. These views have been documented in diverse locations throughout the world, including the early-20th century Trobriand Islands and many indigenous Andean societies through the late 20th century (Weismantel 2001).

In contrast, in Western society, women are expected to start having sex at a later age, have fewer sexual partners, be uninterested in casual sex, and enjoy sex less than men. Well into the second half of the 20th century, scientists also claimed that cerebral and reproductive functions were contradictory in women, such that increasing educational level was thought to correlate with decreasing sexual fulfillment. In more recent decades, as inequalities have narrowed and researchers have paid closer attention to the effects of secrecy and misreporting among female respondents, gender differences in sexual interest and behavior have diminished considerably.

In order to confront the problem of women's unwillingness to respond honestly to questions about sexual behavior, researchers tested responses under three scenarios in which participants received different information about how a questionnaire would be handled. The study found that reported sexual behavior was nearly identical in women and men if participants believed that they would be found out for lying. Differences were moderate if participants believed their responses were anonymous, and large if they believed that the researchers might look at their individual questionnaire (Alexander and Fisher 2003). Another study using an anonymous questionnaire found that male but not female students were influenced both by the gender of the researcher and the inclusion of statements about supposed scientific findings on gender differences in sexual behavior and attitudes. Men reported having had more sexual partners if the researcher was female and the statement read that today's women are more permissive than men. The same study found that women reported having had intercourse at an earlier age than men. Men reported somewhat more permissive attitudes and sexual experience (Fisher 2007).

Recent research also casts doubt on women's purported lack of interest in casual sex. A new study has re-created a classic experiment in which none of the women accepted an offer of casual sex made by a male research assistant, whereas three-fourths of the men accepted offers from a female research assistant. In the revised version, research assistants imitated the behavior of those in the earlier study – which did not take account of the participants' perceptions. Overall, women accepted an offer of casual sex less often than men. However, they ranked the male research assistants posing as prospective sexual partners lower in intelligence and sexual skill than the men ranked the female research assistants. After correcting for the harsher assessment of the male research assistants, the study showed that women and men do not differ in openness to offers of casual sex. In addition, the study found that the gender difference disappears if participants are asked to imagine sexual offers from particular individuals or categories of people such as celebrities (Conley 2011). The study shows that, for casual sexual encounters, women and men share the same motivation – sexual pleasure – and evaluate potential partners according to the same criterion – sexual skill.

Finally, in practice women and men agree on desirable traits in a long-term partner, even though they might verbalize divergent ideals. To illustrate, in the initial phase of a study, women and men adhered to stereotypes in their expressed preferences. However, in a speed dating event and in real life, the women chose partners for reasons other than wealth, while the men were interested in qualities beyond attractiveness (Eastwick and Finkel 2008). In fact, most couples worldwide are similar in age; large age differences are very rare. Across studies including Buss's analysis described above, women and men both tend to choose partners similar or complementary, but not opposite, to them in personality, and to care to the same degree about traits such as kindness, intelligence, and agreeableness, with only minor differences.[5] Through long-term interaction, both partners move towards the realization of personality traits they admire in the other, further illustrating agreement on core values (Rusbult et al. 2009). These findings point to the limited power of childbearing potential and command of resources to explain actual mate choices.

. . . . .

The emphasis on men as the protagonists of evolution distorts the way the past is perceived and the way current human characteristics are evaluated and interpreted. Pictorial representations of human origins almost invariably show an all-male progression of primate and hominid species that culminates with a Western man-of-action such as a business executive or astronaut. Scenes of prehistoric life revolve around males in active, athletic poses, either hunting or stalking game, their eyes trained on the horizon. These fellows embody the courageous individualism of the American self-made man. They evidently were the ones to ensure our species' survival, have the pluck to expand into treacherous new territories, and be the genius behind all tools and innovations including agriculture and complex civilization. Females, if they appear at all, are presented in passive, domestic poses, holding babies and making food or clothing. The limit of their productive capacity is to scan the immediate environment for the ripest berries.

In this imagined environment, females must automatically prefer older males who command more resources. The idea conflicts, however, with the fact that an ancestral male's quality as a father would have declined over time, and not just because age reduced his physical ability to protect others or carry infants. Sperm cells accumulate mutations at the rate of about two per year beginning after age 20 (Kong et al. 2012). Schizophrenia, bipolar disorder, autism, psychosis, attention-deficit/

hyperactivity disorder, academic deficits, and behavioral problems rise in frequency with increased paternal age, as shown through comparisons of earlier-born to later-born children of the same father (D'Onofrio et al. 2014).

The flip side of the evolutionary expectation that women prefer older men is that men are born to desire younger women. Male tastes are even credited with altering female physical characteristics such as breasts, which are seen as sexual displays rather than functional milk-producing organs.[6] This idea leads to misinterpretation of the pleasant feelings that can come from breastfeeding. In reality, breasts are not particularly rich in nerve endings, which is beneficial since breastfeeding can also be painful. People have to learn to associate breasts with sexual feelings. In much of the world, breasts carry no sexual connotations – which explains why they are not covered up – and women and men find the idea of sexual behavior involving breasts bizarre and repulsive, similar to Western responses to the way Chinese culture eroticized tiny feet in the era of foot-binding (Dettwyler 1995).

The uncritical acceptance of the eroticized breast as a natural rather than cultural symbol leads to the notion that men are sexually attracted to ample breasts because they indicate a woman's age and therefore her quality as a breeder. Given that breasts sag with age in proportion to size, large breasts that are still firm are said to indicate more childbearing years ahead. However, there is a major complication: lactation swells the breasts, yet indicates a state of reproductive quiescence. The related assumption that men are by nature more visually oriented and visually stimulated than women also is not supported by evidence. This visual orientation is said to derive from bipedal locomotion, which allegedly caused males to turn their gaze to the breasts, not just the backside – as if only males stood up, and females went about their business and chose mates without looking. Males are not born with better eyes. In early life, boys are less visually capable than girls. In adulthood, on average women and men outperform each other across different kinds of tests. The male advantage with respect to flickering light and small movements in the distance, and the female advantage in stereoscopic close-range vision, reflect gender differences in activities – especially during childhood – rather than inborn differences in visual equipment.[7]

It is true that human females have more permanently visible breast tissue compared to other primate species, but the amount varies considerably within and between populations. The cause is not likely to have been sexual selection through men's attraction to breasts, particularly of a certain size or shape, given that such likes and dislikes are culturally conditioned and changeable over short spans of time – such as the Brazilian preference for small breasts which is now shifting under the influence of Euroamerican media (Edmonds 2013). A more plausible explanation for visible breast tissue would be the metabolic advantage of fat stores for milk production, which would have been helpful over the long span of human evolution when caloric intake was tightly balanced against energy expenditure. Alternatively, the trait could be an artifact of upright posture and the change in demands on the musculature of the upper body.

In a similar manner to large breasts, small waists relative to hips are thought to attract men by indicating youth and fertility potential, and, in addition, lack of pregnancy. However, physically active, muscular women such as foragers do not have small waists to make their hips look wider. In addition, across cultures, thinness is a rare aesthetic ideal. It is far more common for standards of female beauty to emphasize plumpness, which symbolizes health, status, and wellbeing where food is relatively scarce and unreliable (Brown and Konner 1987).

Paradoxically, the presumed evolutionary importance of men's evaluation of women's fertility value through sexual signs of youth contradicts other evolutionary principles. That is, the difference in male and female investment in sperm and egg cells predicts that males should seek to inseminate as many females as possible. This should cause them to disregard the appearance of prospective partners, since it costs little to waste sperm on an undesirable mate.

The focus on female breasts and waists as primary mate-choice criteria fits with the Western habit of objectifying, dehumanizing, and essentializing women by dividing them into disembodied parts, as well as the tendency to prioritize the visual over other sensory fields. In other words, the ideas are congruent with their cultural context, although not necessarily with evidence. In practice, people are attracted to each other in idiosyncratic ways and by many non-visual factors including voice, sentiments, and talents. Being in love causes the brain to develop new preferences for traits embodied by the other person. Even aesthetic tastes change over the lifetime, for instance towards older-looking people as one ages, or from same-sex to opposite-sex partners. Among biological explanations, smell may be more important than looks.

Body odor varies in relation to major histocompatibility complex (MHC) genes that regulate immunological responses to foreign and self antigens, and consequently may signal immunological difference that confers increased protection against disease to the next generation. In an experiment designed to test the hypothesis that women prefer an immunologically different mate, young women sniffed shirts worn by various men for two nights. The men whose odors the women found more pleasant differed from them in more than twice as many genes on average than the men whose odors were ranked as less pleasant. Moreover, the more pleasant odors were more likely to remind the women of their own past or present partners than the less pleasant odors, indicating a consistent preference for difference. Women on oral contraceptives did not share the preference for immunologically dissimilar men, suggesting that during pregnancy and lactation women prefer the company of relatives (Wedekind et al. 1995). The study points to the role of female choice and the importance of factors other than visible age as a marker of wealth. It further suggests that a brain hardwired with specific visual attractions is not very helpful for understanding actual partner choices.

Beneath the idea that males prefer younger but females older age in a mate lies the assumption that ancestral males provisioned decorative females with meat from massive, dangerous animals. The presumption of male provisioning is rooted in the sociobiological models of the 1970s and 1980s, when predation and struggle dominated biological science. Since then, studies of plants and animals have emphasized collaborative behavior as well, calling into question the primacy of competition as the main determinant of survival and evolutionary change. Even bacteria cooperate, as seen in Chapter 4. While themes related to competition are culturally associated with masculinity whereas cooperation is considered feminine, in nature competitive and cooperative behaviors are not linked to one sex or the other. Animals of both sexes help each other but also scuffle over rank and limit other animals' access to food and reproductive opportunities.

Many birds and insects provide food for their mates during special times such as mating or nesting season, but the sex of the provider and recipient varies. Males of some primate species such as baboons and chimpanzees occasionally give gifts of food to female sexual partners, but this does not constitute provisioning. The females see to their own daily nutritional needs. This requires that they range around rather than staying home while the males go it alone in the wide world, as suggested by children's books and the traditional scientific assumption that male animals have larger ranges. Using GPS collars, researchers have shown, to the contrary, that koala females and males have equally large ranges, even though the females carry and nurse the young. Moreover, male nighttime calling does not serve the purpose of communicating territorial information to other males, but rather attracts females from their treetop nests (Ellis et al. 2011). As in the case of people who thought they heard inferior music because the musician's gender or ethnicity did not fit their preconceptions (see Chapter 1), earlier researchers had been hearing what they expected to hear.

As seen in Chapter 2, current knowledge of contemporary and prehistoric foragers likewise challenges longstanding assumptions about provisioning and mobility among ancestral humans. Males and females foraged opportunistically and collected the same food sources. Births were spaced far apart. Mothers and others carried infants while foraging, and fathers helped their pregnant or lactating partners in additional ways such as passing up easily accessible foods and providing protection against dangerous animals. In fact, the very idea of male provisioning contradicts itself, for if a male leaves his family for long stretches of time he cannot also protect it physically. However powerful as a symbol, and as a central element of the economics of gender inequality and the control of women's sexuality, the home as a fixed dwelling has no place in a nomadic society.

As noted in Chapter 2, the transition from herbivory to an omnivorous diet took place long before hunting and involved increased consumption of animal protein in the form of insects, eggs, and small mammals and reptiles. Depending on the food resources available in the diverse ecological zones inhabited by human ancestors, once effective tools were made 75,000–50,000 years ago it may have become possible for one sex to focus on hunting because it could depend on the more predictable food gathered by the other sex. However, it cannot be assumed that hunting was always done by males and gathering by females, given that contemporary foraging societies do not always divide up the tasks this way.

Significantly, while foragers may esteem hunting ability in a man, it does not bring him a larger number of children (Gurven and Hill 2009). In other words, male provisioning does not increase reproductive success. Moreover, hunting has not supplanted gender-mixed activities such as scavenging meat and bones from dead animals, scaring other carnivores away from their kills, and hunting collectively with nets. Finally, at least half of the calories consumed by contemporary and ancestral foragers comes from plant foods, which are accessible to everyone.

. . . . .

The discussion above suggests that commonsense understandings of the evolution of sex and gender may say more about cultural beliefs than empirical evidence. For a further illustration, archeologists have long assumed that so-called Venus figurines were pornographic objects made by men for their own purposes.[8] These statuettes in stone, bone, and clay made 25,000 and more years ago have been found in various locations across Europe and Russia. Some of them show plump women, giving rise to their secondary interpretation as fertility symbols. In reality, the figurines are unlikely to have served their presumed purposes or to have been made exclusively or even predominantly by males.

The meanings of art undoubtedly varied across Paleolithic settings, as they do today, but fertility and male sexual desire are unlikely themes for the Venus figurines. Foraging societies are not known for fertility cults, suggesting that the statuettes may have been used as protective charms during childbirth or as tools for teaching girls about reproduction, which would have been helpful because of the small size of bands and the low rate of reproduction. These and apparent ritual uses suggest manufacture by women. Statuettes found in fire pits had been purposely heated to the point of cracking or exploding, as is done by indigenous peoples with pottery and animal bones such as the scapula in order to divine the future. Non-local materials and special pigments suggest that some statuettes were used for important ceremonies. Those pairing a female figure with animal or supernatural elements indicate a spiritual dimension as well as the role of women as healers and religious leaders. The lack of a face is consistent with the fear of spiritual harm from visual representation that is shared by many non-Western populations today. Finally, some statuettes depict males, but they are not interpreted as pornographic objects.

The projection of contemporary male interests onto Paleolithic art typifies a conceptual habit of allowing dominant assumptions about sex, families, and social roles to set the parameters for interpreting the past, which generates the appearance of timelessness and in turn reinforces the initial assumptions. Pamela Geller (2009) explains that the first question researchers ask about skeletal remains is the individual's sex, as if sex were automatically the same as gender and therefore the main, lifelong determinant of activities, relationships, and social roles. Based mainly on pelvic parts, skeletons are grouped into either/or male and female categories, erasing the overlap in ranges of values, the existence of contradictory elements in a single skeleton, and the convergence of pelvic indicators of sex in older-age specimens.

As a result of categorization practices, all females seem to have died in reproductive age, and reproduction seems to have been the fate and purpose of all females. In contrast, males are associated with production, their skeletal condition evaluated in terms of economic activity. The sexual division of labor emerges as a permanent condition borne of female reproduction and male provisioning, and the primary or only line along which societies organize tasks – as opposed to age, social class, ability, or other differences. Based on the neutral measure of muscle marks on the limb bones, it is possible to more accurately evaluate economic activity in the past, as shown by a study of skeletal remains from post-medieval London that indicates equal involvement of women and men in commercial weaving.

Unconscious assumptions render the heterosexual, monogamous relationship the standard for all humans including our remotest ancestors, as if other kinds of sexual relationship did not exist and all other relationships were secondary. The Laetoli footprints left by a pair of australopithecines are automatically attributed to a heterosexual couple, even though the notable size difference between the prints suggests a child and an adult. Geller notes how any evidence indicating monogamy and nuclear families is seized upon while signs pointing to other relationships go unnoticed. For instance, three graves at the 4,600-year-old Eulau, Germany site contain one male or female adult and 1–3 children, but another grave that consists of a male, female, and two children is the one researchers and the media hold up as the most significant. Likewise, a 5,000-year-old pair of skeletons found in Italy and positioned in an embrace is uncritically accepted as the picture of romantic love between a man and a woman, as if no other interpretation need be considered.

Similarly, bioarcheological evidence from pre- and post-contact Maya sites has been interpreted as showing effects of economic change on men's but not women's bodies as a result of their purportedly separate productive activities and domestic and child care duties, respectively. However, ethnographic and other archeological evidence indicates that the ancient Maya – including female and male rulers – did not have dichotomous, asymmetrical gender roles or behavior, or consider sex equivalent to gender. The case shows that, as in the study of contemporary societies, it is essential to question concepts about the social significance of biological distinctions between people that may appear all the more natural when applied to physical remains, but are nonetheless culturally shaped.

. . . . .

This chapter has shown that women and men do not have opposite inborn priorities for choosing a mate owing to male provisioning among human ancestors. Evolution has not made men choose mates superficially or indiscriminately, for fatherhood entails far more than fertilization and is not something men automatically evade. It has not rendered females unable to make a living or heedless of a potential mate's qualities so long as he is wealthy. To the contrary, women's preference for good relationship and parenting skills makes solid evolutionary sense, considering that in an ancestral environment females had access to the material necessities of life. For both women and men, sexual relationships are not just about procreation, and not the only meaningful human bond.

Patrilineal inheritance rules, patriarchal families, and other means of limiting or precluding women's economic independence and sexual autonomy are the products of certain social and cultural systems, not human biology. As seen in the next chapter, the reasons for today's gender inequalities are close at hand, rather than fixed in the distant past.

Notes

1 On body size and sperm competition across primate species, as discussed in the text and Tables 7.1 and 7.2, see Jolly (1985, 1999).
2 Jolly (1999) reports testes volume as 2.5 ounces in gorillas and humans, versus 4 ounces in chimpanzees, compared to body weights of 450, 175, and 100 pounds, respectively.
3 Regarding hormones, pair bonding, and paternal care, see Gettler et al. (2012); Rilling and Young (2014).
4 On bonobo sexual and social behavior, see De Waal and Lanting (1997).
5 See for example Dijkstra and Barelds (2008).
6 On theories regarding breasts and waists in human evolution, see Singh and Young (1995).
7 On sex differences in visual ability, see Eliot (2009).
8 See Nowell and Chang (2014); Soffer et al. (2000).

References cited

Alexander MG, Fisher TD. 2003. Truth and consequences: using the bogus pipeline to examine sex differences in self-reported sexuality. *Journal of Sex Research* 40(1):27–35.

Brown PJ, Konner M. 1987. An anthropological perspective on obesity. *Annals of the New York Academy of Sciences* 499(1):29–46.

Buss DM. 1989. Sex differences in human mate preferences: evolutionary hypotheses tested in 37 cultures. *Behavioral and Brain Sciences* 12(1):1–14.

Cassell J. 1997. Doing gender, doing surgery: women surgeons in a man's profession. *Human Organization* 56(1):47–52.

Conley TD. 2011. Perceived proposer personality characteristics and gender differences in acceptance of casual sex offers. *Journal of Personality and Social Psychology* 100(2):309–329.

Dettwyler KA. 1995. Beauty and the breast: the cultural context of breastfeeding in the United States. In Stuart-Macadam P, Dettwyler KA, editors. *Breastfeeding: biocultural perspectives*. New York: Aldine de Gruyter. p. 167–205.

De Waal F, Lanting F. 1997. *Bonobo: the forgotten ape*. Berkeley: University of California Press.

Dijkstra P, Barelds DP. 2008. Do people know what they want: a similar or complementary partner? *Evolutionary Psychology* 6(4):595–602.

Dobrin LM, Bashkow I. 2010. "Arapesh warfare": Reo Fortune's veiled critique of Margaret Mead's sex and temperament. *American Anthropologist* 112(3):370–383.

D'Onofrio BM, Rickert ME, Frans E, Kuja-Halkola R, Almqvist C, Sjölander A, Larsson H, Lichtenstein P. 2014. Paternal age at childbearing and offspring psychiatric and academic morbidity. *JAMA Psychiatry* 71(4):432–438.

Eastwick PW, Finkel EJ. 2008. Sex differences in mate preferences revisited: do people know what they initially desire in a romantic partner? *Journal of Personality and Social Psychology* 94(2):245–264.

Edmonds A. 2013. Can medicine be aesthetic? Disentangling beauty and health in elective surgeries. *Medical Anthropology Quarterly* 27(2):233–252.

Eliot L. 2009. *Pink brain, blue brain: how small differences grow into troublesome gaps – and what we can do about it.* Boston: Houghton Mifflin Harcourt.

Ellis W, Bercovitch F, FitzGibbon S, Roe P, Wimmer J, Melzer A, Wilson R. 2011. Koala bellows and their association with the spatial dynamics of free-ranging koalas. *Behavioral Ecology* 22(2):372–377.

Fisher TD. 2007. Sex of experimenter and social norm effects on reports of sexual behavior in young men and women. *Archives of Sexual Behavior* 36(1):89–100.

Fry DP. 2006. *The human potential for peace: an anthropological challenge to assumptions about war and violence.* New York: Oxford University Press.

Gal D. 2012. A mouth-watering prospect: salivation to material reward. *Journal of Consumer Research* 38(6):1022–1029.

Geller PL. 2009. Bodyscapes, biology, and heteronormativity. *American Anthropologist* 111(4):504–516.

Gettler LT, McKenna JJ, McDade TW, Agustin SS, Kuzawa CW. 2012. Does cosleeping contribute to lower testosterone levels in fathers? Evidence from the Philippines. *PLoS One* 7(9):e41559.

Gurven M, Hill K. 2009. Why do men hunt? A reevaluation of "man the hunter" and the sexual division of labor. *Current Anthropology* 50(1):51–74.

Hill KR, Walker RS, Boži evi M, Eder J, Headland T, Hewlett B, Hurtado AM, Marlowe F, Wiessner P, Wood B. 2011. Co-residence patterns in hunter-gatherer societies show unique human social structure. *Science* 331(6022):1286–1289.

Jolly A. 1985. *The evolution of primate behavior.* New York: Macmillan Publishing Company.

Jolly A. 1999. *Lucy's legacy: sex and intelligence in human evolution.* Cambridge, MA: Harvard University Press.

Kilgallon SJ, Simmons LW. 2005. Image content influences men's semen quality. *Biology Letters* 1(3):253–255.

Kong A, Frigge ML, Masson G, Besenbacher S, Sulem P, Magnusson G, Gudjonsson SA, Sigurdsson A, Jonasdottir A, et al. 2012. Rate of de novo mutations and the importance of father's age to disease risk. *Nature* 488(7412):471–475.

Little AC, Jones BC, Penton-Voak IS, Burt DM, Perrett DI. 2002. Partnership status and the temporal context of relationships influence human female preferences for sexual dimorphism in male face shape. *Proceedings of the Royal Society of London B: Biological Sciences* 269(1496):1095–1100.

Mead M. 1935. *Sex and temperament in three primitive societies.* New York: William Morrow.

Nowell A, Chang ML. 2014. Science, the media, and interpretations of Upper Paleolithic figurines. *American Anthropologist* 116(3):562–577.

Reno PL, Meindl RS, McCollum MA, Lovejoy CO. 2003. Sexual dimorphism in Australopithecus afarensis was similar to that of modern humans. *Proceedings of the National Academy of Sciences* 100(16):9404–9409.

Rilling JK, Young LJ. 2014. The biology of mammalian parenting and its effect on offspring social development. *Science* 345(6198):771–776.

Rusbult CE, Kumashiro M, Kubacka KE, Finkel EJ. 2009. "The part of me that you bring out": ideal similarity and the Michelangelo phenomenon. *Journal of Personality and Social Psychology* 96(1):61–82.

Schell H. 2011. The love life of a fact. In Howlett P, Morgan MS, editors. *How well do facts travel? The dissemination of reliable knowledge.* Cambridge, UK: Cambridge University Press. p. 429–453.

Shackelford TK, Goetz AT. 2007. Adaptation to sperm competition in humans. *Current Directions in Psychological Science* 16(1):47–50.

Singh D, Young RK. 1995. Body weight, waist-to-hip ratio, breasts, and hips: role of judgments of attractiveness and desirability for relationships. *Ethology and Sociobiology* 16(6):483–507.

Soffer O, Adovasio JM, Hyland DC. 2000. The "Venus" figurines: textiles, basketry, gender, and status in the Upper Paleolithic. *Current Anthropology* 41(4):511–537.

Todorov A, Mandisodza AN, Goren A, Hall CC. 2005. Inferences of competence from faces predict election outcomes. *Science* 308(5728):1623–1626.

Wedekind C, Seebeck T, Bettens F, Paepke AJ. 1995. MHC-dependent mate preferences in humans. *Proceedings of the Royal Society of London B: Biological Sciences* 260(1359):245–249.

Weismantel M. 2001. *Cholas and pishtacos: stories of race and sex in the Andes*. Chicago: University of Chicago Press.

Wolfe LD, Gray JP. 1982. Latitude and intersocietal variation of human sexual dimorphism and stature. *Human Ecology* 10(3):409–416.

8

HOE AND PLOW, PIG AND COW

Work, family, and gender stratification

The idea that women and men have evolved entirely different sexual and reproductive interests presumes male provisioning and female dependency. The image of men "bringing home the bacon" equates jobs in office buildings and factories with hunting large animals. Meat stands in for money, the source of all the material necessities of life. Work and home are spatially divided into two separate, unequal spheres: a masculine public sphere of self-interest, politics, economics, competition, and thought; and a feminine private or domestic sphere of selfless caregiving, affective relationships, cooperation, and emotion. Women's economic dependence is built into the system, and ensures that men provide only for their own children.

It would seem that paternity certainty, male-headed nuclear families, and patrilineal kin groups are the natural foundation of human societies. However, world societies fail to conform to these allegedly timeless facts of human nature. As we will see, women are not everywhere marginalized from production, or men from family life, whether conceptually or in practice.

. . . . .

Contrary to the assumption of discontinuous sexual, reproductive, and productive roles, long-term relationships between females and males arose millions of years ago along with cooperative parenting of infants born several years apart. For most of human history, males and females both have had access to food they could obtain directly. Both were economically productive and both took care of children and grandchildren. In short, the concept of male provisioning is unsuitable with respect to ancestral foraging societies. It is a poor fit to historical and contemporary populations that forage or practice low-intensity food production, as well.

Kinship organization and gender inequality are interconnected. Whereas kinship in foraging societies is organized bilaterally in the majority of cases, unilateral systems predominate in societies with wealth to be controlled and passed on between generations, such as land, houses, equipment, and herds. Matrilineal or matrifocal societies are common among societies which practice low-intensity agriculture, but virtually absent from societies with intensive agriculture. Intensive agriculture brings wide disparities in rank and roles between women and men as well as between people of different social classes, and is generally associated with patrilineal kinship. Gender stratification is especially pronounced in plow-based societies (Boserup 1970).

Today's industrialized societies grew out of plow-based agricultural societies and carry forward the association of work with masculinity. Work figures prominently in evolutionary theories about social organization, family relationships, and the way our minds function, because work is highly meaningful in industrialized societies. Work not only is the primary source of income for most people, but also is central to social life, personal identity, and status. Older people enter a separate category when they stop working for pay. Jobs with bigger salaries are more highly esteemed than those which pay less. People's worth may even be described in dollar amounts, as in the case of wealthy men ("He's worth four million dollars") or beautiful women ("She looks like a million bucks in that dress").

In a wage-based economy, remuneration demarcates work from non-work, with the consequence that work attains higher social value than non-work. In contrast, from ancient times to the industrial era, work was culturally disvalued as the burden carried by slaves and the laboring classes. Even intellectual labor was considered physically exhausting and injurious.

In foraging and subsistence farming, work and other tasks of daily life are not clearly separated. No one could be considered to work, if only paid labor were counted. Taking a comprehensive view of work as all effort related to the running of economic and household enterprises makes it clear that women work in every society, although there may be social class differences in the amount of work required of both women and men.

In addition to conjuring an imagined past of meat-eating, the image of men "bringing home the bacon" defines hunting and gathering as an opposed pair of economic activities. Yet, many indigenous cultures symbolically link hunting with women's reproductive functions through beliefs and rituals that highlight the shared elements of blood, life, and power and danger. The ancient Sumerian, Greek, and Roman female goddesses who oversaw the hunt were also the goddesses of childbirth (Ninhursag, Artemis, and Diana, respectively). Among the Ndembu of southern Africa, a man's hunting ability may be inherited from either his mother or father, and the spilt blood of hunted animals is equivalent to women's blood wasted in menstruation rather than procreation (Turner 1967).

Moreover, in defiance of the expectation that breadwinners eschew domestic involvement, for hunters there is nothing dishonoring about taking care of babies and children. Aka fathers in central Africa may even calm a fussy baby by putting it to their breast (Hewlett 1991). For men in indigenous Andean societies, active involvement in parenting is a source of pride and social status. Sexuality and masculinity are associated with being a good father to children and other relatives – whether biological or acquired – not the shunning of family life (Weismantel 2001).

The breadwinner-housewife opposition presumes that families are composed of romantically involved couples and their children.[1] Yet, other marriage systems and household structures are not only possible but common. Marriage often unites people for strategic reasons and may not involve sex, as seen below. Not all cultures include a concept of the family as a distinct unit, such as the Zinacantecos of southern Mexico, or prescribe love between relatives – not even between mothers and daughters, as in modern Zambia and historically among the Cheyenne of the Great Plains (Collier et al. 1997). In addition, children in many societies may have multiple fathers or mothers.

Children may have more than one biological father in indigenous societies throughout the world, including the Philippines, India, New Guinea, and South America (Beckerman and Valentine 2002). Shared paternity is customary in the majority of Amazonian societies. It is consistent with foraging and low-intensity food production, in which women and men are mutually interdependent. To illustrate, the Barí of Venezuela combine farming with fishing and hunting. They believe that optimal fetal growth requires additional bathings of semen after conception. To avoid exhausting her husband, a pregnant woman may have a lover or two. These men bring her gifts including meat and fish. They are considered biological fathers, forever linked in substance to the child, and their contribution has the concrete effect of reducing the likelihood of miscarriage and stillbirth.

Children in many African and Australian societies have multiple fathers due to complex kinship systems which intermingle biological and social paternity. For instance, among the early 20th century Nuer of Sudan, men were considered the fathers of all the children born to their wives, including the offspring of lovers taken by their widows. Both men were related to the child, but kinship was determined by the first husband. In the matrilineal Trobriand Islands society, fertilization occurred when the spirit of a dead woman tired of resting and returned to the sea water to enter a woman's body. Sexual intercourse during pregnancy helped the fetus grow and explained why children often looked like their fathers. European scientists of the early 20th century asserted that the first male to fertilize a female animal, including a female human, left an imprint on the appearance of all her subsequent offspring.

In some societies, biological parenthood is unimportant relative to social parenthood. Among the Samo of Burkina Faso young women traditionally would spend a few years with a lover of their choice before joining their arranged husband. They brought their first child to the husband, who thereupon was considered its father. Among the Nuer, the practice of "ghost marriage" ensured that a man who remained childless or unmarried at death would leave descendants. A male relative would use the man's herds to pay bridewealth (discussed below), which thereby defined the woman's offspring as the children of the deceased.

Cultural beliefs about social paternity and multiple biological paternity undermine the supposition that human marriage systems serve the purpose of establishing genetic relatedness as a precondition for men's commitment to fatherhood. They also challenge the assumption that men are hardwired to take lovers in order to improve their own reproductive success. Shared paternity does nothing for the secondary fathers and costs them resources they could devote to their own genetic offspring. As we will see, exclusive paternity is a salient concept where property is kept within male lines of descent, but this also is not a cultural universal.

. . . . .

Cultural expectations about father-headed simple families as the true or natural condition for humankind have cast other family types as aberrations since the first instances of contact between non-Western societies and European colonists and missionaries. Scholars ranked other societies and their ways along an evolutionary scale from savagery to barbarism to civilization. Anything unfamiliar was taken to represent a lower stage of advancement, such as believing in many gods rather than one, using a digging stick instead of a plow, or organizing family relationships along female rather than male lines.

According to anthropologists of the 19th and early 20th centuries such as Lewis Henry Morgan (1877), primitive matrilineal systems automatically gave way to the more elevated masculine institutions of patriarchal civilized society. The reverse – a change from patrilineal to matrilineal organization – was considered impossible. In the New World, this meant that indigenous tribes further south should be patrilineal, whereas those further north should be matrilineal given their shorter history on the continent. Through meticulous research on names, crests, and property among late 19th century Kwakiutl (Kw g'ul) tribes of the Canadian Pacific Northwest, Franz Boas (1966) showed that this progression was false.

Boas found that Kwakiutl kinship combined elements of both the matrilineal clans to the north, such as the Tsimishian and Tlingit, and the patrilineal clans to the south, such as the Nootka and Salish. Rather than becoming more like their southern neighbors, the Kwakiutl had been adopting some of the northern people's matrilineal ways. Furthermore, over the following decades Boas came to the conclusion that it was not possible to classify the tribes as either matrilineal or patrilineal. Through work with many tribes throughout North America, including the Crow, Shoshone, and Hidatsa, Robert Lowie (1920, 1948) concurred that indigenous kinship systems changed in response to contact between societies and that even those which formally appeared unilateral were in fact bilateral.

In the patrilineal societies typical of herding and plow-based agricultural societies, kinship, property, and political relationships are envisioned in masculine terms. Multigenerational, multiple-family households are made up of male relatives and their wives and children, as well as unmarried adult relatives. Women's status and authority are inferior to men's and depend on seniority together with the birth of sons. Access to lovers and divorce is denied to women, while marriages are arranged with property and strategic alliances in mind. The system favors closer relationships within gender and age categories than between them, in contrast to the emphasis on conjugal and parent-child relationships where simple family households predominate.

The patrilineal household or *zadruga* of northern Albanian and western Bosnian Muslims provides an illustration (Byrnes 1976). Traditionally, children slept in their parents' room until the age of 12, after which they were moved to all girls' or all boys' rooms. If a mother left the family, any children over age 7 belonged to the zadruga. Today, marriages continue to be arranged between families. Women work incessantly while confined to the house and immediate area. They remain invisible to guests, their chastity carefully guarded. Men defend their interests through an ancient honor code and blood feuds lasting generations.

In contrast, in matrilineal societies women own land, hold titles, rule over large areas, and dominate trade, religion, and political decision-making – with or without the collaboration of men. Women remain in their natal households their entire lives; men either remain with their sisters or move to their wives' households. Only the children of sisters belong to the family, for the children of brothers belong to their wives' lineages. Men's property goes to their sisters' children. As a result of these rules of residence and descent, children's most important adult male relative tends to be one of their maternal uncles, not their father. To people in matrilineal societies, this way of doing things is as obvious and straightforward as the Euroamerican inclination to trace genealogical links through male relatives.

To illustrate, the Na people (also known as Naze, Mo-So, and Mosuo or Musuo) living in the mountains of China's Yunnan and Sichuan provinces near Tibet are organized in female-centric extended families (Hua 2002). In both affective and economic terms, Na society emphasizes matrilineal relationships over ties created by marriage. Usually the matrilineal household is headed by a woman and her brother, but there can also be just a woman or a male relative in charge. Women and men both have many lovers simultaneously and over their lifetime, until entering a celibate phase after around age 60. As a result, the father of a child may remain unknown. Fathers and children have no formal mutual obligations and are not members of the same kinship groups. However, in practice, fathers engage in parenting activities from direct infant and child care to financial support, and often develop close relationships with their children.

Na men live in their own natal families, with whom they work in fishing and farming. Starting in adolescence they visit women for amorous encounters. Sometimes the visits become more open and committed, and the man is invited to spend time with the woman's family. If either family needs a laborer, a lover may come to live with them. In rare cases there is a feast, after which the couple is considered to be married. The couple's families are not formally united by these relationships, although marriage entails some minimal reciprocal obligations. In both marriage and long-term relationships in which couples live together, individuals of both sexes may continue to have secret liaisons with other sexual partners and publicly-known relationships without cohabitation. Women and men both may maintain several relationships of different kinds at the same time, and they prefer visits to marriage.

Some societies are matrifocal or female-centered without matrilineal kinship. They may be patrilineal, patrilocal, and even polygynous, but women own property such as houses and fields, control food production, market food, and occupy the principal political and social roles. Among the Lovedu of southern Africa, men owned land and held political and prestige positions but the chiefs were women, who generally played a determining role in matters of economics, marriage, and religion. The markets in many West African societies continue to be dominated by women today, with the help of men who haul and transport goods. These women have a relatively high degree of independence and authority within the family, in spite of an overall context of gender inequality.

In matrifocal societies, the husband-father often is absent from the mother-children household, either because he has several families or migrates for work. Examples include horticultural societies in West Africa, Indonesia, and the Caribbean; African-American communities in which single-parent families are prevalent; and historical peasant societies in Europe from which more men migrated for work than women, and stayed away longer.

Marriage systems not only vary from the patrilineal ideal type, but also do not necessarily concern sex or romantic love. For instance, in many pre-colonial African societies a widow could marry another woman to help with running the household. Among the Igbo and Yoruba of Nigeria, elite women could have wives as a way to increase their own status and wealth. These wives would live with men but their children belonged to the female husband. Among the Nuer of the Sudan, an infertile woman had the social status of a man and consequently could marry a woman. Her wife would provide her children through relations with a man paid for the purpose.

Variability in transfers of wealth at marriage also challenges the breadwinner-housewife construction whereby women are defined as an economic commodity and liability. Many African societies practice bridewealth (also known as bride-price), or payments of animals, property, money, and other assets from the groom's family to the wife's family. These gifts are a form of acknowledgment of the birth family's loss of a laborer and may be accompanied by ceremonies in which the community mourns her departure. Some foraging societies, including the Mbuti in Africa, the Au and Gnau in Papua New Guinea, and the Tiwi of Australia, prescribe lifelong gifts from husbands to mothers-in-law and other relatives.

In contrast to bridewealth, dowry tends to denote low female status. Dowry involves payments from the bride's family to the groom's. It was practiced historically in Europe and remains common in Central and South Asia. Where dowry is considered the woman's property, although managed by men, the payments are relatively protective of women. Dowry customs that transfer ownership to husbands and their birth families have the opposite effect. In parts of India, wives have been murdered by their husband or his relatives over demands for dowry disbursements.

Plural marriage appears to support the concept of male provisioning, but it occurs in situations where there are large disparities in wealth and status and consequently is unlikely to have been typical of ancestral human societies. Notably, marriages involving more than two spouses do not account for the majority in any society. In most cases, plural marriage involves one man and more than one woman, properly known as polygyny, after the Greek *gunē* for woman. The term polygamy, from *gamos* for marriage, encompasses both polygyny and polyandry, or marriage between one woman and more than one man, from *andr-* for man.

Polygyny is practiced in parts of Africa, the Middle East, Asia, and Oceania, and existed historically in Europe and North America. It may result from the surplus of widows generated by a later marriage age for men than women, as occurs in some African and indigenous Australian societies. The levirate, a custom recorded in the legal codes of the Ancient Near East and common in many African societies, dictates that widows must marry their husband's brother whether he is already married or not. In other cases, political or economic strategies explain plural marriage. For elite men such as kings or chiefs, multiple wives are needed to oversee different parts of their territory or to represent different family groups, as was the case before colonization in Uganda. Among the Betsileo of Madagascar, wives live in separate houses near the rice fields they individually manage, each contributing to the husband's total wealth.

Polyandry, or multiple husbands, occurs or existed until recently among indigenous societies of Nepal, Tibet, northern China, north India, south India, South America, Arctic Canada, some Pacific Islands, Sri Lanka, southern Arabia, and Kenya and northern Tanzania. It was practiced in northern and southern Europe in ancient times. Polyandry occurs where women control land and production and there is enough of a surplus to create large status differences, as among the Nayar (Nair) of the Malabar Coast in Kerala State, southern India, who have been forbidden by the Indian government to maintain matrilineal households. Alternatively, it is a response to either land scarcity or the chronic absence of men for war or labor migration. By uniting multiple husbands, households are assured that at least one man will always be present to take care of the tasks assigned to males. In fraternal polyandry, a woman marries two or more brothers, the eldest of which is considered the father of all the children. The custom keeps landholdings intact, as in Tibet where the amount of arable land is strictly limited.

Where multiple wives live in the same household, children grow up with multiple mother-figures. In many polygynous African societies, wives choose their husbands' subsequent wives from among their own relatives. Tupi-Kawahíb men of Brazil may marry a set of sisters or a mother with daughters from a previous marriage. In both cases, children's biological tie to a particular mother is submerged in the current of daily living among female relatives who reside, work, and raise children together.

In addition, milk kinship creates multiple mothers in societies throughout the world, including South America, Europe, Africa, South Asia, and the Middle East. Milk kinship forges lifelong relationships between children and the families of women besides their mothers who have breastfed them. In these societies, feeding creates biological connectedness to the same or a greater degree than conception or childbirth, to the point of precluding intermarriage between people related through milk (Khatib-Chahidi 1992).

The variety in family forms and kinship relationships around the world contradicts the presumed universality of concern for exclusive paternity and control over women's sexuality and economic autonomy. Children may have separate biological and social parents and multiple mothers or fathers. Their identity may be defined in terms of maternal relationships, paternal relationships, or both. The marriage bond is not always the locus of romantic love or the most significant relationship for adults, and does not always entail living together. In sum, the breadwinner-housewife is an ideal type familiar to contemporary industrialized societies rather than a biological mandate for gender inequality and male provisioning.

. . . . .

Evidently, the male-headed simple family is not a cultural universal sprouting automatically from evolved human nature, but a social institution that arises in particular circumstances. Likewise, gender stratification is patterned rather than spontaneous or natural; it is the predictable result of proximate factors, not the obligatory outcome of ultimate causes. In particular, gender inequalities arise from systems in which women primarily do work that produces use-value and men concentrate on work that produces exchange-value (Ward 2003). Work that produces use-value benefits family members and includes caregiving, domestic labor, and work for goods or wages consumed within the household. In contrast, exchange-value is the result of work that generates cash, influence, or other resources that can be traded. This kind of work creates obligations and political relationships with people and institutions in the world beyond the family. Cross-culturally, there is a tendency for men to monopolize work that produces exchange-value, do less use-value work than women, and use their earnings independently and strategically as opposed to dedicating them to household needs.

While nomadic foraging favors egalitarian relationships across the board, including between genders, the possibility of food or water storage weakens the need for interdependence and permits incipient forms of social inequality, as seen in Chapter 10. In addition, male control over the distribution of meat can generate inequality, given that meat is a scarce and unreliable food source relative to plants. It is command of a key resource that brings disparities in status and influence, not the absolute caloric value – since that would give women the advantage in many if not most cases (see Chapter 5).

Ernestine Friedl (1978) compares foraging societies along an ascending scale of gender inequality and male control over meat. She observes that the most egalitarian foraging societies are those which practice net hunting and communal gathering in teams. These include the Washo of North America; the Mbuti, Efe, Aka, and other "pygmies" of the Central African Republic; and the Agta of the Philippines.

To illustrate, the Washo living in the Sierra Nevada range about a century ago spent the spring and summer fishing in Lake Tahoe, with everyone participating. As seeds and berries became available, women switched to gathering while men continued to fish. In the fall the community hunted rabbits with nets, and men hunted deer. Couples gathered pine nuts for the winter. As is typical in foraging societies, married men and women both were permitted to have lovers, to divorce their spouse, and to remarry multiple times.

Gender egalitarianism among the Washo is evident in the absence of ritual seclusion of menstruating women. This is significant because menstruation is seen as dangerous and polluting by Native American societies in which women's status is lower than men's – as it is in other stratified societies throughout the world. In addition, the Washo held major ritual celebrations both for gathering and for hunting. While individual men could distinguish themselves through hunting and men tended to lead the group in decisions about migration, women also had leadership roles. Relative gender equality derived from joint participation in most food procurement activities and the lack of centralized distribution. In a word, Washo-style equality is based on cooperation.

The next-most-egalitarian societies on Friedl's scale are ones in which men and women each collect their own food, such as the Hadza of Tanzania. Hadza women and men have access to abundant plant foods and small animals, and consequently can collect food independently. Families share an evening meal procured by women. If men kill a larger animal such as a zebra or impala, they bring it back to split with the whole group. The occasional exchange of meat renders men's status somewhat higher than women's. There are no leaders, although successful hunters tend to have more people in their camp. On the other hand, couples generally live near the wife's mother, towards whom the son-in-law takes on lifelong gift obligations. Plural marriage is rare, and divorce is equally available to women and men. In this kind of society, egalitarianism is based on independence.

Lower on the egalitarianism scale are societies in which men and women work separately but return to camp to share their food, such as the Tiwi of Melville and Bathurst Islands off the northern coast of Australia. Tiwi women gather palm nuts and other plant foods and hunt small animals such as lizards and opossum with dogs. Men go out less often and concentrate on larger animals such as kangaroo and large lizards. They bring in much more meat than women, but less food overall. Whereas plant foods – especially palm nut porridge – are consumed within the family, all meat is cooked by a male or female volunteer and distributed to the entire community by the person who obtained it. Gender-separated economic activities and male control over large game result in inequalities reflected in the betrothal of girls before puberty and the acceptability of polygyny. On the other hand, cross-cousin marriage and residence near both maternal and paternal relatives offset men's advantaged social position. Widows choose their own next husband, and both women and men have a say in the marriage of their children and grandchildren.

Among the Ju/'hoansi of the Kalahari Desert, women's gathered food is consumed within the family, whereas game is divided into shares and distributed first to members of the hunting party, followed by blood relatives, in-laws, and the rest of the community. Able hunters mediate exchange relationships with other bands, have a greater say in group decisions about migrations, and attract more people to their group. On the other hand, women and men's food-procurement activities overlap: men collect water and plant foods, and women provide useful information to hunters. Among the Tiwi and Ju/'hoansi, egalitarianism derives from interdependence and sharing.

The very rare foraging societies in which men provide almost all of the food through hunting, such as populations of the far North, fall last on the continuum. Inland Inuit groups traditionally ate caribou hunted year-round, whereas the coastal diet included whales, seals, fish, and some game. Women processed the animals for cooking, clothing, and other products, whereas men traded whale oil, seal oil, and hides. Low female status and high male status competition resulted in polygyny, mistreatment of women by suitors and husbands, and female infanticide.

It should be noted that gender inequality among the Inuit may not have been as severe as it appeared to Friedl. E.A. Hoebel (1954) concluded that infanticide was a response to high male mortality due to men's greater exposure to danger. He found that, although headmen and shamans led some Inuit bands, the Inuit did not have political hierarchies that supported powerful leaders. Women were sometimes complicit in wife stealing, and they did not always return to their husband after he won a dispute with a rival. In addition, the arctic environment does not necessarily favor male control over food production. For instance, Ainu forager men in northern Japan obtained meat from marine and land sources, but the population depended at least as much on the trapped hares and gathered plants procured by women, who also provided scores of medicinal foods.

In any event, Friedl's analysis shows that gender equality is a function of unrestricted access to valued items; impartial rather than strategic distribution of food resources; and collaboration in food production. The highest degree of subordination of women, as among the Inuit, comes where women have little or no part in obtaining and distributing important resources. In all cases, even those in which women contribute the majority of the calories and procure animal protein, if men trade goods outside the household they gain power through the obligations created in others.

Friedl's framework suggests that, in any society, if women, but not men, use their material and social assets only within the family, their status will be lower. For instance, in contemporary Western society, women without paid employment occupy a lower status position than men, including within the household. In the workplace, jobs which do not provide opportunities to control resources and thereby create obligations do little to improve women's status. This explains why there are fewer barriers to women's work in caregiving and clerical positions compared to managerial and executive jobs.

. . . . .

Food production and the surplus wealth it produces are associated with fundamentally different social and economic relationships than nomadic foraging. As in the comparison above, the degree of stratification rises in step with men's command of scarce resources, even if women do most of the productive labor. The extent of stratification depends also on the way kinship is organized and the intensity of agricultural production.

Low-intensity agriculture, or horticulture, requires a larger land area than agriculture but produces lower yields. It is well suited to tropical areas where plants mature year-round and to areas with abundant additional resources such as fish.

The combination of accessible food and low need for storage tempers the tendency towards social stratification. The use of relatively simple tools such as digging sticks, hoes, and axes ensures that women are not excluded from production. Horticulture is or has recently been practiced in Papua New Guinea, South Asia, Africa, and the Americas. Women tend to be the primary producers or to share responsibility equally with men, who work in plant cultivation to varying degrees and may also hunt and fish. In both of two data sets concerning hundreds of horticultural societies, responsibility for food production is shared equally by women and men in one-third of cases. In 39% and 50% of societies, women are primarily responsible for food production. In the remainder, 17% and 28%, men do the majority of the work.[2]

Many horticultural societies practice shifting cultivation involving the slash-and-burn technique for clearing and fertilizing land used for a few years and then left to recover for much longer. Horticultural populations often raise pigs, which are easy to care for because they do not have to be accompanied to pasture and eat everything including household scraps. Depending on the permanence of settlements, land may be held by temporary use rights or as private property owned by women, men, or both.

The work of a horticultural society is organized in a variety of ways. Some phases of production involve women and men together; others are divided by gender. It is common for women to clear undergrowth and men to slash trees, perhaps with the help of young and old people of both sexes, but duties beyond this phase are less predictable. Among the tribes of the Upper Xingu River Basin in central Brazil, women do the planting, weeding, and harvesting of crops, but Semai boys and men in Malaysia prepare the holes in which women plant seeds. Among the Konyak Nagas in India, men plant seeds which women then cover with dirt. Girls and boys are tasked with weeding, while women and men harvest millet and rice together.

Prestige crops and animals raised for ceremonial or trading purposes may be the purview of men, women, or both. In West Africa, both men and women cultivate and market prestige and subsistence crops. In highland New Guinea, men concentrate on trading prestige crops and pigs, whereas women raise pigs and market subsistence crops.

Martha Ward (2003) observes that horticultural societies do not have automatic brakes on rivalry between women and men, unlike the cooperation and suppression of competitiveness which are essential to nomadic foraging. On the other hand, the appearance of within-gender solidarity and suspicion or disdain of the opposite sex may mask true interdependence and collaboration. With reference to indigenous South American populations, Claude Lévi-Strauss (1963) argues that, because men's work is intermittently but noticeably productive whereas women's work yields reliable but ordinary results, women "are actually cherished, but ostensibly depreciated."

The fact that women are not economically marginalized in horticultural societies suggests that the degree of gender stratification depends less on their work than other factors, namely a higher level of production, pressure on resources, and conflict with neighboring societies. These conditions tend to be associated with patrilineal, patrilocal societies, in which women but not men are separated from their relatives. In contrast, small societies with low population pressure and abundant resources tend to have higher degrees of gender egalitarianism. Crops are grown for use, economic relationships are guided by the principles of reciprocity and redistribution, and there is a stronger tendency towards matrilineal kinship. Matrilineal societies account for 24% of simple horticultural societies but only 12% of advanced horticultural societies and 4% of agricultural societies. Significantly, the likelihood of matrilineal kinship is inversely related to the proportion of the diet obtained through herding or hunting. As the proportion of hunted or farmed animal food increases from up to 15% to 16–25% to 26% or more, the percentage of matrilineal societies declines from 30% (n=60) to 24% (n=54) to 14% (n=29), respectively (Nolan and Lenski 2011).

In sum, horticulture is associated with a variety of economic and kinship systems. Matrilineal kinship and equal access to food sources and tools militate against inequality. Contrariwise, patrilineal kinship and male control over socially and politically valuable resources widens gender disparities.

. . . . .

Compared to foraging and horticulture, herding offers the possibility of relatively large stores of wealth. Historical pastoralists include the Aryans, the Mongols, and the Germanic tribes of early medieval Europe. Recent or current populations include herders in the Middle East, Europe, Africa, Asia, South America, and the American Southwest and Plains regions.

Men in pastoral societies tend to own the herds, provide supplementary animal products through hunting or fishing, and decide whether to use the animals for trade, gift, or slaughter. Women, men, or both may be responsible for accompanying the animals to pasture and carrying out other tasks such as milking, as well as gathering, farming, or trading for plant foods with villagers. Variability in herd size generates competition and status differences between family groups.

Stratification in herding societies varies depending on the environment, social organization, and gender divisions of labor. In sparsely populated areas of the world, such as Scandinavia and northern Eurasia, herders tend to be nomadic or semi-nomadic and relatively egalitarian and unconcerned about boundaries. To illustrate, extended families of Eveny herders and their domesticated reindeer follow wild herds of reindeer across a vast, icy landscape. Women and men in extended-family groups have complementary roles and tasks. Men tend to deal more with live animals, women more with meat, hides, and fur. Women may own herds and be heads or co-heads of families. Both women and men are expected to behave with reserve, respect, and self-reliance. Their perseverance in a harsh, thinly populated environment is favored by cultural codes that emphasize interdependence and mutual appreciation (Vitebsky 2005).

In contrast, pastoral societies of the circum-Mediterranean region (North Africa, southern Europe, and the Middle East) are highly stratified. Herders compete for land and water with each other, agricultural populations, and urban settlements. Herds attract raiders, leading to intense concern about boundaries and property. Men control the economics of herding. Women process animal products and may also tend kitchen gardens and raise small animals such as rabbits or chickens, but their sphere of activity is limited to domestic buildings and grounds. Patrilineal kinship is the rule, with groups of brothers bringing wives into the family. Women enter marriage with a dowry, are not allowed to divorce, and may not remarry if widowed. They may inherit property such as houses and furnishings, but flocks are passed only between men.

These characteristics have been described by John Campbell (1964) in relation to Sarakatsani shepherds in 1950s Greece. Sarakatsani families moved twice a year between summer pastures in the mountains and winter pastures in the lower plains. Brothers and their families consolidated flocks inherited from fathers at around age 60, but often would have to disperse when their wives could no longer get along with each other. Women's only source of income was the sale of eggs. Gender roles were explicitly modeled on religious beliefs about the Holy Family. In particular, collective family honor depended on women's sexual restraint, which related men policed together just as they defended their flocks.

The neighboring Vlachs, a separate ethnic group of herders, were less patriarchal. Women's status was higher and cultural codes about honor were less pronounced. Campbell attributed the difference to more stable settlements, which allowed women a greater degree of social integration and kept them in closer contact with their relatives. In addition, the mixed economy provided women access to a variety of income-generating activities that rendered them more independent. The comparison of two societies sharing a single economic system clearly illustrates the effect of women's financial autonomy and kinship networks on gender roles and behavioral expectations.

. . . . .

While herding and horticulture may be associated with either low or high degrees of gender egalitarianism, agriculture very consistently is accompanied by social stratification, patrilineal kinship, and pronounced gender and socioeconomic inequality – although there are exceptions, as seen below.

Relative to horticulture, agriculture involves more concentrated use of some or all of the factors of production: labor, land, inputs, and equipment. Intensive agriculture is newest system for meeting human nutritional needs, dating only to the last 5,000–6,000 years. It brings greater ecological impacts and faster population growth than the others. Agriculture requires permanent farmlands and settlements, which, along with demographic expansion, generates more competition and conflict within and between societies.

In foraging, horticultural, and herding societies, women's labor in food production is compatible with child care. Mothers carry babies in a sling while older children help with the work. Plow agriculture involving draft animals or heavy machinery, as well as other intensive agricultural practices such as irrigation or terracing on steep hillsides, entails work that is dangerous or hard to do while carrying an infant or looking after small children. For this reason, women's work in agricultural societies tends to involve other kinds of farm and household labor, including the care of animals, the processing and preservation of food, water and fuel collection, and the production of textiles and other goods for use and for sale. As in the other societies considered thus far, the work is not separated from family life.

Agricultural societies reverse the female-concentrated work pattern typical of horticultural societies. In two ethnographic samples, responsibility for food production is primarily male in 59% and 81% of societies, female in 8% and 15%, and shared in 33% and 3%.[3] In terms of specific tasks, plow-based agriculture tends to restrict women's participation in clearing land and harvesting crops, and to exclude women from soil preparation and planting and tending crops.

Intensive agriculture generally places women in a position of social inferiority and institutionalized economic dependence. Women labor significantly more than men (see below), but the work does not give them status, autonomy, or security, given that they are barred from landownership and the most socially valued tasks. Patrilineal kinship and patrilocal residence ensure that related men work together and control property, production, and distribution. Women's work is focused on the homestead and performed in relative isolation, for marriage displaces women from their relatives and childhood friends. Divorce is highly restricted if not disallowed for women.

In patriarchal societies, informal customs and formal laws bar women from the sphere of politics and economics. These societies have religious and philosophical beliefs to match, such as Confucianism in the East and Judaism, Christianity, and Islam in the Middle East and West, each of which advances the view that women are intrinsically inferior to men. The three world monotheistic religions all arose among herders in competitive ecological environments, who tend to worship a distant, harsh, male god who determines the weather and seasons on which animal migrations depend, and whose role in the universe is mirrored by men's role in the society and family. In contrast, agrarian religions throughout the world emphasize fertility and include female goddesses and religious leaders, while foraging and horticultural societies worship ancestor spirits and sacred places and animals, without a gender bias. These comparisons highlight the marginalization of the female in the religions of patriarchal societies and the congruence of religious beliefs with social structures.[4]

Both in ideology and in practice, girls and women of patriarchal agricultural societies must be attached to a father, husband, or other adult male as a matter of survival. Male provisioning is a material-legal reality backed up by cultural codes such as the "honor and shame complex" prescribing reciprocal sexual and economic rights and obligations for women and men. To maintain honor, men must provide economically for their wives, control their wives' and other female relatives' sexuality, and demonstrate their virility through the birth of children. Wives may dishonor their husbands by withholding sex, having affairs, or engaging in economic activity. Shame refers to the social forces pushing women and men to behave appropriately in sexual and economic terms. These ideologies generate tension and danger because in most agricultural societies, women are needed as laborers and must leave their homes, either regularly or periodically, to participate in farm work.

The emphasis on women's sexual probity reflects the importance of legitimate birth to patrilineal societies with permanent landownership. Accordingly, women's sexuality is depicted as predatory and destructive, in need of male control to keep it cool and in check. Menstrual blood is defined as impure, polluting for men, and exceedingly potent and dangerous. Women must remain virgins until marriage and chaste wives thereafter. Their identity is defined by their marital status and marked linguistically and by other means such as ornaments and dress. Men, but not women, may have lovers and abandon their spouses.

Honor and shame beliefs are endemic to geographical areas with weak state control and intense competition over boundaries and property, such as the traditional agro-pastoral societies of the Mediterranean area (Schneider 1971). Related men must unite in defense of shared property and family honor, but at the same time are internally divided by competition over limited assets. Women become objects through which men threaten and compete with each other. It is women's duty to deflect improper sexual attentions. The Hittites' law 197 decrees that, "If a man seizes a woman in the mountains, it is the man's crime and he will be killed. But if he seizes her in (her) house, it is the woman's crime and the woman shall be killed. If the husband finds them, he may kill them: there shall be no punishment for him" (Pearson Education 2004).

By conducting an affair, particularly in the home, a wife emasculates her husband and dishonors her father and brothers. The custom of displaying bloody sheets the morning after a wedding expresses the need for public recognition that the bride has not given precedence to any other man. In patriarchal societies, women continue to be assaulted and killed by husbands, brothers, and fathers as punishment for adultery, being raped, or breaking cultural norms concerning female modesty. These honor crimes occur in the Middle East, North Africa, southern Europe, Pakistan and India, and Latin America, as well as among immigrants elsewhere, and continue to be treated with leniency even where the legal basis for reduced sentencing has been removed (Welchman and Hossain 2005). Traces of honor-and-shame ideologies remain in Western culture, where rape remains underreported, promiscuity is judged negatively in women but positively in men, and a wife's high salary is considered emasculating to her husband.

At the same time as agricultural societies institute male dominance across the board, socioeconomic stratification places men in a continuous competitive struggle for difference rather than equality of rank. Men assert their masculine potency through jokes and threats in all-male environments such as bars and through displays such as cockfighting, sheep raiding, and a posture of sexual aggression toward women. Meanwhile, they must behave submissively toward more powerful patrons who provide them access to jobs and public services including education for their children. In addition, they are expected to actively demonstrate their role as providers and protectors, which conflicts with the symbolic association between nurturance and femininity. In the home, the opposition between masculinity and cooking and cleaning forces men to defer to women for basic needs, and they often find themselves outranked in family decision-making as well.

The tension between the idea of male dominance and the realities of daily existence gives rise to creative outlets for expressing men's fears and vulnerabilities, such as Mexican ballads, Sardinian shepherds' verbal dueling, and cross-dressing during Carnival in Europe and Latin America. These cultural institutions express the ambiguities and contradictory forces at play even where male dominance is institutionalized and actively asserted.

. . . . .

In some cases, intensive agriculture does not lead to the marginalization of women from production and consequently a high degree of gender inequality. For instance, among the Betsileo of Madagascar women do more than half of the work involved in producing food. They pound rice after working with other women or together with men on all the other tasks including transplanting, weeding, and harvesting. Kinship is bilateral. Although couples tend to live near the husband's family, women maintain strong ties with their birth families and wider descent groups. Both men and women are mentioned in offerings to the ancestors, participate in politics, and hold office. Men's political participation is greater, but women have a larger say in marriage alliances. Women market produce, sponsor ceremonial feasts, and buy livestock such as cattle. In short, as is typical of South Asian peasant societies, relative gender equality results from complementary economic roles and kinship systems that emphasize maternal ties equally or more than paternal ones (Kottak 1980).

Similarly, marriage and residence rules counteracted male dominance in mid-20th century southern Italian farming communities. Couples lived near the wife's relatives and women inherited houses as well as land, whereas men inherited only land. Men's loyalties were dispersed from their birth families and subordinated to the relationship between their wives' sisters and their mother-in-law. Women's concentration in towns gave them control over family finances and dealing with government officials, and resulted in their being preferentially hired for office and service jobs. As a result, the precepts of male dominance and honor-and-shame ideology were actively expressed but did not accurately represent the world (Davis 1969).

An example from Portugal illustrates how economic complementarity can result in the absence of honor and shame ideology even in an area of the world known for it. Jan Brøgger and David Gilmore (1997) observe that men are not dominant in ideology or action in Nazaré, on the northwest coast of Portugal. Men fish, oversee the auctioning of fish, and control the town council. Fishing is highly valued socially, which gives men status, honor, and self-esteem as well as the opportunity for male company. However, since the daily buying and selling of fish is done by women, men's work does not allow them to monopolize social, economic, or political life. Indeed, men are less socially integrated than women because couples live near the wife's family. Women in Nazaré rule the household, like other women in Mediterranean societies, but their boldness does not turn to meekness when they step outside. On the streets and at the fish market, women talk in loud voices, use sexual profanities, and even get into physical fights. Men move at a slower pace; they relax in the bars. Virginity is not demanded of brides, and marrying pregnant is neither unusual nor socially condemned. In short, ideas about honor and shame do not resonate in a society in which women and men share responsibility for goods traded outside the household.

Even where ideologies of male dominance appear obvious and uncontested, they do not necessarily correspond to actual gender inequalities or universally-held beliefs. For instance, in working class areas of Mexico City, men are expected to drink, treat women with brutality, and prefer spending time with friends than family, but many men live in companionate relationships and stay close to home. Matthew Gutmann (1996) describes how men often envy their wives' closeness to their children and would like to spend more time with their families, including infants – not just older children and teenagers, as is expected of men in the community. For their part, some women encourage men to take on more domestic responsibilities, but others exile men from their homes and make it awkward for them to express willingness or capability with respect to domestic tasks.

Gutmann explains that even if domesticity is culturally disvalued, in practice it is prized by individual men. Men may champion ideologies of machismo while at the same time admiring women for their activities, achievements, and dedication to family and community. In fact, the neighborhood women are at least if not more involved in paid labor and community activism than the men. Women handle matters involving government offices, are involved in political and religious organizations, and have been responsible for bringing infrastructural improvements such as electricity to the community. They built the road themselves. Their actions show that stated beliefs and everyday realities are not always aligned.

Finally, the transition from agricultural to industrial society highlights elements of both systems that carry positive and negative effects for women and men. By following changes in a town in Andalusia, Spain, from the early 1960s to the early 1980s, Jane Collier (1997) shows how marriage shifted from a union of co-owners to coworkers. From an extended-family, face-to-face society in which women occupied important positions in kin networks and motherhood was highly valued, the town transitioned to a simple-family, urban-anonymity society in which an ideology of maternal sacrifice was eclipsed by an emphasis on women's physical attractiveness. The transition was marked by a change in married women's appearance, from shapeless bodies and drab clothes – including black wool mourning dress worn for the rest of a widow's life – to slim figures, fashionable clothes, and noticeable makeup. This visible change reflected a shift in worldview linked to changed perceptions of the source of social and gender inequalities.

Collier explains that in the 1960s, people's identity and opportunities were understood to depend upon inheritance – of land, social status, and control over resources such as political or professional positions. Legitimate birth was therefore of utmost importance, and procreation was the purpose of marriage. Marriage joined land and other capital derived equally from the wife and husband. Consequently, a woman's standard of living reflected her parents' economic standing rather than her husband's financial worth. Women held considerable authority with regard to family and economic decision-making and were revered in older age. While they did not have much scope for self-realization in an honor-and-shame system that limited the social roles available to them, women's respect for tradition was rewarded with economic security and social esteem.

By the 1980s, socioeconomic inequalities were taken to depend on occupational achievement as reflected in salaries and jobs. Whereas a woman's domestic sphere formerly included her entire neighborhood, now it was limited to an isolated, urban apartment. In the past, wives and husbands spent their evenings apart: women at home or out visiting relatives and the bedridden, men drinking in bars. Now, couples spent their evenings together, for conjugal life no longer represented duty and sacrifice but, rather, the opposite of work and the way to fulfill all social and emotional needs and desires. For wives, marriage no longer meant shared stewardship over property but partnership with a wage-earner whose work was better-compensated than theirs. Couples were structurally unequal and women lost authority over domestic matters, even if they also worked outside the home. Women fretted about gaining weight, for their appearance was now a lifelong concern. The trajectory towards increasing influence with advancing age had changed direction. These common features of industrialized societies reinforce the point that paid labor does not in itself resolve underlying gender inequalities, and that the inequalities in agricultural societies vary across settings in line with differences in kinship, property ownership, and marriage.

. . . . .

As noted above, in industrialized societies work is envisioned as the main pathway to economic advancement and an index of personal capability and value. Work is defined as morally uplifting, a social obligation, and a patriotic duty. The association of work with masculinity recalls the symbolic connection linking men with fields and farm work but women with domestic spaces and duties. This public-private division continues to be taken for granted as a natural, inevitable, or divinely inspired arrangement.

In reality, women have never been absent from the labor force in industrialized societies. Even during the economic boom years in postwar America and Europe, when the proportion of homemakers was unusually high, women made up 30–40% of the official workforce (compared to about one-half today). Industrialization began with predominantly female workers employed in factory labor and piece work, whereas men were more likely to remain employed in agriculture or independent crafts and professions. On the other hand, the class of managers and owners was predominantly male given that men controlled economic and political capital from the start. Over time, men flooded the industrial labor force as mechanization and land consolidation reduced the need for farm workers.

The increased mobility of the labor force demanded by the industrial economy favored simple families as opposed to the multigenerational households of siblings and their families which are typical of farmers; reduced childbearing; and the weakening of patrilineal kinship. For urban industrial workers, marriage no longer had the scope of forging family and economic alliances. The reduced importance of land and legitimate birth to people's life chances made prestige and status ranking systems more fluid and complex, and women's sexual probity less vital to their material wellbeing. Patronage relationships gave way to merit-based systems of advancement. Gossip and reputation lost their power to regulate the behavior of both women and men. Mandatory education distanced young people from family control as state institutions grew in reach and power. Divorce eventually was legalized, as was women's control over property. However, marriage and kinship systems in industrialized societies have retained some of their earlier characteristics, for naming practices and cultural beliefs continue to privilege male lines of descent, and companionate marriage nonetheless concerns property and multiple legal rights and responsibilities.

Within industrialized societies, subpopulations with recent ties to agricultural society are more likely to behave according to its gender expectations. Second-generation immigrant women born in the US and Europe whose parents and husbands' parents came from plow-based societies are less politically and economically active than women whose relatives came from other kinds of societies. Gender beliefs contrary to female paid labor are transmitted more strongly by husbands' than wives' parents, and by couples' mothers than fathers. In other words, parents, and especially mothers of husbands, have a notable impact on the likelihood that wives work outside the home (Alesina et al. 2013).

Cultural beliefs about the incompatibility of work and motherhood draw their authority from alleged roots in nature or history. However, leaving aside the heavier and more dangerous tasks in intensive agriculture, farming and foraging can be done contemporaneously with child care and allow parents of both sexes to remain physically near their children. Much of the work in industrialized societies, by contrast, requires the separation of parents from children. When jobs are scarce, paid work tends to be construed as properly male – leaving aside female-associated professions such as nursing or early-childhood education. Scientific ideas flourish about women's biological unsuitability for work, and the damaging effects of work on women's reproductive functions and children. Emily Martin (1987) shows how scientific studies proclaiming that work is antithetical to motherhood, or the opposite, have appeared in alternating bursts over the last century in response to intense labor competition or a scarcity of male workers, respectively – for example, after and during major wars.

As might be expected based on cross-cultural and historical evidence of women's work as the norm rather than exception, the weight of evidence indicates that *not* working is harmful to women and their families. Mass adherence to breadwinner-housewife roles among middle-class Americans during the 1950s and 1960s brought an epidemic of relationship troubles and psychological distress among both women and men, and resulted in widespread alcoholism and other forms of chemical dependency along with increased child abuse (Whitaker 2016). Recent longitudinal research has shown that women who work full time have a higher level of physical fitness, feel more energetic, and are at lower risk of depression than women who do not work, work part time, or work full time but experience periods of unemployment. After the birth of their first child, women who return to work full time are healthier at age 40, even after controlling for working women's better health beforehand (Frech and Damaske 2012). Their children likewise are advantaged relative to children of non-working mothers. A meta-analysis of 69 studies shows that women's work outside the home after the child's first year has positive effects on children's academic achievement and behavior management at older ages. Results are mixed for the first year of the child's life, but most differences are small and statistically nonsignificant (Lucas-Thompson et al. 2010).

The idea that women's work conflicts with pregnancy and mothering is untenable considering that women do the majority of the world's work while also bearing and raising children. To illustrate, in rural areas in the Ivory Coast, women's total work burden is 3 hours a day longer than men's. Women have less leisure time and, moreover, consume an amount of daily calories that falls well below international nutritional standards and the amount needed to cover their energetic needs (Levine et al. 2001). This is a typical situation for rural societies in impoverished countries worldwide as well as the US and Europe until as recently as the last century. The "breadwinner effect" ensures that husbands and children receive more and better-quality food than mothers, and thereby contributes to persistently high levels of maternal malnutrition, anemia, and mortality. The practice results in growth deficits, chronic health problems, and cognitive defects in the next generation, along with increased infant and child mortality rates among girls (United Nations System Standing Committee on Nutrition 2010).

Rather than being provisioned by men, women in these circumstances provision men, sparing them hunger and physical effort. The higher female than male mortality rates historically associated with agriculture (see Chapter 3), indicate that women have provisioned men in this way for a long time.

Gender inequalities that limit women's economic autonomy are not decreed by nature but arise through social institutions such as patrilineal kinship and male control over tradeable assets. In stratified societies, unequal access to legal rights, education, property, and employment is built on the belief that women and men are differently made. The next chapter focuses on the alleged grounding for this idea in the separate skills needed for hunting and gathering.

Notes

1 Regarding kinship and gender roles described in this chapter, see Godelier (2012); Lévi-Strauss (1969); Ward (2003).

2 Proportions regarding women and men's contribution to production are from Martin and Voorhies (1975); Nolan and Lenski (2011). The first source concerns 104 horticultural and 93 agricultural societies; the second 389 horticultural and 100 agricultural societies. For the original compilations of ethnographic material on hundreds of societies, see Murdock (1967, 1981).

3 See note 2.
4 Regarding religious beliefs across cultures and time, see Adovasio et al. (2009); Durkheim (1915); Evans-Pritchard (1965).

References cited

Adovasio JM, Soffer O, Page J. 2009. *The invisible sex: uncovering the true roles of women in prehistory*. Walnut Creek, CA: Left Coast Press.

Alesina AF, Giuliano P, Nunn N. 2013. On the origins of gender roles: women and the plough. *Quarterly Journal of Economics* 128(2):469–530.

Beckerman S, Valentine P, editors. 2002. *Cultures of multiple fathers: the theory and practice of partible paternity in lowland South America*. Gainesville: University Press of Florida.

Boas F. 1966. *Kwakiutl ethnography*. Codere H, editor. Chicago: University of Chicago Press.

Boserup E. 1970. *Woman's role in economic development*. London: Allen & Unwin.

Brøgger J, Gilmore DD. 1997. The matrifocal family in Iberia: Spain and Portugal compared. *Ethnology* 36(1):13–30.

Byrnes RF, editor. 1976. *Communal families in the Balkans: Zadruga*. Notre Dame, IN: University of Notre Dame Press.

Campbell JK. 1964. *Honour, family, and patronage: a study of institutions and moral values in a Greek mountain community*. Oxford: Clarendon Press.

Collier J. 1997. *From duty to desire: remaking families in a Spanish village*. Princeton, NJ: Princeton University Press.

Collier J, Rosaldo MZ, Yanagisako S. 1997. Is there a family? New anthropological views. In Lancaster RN, di Leonardo M, editors. *The gender/sexuality reader: culture, history, political economy*. New York: Routledge. p. 71–81.

Davis J. 1969. Honour and politics in Pisticci. *Proceedings of the Royal Anthropological Institute of Great Britain and Ireland* 1969(1969):69–81.

Durkheim E. 1915. *Elementary forms of the religious life*. New York: MacMillan.

Evans-Pritchard EE. 1965. *Theories of primitive religion*. Oxford, UK: Clarendon Press.

Frech A, Damaske S. 2012. The relationships between mothers' work pathways and physical and mental health. *Journal of Health and Social Behavior* 53(4):396–412.

Friedl E. 1978. Society and sex roles. *Human Nature* 1:8–75.

Godelier M. 2012. *The metamorphoses of kinship*. Scott N, translator. New York: Verso.

Gutmann MC. 1996. *The meanings of macho: being a man in Mexico City*. Berkeley: University of California Press.

Hewlett BS. 1991. *Intimate fathers: the nature and context of Aka Pygmy paternal infant care*. Ann Arbor: University of Michigan Press.

Hoebel EA. 1954. *The law of primitive man: a study in comparative legal dynamics*. Cambridge, MA: Harvard University Press.

Hua C. 2002. *A society without fathers or husbands: the Na of China*. Hustvedt A, translator. New York: Zone Books.

Khatib-Chahidi J. 1992. Milk kinship in Shi'ite Islamic Iran. In Maher V, editor. *The anthropology of breastfeeding: natural law or social contract*. New York: Berg. p. 109–132.

Kottak CP. 1980. *The past in the present: history, ecology, and cultural variation in highland Madagascar*. Ann Arbor: University of Michigan Press.

Levine JA, Weisell R, Chevassus S, Martinez CD, Burlingame B, Coward WA. 2001. The work burden of women. *Science* 294(5543):812.

Lévi-Strauss C. 1963. *Structural anthropology*. Jacobson C, Schoepf BG, translators. New York: Basic Books.

Lévi-Strauss C. 1969[1949]. *The elementary structures of kinship.* Bell JH, von Sturmer JR, Needham R, translators. Boston: Beacon Press.
Lowie RH. 1920. *Primitive society.* New York: Liveright.
Lowie RH. 1948. *Social organization.* New York: Rinehart.
Lucas-Thompson RG, Goldberg WA, Prause J. 2010. Maternal work early in the lives of children and its distal associations with achievement and behavior problems: a meta-analysis. *Psychological Bulletin* 136(6):915–942.
Martin E. 1987. *The woman in the body: a cultural analysis of reproduction.* Boston: Beacon Press.
Martin MK, Voorhies B. 1975. *Female of the species.* New York: Columbia University Press.
Morgan LH. 1877. *Ancient society: researches in the lines of human progress from savagery through barbarism to civilization.* New York: Henry Holt and Company.
Murdock GP. 1967. *Ethnographic atlas.* Pittsburgh: University of Pittsburgh Press.
Murdock GP. 1981. *Atlas of world cultures.* Pittsburgh: University of Pittsburgh Press.
Nolan P, Lenski G. 2011. *Human societies: an introduction to macrosociology.* 11th ed. Boulder, CO: Paradigm Publishers.
Pearson Education. 2004. *Documents in Western civilization.* Volume 1. Upper Saddle River, NJ: Pearson Prentice Hall.
Schneider J. 1971. Of vigilance and virgins: honor, shame, and access to resources in Mediterranean societies. *Ethnology* 10(1):1–24.
Turner VW. 1967. *The forest of symbols: aspects of Ndembu ritual.* Ithaca, NY: Cornell University Press.
United Nations System Standing Committee on Nutrition. 2010. Sixth report on the world nutrition situation. www.unscn.org/files/Publications/RWNS6/html/. Accessed 23 May 2016.
Vitebsky P. 2005. *The reindeer people: living with animals and spirits in Siberia.* Boston: Houghton Mifflin Company.
Ward MC. 2003. *A world full of women.* 3rd ed. Needham Heights, MA: Allyn & Bacon.
Weismantel M. 2001. *Cholas and pishtacos: stories of race and sex in the Andes.* Chicago: University of Chicago Press.
Welchman L, Hossain S, editors. 2005. *"Honour": crimes, paradigms, and violence against women.* London: Zed Books.
Whitaker ED. 2016. *An analysis of Betty Friedan's the feminine mystique.* London: Macat International Ltd.

9

TALE OF TWO-SPIRITS

Constructing gender and sexuality, aptitudes and inclinations

Besides incompatible sexual/reproductive interests and opposed roles in production versus domestic life, evolution allegedly has generated cognitive differences between women and men. Hunting purportedly has left men intelligent, adventuresome, good at math and science, and adept at visuo-spatial tasks, whereas gathering has made women intuitive, prudent, verbally proficient, and specialized for handicrafts. Media reports and academic research celebrate any evidence of gender differences congruent with these expectations, especially disparities in the size, density, or electrical activity of particular brain structures or regions. Differences with an apparent material basis are taken to reveal something eternal and immutable about masculinity and femininity. Gender consequently appears to be an outgrowth of sex, and behavior a predetermined manifestation of brain anatomy. Studies finding no divergence on a test or neuroanatomical measurement are unlikely to be published and are ignored by the media. As a result, gender differences appear to be more numerous and important than similarities.

The previous chapters challenged the vision of prehistory as a time of dependency and incessant childbearing for females, with food procurement split between plants gathered by women and animals hunted by men. The provider-dependent relationship could not have arisen before people began to cultivate food and settle in villages, and is favored by intensive agriculture and heightened resource competition. This chapter shows that cultures around the world do not uphold identical expectations about the aptitudes and inclinations of women and men. Gender roles vary, sometimes in a mirror-image way. Diversity in on-the-ground behavior and capabilities undermines the idea women and men are born with separate mental traits and faculties.

Moreover, sex and gender both are fluid categories, confounding the search for universal truths about a human race divided neatly into two discontinuous groups. The plasticity of the brain results in anatomical and functional adaptations which challenge the sex/gender binary and the presumed direction of brain-to-behavior causal relationships. Gaps in test performance between females and males change over time, casting doubt on the permanence of gender differences and the underlying idea of inborn, sex-limited mental traits. As we will see, proximate factors such as stereotypes and unequal educational opportunities explain current gender disparities more effectively than ultimate causes rooted in imagined primordial roles and abilities.

. . . . .

The idea that evolution has prepared women and men for different duties is a poor predictor of gender divisions of labor worldwide.[1] In Euroamerican society, sewing is considered a feminine occupation, but men are the ones to make, weave, and decorate cloth in societies such as the Mbuti of the Central African Republic, the Hopi of North America, the Agta of the Philippines, and many populations of West Africa, including the Asante of Ghana. In defiance of the association of building trades with men, women construct and maintain houses among the Maasai in Kenya, the Mbuti, and many historical Native American groups. Hidatsa women made the boats for use on the Missouri River; Pawnee and other Native American women worked wood. Along the Sepik River in Papua New Guinea, where flour made from the pulp of the sago palm is the staple food, some societies consider it women's work to chop and process the trees. Others along the same river just as resolutely believe it is "natural" for men to do this work.

Even stone tools – the presumed achievement of males throughout prehistory – are made exclusively by women in some societies. For instance, Konso women in southern Ethiopia quarry rock and work it into flaked stone tools according to techniques learned through apprenticeship. They transmit the trade from one generation to another along exclusively female lines. The men consider the work beneath them (Arthur 2010).

As noted in Chapter 2, stone tools serve many purposes besides hunting, including cutting and scraping plant and animal foods, cleaning hides, and making shelters and clothing. Additional tools are used for catching and trapping fish and animals, cooking, and transporting goods. It is impossible to know if ancestral males or females made any of these tools to the exclusion of the other sex. The same holds for creative arts and plant and animal domestication. Evidence from current societies suggests a need to rethink the seemingly commonsense assumptions that males were responsible for all prehistoric technological innovation and everyday tool use, and that tools were developed mainly for the purpose of hunting.

The association of masculinity with technical ability and the work world, but femininity with sociality and domesticity, is the fruit of stratified agricultural societies and therefore a recent invention. As seen in previous chapters, foraging societies divide food-procurement tasks in a variety of ways that do not confine women to plants, men to animals. Gatherers and hunters cover similar distances and spend the same amount of time working. Work does not produce durable stores of wealth that engender social stratification. The work of food procurement or dealing with equipment is not separated from social and family life; to the contrary, children learn by observing and imitating parents while they work. Fathers not only care for older children but hold, carry, and comfort babies. There is little specialization, which limits the degree to which work defines people's identity and creates social distinctions.

Another reason to question the impact of work on the evolution of mental traits is that our ancestors' survival did not require devoting the whole day to looking for something to eat. Foraging takes much less time and effort than farming. Even today's foragers, who are forced to live on marginal land, average only a few hours a day collecting food. This leaves 12 or more waking hours for other activities, which also are important for survival and reproductive success. Besides the necessities of daily life, such as building temporary shelters or gathering firewood and water, foragers have ample time for the things people do in all societies – sharing meals, participating in ceremonies and social gatherings, gossiping, philosophizing, creating art, teaching children, playing games, falling in love, strategizing about the future, dealing with conflicts, telling stories. There is no inherent reason to privilege specific types of food procurement over these other activities as the basis for human mental traits and gender differences.

Yet, framing gender traits in terms of hunting and gathering is exactly the strategy favored by researchers working under an evolutionistic paradigm. In particular, studies aim to demonstrate the alleged effects of hunting on spatial ability in men. For instance, American college students' behavior in a shopping mall has been interpreted as the result of gender-disparate navigational methods (Kruger and Byker 2009). That is, women are said to favor object location, whereby they keep track of the position of various low-price items in space. Men, in contrast, are described as using a search-and-destroy approach for finding expensive items such as appliances: they know what they want and dash in and out alone to get it by the most direct route.

In reality, the work of gathering and hunting is nothing like either style of shopping. Gathering does not mean simply picking fruit off of bushes at eye level. Hunted animals do not lie around in plain sight, waiting to be shot and snatched up. If young men and women tend to move differently through a shopping mall, social customs provide a ready explanation. Girls and women are expected to enjoy shopping, whereas boys and men are not encouraged to linger in shopping centers with their friends.

In an attempt to more faithfully reproduce an ancestral environment, some researchers conduct experiments outdoors. A study on mushroom collection in a Mexican forest determined that the women and men returned with the same quantity by weight, but that on average the men ventured farther, went to higher altitudes, visited fewer sites, and gathered fewer species of mushroom (Pacheco-Cobos et al. 2010). They expended more calories and strained their hearts more. This result is taken as proof that women naturally are more efficient gatherers, but social and cultural factors predict it. In Mexico as in most of the world, girls and women tend to be better trained at identifying plants and food in general, and to learn to avoid danger by staying close to home.

Contemporary nomadic foraging populations are the best model for ancestral society, but they do not provide support for the idea that women and men are governed by different orientation styles. For instance, researchers found no difference in spatial skills between indigenous Baffin Island men and women. Women hunted as much as men and used the same navigational techniques to get around on water and land (Berry 1966).

The abilities needed for gathering and hunting are not opposed or mutually exclusive. Both hunting and gathering require the ability to read the terrain and sky for direction, and the ground and vegetation for finding plant foods and tracking animals. Both involve working with others. In the ancestral environment, males did not need special skills for collecting a unique food source; females did not have a monopoly on communication. Women and men have the same visual and verbal equipment. The situation could hardly be otherwise. For natural selection to result in a trait passed genetically only to males or females, the trait must be advantageous to one sex but not the other. Moreover, complex mental functions involve multiple genes, and the undersized Y chromosome is an unlikely location. In short, the idea of sex-limited skills for gathering or physical orientation in a natural environment is biologically implausible and unsupported by ethnographic evidence.

. . . . .

As seen in Chapter 6, measured sex differences in the activity or size of certain brain areas do not necessarily reflect inborn traits. Brain anatomy and functioning are shaped by use, and use, in turn, is influenced by culture. At the same time, plasticity can make people more rigidly and unconsciously attached to habitual ways of seeing and doing things, because repetition solidifies and speeds specific mental processes. Attitudes and behavior consequently may seem ingrained even if they have developed through learning and use instead.

The brain's lifelong responsiveness to gender expectations begins the first day of life, if not sooner, for girls and boys are treated differently from the start. There is no culture-free stage of infant development. Human babies are born before their brains are ready, which makes caregiving an absolute necessity. They seek out adult attention and bend to its influence. Babies are attuned to the voices, smells, and movements of the people around them. They are social, and they use strategies such as imitation and crying to keep caregivers nearby. They understand other people's emotions and motivations and they constantly revise and reformulate their mental constructs through interactions with other people. Babies quickly learn to categorize themselves and others by gender, and are expected to be dressed and to behave in line with established conventions. Separate colors for clothes, toys, and bedroom décor forcefully mark the distinction. All of this management and interpretation of the outside world plays a critical role in brain development. In other words, the differential treatment of babies based on gender has a direct effect on female and male brains.

Parents perceive and handle their children in line with gender stereotypes even during the first 24 hours. This has been demonstrated by Jeffrey Rubin et al. (1974) through a study involving girl and boy babies born in the same hospital and evaluated to ensure that there was no visible difference in size or vigor. The parents were given a checklist of traits. Parents of girls were more likely to tick the boxes for inattentive, passive, weak, delicate, small, and pretty. Parents of boys more frequently described their babies as attentive, alert, coordinated, strong, and active. Accordingly, girls were treated delicately, whereas boys were handled playfully. Verbal communication predominated with girls; physical communication was more likely with boys. Fathers were more extreme in their gendered evaluations than mothers.

More recent studies have shown a decline in parents' and especially fathers' biases about boys and girls. In a study modeled on the one above, parents did not use stereotypes when freely describing their babies (Karraker et al. 1995). However, the stereotypes came through in parents' ratings of their newborns on a prepared scale. As in the previous study, girls were more likely to be described in terms of beauty and delicateness, boys in terms of alertness and vigor, although the differences were much smaller.

Experiments in which babies are dressed or named oppositely to their true sex uncover the same gender associations. When adults think the child is a boy (even though a girl), they see strong facial features, attentiveness, robustness, irritability, and anger. When a girl is accurately presented as a girl or when a boy is dressed as a girl, adults perceive a delicate, placid, happy, and socially oriented child (Stern and Karraker 1989).

Besides placing the sex of the child foremost, birth announcements for girls are more likely to express happiness whereas for boys they express pride. Gonzalez and Koestner (2005) suggest that these feelings are linked to different "motivational systems" surrounding attachment and status, respectively. Parents unconsciously channel their children's treatment and opportunities in line with the expectation of amiability from girls, accomplishments from boys.

In a study of 11-month-old babies presented a downward-sloping carpeted ramp, researchers found that the boys and girls had the same physical ability, but the girls were willing to attempt steeper slopes than the boys. The mothers were a different matter. Asked to regulate the angle of the slope before their child was challenged with it, mothers of girls significantly underestimated their children's ability, placing the ramp at a much gentler angle – 9 degrees lower on average – than did mothers of boys, who were off by less than one degree (Mondschein et al. 2000).

Parents' assumptions about children's strength are out of line with the relative biological weakness of male children, which causes more failed conceptions, stillbirths, and deaths in infancy. Boys score lower than girls on the APGAR and Brazelton scales for assessing wellbeing after the stresses of delivery and contact with the outside world. Boys are born larger but less mature than girls, with negative effects on respiratory, immune, and neurological functioning. Until school age, boys are less adaptable, more vulnerable to infectious diseases, and fussier.

Evidently, the reason girls are given fewer opportunities for physical play and training is cultural beliefs rather than natural limitations. Differences in adult athletic performance are not indicative of inborn female weakness, given that a lack of early training leads to reduced performance in adulthood. Over the last several decades, as girls' participation in sports has risen dramatically, female athletes and military recruits have challenged established ideas about the female body. In sports such as swimming and running, today's female professional athletes surpass the level of all of the top male professional athletes of two or three generations ago. In addition, military recruits have shown that women are not more susceptible to sports injuries, after all (Jones et al. 1990). The higher rate of injury among women military recruits in the past turns out to be due to a difference in the average level of physical conditioning of the research subjects; women and men of the same fitness level have the same injury rate. In sum, whether or not true sex differences affect muscular strength or other measures of athletic ability, an individual's ability to do pull ups or run a marathon depends far more on training than sex.

As long as people believe that girls and boys have different physical and cognitive abilities it will be impossible to know whether or not they truly do, for unequal experience will continue to affect the ways in which their bodies and brains are constituted and operate. Rapid changes in athletic performance over the last several decades have not been the product of population-wide changes in human biology, but altered social investment in girls' opportunities for training and practice. These and other changes discussed below challenge traditional wisdom about women and men's natural endowments.

. . . . .

In addition to the impact of differential treatment on children's physical and mental development, the assumptions that humans come in only types, and that sex determines gender, cast doubt on the validity of purported evidence of essential differences between women and men. To the contrary, as seen in Chapter 6, many people are born with mixed genetic and phenotypic sexual traits, while in others phenotypic sex does not match with chromosomal sex. In addition, there are cultural systems around the world in which multiple sexual and gender identities coexist.[2]

The idea that gender identity stems directly from sex and is established before birth draws support from the adverse experiences of some individuals subjected to surgical sex reassignment in infancy due to intersex conditions or complications during a circumcision. This was standard practice in some US hospitals from the 1960s–1980s, when it was also applied to boys born with a very small penis. David Reimer, who was born in 1966, was surgically and hormonally reassigned as female after an unsuccessful circumcision.

Reimer grew up with a female appearance but never took to his assigned sex, and committed suicide at age 38. Reimer's case suggests that developmental processes during gestation affect gender identity in enduring ways. On the other hand, in other cases of male-to-female gender reassignment the children have grown up completely comfortable with their female identity. Moreover, Reimer had an identical twin brother and was nearly 2 years old when his gender change was made – an age by which infants have developed a strong sense of gender. Reimer's physician, John Money, spent many sessions with Reimer and his brother over the ensuing years, and has been blamed for causing severe psychological distress in them both.

Without excluding the possibility of a "hardwiring" influence on gender identity, the varied life experiences of intersex, transgendered, and transsexual people demonstrate the fact that gender is not embodied as only one of two mutually exclusive forms, and does not necessarily remain fixed for life. Just as individuals may radically change their sex/gender identity over time, societies may change the categories defining sex/gender groups. For instance, in Cuba, the revived sex trade, which had been suppressed until the 1990s, generated multiple and shifting categories of nonconforming sexual identity, behavior, and emotional attachment. Now, under the force of increasing contact with the outside world, these variegated ways of being and living are changing again in line with homogenizing international definitions of the meaning of gay and transsexual (Stout 2014).

Evidently, sex and gender categories, and the relationship between them, are culturally defined. Even in societies with a rigid sex/gender binary, it may be possible for some individuals to change their identity or combine gender and sexuality in nonstandard ways. For instance, in parts of northern Albania, families without a male heir may designate a young daughter to assume the social role of a man. The "sworn virgin" dresses and behaves as a male, with all the usual masculine duties and privileges, from owning land and engaging in blood feuds to smoking, drinking, and acting as host to any guests who come to the compound. These women may marry another woman if someone is needed to fulfill female functions in the household. The relationship is not sexual, similarly to marriage between women in other societies mentioned in the last chapter.

Albanian sworn virgins have explained to Antonia Young (2000) that being a woman involves so much toil and subordination that they do not hesitate to become a man if offered the chance. Sometimes the conversion is so complete that the woman does not develop breasts and never starts her menstrual cycle. One of the women told Young that her greatest satisfaction in life was the knowledge that she would be buried in men's dress upon her death. These women's lives as undisputed males demonstrate the cultural constructedness of gender, a template so compelling that it can alter biological sex characteristics.

In parts of Afghanistan and Pakistan, families with many girls or no sons may allow one of their daughters to live as a *bacha posh*, a girl "dressed up as a boy." The parents are treated with more respect, and the putative son relieves the father of tasks forbidden to girls because they require going out in public, such as shopping. Girls dressed as boys can work and attend school. While in their boy identity, they are self-confident, unafraid, and domineering towards their sisters. At puberty or sometimes later, their parents force them to return to being girls, usually because of an arranged marriage, but they struggle with the loss of status and the imposed confinement of their clothes and domestic space. Unlike Albanian sworn virgins, they do not have the option of living permanently as males unless they emigrate.

In contrast to traditions by which some individuals assume completely, if temporarily, the attributes of the other gender in a binary system, the Native American two-spirit tradition permits the combination of gender characteristics and sexuality in creative, idiosyncratic ways. The term refers to the presence of two opposite spirits in the same person, whether animal-human or male-female. Virtually all Native American tribes covering all parts of the North American continent have included two-spirits or at a minimum lacked beliefs that would have precluded their existence.

Early European observers assumed that the tradition had to do with homosexuality, deviance, and low status. They referred to the two-spirit as a *berdache,* the French version of a Persian word used to describe the younger or passive man in a homosexual relationship (in contrast to *bougre*, for the active partner). In reality, two-spirits were highly esteemed – although, by now, this has changed due to integration into the larger society. Two-spirits were often wealthy, accomplished people. They would take on their gender identity at puberty as a personal choice, freely combining male and female dress and activities and swapping them at will over time. Two-spirits did not form sexual relationships with other two-spirits, and their sexual partners did not consider themselves homosexual. In general, two-spirits had partners or spouses of the same sex, although male-bodied two-spirits sometimes had relationships with women.

Male-bodied two-spirits could go to war even though they cooked and made craft items such as pottery or textiles. Female-bodied two-spirits could cook even though they went to war or hunted. Two-spirits also had special spiritual duties such as healing, divination, ceremonial functions, and singing and storytelling. They were not just accepted or tolerated, but revered and honored as powerful individuals with special connections to the supernatural – a reason for which they sometimes were feared as well.

In India, the state recognizes *hijras* as a "third sex." This category has existed for many centuries, as indicated by religious and literary sources. Hijras are women born male, or, more rarely, with intersex characteristics. Some undergo surgical removal of the external genitalia during an initiation ritual, but others do not. Many live communally with other hijras and a guru, who leads them in Hindu rituals for both women and men. The choice of hijra identity is motivated by complex and variable factors, and is not primarily about sex. Some hijras renounce sexuality altogether, although many are forced to engage in sex work to make a living. In contrast to two-spirits, hijras tend to be socially marginalized, and increasingly so, as indicated by the re-criminalization of homosexuality.

Cultural traditions involving multiple sexual/gender identities show that nonconforming roles and relationships may be institutionalized and socially valued. In global perspective, categories and behavioral expectations are fluid rather than fixed. In short, the relationships linking biological sex, sexuality, and culturally constructed gender, are indeterminate rather than obligatory.

. . . . .

The discussion above has shown that sex and gender categories are variable and porous. Moreover, all people grow up in a cultural environment that shapes the way their brains are used. As a result, evidence of inborn differences in women and men's mental abilities is inherently unreliable. Brains do not come in two sexes. While quantitative measures of a few brain structures or activity patterns may yield more male-typical or more female-typical ranges, individual brains are composites of both (see Chapter 6). On the other hand, there are some small differences between babies due to boys' prenatal exposure to testosterone. The differences may either be amplified or eliminated through gendered treatment of infants and children.

Boys are born larger than girls on average. The faster body growth in the womb comes at the expense of the brain, meaning that boys are born at an earlier stage of neurological development. Together with the early effects of testosterone on the configuration of male brains (see Chapter 6), this developmental discrepancy explains the main differences in children's cognition and behavior. It is the reason the physical senses including hearing, smell, and touch are more advanced in girls than boys for the first year of life. Lise Eliot (2009) reports that baby girls score higher on tests of fine-motor skills, communication, and memory, and are slightly better than boys at discerning emotions in others. Thanks to their larger size, boys keep up with girls in gross motor skills needed for sitting up and learning to move around on their own. On the other hand, boys are comparatively ill-equipped to deal with life outside the womb, which makes them more irritable and ill-tempered. It is harder to calm boy babies, and they have more trouble learning how to soothe themselves.

During infancy and early childhood, boys catch up to girls and the differences in cognitive functioning diminish, unless environmental influences maintain or magnify them. For instance, parents tend to respond to baby boys' greater crankiness with more solicitude than they display towards girls. Parents play more with boy babies and distract them with interesting games and toys. At the same time, parents tend to ignore or respond more harshly to boys' complaints of pain, but to be more indulgent regarding outbursts of anger. In sum, parents tend to devote more effort to managing boys' emotions and exposing boys to visual and physical stimulation.

With girls it is the reverse: parents are more likely to leave a baby girl alone. Girls' relative placidity makes it easier for parents to interact with girls verbally and less necessary for them to distract girls with toys. In line with stereotypes about female delicateness and emotions, parents generally are less responsive to and accepting of expressions of anger than pain in girls. In sum, parents of girls tend to concentrate on verbal and social engagement.

As they grow, boys spend more time participating in "rough and tumble play" than girls on average, as do male animals in general. Because "rough and tumble play" is culturally valued as masculine behavior that indicates assertiveness and athleticism, it tends to be reinforced in male children but discouraged in female children – for whom friendly interaction and fine-motor activities are rewarded due to their association with femininity and sociality.

Expressions of anger and contentment occur at similar frequencies in girl and boy babies. However, girls show interest in situations and surroundings more often than boys, a difference which tends to reinforce parents' belief that girls are naturally more sociable than boys. This idea dovetails with the assumption that women are "hardwired" for social interaction, which, as Eliot explains, is based on a flawed psychological study. The study found that newborn boys showed greater interest in looking at a colorful mobile than did girls, who spent more time looking at a human face. However, the study was never replicated and was compromised by the fact that the face presented to the babies was that of the researcher, who knew the sex of the children she was studying.

The assumption that boys are more object-oriented and possess better object-manipulation skills is not supported by research on babies. Boys have not done better than girls on tests verifying that young infants can count and that they understand physical laws governing the movement of objects (gravity, speed, momentum). Sometimes they have done worse. Other studies have found no difference in the amount of gazing at faces done by newborn girls and boys, although after a few months boys look less at faces and avert their gaze more often. These findings attest to the responsiveness of infant behavior to social cues.

Children learn gender-based toy preferences from an early age. At 12 months of age, children of both sexes look more at dolls than toy cars, and prefer dolls over other toys to virtually the same degree: 57.2% of girls and 56.4% of boys. By 24 months, girls are more likely to look first at dolls: 52.7% versus 47.9% (Jadva et al. 2010). Throughout childhood, boys show interest in a narrower range of toys than girls, reflecting stronger social pressure on boys to avoid opposite-gender play.

Differences in play during the first 3 years of life have an impact on brain development during a time of especially rapid growth. By being encouraged to take an interest in dolls from an early age, girls may develop greater capacity in the right brain areas that deal with relationships, nonverbal communication, and visual discernment of the emotions and faces of others. Toys such as blocks and other construction materials which are offered more often to boys may favor development of left-brain areas involved in linear, analytical, conscious thought. Since brain plasticity is competitive, training can develop some areas at the expense of others, leaving culture's mark on cerebral anatomy and functioning.

As children grow, free-time activity may amplify these differences. Boys throughout the world have more time to play than girls, who are more likely to be given chores. Among children given chores, boys spend more time playing than doing chores, but girls spend more time doing chores than playing. Not only are girls' chores more time-consuming, but they are less likely to be compensated with money. Girls learn that they are expected to take care of others and the household, whereas boys learn to expect payment for tasks that take them away from their own interests. The gender difference in responsibility for chores persists into adulthood. In the US, for instance, adult men spend about 7 hours a week on housework, compared to about 25 among working women (Stafford and Swanbrow 2007).

Differences in the educational and recreational activities that occupy girls and boys beginning in babyhood explain why boys tend to score higher on tests of mental rotation, which is considered an indicator of visuo-spatial abilities possessed in greater measure by males. However, as Eliot (2009) explains, the gap in scores grows with children's age, indicating that boys receive more training in this area than girls. Historical improvements in girls' performance on other visuo-spatial tasks such as the water-level test – in which the child draws a line where water should rest in a tilted glass – likewise reflect the impact of experience and training.

Some but not all math tests yield a larger gender gap with respect to geometry than arithmetic, and girls often outperform boys in the latter. This pattern is taken to support the association of males with visuo-spatial skills, but females with verbal ability, given that math computation tends to be processed in the same hemisphere as language. However, it is more likely the result of disparities in training related to the gendered treatment of girls and boys, for instance through unequal involvement in sports and outdoor activities that involve orienteering.

Guided practice improves performance on tests of all kinds of mental skills, including visuo-spatial ones. To illustrate, girls' lower average score on a pretest given to first graders was eliminated in the post-test among girls who received training in visuo-spatial manipulation and interpretation, but not the control group (Tzuriel and Egozi 2010). In a study in which adults were trained in visual monitoring and attention skills which they practiced for 10 hours using a 3-D video game involving shooting, both males and females improved their scores on tests of mental rotation and spatial attention. The gender divergence on the pretest was nearly eliminated for spatial attention and greatly diminished for mental rotation. The control group, which played a 3-D maze-type game and was not trained, did not improve its scores (Feng et al. 2007).

Visuo-spatial skills are culturally associated with masculinity and consequently with rational thought and intelligence, whereas femininity lines up with oppositely categorized traits, especially sociability and emotionality. Women and men are expected to experience different amounts and types of emotions. Excitement and frustration are considered proper to men, sadness and apprehension typical of women. Men are expected to experience positive emotions such as pride and contentment in reference to the self, but women are assumed to experience positive emotions in relation to others.

These associations have long been assumed to derive from inborn differences. In their "six cultures study," Beatrice and John Whiting (1975) concluded that, on average, boys tend to be more self-oriented and less altruistic than girls, and more aggressive and less nurturing. However, these distinctions did not apply to all societies in the study. In-depth studies elsewhere have shown that gender-associated emotions vary across cultures.[3] Moreover, inequality plays a preponderant role in gender differences in emotion. Western women's higher frequency of negative emotions and Western men's greater likelihood of experiencing positive emotions reflects women's lower socioeconomic status (Simon and Nath 2004). Likewise, divergent gender-role expectations and degrees of inequality explain why there are larger gender gaps in emotional experience, emotional expression, and emotional literacy in Western than non-Western societies (Fischer and Manstead 2000).

Outward emotion is deceptive because women and men are expected to express their emotions in different ways. Boys learn to avoid crying by school age and especially after about the age of 10. They are discouraged from betraying their feelings through facial expressions, aside from anger. Paradoxically, repressed emotional expression is demanded of the sex which is predisposed to heightened feeling (see Chapter 6). In experimental situations, when challenged with violent images or the threat of pain, such as an electric shock, men respond with stronger emotions than women as measured by heart rate, sweating, and blood pressure (Manstead 1992).

These findings challenge the image of men as naturally rational and cool-headed, and women as irrational and driven by emotion. Similarly, experimental and cross-cultural evidence refutes the assumption that men are born competitive but women collaborative. As noted in earlier chapters, women behave assertively and competitively in societies in which they control property and economic decision-making. Economic games confirm that the strength of women's competitive spirit increases with greater economic independence. To illustrate, participants were presented an unfamiliar game involving tossing balls into a bucket. They could either play for a sum of money that depended on their performance alone, or a greater amount if they outperformed a competitor chosen at random. Among participants in the US and the Maasai in Tanzania, far fewer women than men opted to compete against a rival: 30% and 26% of US and Maasai women, versus 69% and 50% of US and Maasai men, respectively. In contrast, among the matrilineal Khasi of northeastern India, 54% of women and 39% of men chose the competition option (Gneezy and List 2013).

In sum, females and males both are born with necessary abilities for interacting with others and the physical environment. In childhood, parents and others may train girls to develop visuo-spatial skills, and boys to control anger and desire. Alternatively, social environments may channel the behavior of children and adults in line with the image of women as supportive, cooperative, other-oriented, and verbally proficient, but men as productive, hierarchical, self-oriented, and interested in objects. In the present historical moment, fields involving science, technology, and finance are highly prestigious and remunerative. Math ability, as a requirement for entry, has become a contested gender attribute even though, as seen below, current gender differences in verbal skills are much larger.

. . . . .

Scores on tests of knowledge or mental skills often turn up a gender difference, but they cannot be taken as proof of biological sex differences for the reasons discussed above. In addition, objectification and gender stereotypes distort women's performance on tests of intellectual ability. The effect is particularly strong with respect to math.

Where femininity is equated with sexuality and reproductive potential, women are placed in the role of objects that exist to satisfy the desires and ambitions of men, who are unequally endowed with subjectivity and agency. Objectification has concrete effects both on women and those who regard them as objects. If women are asked to introduce themselves to a man who can only see their body, they restrict their role in conversation (Saguy et al. 2010). When talking with male colleagues, women scientists express themselves less capably and experience reduced personal engagement if the topic concerns their work. There is no similar effect if the conversation revolves around other topics, or if women scientists discuss their research with female colleagues. The alteration occurs even if the men do not express negative gender beliefs in any way (Holleran et al. 2011).

Women who self-objectify or are induced to self-objectify see themselves as less competent, experience more negative emotions and less motivation, and perform less well than women who do not evaluate themselves based on appearance. As early as first grade, girls perform less well on math tests if shown images or words that cast girls and women in domestic or decorative roles. Women college students given a swimsuit to try on score lower on math tests taken alone in a dressing room than women given a sweater; the same scenarios presented to men have no effect on test scores. Women who self-objectify are more likely to condone systems of gender inequality and less likely to engage in gender-based activism. Among heterosexual women, self-objectification is associated with greater enjoyment of sexualization, which is further associated with increased perceptions of objectification by the male partner and, *in fine*, reduced relationship satisfaction.[4]

Objectification deprives its targets of personhood, individuality, and self-efficacy. By rendering the other less human, it blocks empathy and legitimizes aggression (see Chapter 11). Objectification causes people, including women, to see women as deficient in moral sense, intelligence, and capability. Only attractive women are evaluated positively, yet their attractiveness is perceived by both women and men as inversely proportional to their competence – as is the provocativeness of their dress. In psychological experiments, priming men with sexualized images of women before presenting them pictures of working women results in lower judgments of competence.[5]

Like objectification, cultural beliefs about group-wide deficiencies dampen performance when triggered during a test of skill or knowledge. Stereotype threat occurs wherever an individual is reminded of belonging to a group considered inferior in some way, such as whites assessed for athletic ability, old people challenged with memory tasks, and minority and lower-class students tested for cognitive or academic skills. People unconsciously reminded of stereotypes that apply to their group perform worse than equally skilled people who do not fall under the stereotype and worse than people matched for the same identity characteristic and skill level but shielded from stereotype threat (Steele 2010).

Table 9.1 summarizes the way stereotype threat is elicited experimentally through specific scenarios. The numbers are only indicative of the differences that occur in the various situations; they do not come from any particular study. Two groups of people, A and B, are given a test. The stereotype in question applies to Group B, but not Group A. The individuals in both groups are matched for ability, for example by having completed certain math courses with a high grade or having entered university with SAT (Scholastic Aptitude Test) scores above a certain

TABLE 9.1 Effect of stereotype threat on performance

		Score with stereotype evident	*Score with no stereotype threat*	*Score with stereotype counteracted*
High performers	Group A unaffected by stereotype	80	80	75
High performers	Group B subjected to stereotype	50	80	85
Low performers	Group A unaffected by stereotype	50	50	n/a
Low performers	Group B subjected to stereotype	50	50	n/a

percentile. Participants are given a challenging test that is beyond their ability. For instance, college students in their early years of study may be administered a set of questions from tests intended for upper-level students applying to graduate school, such as the GRE (Graduate Record Examination), or the GMAT (Graduate Management Admission Test).

Before taking the test, participants are prompted either in terms that elicit the stereotype or not. For instance, stereotype threat may be activated by a pretest demographic questionnaire, statements about how the test measures intelligence, or communication of the idea that the test normally turns up a difference in favor of the advantaged group or against the disadvantaged one. Alternatively, stereotype threat may be reduced or counteracted by statements affirming that the test is being conducted purely for research on learning or problem-solving, or that it does not typically yield differences between groups.

The table shows that stereotype threat occurs only if the person cares about the task at hand. Being reminded of negative stereotypes makes no difference to low performers with little at stake, but high performers under stereotype threat may score the same as low performers. This is important because lower test scores are considered proof that stereotyped groups are less capable than others, which further reinforces negative stereotypes.

In addition, stereotype threat only affects high performers if the task is challenging. When mixed-gender groups of college students with demonstrated math competence are given either an easy or hard math test, no gender difference in scores emerges on the easy test but a gap favoring men appears on the hard one. Researchers then give the same test to another batch of participants. Among those told that the test has resulted in a gender difference in the past, women score lower than men. In contrast, women score the same or slightly higher than men in groups informed that the test does not typically yield a disparity.

Stereotype threat may be counteracted to the point where a disadvantaged group outperforms the other, for instance through statements that call attention to positive elements of an individual's identity. Asian-American women's scores on math tests increase if pretest questionnaires ask about ethnicity. They decline if the questionnaires request gender identification (Shih et al. 1999).

Stereotypes trigger vigilance, which interferes with thought and distracts the mind. The resulting frustration further impairs performance. Anxiety raises blood pressure, heart rate, and sweating. Sensing stress, the brain secretes cortisol, which increases activity in areas involved in social and emotional functions while decreasing activity in areas associated with learning abstract concepts and processing working memory – the type called upon for short-term tasks such as math tests. Negative psychological states suppress the brain's pleasure centers and thereby further impair performance. In contrast, in felicitous circumstances the brain's pleasure centers are active and there is a rise in dopamine and serotonin, which favors cognitive functions and consequently boosts learning and performance.

Since stereotype threat operates through unconscious effects, deliberate effort is ineffective relative to social changes such as reductions in inequalities and elimination of visual and spoken cues from the environment. It also may be counterbalanced by values affirmation, as shown by a semester-long experiment involving college physics students. The students were given writing exercises about individual values in general as a way to foster feelings of self-worth and personal integrity. Women in the experimental group received higher course grades than those in the control group. In addition, values affirmation brought women's improvement in physics knowledge over the semester in line with men's, as measured by a standardized test of physics knowledge given at the beginning and end of the term. The improvements were greatest among the women who started the term most inclined to agree with stereotypes about men being better at physics (Mikaye et al. 2010).

By reducing women's scores on math and science tests, stereotype threat contributes to the very prejudices that engender it. Together with chronic objectification, stereotype threat pushes women from male-dominated fields, as discussed below. Their unequal presence in these fields, in turn, fuels cultural beliefs about women's purported natural unsuitability for pursuits defined as masculine.

. . . . .

Stereotype threat calls into question the validity of test results as a measure of gender differences in intelligence or ability. There are other problems, besides. Apart from the effects of human choices that influence how quantitative data are produced and analyzed, differences in average scores between two groups may be the result of any number of factors, or simply chance. For a difference in test scores between groups of people wearing shirts with stripes versus polka-dots to be attributed to the cloth, a causal relationship between it and brain activity would have to be demonstrated. Analogously, gender differences in scores cannot legitimately be chalked up to sex without evidence of a mode of action. Moreover, comparison of the average scores of women and men on a particular test collapses the range of values into a single number, giving the appearance of discontinuities or absolute differences – as if one gender had the trait all to itself. Comparison of averages creates the impression that all members of one group differ from all members of the other group in the same way, and that differences are more meaningful or important than similarities.

Psychologists express gender differences on tests and experiments in terms of *d* ("difference") values, calculated by subtracting the mean score of females divided by its standard deviation from the mean score of males divided by its standard deviation. The male mean is the one to which the female mean is compared, such that positive *d* values signify that males scored higher, while negative values indicate that females scored higher. When *d* is above 0.8, either positive or negative, it is considered high. Values between 0.66–0.79 are moderately high; those between 0.36–0.65 are moderate; and ones between 0.11–0.35 are low. Values up to 0.10 are considered to reflect little or no difference (Eliot 2009).

Compared to the average size difference between women and men, gender differences in behavior and ability as measured by tests and experiments are 7–10 times smaller: 2.0–2.6 for height, as opposed to under 0.35 (positive or negative) for the vast majority of cognitive traits. This means that the bell curves for women and men are relatively detached for stature but practically superimposed for psychological tests. If the difference in height were similar to the difference in scores on psychological tests, it would be impossible to tell with the naked eye that, on average, men are taller than women.

The following *d* scores from a textbook by Randy Larsen and David Buss (2009) provide a sample of the types and magnitude of gender differences examined by psychologists. Characteristics with absolute *d* values below 0.11 include more male impulsiveness and openness to experience. Ones with very small *d* values, below 0.21, include somewhat higher female gregariousness and conscientiousness. Small differences, below the 0.35 level, include higher trust and anxiety among women, and greater self-esteem among males during late adolescence (*d* values for childhood and adulthood are lower). Moderate values from 0.36–0.65 include more smiling among women and more assertiveness among men. Large differences include more tender-mindedness among women (-0.97), and, among men, more interest in casual sex (0.81) and a higher number of desired sexual partners over the lifetime (0.87).

Tests of math and verbal ability (written and spoken) generate small *d* values. Differences in performance on tests of spatial ability such as mental rotation and the water-level test fall in the moderate range, 0.40–0.50, with some studies yielding higher values such as 0.90. On the other hand, *d* scores are negligible or nonexistent for other visuo-spatial tests such as the embedded figure test of spatial visualization, at 0.13 (Eliot 2009).

Unlike some test results which lend support to the idea of male superiority in math, other tests as well as classroom performance suggest that, where girls' scores are lower, the reason is gender inequality rather than inborn differences in intellectual endowments. In addition, the math gap is much smaller than the reading gap favoring girls. Across countries, higher degrees of gender stratification are accompanied by wider math gaps, whereas gender equality is associated with equal or better performance on the part of girls.

Since 2000, the Organization for Economic Development (OECD) has carried out an educational assessment of hundreds of thousands of 15-year-olds in dozens of countries every few years through its Programme for International Student Assessment (PISA). The testing consistently has revealed a pooled verbal gap in favor of girls that is at least three times larger than the math gap in favor of boys – around 2% of possible points versus more than 6% of possible points. While there is substantial variation in the size of the gaps between countries, in all countries the gender difference in verbal scores is larger than the difference in math scores.

Gender differences in math performance on PISA tests correlate with the World Economic Forum's "Gender Gap Index," independent of national economic well-being. In Iceland, girls score higher than boys on the math test. The difference in favor of males is miniscule in the Scandinavian nations and small in the US and parts of Europe, but much larger in countries with greater gender inequality such as Turkey and Korea.

On the 2012 test, girls performed as well or better than boys in math in 28 of the 65 countries, outperformed boys in reading in nearly all countries, and performed roughly equally with boys in science across countries (OECD 2014). The same proportion of girls and boys (4%) achieved the top level of performance in all three subjects. As in earlier versions of the test, there was a wide range of average scores across countries (from the upper 300s to the high 500s or low 600s), and a far greater amount of variation within than between genders. In fact, socioeconomic class was a far more salient factor than gender with respect to math scores, which differed by 39 points between socioeconomically disadvantaged and advantaged students as opposed to 10.5 points between girls and boys. Between students who attended more than one year of pre-primary school and those who did not, the gap was 53 points.

Differences in levels of math anxiety and math self-confidence explain why, across countries, there was a 19-point gap between high-achieving girls and boys. Among students of the same ability level, boys scored higher on assessments of competitiveness, responsiveness to outside incitement, and self-belief, and were less prone to blame themselves for failure in math. There was no difference in math scores between students of different gender but the same level of math anxiety and math confidence.

The 2012 PISA assessment verifies that, at school, girls receive higher grades than boys across all subjects – with the exception of France, where boys received higher grades in math than girls. Significantly, girls' grades in math were not as high as predicted by the ratio between school grades and performance on PISA reading scores. In other words, gender stereotypes dampen teachers' evaluations of math performance among girls.

Parents also tend to discourage girls with respect to math and science. For both girls and boys, parental attitudes influence self-belief and math self-confidence, and, in turn, scores on math tests. Math self-confidence has an effect on scores that is three times larger than gender among girls in general, and nearly four times larger among high achievers (31 and 39 points, respectively). Across countries, parents are more likely to expect their sons than daughters to work in scientific research or applied science. Not surprisingly, 39% of young men but only 14% of young women who started college in 2012 enrolled in fields related to science, engineering, manufacturing, or construction.

At the same time, boys tend to be overrepresented at the lowest levels of academic performance at school and on tests. Aside from a handful of countries in which the proportions were roughly equal, the 2012 PISA assessments showed a higher proportion of male than female low achievers across the three subjects (math, reading, science): 14% of boys versus 9% of girls. In some countries virtually all low performers in reading were boys, and in many countries most low performers in math were boys. The assessments also showed that boys spend less time studying and reading for pleasure than girls, and far more time on video games and other computer-based activities. Boys are less punctual and well-behaved at school, less likely to report being happy at school, and more likely to consider school a waste of time. Evidently, societies not only fail girls through stereotypes and gender-unequal opportunities, but also invest insufficient effort in engaging boys academically, especially at the lower levels of achievement.

The PISA tests show that math gaps close with declining gender inequality across countries. Other standardized tests confirm that historical declines in inequality are accompanied by shrinking gender gaps in math test scores. For instance, in the US, gender disparities (along with ethnic-group differences) in scores on math tests, math course grades, and the number of high school math and science courses taken have narrowed dramatically over the last several decades. This shift has been observed through national tests such as the SAT, Advanced Placement tests, the GRE, and the GMAT. It has coincided with the restoration of the gender balance at US universities that prevailed during the first three decades of the 20th century but was upset during the late 1940s and 1950s, when men significantly outnumbered women (Goldin et al. 2006).

The College Board reports that, in the US, female high school students have higher grade-point-averages than male students, that more girls take advanced-placement or honors math courses than boys, and that more girls are in the top 10% of their classes. On the other hand, although the gaps have narrowed dramatically in recent decades, males continue to score slightly higher on average than females on standardized math tests such as the SAT and GRE. Males are more likely than females to score in the top 1% and to earn a perfect score (Wai et al. 2010).

The mixed results discussed above suggest that neither girls nor boys have an innate advantage with respect to math and science. Differences in knowledge or ability consequently do not explain the unequal representation of women and men in scientific fields. While women earn 25% or fewer of American doctoral degrees in physics, math, computer science, and engineering, they earn 50% or more of the doctoral degrees in the life sciences, social sciences, and psychology, as well as medicine and veterinary medicine. All combined, women earn 41% of advanced degrees in STEM (science, technology, engineering, and math) fields, but they account for only 28% of tenure-track and tenured university positions. Women's representation at the higher ranks is especially low. For instance, in the top 100 American universities women hold 9–16% of tenure-track positions in math departments, and less than 10% of full professor positions (Ceci and Williams 2011).

Even scientists, whether male or female, unconsciously perpetuate gender stereotypes about women's alleged weakness in math and science. They may accuse female students of cheating if they solve complex problems or do well on math tests, as neuroscientist Ben Barres learned by living into young adulthood as a woman before changing his gender identity (Eliot 2009). When evaluating potential employees, scientists are biased towards male candidates, as shown by a study in which professors of chemistry, physics, and biology were sent fictitious applications for a lab manager job from male and female students with identical backgrounds. The professors favored the male candidate on all three measures: perceived competence, level of compensation and mentoring offered, and willingness to hire. Male preference was independent of the professors' gender, scientific field, age, or ethnicity. There was, however, a modest relationship between the degree of gender bias on a pretest questionnaire and unequal evaluation of the candidate, suggesting that counteracting stereotypes could lessen the effects of prejudice (Moss-Racusin et al. 2012).

In the workplace, women in scientific fields are penalized by institutional factors that result in lower publication output compared to men, with cascading effects on career advancement in terms of rank and research sponsorship. For instance, in the US and Australia, men accumulate 40% more publications during their early careers as a result of having more time and support for writing. Women write fewer articles but on average the quality is higher, as measured by the frequency with which a publication is cited, but academic promotion depends on quantity more than quality (Symonds et al. 2006). In addition, women scientists, like all working women, often endure sexual harassment, which impairs performance and has negative effects on health and job satisfaction. Severe harassment affects up to half of working women, but is so familiar that few women deem it sufficiently grave to report. Institutional responses tend to be disappointing. Women who have dealt with harassment through formal channels have a lower perception of justice than women who do not take action (Adams-Roy and Barling 1998).

The topic of harassment brings us back to the themes of objectification and gender constructs by which women's work is construed as contrary to their sexual/reproductive role. In fact, women are penalized materially if they fail to conform to prevailing standards of physical attractiveness, as seen in the inverse relationship between body weight and income for female workers in the US, Germany, Finland, and other industrialized countries. The decline in income is most drastic between underweight and normal weight, after which further declines are less pronounced. Women's income increases with height, although the relationship is weaker than it is for men, for whom salaries rise in step with height and weight (except in the obesity range), in accordance with the symbolic association of height and bulk with masculine potency (Judge and Cable 2010). For both women and men, stereotypes and assumptions about natural gender roles can have concrete negative effects on the way their work is perceived and compensated.

. . . . .

The last three chapters have shown that women and men vary in terms of average body size, aggressiveness, and degree of motivation towards, and experience of, physical pleasure. Other differences in behavior and ability are small, changeable, and equivocal. Performance on tests of skills and knowledge is elastic and responsive to training; sustained focused effort alters brain anatomy and physiology. For the same reason, cultural expectations about gender attributes which cause girls and boys to become proficient at different tasks can lead to modifications that appear to constitute evidence of inborn sex differences. In a perpetual cycle, differences appear natural, timeless, and universal, further justifying disparities in the training and opportunities presented to girls and boys.

Contrary to ideologies of essential difference, natural selection has not endowed women and men with different intellectual abilities or brain power. The capabilities employed by hunters and gatherers to procure food are not useful to people of only one sex and could not have been transmitted exclusively to male or female offspring. Moreover, the picture of gender roles in prehistory that emerges from ethnographic and paleo-archeological evidence is nothing like the scenario that is supposed to account for so much about the human species. Until recently, virtually all humans lived in mobile social groups in which females and males shared the work of food procurement and parenting. This way of life required a flexible brain able to handle complex, shifting social and ecological conditions, not a hardwired one.

The idea of fixed differences serves stratified societies in which privileged groups defend institutionalized inequalities, but it is damaging to women and men and incompatible with the variability in gender roles and the capabilities of real human beings around the world.

Notes

1 Regarding women's and men's work in different societies, see the sources in Chapter 8.
2 Regarding intersex conditions and multiple human sexualities and genders discussed in this section, see Jacobs et al. (1997); Kalra (2012); Karkazis (2008).
3 On gender and emotion in non-Western societies, see Lutz (1988) and Chapters 8 and 11.
4 On the effects of self-objectification discussed in this paragraph, see Calogero (2013); Fredrickson et al. (1998); Quinn et al. (2006); Ramsey et al. (2016).
5 On the way objectification affects how women are perceived by others, see Glick et al. (2005); Loughnan et al. (2010); Rudman and Borgida (1995).

References cited

Adams-Roy J, Barling J. 1998. Predicting the decision to confront or report sexual harassment. *Journal of Organizational Behavior* 19(4):329–336.

Arthur KW. 2010. Feminine knowledge and skill reconsidered: women and flaked stone tools. *American Anthropologist* 112(2):228–243.

Berry JW. 1966. Temne and Eskimo perceptual skills. *International Journal of Psychology* 1(3):207–229.

Calogero RM. 2013. Objects don't object: evidence that self-objectification disrupts women's social activism. *Psychological Science* 24(3):312–318.

Ceci SJ, Williams WM. 2011. Understanding current causes of women's underrepresentation in science. *Proceedings of the National Academy of Science* 108(8):3157–3162.

Eliot L. 2009. *Pink brain, blue brain: how small differences grow into troublesome gaps – and what we can do about it.* Boston: Houghton Mifflin Harcourt.

Feng J, Spence I, Pratt J. 2007. Playing an action video game reduces gender differences in spatial cognition. *Psychological Science* 18(10):850–855.

Fischer AH, Manstead AS. 2000. The relation between gender and emotions in different cultures. In Fischer AH, editor. *Gender and emotion: social psychological perspectives.* Cambridge, UK: Cambridge University Press. p. 71–94.

Fredrickson BL, Roberts T-A, Noll SM, Quinn DM, Twenge JM. 1998. That swimsuit becomes you: sex differences in self-objectification, restrained eating, and math performance. *Journal of Personality and Social Psychology* 75(1):269–284.

Glick P, Larsen S, Johnson C, Branstiter H. 2005. Evaluations of sexy women in low- and high- status jobs. *Psychology of Women Quarterly* 29(4):389–395.

Gneezy U, List JA. 2013. *The why axis: hidden motives and the undiscovered economics of everyday life.* New York: PublicAffairs Books.

Goldin C, Katz LF, Kuziemko I. 2006. The homecoming of American college women: the reversal of the college gender gap. *Journal of Economic Perspectives* 20(4):133–156.

Gonzalez AQ, Koestner R. 2005. Parental preference for sex of newborn as reflected in positive birth announcements. *Sex Roles* 52(5–6):407–411.

Holleran SE, Whitehead J, Schmader T, Mehl MR. 2011. Talking shop and shooting the breeze: a study of workplace conversations and job disengagement among STEM faculty. *Social Psychology and Personality Science* 2(1):65–71.

Jacobs S, Thomas W, Lang S, editors. 1997. *Two-spirit people: Native American gender identity, sexuality, and spirituality.* Urbana: University of Illinois Press.

Jadva V, Hines M, Golombok S. 2010. Infants' preferences for toys, colors, and shapes: sex differences and similarities. *Archives of Sexual Behavior* 39(6):1261–1273.

Jones BH, Bovee MW, Knapik JJ. 1990. Associations among body composition, physical fitness, and injury in men and women army trainees. In Marriott BM, Grumstrup-Scott J, editors. *Body composition and physical performance: applications for the military services.* Washington, DC: National Academy Press. p. 141–173.

Judge TA, Cable DM. 2010. When it comes to pay, do the thin win? The effect of weight on pay for men and women. *Journal of Applied Psychology* 96(1):95–112.

Kalra G. 2012. Hijras: the unique transgender culture of India. *International Journal of Culture and Mental Health* 5(2):121–126.

Karkazis K. 2008. *Finding sex: intersex, medical authority, and lived experience.* Durham, NC: Duke University Press.

Karraker KH, Vogel DA, Lake MA. 1995. Parents' gender-stereotyped perceptions of newborns: the eye of the beholder, revisited. *Sex Roles* 33(9/10):687–701.

Kruger D, Byker D. 2009. Evolved foraging psychology underlies sex differences in shopping experiences and behaviors. *Journal of Social, Evolutionary, and Cultural Psychology* 3(4):328–342.

Larsen R, Buss D. 2009. *Personality psychology: domains of knowledge about human nature.* 4th ed. Boston: McGraw-Hill.

Loughnan S, Haslam N, Murnane T, Vaes J, Reynolds C, Suitner C. 2010. Objectification leads to depersonalization: the denial of mind and moral concern to objectified others. *European Journal of Social Psychology* 40(5):709–717.

Lutz C. 1988. *Unnatural emotions: everyday sentiments on a Micronesian atoll and their challenge to Western theory*. Chicago: University of Chicago Press.

Manstead AS. 1992. Gender differences in emotion. In Gale A, Eysenck MW, editors. *Handbook of individual differences: biological perspectives*. Oxford: John Wiley & Sons. p. 355–387.

Mikaye A, Kost-Smith LE, Finkelstein ND, Pollock SJ, Cohen GL, Ito TA. 2010. Reducing the gender achievement gap in college science: a classroom study of values affirmation. *Science* 320(6008):1234–1237.

Mondschein ER, Adolph KE, Tamis-LeMonda CS. 2000. Gender bias in mothers' expectations about infant crawling. *Journal of Experimental Child Psychology* 77(4):304–316.

Moss-Racusin CA, Dovidio JF, Brescoll VL, Graham MJ, Handelsman J. 2012. Science faculty's subtle gender biases favor male students. *Proceedings of the National Academy of Sciences* 109(41):16474–16479.

OECD. 2014. PISA 2012 results in focus: what 15-year-olds know and what they can do with what they know. OECD Publishing. www.oecd.org/pisa/keyfindings/pisa-2012-results-overview.pdf.

Pacheco-Cobos L, Rosetti M, Cuantianquiz C, Hudson R. 2010. Sex differences in mushroom gathering: men expend more energy to obtain equivalent benefits. *Evolution and Human Behavior* 31(4):289–297.

Quinn DM, Kallen RW, Twenge JM, Fredrickson BL. 2006. The disruptive effect of self-objectification on performance. *Psychology of Women Quarterly* 30(1):59–64.

Ramsey LR, Marotta JA, Hoyt T. 9 February 2016. Sexualized, objectified, but not satisfied: enjoying sexualization relates to lower relationship satisfaction through perceived partner-objectification. *Journal of Social and Personal Relationships*. doi:10.1177/0265407516631157.

Rubin JZ, Provenzano FJ, Luria Z. 1974. The eye of the beholder: parents' views on sex of newborns. *American Journal of Orthopsychiatry* 44(4):512–519.

Rudman LA, Borgida E. 1995. The afterglow of construct accessibility: the behavioral consequences of priming men to view women as sexual objects. *Journal of Experimental Social Psychology* 31(6):493–517.

Saguy T, Quinn DM, Dovidio JF, Pratto F. 2010. Interacting like a body: objectification can lead women to narrow their presence in social interactions. *Psychological Science* 21(2):178–182.

Shih M, Pittinsky TL, Ambady N. 1999. Stereotype susceptibility: identity salience and shifts in quantitative performance. *Psychological Science* 10(1):80–83.

Simon RW, Nath LE. 2004. Gender and emotion in the United States: do men and women differ in self-reports of feelings and expressive behavior? *American Journal of Sociology* 109(5):1137–1176.

Stafford F, Swanbrow D. 2007. Time, money, and who does the laundry. University of Michigan Institute for Social Research. http://deepblue.lib.umich.edu/html/2027.42/61984/chores.pdf.

Steele CM. 2010. *Whistling Vivaldi: and other clues to how stereotypes affect us*. New York: Norton.

Stern M, Karraker KH. 1989. Sex stereotyping of infants: a review of gender labeling studies. *Sex Roles* 20(9/10):501–522.

Stout NM. 2014. *After love: queer intimacy and erotic economies in post-Soviet Cuba*. Durham, NC: Duke University Press.

Symonds MR, Gemmell NJ, Braisher TL, Gorringe KL, Elgar MA. 2006. Gender differences in publication output: towards an unbiased metric of research performance. *PLoS One* 1(1):e127. doi:10.1371/journal.pone.0000127.

Tzuriel D, Egozi G. 2010. Gender differences in spatial ability of young children: the effects of training and processing strategies. *Child Development* 81(5):1417–1430.

Wai J, Cacchio M, Putallaz M, Makel MC. 2010. Sex differences in the right tail of cognitive abilities: a 30 year examination. *Intelligence* 38(4):412–423.

Whiting BB, Whiting JW. 1975. *Children of six cultures: a psychocultural analysis.* Cambridge, MA: Harvard University Press.

Young A. 2000. *Women who become men: Albanian sworn virgins.* New York: Berg.

PART IV
Conflict and violence

10

SAVAGE EMPATHY

Sources of competitiveness and cooperativeness, greed and generosity

Images of human nature as combative and violent mesh very well with contemporary news reporting, which revels in stories of assault, gang violence, warfare, sex crimes, vehicular and industrial accidents, and other forms of death and destruction. Like today's seemingly bloodthirsty humans, our ancestors are pictured as incessantly battling each other – when not killing enormous animals practically with their bare hands. Together with the conjured violence of video games, movies, and novels, these representations make it appear as if humans were born with an appetite for fighting. Warfare appears to be as old as humankind itself.

There is no shortage of evidence that people can be hierarchical, aggressive, and competitive. On the other hand, people spontaneously and willingly cooperate with others, including strangers. As a mathematical proposition, it cannot be argued that human nature is predominantly murderous. Violent behavior is very rare for the female half of the population, and unusual for the male half as well. Across societies, nonviolent interactions are more common than violent ones.

Although males are more likely than females to engage in violent behavior, the biological mechanisms involved in aggression and violence are the same for both. Like other primates, both sexes have an evolutionary history of competing with individuals of the same sex and defending themselves and their offspring against threats. As shown below, however, mate competition is not likely to have regularly involved dangerous combat, given that lethal violence is more likely to reduce than increase the number of offspring.

Throughout human evolution it has been indispensable for individuals to live in communities, for living alone in an unbuilt environment is inefficient and dangerous. As in other social animals, community living has resulted in traits such as empathy, reciprocity, and forbearance, along with vigilance about fairness, cheating, and opportunism. Significantly, social connectedness is positively associated with health and wellbeing, whereas inequality and social isolation are harmful to individuals and communities.

Variability in the frequency of bloodshed indicates that wanton violence is not an evolved trait – except in the sense that evolution has given rise to all our behavioral options. Violence between populations was extremely rare until humans began to cultivate food instead of collecting it. Historically and cross-culturally, violence within and between societies is linked to factors including intensive production, social and gender inequality, political and economic instability, and cultural beliefs favorable to aggressive behavior. In short, violent behavior is patterned rather than spontaneous – which means that it can be prevented.

. . . . .

This chapter lays the groundwork for an anthropological analysis of violence by examining questions related to the alleged human instinct for hierarchy and lethal competition. We will begin by analyzing commonsense beliefs about spontaneous biological drives towards extreme treachery, in the form of cannibalism, and tenderness, in the form of maternal love.

In the Western imagination, cannibalism signifies the ultimate exercise of dominance.[1] To describe people as cannibals is a form of "othering" that marks a boundary between "us" and "them." The folklore of societies around the world, including reputedly cannibalistic ones, regularly defines other groups as depraved, uncivilized cannibals. At the same time, cannibalism symbolizes panhuman evil, the wickedness lurking within. In mid-20th century Papua New Guinea, white intruders were envisioned as ancestors come back among the living – both fearsome and familiar, us *and* them.

Cannibalism as a trope for bloodthirstiness is different from anthropophagy, or the actual consumption of human flesh. To illustrate, kuru, a transmissible spongiform encephalopathy that spread among the Fore people of Papua New Guinea between the 1920s–1960s, is known to Western medicine as a disease caused by cannibalism. That was the conclusion reached by Daniel Carleton Gajdusek, who visited as the disease was disappearing and recorded its effects on film. Yet, the cannibalism at issue involved the respectful handling of human remains. Informants told Shirley Lindenbaum (1979) that it had been women's task to remove the brain, organs, and muscle tissue, and steam or roast them over hot stones. The women ingested the cooked matter with specific relatives according to established rules. In particular, the ashes from the brain were sipped in a tea as a form of communion with the dead. The practice was abandoned once Europeans arrived in the area in 1961, but the latent infection continued to affect older women for several years after. In the end, anthropophagy may not even have been the true route of transmission, which more likely occurred through skin lesions or mucous membranes such as the eyes.

There is no doubt that anthropophagy has in fact been practiced by some individuals and societies. At archeological sites in the southwestern US dated between 900–1300 CE, bones marked by knives and human teeth strongly indicate human consumption, as does the presence of myoglobin on cooking pots and a lump of fecal matter.[2] In the mid-1500s in northern Arizona, 30 people – mostly women and children – were massacred, many of their bones broken, cut, roasted, and boiled. However, the Hopi ("peaceful") and their Anasazi ancestors are not known for violence, and no oral tradition among dozens of clans makes mention of cannibalism. Women and children were not normally targeted during conflicts, raising questions about how ordinary this type of massacre could have been. Increased intertribal tensions as a result of the Spanish conquest could account for it and also explain the presence of men among the victims, as they may have been missionaries blamed for sorcery.

As seen in the next chapter, skeletal evidence of anthropophagy is often equivocal and open to sensationalistic interpretations. To illustrate, in reference to the discovery of 14,700-year-old skull-cups found in England near butchered animals whose mandibles had been separated from the skull in the same way – suggesting ingestion of bone marrow and brain matter – a brief in *Science* (2011) says the eyes were "gouged out," the faces "smashed off." However, as indicated by the kuru example, the drinking vessels may have been made to honor the dead. Indeed, the tales of cannibalism told to European explorers, colonists, and missionaries in centuries past emphasized the ritual consumption of witches or enemies killed in battle as a way to appropriate their special powers or life force. Mystical motives reflect awe and respect, although in some cases informants claimed that the enemy was eaten with no more fanfare than any other food as a display of dominance to humiliate enemies. At all events, the veracity of these stories remains in doubt, given that outsiders did not witness cannibalism and the purported custom disappeared as soon as they arrived.

Western culture itself is not immune to accusations of cannibalism. The Christian sacrament of communion entails the ingestion of the body and blood of a human being, which, to Catholics, is not just symbolic. Medicinal cannibalism was a mainstream healing method in Europe from the 16th–18th centuries, and some remedies persisted until the early 20th century. Europeans ingested human organs, muscle, blood, bone, and bone marrow for a range of ailments including epilepsy, which in ancient times had been treated with blood taken immediately from dead people. Experts advised procuring medicines from people killed suddenly, such as criminals, prisoners of war, or victims of fatal accidents, and provided detailed instructions for cutting the body and extracting prized substances (Gordon-Grube 1988). Even now, some standard medical practices could be seen as a form of medicinal cannibalism, such as blood transfusion and organ transplantation. One person's biological matter is incorporated into another's body, and many recipients and donor families believe that spiritual and personality traits travel with it (Sharp 2001).

Cannibalism is a powerful idea, and the source of many myths and legends. Sometimes it actually occurs. Yet, the evidence does not suggest that, deep down, people would eat each other if allowed, or that they made it a regular habit until recently. The act, and its meaning, depends on the social context.

. . . . .

While the presumed instinct for killing and eating enemies points to the worst in humankind, all-powerful maternal love exemplifies the best, or, alternatively, an irresistible drive to safeguard the vessel carrying one's genes into posterity.[3]

However, mothers do not always bond with their babies. Under some circumstances, they kill, fatally neglect, or abandon their newborns. This has occurred in many different times and places, including impoverished countries in Asia, the Middle East, and Latin America today.

Sometimes the reason is a very rare psychological disorder; far more frequently, it is the cruelty of a woman's life circumstances. Babies may be killed as a result of extreme poverty, or because of social stigma where pregnancy outside of marriage presents an intolerable threat to personal survival and family honor. Female fetuses and babies are targeted for infanticide and neglect in countries such as India and China where girls are disvalued, dowry customs make girls a financial burden, and a lack of state protections for the elderly combined with gender disparities in access to income leaves parents dependent on sons in older age (see Chapters 3 and 8).

Until well into the last century, church doors in Europe had revolving trays for receiving abandoned newborns, who were taken to orphanages where the majority died. Physicians wrote that rolling over onto the child during the night – a frequent official cause of infant death – was really a mask for infanticide. Large impoverished families sent children into domestic service or farm labor at the age of 5 or 6, or left them at orphanages. Wealthy mothers handed their newborns off to wet nurses in the countryside, knowing full well that they were unlikely to survive.

Nancy Scheper-Hughes (1992) explains that some mothers in the northeastern Brazilian shantytowns she studied from the 1960s–1980s lived so close to the edge of existence that they could not afford to become emotionally attached to a baby who appeared weak or unhealthy. Over their reproductive lives, these mothers had an average of 9.5 pregnancies, 1.5 stillbirths, and 3.5 child deaths. Most deaths were concentrated in the first few months, four-fifths in the first year. Mothers raised children on their own without help from their male partners, family, or society. They worked on sugar plantations or in wealthy people's homes, both of which excluded breastfeeding and forced mothers to leave babies at home alone. Older children were away at school or work.

Mothers responded by not wasting effort on babies with an insufficient "taste for living." They delayed attachment until it seemed clear that they were not going to have to deal with another infant death. Babies left to waste away were considered "little angels" – beings who had been born with a will to die, and who were called to heaven by a particular saint. This helped the mothers remain resigned and detached in the face of loss. Mothers and health professionals attributed the deaths to a variety of locally defined sicknesses, most of which were recognizable to Scheper-Hughes as starvation, dehydration, and diarrheal diseases. The state remained indifferent: it was much simpler and quicker to register a child's death than a car. The Catholic Church consoled women with rushed baptisms of moribund babies and funeral processions accompanied by church bells, but these practices were abolished in the 1980s, abandoning women to their grief and to more of the same, for there was no change in the Church's stance on birth control.

Infanticide and fatal neglect indicate that maternal love cannot be taken for granted as a biological inevitability or human universal. This view, in fact, is recent to European culture. Reacting to a culture of resignation and fatalism, Enlightenment scholars and political leaders exalted the ideal of direct, affectionate maternal care as a public health and moral obligation even for wealthy women. Over time, medical advice and popular norms regarding swaddling, feeding, and holding infants have come and gone, each one considered "natural" in its turn. Traces of mid-20th century scientific mothering remain in today's idea that too much solicitude towards newborns and infants is bad for children and a sign of pathological attachment on the part of mothers (or fathers). This kind of care appears detached and neglectful to parents in non-Western societies, who constantly and unreservedly hold and comfort small children.

Evidently, what constitutes natural maternal behavior varies across time and space. Women may be "programmed" like all mammalian mothers to take care of their newborns, but they are capable of killing babies or leaving them to die. As shown also by the discussion of cannibalism, human feelings and behavior do not emerge from a well of primal instincts, pure and unfiltered. This is an important point to keep in mind as we examine contrasting assertions about the origins and naturalness of violence.

. . . . .

We may now consider theories of innate killer instincts, beginning with the proposition that violence brings reproductive benefits to males. Males allegedly are driven to fight each other for rank but also to band together to attack other males and appropriate their mates and territory. The increased food supply is said to benefit resident females and attract new ones, further increasing the males' reproductive success. In this view, females represent passive objects of masculine strategizing and domination. In short, their capture is the evolutionary purpose of warfare (Wrangham and Peterson 1996).

As proof, Napoleon Chagnon (1997) argues that lethal violence correlates with increased reproductive success among Yanomami men living in the rainforests along the border between Venezuela and Brazil. According to Chagnon, who made several research trips to the area from the 1960s–1990s, headmen and men who have participated in a killing, thereafter given the title of *unokai*, have more wives and children than other men.

A first concern is that Chagnon's arguments concern a single society that is unrepresentative of ancestral human populations. The Yanomami are not nomadic foragers, but rather a collection of village-based patrilineal tribes. In food-producing societies of this type, women may be considered property to be exchanged or stolen along with other objects, but in foraging societies, women and men are autonomous and enter intimate relationships by choice. As seen in the next chapter, people of both sexes sometimes fight about lovers but it is rare for anyone to be badly hurt, and if men fight over women they fight about specific women. Groups of men do not fight other groups to gain control of women they do not know. The idea that men are hardwired to raid other groups and steal their women does not fit with the behavior of people in real-world foraging societies.

Secondly, the Yanomami are on the extreme end of gender stratification among horticultural societies. Compared to other indigenous populations in the same region, they are more hierarchical within and hostile between tribes. Men are dominant politically and within the family. They may have more than one wife, and they consider it within their rights to use physical violence against women.

Not only are these "fierce people" unrepresentative of ancestral societies, but the amount of violence remains controversial. Other anthropologists and missionaries working in the area have judged the Yanomami to be far less brutal than implied by Chagnon, who has been accused by Patrick Tierney (2000), among others, of inciting violence and consequently helping to create the conditions he expected to find. Whether or not Chagnon's behavior played a determining role, he openly admits to trading weapons for information and biological samples. There is no doubt that effective weapons obtained through several generations of contact with Westerners, including Chagnon, along with a shrinking resource base due to mining and other extractive industries, has increased the frequency and lethality of Yanomami violence.

While it sometimes happens that one village's men raid another village and forcefully take women, this is not the kind of customary or frequent event suggested by Chagnon, and the number of deaths is lower than he implies. Douglas Fry (2006) points out that two-thirds of the men in Chagnon's data set had not killed anyone. Of the one-third who were unokais, three-fifths had participated in one killing, one-fifth in two, and one-fifth in more than two. Hence, it was more common *not* to be a unokai than to be one, and for unokais to have participated in one killing rather than multiple homicides.

Fry shows that Chagnon's strategic organization of the numbers obscures important differences in the age of the men in the two groups. For instance, Chagnon sorts the men into five unequal age ranges that stretch from 5 years to more than 30, and presents an average for each grouping. This is an unusual thing to do with data, as is comparing vastly different sample sizes such as five unokais against 78 non-unokais in the 20–24 age group. Chagnon's quantitative presentation conceals the fact that the majority of the non-unokais (56%) were 20–30 years old, whereas the majority of the unokais (55%) were 41 years old or older. Men younger by well over a decade are bound to have fewer children to date. Furthermore, Chagnon included headmen in the unokai totals. Amazonian headmen have more wives and children than commoners, but that is because of their social status, not murderousness.

Combining the age and headmen effects, including correcting for the fact that headmen tend to be older than commoners, Fry finds that at least 95% of the alleged 3:1 unokai reproductive advantage disappears. Moreover, Chagnon's analysis includes only living unokais. Those who have died, their reproductive lives cut short, are left out, thereby preventing them from reducing the group average. Warriors in other preindustrial societies, such as the North American

Cheyenne, had fewer children than non-warriors, due largely to the fact that they lived significantly fewer years as a result of fighting and the increased risk of retaliation. A birth-cohort comparison would very likely show that unokais fare worse than men who do not kill other men.

.....

The other main evidence for primeval coalitional violence consists of sporadic reports on chimpanzees which have engaged in intergroup violence. At this point a note on language is in order. As in earlier chapters, the following discussion avoids the standard term, "troops," in light of its gender and military connotations and the related implication that these animals are equivalent to organized warrior bands.

Chimpanzee "warfare" is taken to signify that the trait was present in the common ancestor with humans and consequently is over 6–7 million years old. However, there are few instances, and one of them concerns a group three times larger than average: the Ngogo group in the Kibale National Park in Uganda, which has 145 animals instead of the usual 50. Over a decade of observation, researchers have documented a large number of scuffles between this group and its neighbors, commonly when they run into each other at feeding sites such as fruit trees. In these scuffles, generally the males fight but females and infants also may be attacked. In addition, during two of the years in which observations were made (2002 and 2004) researchers documented five lethal attacks on lone males encountered by a group of Ngogo males, four of which were observed, and one inferred from circumstantial evidence (Mitani and Watts 2005).

To study the formation of male coalitions, researchers followed males over a total of 24 months in periods spread over 5 years. They expected to find that patrols formed in response to factors such as female fertility, food availability, or the presence of intruders, but instead there was no pattern except for numbers. That is, if enough males congregated in one area (about 20), they would start out in a line to patrol the forest silently, stopping now and then to groom each other, embrace, and rub genitals. If they encountered an unaccompanied male they would attack, but if other males were present they retreated.

This behavior shows that male chimpanzees will join up to watch and defend territory provided they are numerous enough not to risk injury in a conflict. Previous studies have also confirmed that chimpanzees collaborate for the purpose of hunting colobus monkeys and bush babies. However, the behavior at Kibale does not constitute warfare or an attempt to expand territory, given that groups only attacked if they came across a lone male.

The other principal example of chimpanzee violence comes from Jane Goodall's (1986) observations in Tanzania's Gombe Game Reserve. Goodall spent 9 years observing the group before it split in 1969. The original group remained under the leadership of the alpha male. Within 2 years, its eight males appear to have killed all seven of the secessionist group. The secessionists had tried for years to challenge the alpha male before leaving as a group. Thereafter, they continued to overlap their former territory. The simplest explanation is that the secessionists insisted on encroaching upon the original group's territory. Similar to the Ngogo group in Kibale, proximate ecological and demographic pressures are more pertinent to the escalation of tensions than final causes such as inborn propensities for coalitional warfare.

The evidence for chimpanzee "warfare" at other sites is scarce and equivocal, in large part because researchers have not witnessed the violence or found bodies of chimps killed by other chimps. In any case, its frequency is very low considering how rarely it has been reported. Chimpanzee coalitional violence does not constitute an evolutionary basis for human warfare, not least because attacking individuals singly is fundamentally different than attacking a group and consequently does not qualify as warfare. Moreover, females carry out organized violence in other species including white-faced capuchins, western red colobus, and diana monkeys. In species such as macaques and baboons, the elderly females are the ones who protect the group from predation.

To reduce chimpanzee-ness to a tendency to confrontational violence obscures the complexity of social relationships and individual temperaments in these animals. Chimpanzees may be competitive, political, and vigilant about fairness, but they are also caring and solicitous to each other. They make long-term friendships and look out for each other. To illustrate, chimpanzees trained to trade color-coded lengths of PVC pipe for either a single or double portion of bananas more often procure food for themselves plus a friend than just for themselves. All seven animals in the study did this both spontaneously and in response to mild solicitation by the three different partners successively paired with them, although they responded less well if the partners were overtly demanding or put pressure on them (Horner et al. 2011).

Chimpanzees mourn the dead, teach each other, and share food. Particular groups have their own cultural knowledge and technology which is transmitted across generations, including distinctive tools and techniques such as sticks for termite or ant fishing, crumpled leaves that serve as sponges to soak up drinking water, and tree bark worn on the feet like sandals for walking over the spiny needles of fruit-bearing trees. Populations in West Africa are the only ones known to use rocks to crack nuts. Such cultural variations speak to chimpanzees' adaptability, creativity, and ability to communicate learned skills and information (Horner et al. 2006).

Most tellingly, nothing similar to warfare has been found among gorillas, orangutans, or bonobos. Neither lowland nor mountain gorillas display aggression toward neighboring groups. Orangutans are solitary except for mother-infant pairs. Bonobos live in large mixed-sex groups as do chimpanzees, but are sociable and averse to conflict.

Humans are equally closely related to bonobos and chimpanzees. The latter two were separated by the Congo River 1–2 million years ago, leaving bonobos on the south side. Their appearance is similar – except for the smaller size and more elongated shape of bonobos – and they both live in mixed-sex groups from which most females migrate out when they mature. However, in other ways chimpanzee and bonobo social organization and behavior vary dramatically. For instance, territorial defense on the part of chimpanzees, noted above, is unusual for a species organized into multi-male groups, for single-male groups such as gorillas generally are the territorial ones. Bonobos, which do not maintain boundaries, are more typical of multi-male groups.

Chimpanzees are far more hierarchical than bonobos, as seen in formulaic aggressive displays answered with submissive physical and vocal groveling. Males fight with each other and sometimes attack females as well; females scuffle and have been known to kill each other's offspring. Chimpanzee males are dominant over females, although in many groups females choose the alpha male. For both sexes, rank depends more on political skills than physical size and is achieved through effort. Higher-ranking males have first priority in feeding and get more mating opportunities on peak fertility days – although females manage to mate with all the males in the group during estrus. Chimpanzee males rarely venture out alone, whereas females often roam either by themselves or with their offspring, indicating that males do not habitually attack females.

Bonobos grow and mature more slowly than chimpanzees. The males take longer than females to begin ranging away from their mothers, and do not go as far. Whereas chimpanzee males become socially oriented toward other males as adolescents and adults, bonobo males stay near their mothers their whole lives.

Bonobo society is dominated by females. Females feed freely and tend to eat first, whereas males must defer to each other and to females, including the alpha male to the alpha female. Female dominance hierarchies take the implicit, understated form of respect for older females and are reinforced only under rare, highly disruptive circumstances such as rank changes among males, the outcome of which is determined by females. Males assert their status more often, but without the ritualized displays and political maneuverings used by chimpanzees. After a dispute, males mount each other or engage in back-to-back "rump rubbing" that is by definition equitable, whereas chimpanzee males reconcile less readily and with mounting that reaffirms their position in the hierarchy.

Bonobos actively avoid and alleviate social tensions associated with food or political changes, such as the arrival of a new female, by grooming each other and engaging in sexual activity with same-sex and opposite-sex individuals. Bonobos are highly sensitive to emotional cues from each other, and very adept at managing social relationships within the group and with other groups. They readily give each other affection and other signs of attachment, and they avoid fights and displays of power. Couples look each other in the eye before and during mating, which includes front-to-front copulation more often than occurs among other great apes.

Bonobos go out of their way to welcome strangers, as shown through a series of experiments at the Lola Ya sanctuary in the Democratic Republic of the Congo. A hungry bonobo was placed in a central enclosure with adjoining areas on either side: one for a stranger, the other for a familiar animal, each of which was separated from the central room by gates that could be opened only from the inside. The test animal was presented with food. After many repetitions with different animals, the results showed that the test animal not only saved most of the food to share with another animal, but was more likely to open the gate to the stranger than the familiar animal. In addition, the two bonobos would subsequently open the gate to the third animal. The stranger was more likely to do so than the test animal. Through other scenarios, the researchers also showed that the animals were willing to forego their own food only if presented an opportunity for social interaction with another animal. There was no aggression observed during any of the experiments (Tan and Hare 2013).

Genetic evidence indicates that humans are more like bonobos than chimps with respect to interest in strangers. The repetitive DNA sequence or microsatellite which modulates the expression of the gene for the vasopressin 1a receptor (*aypr 1a*) is virtually the same between humans and bonobos but differs by a few hundred base pairs in the case of chimpanzees. As noted in Chapter 7, vasopressin promotes sociability, parenting, and pair bonding. It stimulates social interest and improves the ability of animals to recognize one another through the sense of smell. In fact, male montane and meadow voles can be made to behave like highly social, pair-bonded prairie voles through genetic manipulation of the microsatellite. Treated animals more frequently lick and groom their pups and display more social interest in response to the odor or presence of another vole. Contrariwise, mutations in the microsatellite affecting *aypr 1a* in humans are associated with autism, which is associated with extreme social isolation and difficulties understanding and getting along with people (Hammock and Young 2005).

. . . . .

The comparison between bonobos and chimpanzees suggests that choosing one species as a model for human society is hazardous because of the variability in behavior between even very closely related species. In addition, conditions observed at one site may not be representative, given that demographic and environmental conditions may change. The presumed driving force for dominance hierarchies and warrior coalitions – the potentially extreme variability in male lifetime reproductive potential – does not universally result in pronounced, contested ranking systems among primate species. For males, increased status may or may not pay off in terms of reproductive and resource gains: for baboons it does, for bonobos it does not. Even where it does, top rank may be as stressful as bottom rank, as in savannah baboons, for whom second rank is better than first in terms of both reproductive opportunities and the physical harm caused by psychosocial stress (Gesquiere et al. 2011). In other words, the inverse relationship between rank and levels of adrenal steroid hormones (glucocorticoids) such as cortisol is not necessarily continuous. Moreover, while higher rank is experienced by primates as rewarding – as indicated in experimental situations by less self-medication with psychoactive drugs such as cocaine, thanks to higher levels of endogenous neuropeptides such as dopamine – falling down in rank brings a rise in atherosclerotic plaque formation and an increase in abdominal fat, two effects of stress seen also in humans.

Rank is not a simple question of size or aggressiveness, and challenging another animal physically is less common than posturing and aggressive displays. In species such as rhesus macaques, both the least and most aggressive animals have higher reproductive success than moderately aggressive monkeys. Compared to aggressiveness, sociability as demonstrated by friendships and alliances is more consistently linked to survival and reproductive success (Brent et al. 2013). In chimpanzees, males of a given rank who join alliances have higher reproductive success than those which do not. The greatest advantages accrue to chimpanzees who manage to unite individuals that are not inclined to join up with each other (Gilby et al. 2013).

The complexities of ranking systems and reproductively beneficial affiliative behavior have moved primatology beyond an earlier absorption with hierarchy and competition. Yet, human behavior continues to be seen in terms of male-male fighting over females. For instance, male-biased sex ratios are thought to bring increased violence due to intensified competition and stepped-up mate guarding. Finding that an equal number of studies show lower rates of violent crime, including homicide, rape, and sexual assault, Schacht et al. (2014) argue that male scarcity can result in lower rates of violence because men expend less energy on competition and are pushed to maintain stable relationships and provide more parenting effort. In both cases, violence is understood as mechanically responsive to the numerical availability of females, and every male trait or behavior, from creativity to crime, is interpreted as a strategy for obtaining mates, whether by charm or by force. As seen in Chapter 7, ultimate explanations fit poorly with actual mate-choice behavior. That opposite relationships between sex ratios and violence can be attributed to the same final cause – male reproductive interests – further highlights the need for other approaches to explaining human behavior.

In particular, a focus on the reproductive interests of males is unhelpful for understanding prosocial characteristics. Traditional evolutionary theory is constrained to explain all other-oriented behavior as beneficial to the survival and reproduction of the self or indeed to individual genes. More recent models attend to group or "multilevel" selection, which E.O. Wilson (2012) argues is better equipped to explain cooperative behavior than inclusive fitness (the principle by which helping behavior promotes the survival of genes shared with the recipient). That is, traits such as empathy evolved because cohesive groups did better than groups of selfish individualists who could not put aside their own interests in a confrontation with another group.

Wilson argues that evolution has left us with conflicting impulses between competing with members of our own group and collaborating in the face of threats from other groups. As evidence, he points to the tendency for people to believe that members of their own group are more competent, ethical, and trustworthy than people in other groups. Indeed, babies and children are inclined to favor people who are similar to them in any recognizable way – language, physical appearance, even colored clothing. This in-group preference is evident also in phenomena such as racism, sexism, nationalism, and religious and other kinds of bigotry.

On the other hand, people routinely respond to strangers with curiosity, friendliness, and openness to new ideas and customs. Interest in social interaction and learning from unfamiliar others is widespread across animal species. Whales abandon the habits of their natal group in favor of those observed in new associates, even without any material benefit such as a more efficient fishing technique (Allen et al. 2013); adolescent wild vervet monkeys taught a preference for colored corn in infancy switch to their new group's color preference upon in-migration, even when eating unobserved by other animals (van de Waal et al. 2013).

Prosocial behavior in humans and other animals suggests that empathy and other-orientation are not reducible to the necessity to get along in the face of outside threats, just as collaboration did not grow out of all-male coalitions organized for the purpose of fighting other males for territory and females. Life in small, face-to-face societies favors empathy, reciprocity, and fairness behavior for the good of the group and individual, as ends in themselves. These traits and behaviors are not directed only to insiders but extend outward, as well.

Experiments eliciting consolation behavior in prairie voles indicate that empathy does not require advanced cognition but rather is linked to ancient neurological pathways common to social species (Burkett et al. 2016). The same behavior does not appear in meadow or montane voles, which do not form pair bonds, live in organized social groups, or provide long-term parental care by both females and males. In the experimental situation, researchers repeatedly stress a prairie vole with electric shocks preceded by a warning sound. The mole is then united with another vole which has not been exposed to the stressor. Provided the distressed animal is familiar, although not necessarily a relative, the consoler mole licks and grooms it more immediately and for a longer period than if placed with a vole that has not been stressed. The care eliminates the anxiety behavior that develops in stressed voles left alone in a cage.

In addition, the consoler mole mimics the stressed vole's anxiety-induced rise in self-grooming and its freezing upon hearing the warning sound. If the consoler mole is denied physical contact with the distressed mole by a clear, perforated partition, its glucocorticoid levels rise like those of the distressed vole, indicating that empathetic behavior reduces stress in the consoler as well. Finally, injecting an oxytocin-receptor antagonist into the consoler mole's brain prevents the rise in grooming and licking behavior.

In voles as in other animals, oxytocin promotes nurturing, touching, and grooming. It induces more approach and less avoidance behavior. In humans, a variant of the oxytocin-receptor gene is associated with a higher likelihood of depression and lower levels of psychological resilience, self-esteem, impulse control, and optimism.

Oxytocin levels rise in response both to being trusted and trusting others. Research participants given a nasal spray of oxytocin improve their ability to discern emotional expressions in others and become more inclined to bond with their associates. Oxytocin administered before a game increases the level of trust participants demonstrate towards the other player, even if the game is played on a computer and the other player remains anonymous. These findings regarding the oxytocin system indicate that empathy is a very old mammalian trait.

Unconscious imitation during social interaction demonstrates that humans and other primates do not limit empathy and trust to individuals they know personally. Studies on experimental animals including macaque monkeys show that even if the animal is constrained to stay still, its "mirror neurons" behave as if it were imitating an observed action (Rizzolatti and Craighero 2004). Mimicking emotions causes psychological responses equal to the true experience of the same emotion, such as faster heartbeat, increased blood pressure, and hot and clammy hands in response to anger and distress. If people are forced to smile by clenching a pen between their teeth, they find the same cartoons much funnier than people who are prevented from smiling by holding the pen between their lips. Grasping the pen after the cartoon yields opposite reports: smilers rate the cartoons as less funny than those unable to smile, indicating that current emotional states modify perceptions of past situations (Strack et al. 1988). In sum, witnessing someone else's emotions provokes identical emotions; and emotional expression, whether genuine or feigned, has the same psychophysical impact.

Evidently, social competence does not require language. Indeed, it emerges first in infants.[4] Babies younger than one year know the difference between beings with faces and inanimate objects and that these categories of things behave in distinct ways; and they demonstrate empathy in the face of other people's emotions. They can read people's intentions (as in looking for a hidden object), which shows that they have theory of mind. They have a sense of right and wrong in human interactions, and they prefer helping behavior to interference. In experimental situations, if infants observe unfair behavior they train their eyes on the punisher responsible for dealing with the miscreant.

Children and adults unconsciously adjust their behavior in line with the expectations of authority figures such as parents and educators. Children score higher on tests if they know they are being observed or if their teachers have been primed to expect that they will perform well. This Pygmalion (or Rosenthal) Effect is similar to the Hawthorne Effect, which causes worker productivity to rise in response to any experimental alteration of the workplace, including changes designed to be neutral or negative such as fewer work hours. Termination of the experiment brings a decline in productivity. These measurable impacts of social contexts on individual perceptions and performance demonstrates a sensitivity to human interaction that goes beyond in-group preference.

. . . . .

Experiments involving economic games modeled on the prisoner's dilemma highlight the importance of other-orientation and fairness in human relationships. These studies suggest a stronger tendency towards reciprocal respect than unpunished opportunism. They reliably generate sharing and fairness behavior to a greater degree than hoarding and cheating.

In the dictator game, one player offers a portion of a sum of money to an unseen other; the other player decides whether to accept or reject the offer. The ultimatum game is the same except that the second player sets the limit for rejection in advance. In the case of rejection both finish the game with nothing. Players from industrialized societies generally share 40–50%, and most often offer one-half. The other player tends to reject the offer if it falls below one-fifth. In general, the proportion of rejected offers falls well below one-third. The rate of fairness and punishment behavior increases if research participants are permitted to communicate during the game. Rejection is less likely if responders are told that the offer came from a computer.

Compared to players accustomed to abstract financial transactions, players from non-Western societies behave in more variable ways, and often require several rounds of explanation and pre-testing to understand the rules. Au and Gnau forager-horticulturalists in northern Papua New Guinea offered the other player just over 40% on average, and one-third of offers were rejected. The rate of rejection was not only relatively high, but its pattern was different from industrialized societies, where players rarely reject fair or overly-generous offers. In addition to refusing most low offers (20% of the initial sum), recipients rejected three-fifths of high offers (70% of the initial sum). The latter speaks to the importance of honor and obligation in small, face-to-face communities where people are expected to respond open-handedly to any request but also not to impose obligations on others through immoderate gifts (Tracer 2003).

A study of three games played in 15 societies found that increasing degrees of market integration bring a higher likelihood that players will make fair offers, with the exception of a foraging society with low market integration but high rates of fair offers (Henrich et al. 2010). In addition, the larger the size of the community, the more likely is unfairness to be punished through rejected low offers in a two-player game or intervention by a third player who controls half the initial sum. Put another way, people from the smallest-scale societies tend to be the least severe about punishing low offers.

Comparison of games to economic behavior in everyday life sheds light on these results. Among Tsimane' forager-horticulturalists in two Bolivian villages, levels of giving in games does not correlate with degrees of fairness in actual behavior including work on a public well, social visits, and participation in and contributions of beer and food to village feasts (Gurven and Winking 2008). Evidently, the games do not accurately model the complex social field in which actual behavior occurs. The same reason explains why research participants rarely penalize the other player in games that include a punishment component. In real life, unacceptable behavior does not go unnoticed, but the game does not resemble a situation in which a familiar social norm is violated. Moreover, in the local context enforcement occurs through public damage to personal and family reputation rather than private financial penalties.

Studies on forests and fisheries here have demonstrated that in experiments as well as real-world situations, cooperation increases as people observe others choosing to cooperate, especially if the number of free riders is kept low (Poteete et al. 2010). Over time, the level of individual compliance and investment in enforcement rises where there are trustworthy institutions, respected leaders, and a high proportion of people who are willing to cooperate. These findings suggest that low social integration, unchecked corruption, and institutionalized unfairness promote conflict and resource degradation, which together increase the likelihood of violence, as seen in the following chapters.

. . . . .

The high level of social awareness and other-orientation described above is congruent with evidence that social integration is beneficial to individuals and societies, whereas social isolation is injurious. The benefits and costs convey the evolutionary importance of human prosocial characteristics and cast doubt on the advantageousness of hierarchy.[5]

Individual wellbeing depends to a great degree on social relationships. Behaviors and health outcomes link people to others in their social universe, even at the farthest reaches; these include smoking, overweight/obesity, immunization compliance, diet and physical activity, heart disease, and happiness.[6] People who provide social support to others have better self-reported health, lower sickness and death rates overall, and reduced risk of specific diseases such as diabetes or heart attack. Their blood pressure is lower. People in long-term intimate relationships have better health and mortality rates than those who are single – whether never-married/partnered, separated or divorced, or widowed.

High levels of social integration are associated with lower risks of mortality, depression, and, among older people, risk of falling down, as well as greater emotional wellbeing, life satisfaction, and self-reported mental health. Subjective wellbeing is associated, in turn, with better physical health, more years of life, lower frequency of accidents and suicide, and increased resiliency in the face of adverse life events. In contrast, social isolation has an effect on mortality risk roughly equivalent to smoking, and greater than obesity or any lifestyle factor such as physical inactivity.

Inclusion and participation in a social group stimulate the same pleasure-and-reward areas of the brain that deal with important behaviors such as eating and sex, and activate the same endogenous opiates. In contrast, rejection and social isolation are processed by the brain in the same way as physical pain, and dampen activity in the prefrontal cortex that handles restraint and impulse control. Drugs such as cocaine and marijuana bind to the same receptors as mood-enhancing neuropeptides such as dopamine and serotonin, which explains high rates of substance abuse in isolating, stratified environments. Even fruit flies drink more alcohol if subjected to social isolation, rejection, or sexual deprivation (Shohat-Ophir et al. 2012).

Chronic social isolation alters brain activity during interpersonal interactions, rendering even friendly encounters and activities less satisfying. Activated areas of the brain concerned with threat detection, such as the amygdala, bring heightened alertness to negative social cues such as facial expressions and pejorative words. This further increases anxiety and, combined with reduced impulse control, the likelihood of lashing out in response.

Psychosocial stress triggers the threat-and-danger response including the secretion of epinephrine and glucocorticoids such as cortisol. Workers at the lowest job ranks, with the least amount of control over their work, have the highest cortisol levels. Those in the top ranks, such as leaders in business and government, have the lowest levels. Among these least-stressed workers, cortisol levels are lowest in people with the most independence and scope for directing others (Sherman et al. 2012).

In limited amounts, stress is an appropriate response to adverse circumstances. It generates higher levels of resilience than the absence of stress, as seen in laboratory animals exposed to short separations from their mothers in infancy compared to those never left alone. Over time, however, chronic stress provokes widespread damage because cells in the nervous and immune system communicate with each other, produce some of the same substances, and have far-reaching effects throughout the body. For instance, increased vascular resistance causes increased blood pressure, with consequences for organs such as the heart and kidneys. Prolonged stress causes genes associated with inflammation to become more active, but genes associated with suppressing inflammation to become less active, increasing the likelihood of a wide range of health concerns including heart disease and some cancers.

Chronic stress leaves its mark on the telomeres, the clusters of short DNA repeats at the ends of the chromosomes that keep them from binding together, indicating faster aging and therefore higher all-cause mortality risk. The length of the telomeres declines with successive cell divisions, until the cell can no longer divide and either self-destructs or enters a restful state of limited activity. Psychosocial stress impinges on telomere length by generating more free radical molecules, which cause oxidative stress, and less of the enzyme telomerase that can attach DNA segments to telomeres and thereby forestall their degradation. Accelerated cellular aging has been verified in many groups subjected to severe stress, including children whose mothers endured traumatizing events during pregnancy; children exposed to maltreatment, neglect, or trauma (or adults who experienced adversity in childhood); adult victims of physical abuse; and mothers of chronically sick children (Blackburn et al. 2015).

The connection between stress and inequality has been well established since the original Whitehall studies on British civil servants led by Michael Marmot beginning in the late 1960s (Marmot et al. 1991). The first studies concerned men only. At the time, heart disease was considered an affliction of powerful men, but the studies found that lowest-ranking men die from cardiovascular disease at 3 times the rate of highest-ranking men. In between there is an inverse gradient between employment grade and heart disease mortality. In addition, as job rank decreases, the risk of a number of other conditions and diseases rises, including back pain, certain cancers, diseases of the lung and gastrointestinal tract, depression, suicide, and poor perceived health. Lack of material wellbeing clearly is not the reason, given that staff members of every grade have job stability, adequate income, and access to medical care. Less favorable lifestyle and health indicators among people in the lower job positions likewise do not account for the difference. After controlling for smoking, high blood pressure, low levels of exercise, and obesity, two-thirds of the increased risk of heart disease remains.

Social inequality has direct effects on wellbeing due to unequal living conditions and exposures to health threats (see Chapter 3), but the information above shows that inequality is harmful even where material needs are broadly met. One cause involves relative deprivation, or the sense that others have more of the good things in life: status, material objects, schooling, leisure time, even space – such as bigger offices and houses. The effects are evident in levels of stress-related biomarkers, as shown in South Pacific islands where young people in the most remote areas are less stressed than those in semi-rural areas near cities, who, in turn, are less stressed than young people in urban areas with the most exposure to globalized culture and consumer products (McDade et al. 2000). In addition, social divisions are noxious to groups marked as different (see Chapters 6 and 9), as seen in the worse health of minorities living in majority neighborhoods compared to individuals of the same minority who live in minority neighborhoods, even though the former enjoy a higher standard of living. Media saturation in hierarchical societies increases people's vulnerability to invidious comparisons, earnest status competition, and all-consuming investment in the pursuit of grandiose but unrealizable goals, and therefore to psychosocial stress and depression (Nesse 2000).

For marginalized groups, the uneven distribution of high-quality food in stratified societies can exacerbate the effects of psychosocial stress and contribute to aggressive behavior. Dietary deficiencies are linked to defects of attention and learning, reduced impulse control, and physical aggression. Combined with a diet poor in vitamins, minerals, and fatty acids, excessive sugar intake is associated with a much higher frequency of conduct disorders. Contrariwise, programs that provide nutritious food to low-income schoolchildren, homeless people, and prisoners bring reductions in antisocial behavior, violence, self-harm, and mental distress. Young male prisoners in the UK committed fewer offenses after receiving nutritional supplements than before, and fewer offenses than the control group. In psychological tests, they showed more restraint and better impulse control (Gesch et al. 2002).

Across wealthy nations and within the US, higher levels of socioeconomic inequality correlate with poorer population health, lower-quality social relationships, and higher rates of violent crime (Wilkinson and Pickett 2009). Life expectancy is lower and infant and general mortality rates are higher. More specifically, there are higher rates of disease-specific morbidity and mortality from causes including obesity and overweight, heart disease, hypertension, cancer, diabetes, and chronic lung disease. More unequal societies have higher rates of depression and anxiety.

Higher degrees of inequality are associated with lower levels of social cohesion, civic engagement, and mutual trust. Lower scores on these measures of social capital are associated with more low-birth-weight babies, less seatbelt use, and poorer provision of medical services. People work more hours and have fewer vacation days. There is less, not more, social mobility. More unequal nations and states within the US have lower levels of educational performance and literacy.

They have higher rates of imprisonment, teenage pregnancy, and illicit drug use, and more conflict and trouble such as bullying among children and adolescents. Women's status is lower, and there are more violent crimes such as robbery and rape. The extra burden of crime and health and social problems requires more government services. Greater inequality brings not only more violence but also more worry and dread of it, resulting in diminished quality of life. Socially disadvantaged groups, such as women, ethnic minorities, and the elderly, are more likely to fear violence than are high-status groups.

Compared to other high-income countries including England, the US has lower life expectancy and higher disease and injury rates. This is not due to health disparities that result in worse health outcomes for minorities and lower-income groups, but rather applies across all socioeconomic categories including the well-off (Woolf and Aron 2013). Consequently, even the top tier of stratified societies would be better off along with everyone else under circumstances of lessened inequality.

. . . . .

Stratification is related to cultural beliefs about interpersonal interaction which influence the likelihood of confrontational versus peaceful behavior. As seen in the next chapter, face-to-face, egalitarian societies cultivate values emphasizing modesty and consideration for others. To illustrate, Fry (2006) describes the Semai, who live in groups of up to 100 people in Malaysia. They grow crops using slash-and-burn horticulture and collect wild foods such as fish, game, and plants. There is a village leader (male or female) who has moral influence over others but is not supported by any formal political structure. Children learn about peaceful interactions beginning in early childhood. At most, any misbehavior brings a gentle pinch or a pat on the hand. Children are never struck, for adults believe that it would cause fatal illness, and they are not permitted to use violence in their relationships with others.

Violence is not a behavioral alternative presented to Semai children. Neighbors do not get into disputes, spouses and other adults do not hit each other, and the villages have no history of external violence such as feuds or wars with other groups. Children grow up sharing the horror adults feel at the very idea of physical aggression.

The Semai example shows that gentleness in human relations depends on a favorable social context, not that people are naturally good. In fact, when enlisted by the British military for counterinsurgency campaigns in the 1950s, individual Semai adapted to the necessity of killing enemies with alacrity. That is, even people raised to abhor violence can be brought to brutality through changed circumstances.

Psychological experiments demonstrate that people who learn to control their impulses in childhood are better equipped to get along with others and handle the responsibilities of life. For instance, Walter Mischel et al. (1989) presented 4-year-old children a choice between ringing a bell to call a researcher into the room and be able to enjoy a treat left on the table immediately, or wait until the researcher returned after about 15 minutes and be given a greater treat instead. The difference in the amount or value of toys or sweets was calculated to place the child in a dilemma. A decade later, the adolescents who had been able to delay gratification in the "marshmallow test" received more favorable parental assessments of their cognitive and social proficiency, including concentration and reasoning capacity, tolerance for frustration and stress, ability to think ahead and plan, and avoidance of problems in interpersonal relationships or with substance abuse.

Mischel's studies highlight the role of training in early childhood, for delay time was longer in children who spontaneously diverted themselves by covering their eyes, playing, or singing, or who were advised by the researchers to use distracting thoughts in order to endure the wait. In line with the relationship between small stresses and increased resiliency mentioned earlier, this suggests that children would benefit from being forced to deal with temporarily unmet requests such as permission to interrupt an adult conversation, rather than being instantly obliged in order to cultivate their assertiveness and exceptionality.

In every society, individuals are embedded in family and social relationships, yet concepts of personhood vary widely. Where individuals see themselves in relation to others, conflict is less likely and remediation more probable. Where personhood is defined in radically individualistic terms, interests are more likely to collide. Paradoxically, the latter type of personhood is more typical of mass societies in which there is no escape from systems of domination and control, and which therefore do a relatively poor job of safeguarding personal autonomy.

As Clifford Geertz (1983) explains,

> The Western conception of a person as a bounded, unique, more or less integrated motivational and cognitive universe, a dynamic center of awareness, emotion, judgment, and action organized into a distinctive whole and set contrastively both against other such wholes and against its social and natural background, is, however incorrigible it may seem to us, a rather peculiar idea within the context of the world's cultures.

Geertz contrasts this ideal against more explicitly socially embedded understandings in other ethnographic settings. He describes a high sense of civilized conscientiousness with regard to protecting one's own and other people's emotional equilibrium in Java; a controlled, self-effacing performance of standardized behavior by persons defined according to birth order, caste, sex, and kinship in Bali; and a conditional identity dependent on associations to people, profession, and place in Morocco that shifts in line with immediate circumstances.

In contrast to socially embedded personhood, autonomous personhood construes the self as a bounded, fixed essence. Combined with constant exposure to status differences inherent in stratified societies, this view encourages individuals to assert and defend their interests rather than defer to others. A confrontational attitude is embedded in the language itself, allowing violence to be seen as a legitimate response to conflict. English-language literature, politics, and everyday conversation are replete with metaphors of battle and violent sports, as in words such as ambush, attack, fray, aim, strike, shoot, parry, counterattack, surrender, and so on. Military imagery is highly meaningful to Western culture, as is evident in historiography, mythology, and entertainments which celebrate heroic narratives of violent conflict.

As noted in Chapter 1, language and cultural metaphors profoundly shape perception. In fact, if researchers use more brutal words while asking people to recall an incident such as a car accident they watched on a screen, respondents remember the event in more violent terms – higher speeds, greater impact, even broken glass where there was none. The everyday use of confrontational, aggressive language consequently channels how people interpret interactions and communicate with each other. It appears as if everything is a battle with only two sides and only one winner. Tolerance of ambiguity and open-endedness is cast as weakness or indecisiveness, a willingness to yield dishonoring – as if compromise in language were the same as inconstancy in substance. If a disagreement is set up as a conflict, then neither side can acquiesce or withdraw gracefully. As Deborah Tannen (1999) explains, cooperation comes not from spontaneous harmony but rather represents the successful control of discord. Constraint is more feasible where differences are not set up as win-lose situations.

As seen in the next chapter, neither confrontation nor spontaneous harmony is inherent in the human condition. Control of discord requires individual and social investment. Egalitarian societies maintain a relationship matrix that prevents individuals and groups from dominating others. Children do not expect inequalities, and as adults they do not seek to create them in their turn.

. . . . .

The strands of evidence collected in this chapter indicate that hierarchy and violence are not the product of primal raiding behavior in our distant ancestors. The degree of hierarchy varies among primate species, and competition for rank is not always beneficial or more effective than collaborative behavior for increasing reproductive success. The well-established traits of empathy, concern for fairness, and interest in strangers which humans share with chimpanzees, bonobos, and other mammals cast further doubt on the assumption that people cannot help trying to dominate or eliminate each other.

Stratification is harmful to individuals and societies and plays a key role in the health transitions discussed in earlier chapters. Previous mortality transitions depended predominantly on living conditions that affected nutrition, hygiene, and infectious diseases. Today, social inequality continues to maintain uneven standards of living while also generating psychosocial stress through status competition and real and perceived differences in opportunities and material assets. Hierarchy hurts.

Notes

1 On stories and interpretations of cannibalism, especially in Papua New Guinea, see Goldman (1999).
2 On anthropophagy in the American Southwest, see Lally (2005); Marlar et al. (2000).

3 This section on mother love is based on Whitaker (2000).
4 On the minds of babies, see Bloom (2004).
5 On social connectedness, resiliency, and psychosocial stress, see De Dreu et al. (2010); Norman et al. (2011); Saphire-Bernstein et al. (2011).
6 On connections between health and social integration, see Brown et al. (2003); Smith and Christakis (2008); Weitoft et al. (2000).

References cited

Allen J, Weinrich M, Hoppitt W, Rendell L. 2013. Network-based diffusion analysis reveals cultural transmission of lobtail feeding in humpback whales. *Science* 340(6131):485–488.

Blackburn EH, Epel ES, Lin J. 2015. Human telomere biology: a contributory and interactive factor in aging, disease risks, and protection. *Science* 350(6265):1193–1198.

Bloom P. 2004. *Descartes's baby: how the science of child development explains what makes us human.* New York: Basic Books.

Brent LJ, Heilbronner SR, Horvath JE, Gonzalez-Martinez J, Ruiz-Lambides A, Robinson AG, Skene JP, Platt ML. 2013. Genetic origins of social networks in rhesus macaques. *Scientific Reports* 3:1042. doi: 10.1038/srep01042.

Brown SL, Nesse RM, Vinokur AD, Smith DM. 2003. Providing social support may be more beneficial than receiving it: results from a prospective study of mortality. *Psychological Science* 14(4):320–327.

Burkett JP, Andari E, Johnson ZV, Curry DC, de Waal FB, Young LJ. 2016. Oxytocin-dependent consolation behavior in rodents. *Science* 351(6271):375–378.

Chagnon N. 1997[1968]. *Yanomamö.* 5th ed. New York: Harcourt Brace.

De Dreu CK, Greer LL, Handgraaf MJ, Shalvi S, Van Kleef GA, Baas M, Ten Velden FS, Van Dijk E, Feith SW. 2010. The neuropeptide oxytocin regulates parochial altruism in intergroup conflict among humans. *Science* 328(5984):1408–1411.

Fry DP. 2006. *The human potential for peace: an anthropological challenge to assumptions about war and violence.* New York: Oxford University Press.

Geertz C. 1983. *Local knowledge: further essays in interpretive anthropology.* New York: Basic Books.

Gesch CB, Hammond SM, Hampson SE, Eves A, Crowder MJ. 2002. Influence of supplementary vitamins, minerals and essential fatty acids on the antisocial behaviour of young adult prisoners. *The British Journal of Psychiatry* 181(1):22–28.

Gesquiere LR, Learn NH, Simao MC, Onyango PO, Alberts SC, Altmann J. 2011. Life at the top: rank and stress in wild male baboons. *Science* 333(6040):357–360.

Gilby IC, Brent LJ, Wroblewski EE, Rudicell RS, Hahn BH, Goodall J, Pusey AE. 2013. Fitness benefits of coalitionary aggression in male chimpanzees. *Behavioral Ecology and Sociobiology* 67(3):373–381.

Goldman LR, editor. 1999. *The anthropology of cannibalism.* Westport, CT: Bergin and Garvey.

Goodall J. 1986. *The chimpanzees of Gombe: patterns of behavior.* Cambridge: Belknap Press.

Gordon-Grube K. 1988. Anthropophagy in post-Renaissance Europe: the tradition of medicinal cannibalism. *American Anthropologist* 90(2):405–409.

Gurven M, Winking J. 2008. Collective action in action: prosocial behavior in and out of the laboratory. *American Anthropologist* 110(2):179–190.

Hammock EA, Young LJ. 2005. Microsatellite instability generates diversity in brain and sociobehavioral traits. *Science* 308(5728):1630–1634.

Henrich J, Ensminger J, McElreath R, Barr A, Barrett C, Bolyanatz A, Cardenas JC, Gurven M, Gwako E, Henrich N, et al. 2010. Markets, religion, community size, and the evolution of fairness and punishment. *Science* 327(5972):1480–1484.

Horner V, Carter JD, Suchak M, de Waal FB. 2011. Spontaneous prosocial choice by chimpanzees. *Proceedings of the National Academy of Sciences* 108(33):13847–13851.

Horner V, Whiten A, Flynn E, de Waal FB. 2006. Faithful replication of foraging techniques along cultural transmission chains by chimpanzees and children. *Proceedings of the National Academy of Sciences* 103(3):13878–13883.

Lally EF. 2005. Hopi and the cannibalism issue: science and oral history in conflict. *Anthropology News* 46(4):13–15.

Lindenbaum S. 1979. *Kuru sorcery: disease and danger in the New Guinea Highlands.* Palo Alto: Mayfield.

Marlar RA, Leonard BL, Billman BR, Lambert PM, Marlar JE. 2000. Biochemical evidence of cannibalism at a prehistoric Puebloan site in southwestern Colorado. *Nature* 407(6800):74–78.

Marmot MG, Stansfeld S, Patel C, North F, Head J, White I, Brunner E, Feeney A, Smith GD. 1991. Health inequalities among British civil servants: the Whitehall II study. *The Lancet* 337(8754):1387–1393.

McDade TW, Stallings JF, Worthman CM. 2000. Culture change and stress in Western Samoan youth: methodological issues in the cross-cultural study of stress and immune function. *American Journal of Human Biology* 12(6):792–802.

Mischel W, Shoda Y, Rodriguez ML. 1989. Delay of gratification in children. *Science* 244(4907):933–938.

Mitani JC, Watts DP. 2005. Correlates of territorial boundary patrol behaviour in wild chimpanzees. *Animal Behaviour* 70(5):1079–1086.

Nesse RM. 2000. Is depression an adaptation? *Archives of General Psychiatry* 57(1):14–20.

Norman GJ, DeVries AC, Cacioppo JT, Bernston GG. 2011. Multilevel analysis of stress. In Contrada RJ, Baum A, editors. *Handbook of stress science: biology, psychology, and health.* New York: Springer. p. 619–634.

Poteete AR, Janssen MA, Ostrum E. 2010. *Working together: collective action, the commons, and multiple methods in practice.* Princeton, NJ: Princeton University Press.

Rizzolatti G, Craighero L. 2004. The mirror-neuron system. *Annual Review of Neuroscience* 27:169–192.

Saphire-Bernstein S, Way BM, Kim HS, Sherman DK, Taylor SE. 2011. Oxytocin receptor gene (OXTR) is related to psychological resources. *Proceedings of the National Academy of Sciences* 108(37):15118–15122.

Schacht R, Rauch KL, Borgerhoff Mulder M. 2014. Too many men: the violence problem? *Trends in Ecology and Evolution* 29(4):214–222.

Scheper-Hughes N. 1992. *Death without weeping: the violence of everyday life in Brazil.* Berkeley: University of California Press.

Science. 2011. Untitled brief. *Science* 331(6020):994.

Sharp LA. 2001. Commodified kin: death, mourning, and competing claims on the bodies of organ donors in the United States. *American Anthropologist* 103(1):112–133.

Sherman GD, Lee JJ, Cuddy AJ, Renshon J, Oveis C, Gross JJ, Lerner JS. 2012. Leadership is associated with lower levels of stress. *Proceedings of the National Academy of Sciences* 109(44):17903–17907.

Shohat-Ophir G, Kaun KR, Azanchi R, Mohammed H, Heberlein U. 2012. Sexual deprivation increases ethanol intake in Drosophila. *Science* 335(6074):1351–1355.

Smith KP, Christakis NA. 2008. Social networks and health. *Annual Review of Sociology* 34:405–429.

Strack F, Martin LL, Stepper S. 1988. Inhibiting and facilitating conditions of the human smile: a non-obtrusive test of the facial feedback hypothesis. *Journal of Personality and Social Psychology* 54(5):768–777.

Tan J, Hare B. 2013. Bonobos share with strangers. *PLoS One* 8(1):e51922.

Tannen D. 1999. *The argument culture: moving from debate to dialogue.* New York: Ballantine Books.

Tierney P. 2000. *Darkness in El Dorado: how scientists and journalists devastated the Amazon.* New York: Norton.

Tracer DP. 2003. Selfishness and fairness in economic and evolutionary perspective: an experimental economic study in Papua New Guinea. *Current Anthropology* 44(3):432–438.

van de Waal E, Borgeaud C, Whiten A. 2013. Potent social learning and conformity shape a wild primate's foraging decisions. *Science* 340(6131):483–485.

Weitoft GR, Haglund B, Rosén M. 2000. Mortality among lone mothers in Sweden: a population study. *The Lancet* 355(9211):1215–1219.

Whitaker ED. 2000. *Measuring mamma's milk: fascism and the medicalization of maternity in Italy.* Ann Arbor: University of Michigan Press.

Wilkinson R, Pickett K. 2009. *The spirit level: why greater equality makes societies stronger.* New York: Bloomsbury Press.

Wilson EO. 2012. *The social conquest of Earth.* New York: WW Norton.

Woolf SH, Aron L, editors. 2013. *US health in international perspective: shorter lives, poorer health.* Washington, DC: National Academies Press.

Wrangham R, Peterson D. 1996. *Demonic males: apes and the origin of human violence.* Boston: Houghton Mifflin.

11

WHY STRATIFY?

Inequality and interpersonal violence

The last chapter showed that strict dominance hierarchies are not a requirement of primate existence, and are harmful on the downward path and to those at the bottom. Across human societies, increased inequality brings worse health and more severe social problems, including violence. In addition, beliefs and values about the place of violence in managing frustration and self-interest contribute to cross-cultural variability in the way people deal with disagreements and obstacles.

This chapter examines connections between stratification and interpersonal violence. It shows that, contrary to the popular image of prehistoric life as a battle of bloodthirsty opportunists, nomadic foraging is incompatible with lethal interpersonal violence and the formation of violent male coalitions. Foraging and food sharing favor interdependence instead of unbridled competition. Aggressive, domineering individuals are selected against, not for. Small societies with open, fluid membership are tied to other groups through kinship, reciprocity, and friendship, and consequently have little incentive to assault them. The absence of significant wealth and landownership precludes raiding behavior.

In contrast, permanent settlement together with intensive food production favors territoriality, wealth accumulation, class hierarchy, and political domination. Competition for wealth and status generates self-aggrandizing behavior that divides and isolates people. Agricultural and industrial societies have the means and beliefs to carry out forms of inhumanity without any parallel in smaller-scale societies, such as the wars and genocides of the last century. As shown below, the roots of monstrous behavior lie close to the surface in social and economic systems, not deep in an atavistic inhuman nature.

. . . . .

The following discussion concerns violence from a population perspective, and consequently leaves aside cases of genetic variants or psychopathologies that predispose rare individuals to violence and can arise in any society. It also sets aside modern terrorism due to its incomparability to warfare or terror tactics used by political regimes to subdue or control populations. The analysis follows Douglas Fry's (2006) definitions of conflict, aggression, and violence. To Fry, conflict denotes colliding interests with respect to anything from tangible objects – such as a contested boyfriend or boundary – to moral concerns, such as how to discipline a child. Aggression concerns intentional behavior aimed at harming others, although not necessarily through physical injury – as in emotional or social aggression. Physical aggression refers to the use of force against another person. Violence involves a more severe use of direct physical force that is meant to be very injurious and possibly fatal.

Fry divides violence into two types. Internal violence refers to within-society violence such as spouse abuse, fighting and homicide, and feuding. It is primarily one-on-one violence, although other people sometimes get involved. External violence refers to warfare and raiding. It involves groups of people fighting other groups for political rather than personal reasons. This and the next chapter focus on direct physical harm, even though, as seen in previous chapters, structural violence exerted through politico-economic systems can just as assuredly hurt and kill people – for example, through exposure to hunger, unsanitary conditions, psychosocial stress, or lack of access to medical care.

Internal and external violence are fundamentally unalike. The first is caused by aggression; the second causes individuals to behave aggressively. In warfare, usually the decision-makers are not directly involved in the fighting. Soldiers are expected to kill enemies out of duty, not because they like to murder other people. Their participation may be involuntary or offered willingly, not just out of patriotism but also for practical reasons. Soldiers who turn out to relish killing are expelled or disciplined.

In order for warfare to work, in fact, people have to be trained to overcome a very strong, virtually universal aversion to killing. Only 1–2% of humans, including soldiers, would rather kill someone else than be killed. As a result, psychological distress and suicide have become far more frequent among soldiers as the lethality of weapons has increased along with the pool of people considered enemies. Murderousness may be glorified by the media and entertainment industry, but it is not most humans' preferred state and it has disastrous effects on those who are encouraged or forced to embrace it (Grossman 2009).

. . . . .

Interpersonal conflict is common enough cross-culturally, but in peaceful societies violence is extremely rare and social disapproval of physical assault very heavy. There are at least 80 such societies in the ethnographic record (Fry 2006). They span all the major world regions, including: Africa (Mbuti, G/wi, Ju/'hoansi); Asia (Batak Agta, Ladakhi, Semai Senoi, Semang); Europe (Icelanders, Norwegians, Saami/Lapp); Oceania (Arapesh, Ifaluk, Tikopia); North America (Amish, Canadian and Greenland Inuit, Taos Pueblo); and, South America (Kuikuru, Siriono, Wauju/Waura).

Internally peaceful societies stress the importance of a calm, conscientious demeanor. Aggressiveness is so destabilizing to small, face-to-face societies that individuals who repeat violent behavior are disciplined through banishment or, in extreme cases, capital punishment. Violent individuals have been executed for the safety of the group in indigenous North American, African, and Australian societies. To illustrate, among the Netsilik of the Central Canadian Arctic, disputes – often between two men over a woman – sometimes led to violence. Usually the conflict was resolved in nonlethal ways, as in ritualized fights or song duels (see Chapter 12), but sometimes there was a homicide. It was acceptable for a man to kill once, but any further killing showed that he was mentally unstable and dangerous to others. The man's family would make the decision to kill him. Since his own relatives were involved, the punishment did not set off the usual chain of revenge killings.[1]

The cultural expectation of mildness in peaceful societies is not a guarantee against disagreements and hostilities.[2] Quarrels erupt over failures of generosity, humility, and productiveness, as well as clashes over sexual partners. Women and men bicker with each other or other women and men over jealousy, indiscrete adultery, or withholding of physical affection, and sometimes they fight. Disputants may scuffle with each other, throw objects, or hit each other with a stick. Their friends or relatives may join them, but eventually onlookers intervene and bring the conflict to an end before anyone is badly hurt. Significantly, male violence against women is not culturally condoned.

Over a period of 3 years among the Ju/'hoansi in southern Africa, Richard Lee (1979) recorded 34 physical fights in a combined population of around 400 people. None involved deadly weapons, even though spears and poisoned arrows were readily available. In six cases, an implement such as a stick was used during the tussle. In all but two cases, the people walked away with nothing but a few scrapes or minor cuts. There were no fatalities.

Colin Turnbull (1965) described fights but no violent deaths in a population of about 250 Mbuti foragers of the Central African Republic during his 14 months of research. Someone seemed to bicker just about every day. A more serious dispute would erupt every 3–4 days, for a total of 124 conflicts. Physical fighting never involved an implement other than wood (stick or log), although sometimes people would use a spear as a threat. More than half the conflicts were about food (67). The others concerned sex (37), relations with villagers (11), theft (5), and territory (4). These lesser causes grew out of the regular contact between Mbuti foragers and villagers on the edge of the forest.

The food-related conflicts revolved around unfair contributions to work such as net hunting, disputes over the distribution of shares, and contributions to family meals through provision of food or competent cooking. The conflicts about sex concerned men who put off marriage or married men's neglect of their wives or obligations to in-laws. Adultery was *not* a common reason, as affairs were acceptable for women and men as long as they were carried out with discretion, as was premarital sex.

Turnbull took a representative sample of 34 interpersonal conflicts to analyze in depth. Of the 15 quarrels which resulted in physical fighting, 10 involved two people while five involved two to five pairs of disputants. Only one of the one-on-one fights involved sticks or firewood, compared to four of the five multiple-pair skirmishes. Both men and women were involved in physical aggression, but where spouses were concerned it was always the men who started it. No implements were used between spouses, except in one case in which a wife fought back wielding a burning log.

People exercised restraint in all cases, even the bigger brawls involving several disputants. Other people intervened as the fight became serious, mostly verbally but physically if necessary. This was done especially if one of the combatants drew blood or struck someone in the face, both of which were considered unacceptable. The non-disputants shouted abuse at the people fighting until they either broke down in laughter because the comments became more and more outlandish, or they walked off and sulked for a day.

The scenarios described by Lee and Turnbull show that arguments are common even in foraging societies, but can be kept from escalating to severe violence by restraint and onlooker intervention. In contrast, in large urban societies violent crimes occur under the watch of unresponsive witnesses; looters run amok after natural disasters. Such behaviors reflect a relative dearth of both social control and helping behavior in anonymous mass society.

. . . . .

While most conflict between people is resolved without harm, it sometimes leads to homicide even in peaceful societies. Some homicides occurred in prehistory, as well, although the frequency is unclear due to ambiguous evidence and the tendency for skeletal damage to be interpreted as owing to murder and cannibalism rather than ordinary causes such as hungry animals or shifting earth.[3] Paired punctures in skulls are attributed to violence even though it would be difficult to land such a blow – assuming a proper tool existed – and even though the holes match the canines of tigers or saber-toothed cats. Scratch marks assumed to be due to scalping have ended up being caused by laboratory workers. The perforations on the skull of the 3- or 4-year-old australopithecine "Taung child" found in South Africa are now known to have been made by the talon of one of the enormous eagles inhabiting the landscape at the same time. The damage to *Homo erectus* skulls found at China's Zhoukoudian cave points to the way hyenas feed on prey, not how human ancestors brutalized and ate each other.

Even where the damage speaks clearly of projectile points, such as the arrow tip embedded in the shoulder of the 5,000-year-old "Ice Man" found in northern Italy, the cause may have been accidental, as occurs among hunters today. Instead, bone fractures and scars suggesting spears used by Neanderthals 50,000–40,000 years ago at the Shandihar site in Iraq, or projectiles used by modern humans at various locations in Europe, North Africa, and North America from 30,000–2,000 years ago, are routinely attributed to malice. In any event, even if all of the evidence were caused by deliberate violence, it would only mean that human ancestors sometimes killed each other – not that they were homicidal maniacs or that they engaged in warfare. As noted in Chapter 3, increased rates of forearm and skull fractures from after the advent of agriculture suggest a much higher rate of violence once human groups founded permanent settlements.

Homicide rates for small societies are unreliable for a variety of reasons, including the fact that they are based on oral testimony that generally concerns past events. Miscalculations have led to the idea that these societies are more violent than state societies – a notion that falls on very receptive ears given its implications for theories about human nature. For instance, among the Semai discussed in the last chapter, two murders occurred in the period from 1955–1977. Based on a local group of 300 rather than the true population of 15,000, it appears as if the homicide rate were 50 times higher than the correct one, or nearly 30 instead of 0.56 homicides per 100,000 inhabitants per year. It is significant that one of the two homicides consisted of the abandonment of a terminally ill individual, as opposed to an instance of direct violence (Fry 2006).

Ju/'hoansi informants told Richard Lee that 22 people died from 1920–1955 in 37 conflicts involving weapons. This number has been used to calculate a homicide rate of 30–42 per 100,000 per year, even though during Lee's stay there were no homicides – a rate of zero. Similar stories told to ethnographers have led to statistics such as 300–500 or more violent deaths per 100,000 among the Copper Eskimo and the Enga and Gebusi of Papua New Guinea (Kelly 2003).

Homicide rates are inherently incomparable between small and large populations. In large populations there are homicides every year, from which rates can be calculated that do not fluctuate drastically over time. In small populations, many years may go by without a single homicide. This time dimension, together with sampling effects where the number of people is low, makes it unlikely that homicide rates in any year or string of years faithfully represent the true probability of homicide in a small society. Moreover, capital punishment and accidental killing of peacemakers or bystanders are counted as homicide in the case of indigenous societies, but not state societies. Most reported killings in foraging societies are of these two types, including those analyzed by Lee (1979). Finally, indigenous societies do not have medical examiners and bureaucrats who certify and register deaths, which means that purported homicides may have resulted from other causes. Where homicide counts are based on oral testimony, the numbers may be inflated by sorcery beliefs according to which several people may take credit or blame for the same death, or maintain that their actions caused a death that in reality occurred for other reasons.

Overall, homicide rates for foraging societies tend to be exceedingly low – below 1 per 100,000 per year. Agricultural societies have homicide rates on the order of 4–6 per 100,000 per year, but in areas without effective state governments the rates can reach the 20s and higher – far higher than rates in industrialized societies. Homicide rates swing from moderate to very high where state control breaks down, as in Russia (around 30), or where there is severe political turmoil, as in Venezuela (32–37) and Colombia (46–61).

Homicide rates are highly elastic, even over short periods of time. Among the Waorani of Ecuador, the murder rate declined by more than 90% in just a few years after two of the women brought a pair of American missionaries into their territory. As a result of these women's efforts, the people became convinced that peace was possible, and managed to halt the cycle of feuding and revenge homicides (Fry 2006). A similar drop in violent deaths is under way among the Enga of Papua New Guinea, as seen in Chapter 12.

National comparisons show that homicide rates fall within a narrow range in some world regions, such as Western Europe, with 0.2–3 homicides per 100,000 per year in all countries (United Nations Office on Drugs and Crime 2006). Regions with high rates in many countries, exceeding 13 per 100,000 per year, include Southern Africa, Central America, and the Caribbean. In other regions there are countries spanning a wide range, such as Oceania, with rates below 3 in Fiji but above 15 in Papua New Guinea, or East Asia, with Japan's rate of 0.5 alongside the Philippines' rate of 12–21. In North America, rates increase from north to south: around 2 in Canada, 6 in the US, and 11 in Mexico.

In sum, homicide rates are highly variable across societies and time periods. They are sensitive to social and economic conditions, political unrest, and cultural beliefs. Homicide is not a random or inevitable fact of nature.

. . . . .

Rates of domestic violence, like homicide, vary across cultures. The degree of gender stratification is a primary factor that also plays a role in the patterning of warfare, as seen in the next chapter. Violence is rare between spouses – and people in general – in relatively egalitarian foraging societies such as the Mbuti and the Ju/'hoansi. Horticultural groups with complementary or shared labor also have low levels of domestic violence, such as the Semai of Malaysia, the Balinese, the Central Thai, and indigenous Tahitians. In contrast, complex horticultural, herding, and agricultural and industrial societies tend to generate more interpersonal violence overall, including physical abuse of women by male partners. Examples of societies with very high levels of domestic violence include Samoans, Maasai, Kurds, and Gheg Albanians.

Lori Heise's (1997) meta-analysis of domestic violence research shows that one-third to two-thirds of women in agricultural and industrial societies experience physical abuse, and in some cases the proportions reach four-fifths. At the high end, in Jullundur District, Punjab, India, three-fourths of lower-caste men report having beaten their wives. Lower amounts, around one-fifth, have been reported for Colombia and New Zealand. In the US, the proportion tends to fall between one-fourth and one-third. Throughout the world, intimate partners also are responsible for the majority of violent deaths among women. In the US, femicide is the top cause of injury-related death for women of reproductive age, and a leading cause of death for women during and after pregnancy – at a rate of 1.7 per 100,000 live births, comparable to some national homicide rates (Chang et al. 2005).

Domestic abuse not only harms individual women through acute injuries, psychological trauma, and chronic stress, but brings a cascade of exponentially increasing violence through their children, who are also frequent targets of abuse. Effects on children include increased risk of suicide, drug use, criminal behavior, teen pregnancy, and relationship and parenting difficulties – including partner and child abuse. In sum, the costs of domestic violence multiply over time.

Heise shows that, across societies, higher rates of domestic violence are associated with gender inequalities in income and economic status, lower female decision-making authority within the family, cultural ideas of dominant masculinity, and the acceptability of violent conflict resolution. Contrariwise, lower rates emerge where violence is actively counteracted by the community, women have powerful roles outside the family, there are all-female social or work groups, and women have access to supportive institutions, family, and friends. The first set of factors corresponds with the features of patrilineal societies with patrilocal residence rules, which isolate women from relatives and friends, preclude women's economic independence, and foster cultural beliefs that define masculinity and femininity as mutually exclusive opposites of unequal value.

Paradoxically, the same social and ideological structures that preclude women's economic independence establish men as both the protectors of women and a principal danger to them. With allowance for the unreliability of data, especially where women's status is low, it is clear that rape is more frequent in more unequal societies. The rate is about five times higher in the US than Finland (Fry 2006). According to a popular theory, rape is a biological necessity for disadvantaged men who have few chances of mating, but evolutionary processes could not have selected for it, and normally the brain processes sex and violence separately.[4] Beyond individual psychopathologies, gender inequality plays a significant role, as seen in wartime, when women both symbolize the homeland and are cast as booty to be abused at will or even raped strategically to humiliate the enemy and contaminate it biologically.[5] Men who otherwise would abhor rape commit sexual violence on a mass scale. Biologically, the dopamine secreted in response to constant aggressive excitation suppresses perception of aversion and pain. Cognitively, the subordination of the female at the core of military culture and masculine camaraderie, together with the dehumanization of the enemy, permits the double objectification and exploitation of enemy women.

With reference to domestic violence, W. Penn Handwerker (1998) explains that power resides in structural relationships which determine the flow of necessary resources. Power equalities emerge where people are able to bypass gatekeepers; inequalities emerge where gatekeepers are able to restrict access. For gatekeepers, power is proportional to the importance of the resources they control, the scarcity of alternative routes to access, and the number of people who need their assistance. Gatekeepers' power allows them to exploit resource seekers by making demands on them or using violence against them.

In the case of spouses, power inequalities generate violence against women, whereas power equalities bring affection. Handwerker shows how the balance between the two types of interaction shifted in Antigua and Barbados during an economic transformation in the 1950s–1960s involving a decline in the sugar industry and a rise in manufacturing and tourism. Increased economic wellbeing and education fueled a health transition to lower fertility and infant mortality rates, along with more equitable economic conditions for women and men. Within one generation, these changes brought a 40% decline in domestic violence.

Before the shift in the island economy, men had exclusive access to gatekeeper positions in finance and government. Women were resource seekers, limited to low-paying physical jobs such as agricultural labor, road work, and domestic service. Men were abusive, violent, and irresponsible. Wife abuse was expected and socially acceptable, and some fathers acted upon men's conventional right to demand sex from their daughters.

As power inequalities declined during the transition, the chance that a man would act violently fell by one-half while the chance that a man would behave affectionately increased by 9 times. In the rarer cases in which power inequalities increased between spouses, so did domestic violence. The frequency of violence by "rotten" men increased by more than 4½times, while the chance that they would act affectionately declined by three-fourths. These relationships between power inequalities and violence, and between equalities and affection, were not a function of social class or degree of poverty. In addition, they were independent of men's variations in temperament – in other words, whether their baseline was violent or affectionate.

With reference to the intergenerational effects of domestic violence, Handwerker observes that children grow up within either an exploitative or non-exploitative matrix of human relationships. In Antigua and Barbados, men who had grown up highly attuned to power tended to be the rotten ones. As children they had witnessed, at a minute level, the workings of power between people of different status, and learned to detect power inequalities in order to seize opportunities and avoid finding themselves on the wrong end of exploitation. In contrast, children raised in a context of equalities, or who are exposed to them later in life, are less proficient at seeing power and less likely to react to people and situations with aggression or fear. Consequently, the cycle of violence is not simply about one diseased or damaged person passing the trait on to another, but rather the transmission of social relationships as a whole from one generation to the next.

Fry's (2006) comparison of two adjacent Zapotec towns in Mexico's Oaxaca Valley provides an illustration of Handwerker's arguments. The towns, which Fry calls San Andrés and La Paz, have very different systems of gender relations. Each is considered perfectly natural and right in its own context. The one with gender inequalities fosters aggression; the one with equalities, affection.

In San Andrés, an honor-and-shame system (see Chapter 8) gives rise to jealousy, suspicion, and reinforcement of social norms through gossip. Women and men do not talk to each other or look one another in the eye, much less smile, in order to avoid giving anyone the wrong idea about their sexual intentions. Husbands order wives around, and couples do not show physical affection. They do not even touch each other while dancing. Wives guard their reputation closely by never allowing a man into their house or garden if their husband is not home. They know that if they do, the price will be a beating. Men fight each other as well, and sometimes kill one another.

The situation is entirely different in La Paz, where women invite Fry into their homes for a chat as he walks by. There is more trust between women and men, and the men show more respect and admiration for women. Children's play involves less aggression and physical combat. The frequency of wife abuse is lower.

Fry attributes the difference to women's economic position in La Paz, where there is an exclusively female ceramics tradition that brings money and goods into the family. The trade is transmitted from mother to daughter, leaving men cognizant of their lack of ability and appreciative of their female relatives' skill. In contrast, men in San Andrés earn all of their family's income through work in nearby mines, from which women are entirely excluded. While jealousy is in the air people breathe in San Andrés, in La Paz it is not a taken-for-granted emotion, but one that is dealt with nonviolently in youth and outgrown in adulthood.

Matthew Gutmann's (1996) work in Mexico City provides further insights into the processes that increase the likelihood of domestic violence, including men's experience of socioeconomic changes as humiliating and disempowering. As noted in Chapter 8, women in the urban shantytown he studies are heavily involved in community and religious activism, dealing with government officials, and work outside the home. Gutmann explains that some men resent what they perceive as a loss of authority and strike out whenever they do not receive the respect or obedience they believe is their due. They blame their behavior on the culture of machismo, but at the same time are ashamed by their loss of control, making it much harder for men to talk about domestic violence than women. Gutmann surmises that, although it is ever-more culturally unacceptable, domestic violence is becoming more frequent as men struggle with changing family and economic roles.

The analysis of domestic violence above indicates that any hierarchy will give rise to exploitation and displaced aggression directed against those in a structurally inferior position. Men frustrated by the necessity of submission to men ranked above them may turn their rage on their wives and children; women, in turn, may take out their anger and humiliation on their children. Organizations such as hospitals, armies, and schools generate displaced aggression down the line. These hierarchical environments, and stratified societies as a whole, not only make subjugation and humiliation more likely but also fail to provide the social support and sense of mutual responsibility needed to resolve painful feelings of anger and impotence. Violence represents an attempt to restore self-respect and pride, and to recover from the shame of losing face. In the tense social environment of prisons and urban gangs, it erupts over the smallest of perceived slights or violations of etiquette, as seen in a Brazilian juvenile-reform institution where boys' resentment over being denied adult status leads them to remorselessly beat and kill other boys in defense of their self-image as "man-subjects" (Drybread 2014).

Social hierarchies can even block the brain's perception of another individual as a human being. Normally the sight of a person activates the prefrontal medial cortex, but not if the person belongs to a stigmatized, despised category such as drug addicts or the homeless. In that case, the brain behaves as if it were not seeing a human being at all. Susan Fiske (2011) explains that people tend to see their own group as both likable or "warm" and competent. Other groups are perceived as likable but not competent, such as the sick or elderly; or competent but not warm, such as the wealthy and powerful. These others elicit pity and envy, respectively, but the brain nonetheless recognizes them as social actors. In contrast, the sight of people who do not register as either competent or likable fails to spark a neural response.

This mechanism underlies the maltreatment of groups of people based on cultural categorizations and is easily evoked experimentally, as Jane Elliot showed in the 1960s with her third-grade students. Elliot offered some children special privileges but imposed limitations on others based on eye color. The children designated as superior behaved monstrously towards the others, whereas those defined as inferior became timid, submissive, and reluctant learners. The effect came within a single day and was reversed the next day when the designations were switched.

Similarly, in 1971, Philip Zimbardo (2007) divided male student volunteers at Stanford University into prisoners and guards and confined them to a basement on campus for an experiment. Within days they were all transformed, including Zimbardo himself, who unintentionally assumed the demeanor of a warden. The prisoners revolted; the guards implemented brutal procedures and escalated the psychological abuse. These experiments indicate that social divisions cause curiosity, trust, and interest in others to be suspended in favor of indifference, contempt, and violent hostility.

.....

In order to identify some of the ways in which unequal societies engender violent interpersonal and between-group interactions, the following section considers different types of sociopolitical organization based on Elman Service's (1962) categories of foraging bands, horticultural tribes, and agricultural chiefdoms and states. The comparison is not meant to imply any directionality or progression between types of society, or that societies classified together are the same and completely distinct from other categories. As we have seen, in many respects settled foragers are more similar to agriculturalists than nomadic foragers, even though both subsist on wild foods; virtually all contemporary indigenous societies, including relatively isolated ones, are also embedded in state societies. Moreover, the emphasis on politico-economic organization is not meant to suggest that modes of production determine social institutions and cultural beliefs, for causal influences flow in both directions.

As noted earlier, foraging bands tend to consist of 30–50 people, although the number may range from 15–150. Contrary to the assumption that gangs of related males were the foundation of warfare and human society itself, the people in foraging societies tend not to be relatives. This is because of bilateral kinship, which gives each person a unique, broadly dispersed kinship network. Family ties interlink neighboring bands, making it easy for people to change residence in case of conflict.

Entire bands may split over an internal conflict that cannot be resolved, even with the help of third-party mediators from other bands, only to coalesce with others or grow by attracting new members. Shifting band composition provides opportunities for diffusing conflict that are not available to sedentary societies.

People in foraging bands are obliged to each other through established norms of reciprocity and fairness. The system works against shirking and any behavior that would put another person in a submissive or servile position. For instance, norms for distributing meat prevent hunters from taking credit or using gifts of food strategically, although that is not their express purpose. Rather, the rules serve needs such as protecting hunters' skills or luck, or demonstrating respect to wildlife and the spirits.[6] They include taboos against hunters eating animals they have killed, as among the Aché (or Guayaki) of Paraguay or Au and Gnau forager-horticulturalists of Papua New Guinea. Hunters may be required by a prohibition against carrying game they have procured to hand the animal off to a relative, as among the Matsigenka (or Machiguenga) of Peru. Responsibility for distributing portions may fall by rights to the person who owned the arrow, including a woman or man not present when the animal was killed, as among the Ju/'hoansi.

These customs prevent individuals from rising above others, and in some cases from even being identified as the one responsible for killing an animal. Men who have been successful at hunting minimize their accomplishments and avoid talking about them. The same humility is expected of anyone with good fortune or special talents such as a skillful singer or an able healer, man or woman. These people may be admired more than others, but they are not placed above them. Through mutual respect and interdependence, together with the unacceptability of power, foraging societies protect individual autonomy and foster social trust.

In addition to sharing meat throughout the band, foragers exchange food, decorative objects, and other resources with other bands. Reciprocity occurs informally and according to customs such as the *hxaro* of the Ju/'hoansi, which ensures a continuous exchange of gifts back and forth over long spans of time. While the practice conforms in some ways to gift-giving throughout the world, in that it creates reciprocal obligations, it is open-ended and cannot be terminated with an immediate return gift. In addition, it is not a mechanism for showing off or exercising power over the receiver. In fact, if a proffered gift is too lavish it will be rejected.

Sharing spreads excess in times of plenty and provides security in times of need. Even foraging bands which speak different languages engage in exchange relationships and intermarriage. Similar forces drawing bands into friendly relationships are evident in regularized exchanges of goods among Upper Paleolithic foragers as long as 40,000–30,000 years ago, such as decorative beads traded at several convergence sites in the Dordogne River Valley in France, or personalized projectile points exchanged in the Kalahari Desert (d'Errico et al. 2012).

The meaning and purpose of sharing in foraging societies became clear to Richard Lee (1969) through an incident at the end of his fieldwork among Ju/'hoansi foragers during the 1960s. To publicly display his thanks to the community,

Lee bought the biggest possible ox for the Christmas feast attended by foragers and villagers. In the days leading up to the event, a series of individuals and small groups teased him about his choice of a scrawny beast, which all could see was quite fat. They were trying to cut Lee down to size. Only then did he grasp the extent of social investment in teaching everyone not to be boastful or to raise themselves above others. As the people told Lee, pride only leads to conflict and violence.

In foraging societies, there are neither ranks nor rulers, and decisions are reached by consensus. This means that everyone must agree, even if it takes a long time. Older people are revered, not marginalized. They keep interpersonal conflicts from getting out of control, communicate with the spirit world, and guide collective decision-making. Full participation in community life reflects and reinforces cooperative, egalitarian relationships between women and men, and among all people in the group.

Contrary to the assumption that people inevitably view other groups as either threats or opportunities, foraging bands reach out to other groups. If they come across an abundant source of food, such as plentiful nuts or fruit, they share it. A group in Australia that came upon a beached whale lit fires to attract other bands to the site. Foragers in Australia, Africa, South America, and elsewhere split not only surplus but also scarce resources with other bands, who need only ask permission in advance. For instance, among the Ju/'hoansi, watering holes are held in trust by an individual "owner," such as an elderly woman, who grants use rights to other bands during the dry season.

Most band societies interact positively with other groups, given a generally low level of territoriality. However, some societies such as the Semang of peninsular Malaysia and the Siriono of Eastern Bolivia prefer to keep their distance and move on when they encounter other bands. Occasionally, groups have assaulted trespassers, although only under unusual circumstances such as the continuous onslaught of invaders arriving by boat to the Andaman Islands, or the expansion of the Cree people who pressed the Slavey out of their territory in Canada (Fry 2006).

Unlike tribal and state societies, there is no coordinating structure governing bands of foragers, just as there is no internal system of formalized political control. Foraging societies maintain order without police or courts, in large part because egalitarianism and personal autonomy prevent dangerous conflict in the first place. However, safety and fairness do not come without effort. They must be assiduously defended through social pressure against manifestations of greed, arrogance, and power.

Any amount of farming or food or water storage loosens the need for long-term interpersonal and intergroup interdependence, rendering accumulation, self-aggrandizement, and social hierarchy and gender inequality more tolerable.[7] To illustrate, unlike other San peoples such as the Ju/'hoansi, //Gana foragers in the northern and eastern parts of the Kalahari Game Reserve grew beans, maize, and melons, in addition to keeping herds of goats (Cashdan 1980). These stores of water, protein, and other nutrients buffered the //Gana against seasonal and spatial variability in resources. Whereas other foragers in the area disbursed all animal products for immediate consumption and carried only limited quantities of water in ostrich eggs, the //Gana stored water and food including dried meat at a year-round site. Their stocks allowed them to remain at the site for many months at a time, which permitted the collection of wealth objects such as furs and skins that could be sold outside the Reserve. Some people used the proceeds to buy barrels which further alleviated water scarcity, as well as cattle, horses, and donkeys kept by relatives living in less arid areas. While 73 people had none of these wealth objects, 10 had 1, 17 had 2–5, and 5 had 6–11.

Even though it was still the norm for people to informally share both wild and cultivated food, accumulation was accepted in //Gana society. Whereas polygyny was very rare among other San peoples, about one-fourth of the married men had two to three wives and therefore enough goats to pay bridewealth more than once. Along with a few younger men who periodically left the Reserve for work in the mines, these wealthy, older men styled themselves as leaders, although their position was not formalized and they did not exercise any of the functions of tribal headmen. Significantly, they were respected, rather than reviled for keeping instead of dispensing with personal wealth. The case shows how a measure of food and water storage results in relaxed social vigilance with regard to self-advancement and the emergence of stratification.

.....

Food production generates distinctive psychological and social challenges related to permanent settlement, social stratification, increased population density, and particular risks to health and the food supply (see Chapter 3). The increase in the size of communities stretches the brain's capacity to recognize and retain personal information about others, and therefore to monitor fairness behavior and discipline cheaters, beyond the limit of 150 confirmed by economic and psychological studies (Dunbar 2003). These factors create a need for more formal organization into tribes and clans, or chiefdoms and states. Tribes practicing low-intensity cultivation (horticulture) are found in warm zones and resource-rich areas around the world, including the Americas, Papua New Guinea, Melanesia, Africa, and South Asia. They are bigger than nomadic foraging bands, with a hundred to several hundred people. These societies do not have social classes but are divided into lineages of people related to an apical ancestor or otherwise considered to share a kinship bond. Tribes may be either matrilineal or patrilineal, and consequently may have low to high degrees of gender inequality. Family relationships define personal identity.

The food produced by horticultural societies generally cannot be stored, unlike grains produced in cooler, drier places. In addition, villages may be moved every few years or every few generations depending on the terrain and the distance people are willing to travel to reach new plots of land. As noted in Chapter 8, hoes and other equipment are relatively simple and accessible to everyone. The combination of mobility and lack of durable surplus crops with which to pay tribute or tax explains why horticultural societies are able to remain outside the control of chiefdoms and states.

Horticultural tribes engage in extensive trade and ceremonial networks involving other villages, which provide opportunities for marriage partners to meet and result in a reduced likelihood of conflict. Big men or headmen, which in some cases are women, do not rule by coercive force but guide others through persuasion and example. Their position is the result of personal qualities and is neither permanent nor institutionalized.

Reciprocity is a core economic principle within and between tribes, as it is for nomadic foraging societies.[8] For example, in the Sepik Coast area of New Guinea, gifts are distributed across a wide area through complex family exchange networks. Gifts include handmade baskets and bowls, tobacco, and sago. The *kula* ring famously described by Bronislaw Malinowski involved the circulation of decorated white shell armbands and red shell disc necklaces in opposite directions among Melanesian islands of the Massim Archipelago, including the Trobriand Islands. In some cases only big men were involved, but in others all men participated. Gifts were carried over long distances by canoe. Their value rose by having been previously held by esteemed people.

Trade and barter occur alongside reciprocal exchange in tribal societies. All these practices reflect the existence of concepts such as debt, credit, and interest, for all involve established standards of value. At the same time, many tribes practice redistribution. Big men collect tribute from the population only to give their wealth away during periodic feasts. In the Mount Hagen area of Papua New Guinea, big men traditionally distributed pigs through a system of ceremonial exchange called *moka*. In recent decades, pigs have been replaced by exorbitant sums of money and consumer goods. The idea is to display status and power by dispersing wealth rather than accumulating it.

Redistributive feasts benefit all villages over the long term. Since any group may be struck by local shortages of food at some time or other, villages alternate between hosting and attending feasts. Although the receiving tribe experiences a decline in prestige, they make it up later when the tides turn. Notably, giving away the tribe's wealth also helps to prevent the deepening of internal divisions – in other words, social classes.

Reciprocity and redistribution lose ground in societies which practice intensive agriculture and therefore produce surpluses that can be stored and accumulated. These societies are organized as chiefdoms and states. Instead of scores or hundreds of people, there are thousands or millions. Chiefdoms emerged about 6,500 years ago in many areas of the world, including the Americas, Polynesia, and pre-classical and medieval Europe. They were prevalent in West Africa at the time of colonization. The first states arose with the complex civilizations of the ancient world 6,000–5,500 years ago, starting in Mesopotamia and followed by Egypt, the Indus River Valley, northern China, and, later, West Africa, Cambodia, Mesoamerica, and the Andes Mountains. Some but not all of these civilizations depended on irrigation agriculture. While chiefdoms and states are vulnerable to instability due to the intensive use of natural resources, size of populations, and pernicious effects of stratification, ancient civilizations did not all fail suddenly and dramatically through starvation or annihilation by way of enemy weapons and diseases (McAnany and Yoffee 2010). To the contrary, many persisted beyond the phases of ardent monument-building allegedly marking their disappearance, including the late Roman Empire and the Hohokam of the American Southwest. Others have left descendants to the present day, including Easter Islanders and Mayas and other indigenous peoples of the Americas.

Sedentary (or complex) foraging societies, which emerged 13,000 or more years ago in a few especially resource-rich parts of the world (see Chapter 2), were similar to chiefdoms in that they had permanent villages, social classes, and formal leaders. The category includes equestrian foragers such as the North American Apache, who also had a large inventory of valuable animals. On the other hand, these populations' economic behavior overlaps with redistributive tribal systems. For instance, populations of the Pacific Northwest such as the Salish and Kwakiutl (Kwāg'ul) took turns hosting feasts, or potlatches, during which chiefs gave away huge quantities of gifts such as food and copper plates. Valuable goods could even be destroyed or thrown into the sea as a demonstration of the leader's political power and wealth. The sponsor's prestige increased in proportion to the extravagance of the potlatch; that is, from expending rather than hoarding wealth.

The potlatch expressed a worldview according to which chiefs represented separate lineages and therefore qualitatively incomparable connections to the spirits. Marshall Sahlins (1999) explains that this is why competitive gifting took the form of a quantitative display of uniform wealth objects, most famously thousands of Hudson's Bay Company blankets at the height of the 18th-century fur trade. Sahlins contrasts the Kwakiutl redistributive system to the behavior of Hawai'ian chiefs also drawn into international trade. As descendants of the gods with quantitatively equal claims to divine status, they distinguished themselves through qualitatively different wealth objects. Chiefs obtained ostentatious furnishings and fine cloth for their personal adornment from British and American ships in need of provisions and sandalwood on their way to China. The contrast between Kwakiutl and Hawai'ian chiefs highlights the difference between a system in which accumulation remains unacceptable notwithstanding the existence of disparities in political and social status, and a proper chiefdom in which leaders are permitted to stockpile and display wealth.

Chiefdoms and states depend on satellite populations that produce transportable rice, wheat, and other grains, and pay tax and tribute to the center. Whereas in tribal societies leadership depends upon personal qualities, in chiefdoms and states the political position itself conveys power and authority and is supported by a permanent political and governmental structure. Ceremonies, clothing, and special privileges accentuate the differences between leaders and the rest of the population. Religious and royal elites invest in infrastructure and monument-building, often accomplished with forced labor. They fund a professional police and military force to control long-distance trade routes and meet the relentless need for additional land that results from rapid population growth.

Economic specialization in a complex economy excludes many citizens from direct contact with food production or the land, and contributes to social class and gender differences that unequally distribute material and social goods. Ranked status differences depend on kinship, occupation, gender, and generation, and, in modern states, ethnicity. There is a strong tendency towards patrilineal rules of inheritance and descent. Individual-oriented values support private ownership and permit wealth accumulation for personal status and security.

Low mobility and autonomy are balanced by a strong emphasis on citizenship in a kingdom or nation, which solidifies psychological boundaries separating outsiders from insiders. Through a monopoly on force, states discipline the population by way of control over the body, whether in relatively benign forms such as mandatory school attendance and health surveillance, or brutal ones such as torture, imprisonment, and capital punishment. These methods suggest implicit agreement with the principle that violence is a legitimate means to a political end. The combination of totalizing control, territoriality, and demographic expansion predisposes chiefdoms and states to internal and external violence.

More controlling institutions and "tighter" cultures go hand in hand, as shown by surveys distributed in 33 relatively wealthy and technologically advanced countries throughout the world, including Spain and Singapore, India and Israel (Gelfand et al. 2011). The looseness or tightness of culture was calculated according to the average number of 12 behaviors, such as eating or laughing, which respondents rated as appropriate in 15 situations, such as a funeral or party. The national scores were compared to data regarding church attendance, control of media and individual access to information technology, political activism, civil liberties, police presence, and legal rules and punishments. The results affirmed the relationship between the degree of internalized behavioral control and the reach of political and other institutions.

In addition, tightness of culture was associated with current or past threats including high population density, war and territorial conflict, resource scarcity, low environmental quality, natural disasters, high historical or current infectious disease burden, and high infant and child mortality rates. In short, pressures and threats result in more controlling institutions and a tighter culture that encourages compliance, self-censorship, and comfort with structure. More fortunate societies permit more behavioral noncompliance and can manage with less-intrusive institutions. As indicated above, these societies are less concerned about borders, and less likely to engender internal and external violence.

. . . . .

The downsides of social stratification, which are evident both in retrospect and as it develops, beg the question of why early human societies allowed it to spread. Computer simulations suggest that the reason is that stratified foraging societies outcompete egalitarian ones through migration (Rogers et al. 2011). This is in spite of the smaller size of stratified societies resulting from higher mortality among the lower classes and faster resource depletion by the upper classes. The long-term demographic advantages of stratification hold whether the scenario involves two or five classes.

The simulations show that, in a constant-environment scenario, egalitarian societies are more stable demographically. The total population size remains within 5% of the mean for at least a century, and there are fewer extinctions and population crashes (loss of more than one-fourth of the population in a year or series of years). Population stability arises through a feedback loop linking fertility to resource availability. Stratified societies disrupt the loop through inequality, and demographic and ecological instability drives them to migration in spite of their smaller population size.

In variable environments that have fluctuating resource availability year to year, stratified societies fare better than egalitarian ones. This is because people in egalitarian societies are all equally at risk, leading to more crashes and extinctions. In stratified societies, elites survive by pushing mortality onto the lower classes. If food storage is introduced into the simulations, it buffers against population instability in stratified societies but causes egalitarian societies to deplete resources more rapidly. As in a constant environment, under variable environments stratified societies are more likely to migrate. Finally, in scenarios involving peaceful migration into unoccupied sites in response to high mortality, deprivation, or environmental resource depletion, stratified societies migrate and move more rapidly than egalitarian ones. In other words, egalitarian societies are less likely to deal swiftly with stress by migrating.

To check the validity of the model, the researchers analyzed a sample of 15 archeological case studies and found the same pattern of internal population dynamics fueling expansion or migration by stratified societies, in both constant and variable environments. They also examined a study on numerous early Polynesian agricultural societies that confirms the relationship between stratification and lower equilibrium population size. That study shows, in addition, that higher fertility, labor productivity, and population growth are associated with reduced wellbeing.

The congruence between the model and archeological and historical cases strongly suggests that stratification spread in the past because of the rapid expansion of class-based societies. There is no need to speculate about rapacious human nature, or whether egalitarian groups were constrained or disposed to emulate the ways of stratified societies. Demographic processes set in motion by settlement, food cultivation, and incipient social classes were enough to ensure the spread of stratified societies at the expense of egalitarian ones.

. . . . .

Ethnographic case studies can open a window on the processes connecting inequality to reduced wellbeing, including increased interpersonal conflict, as they unfold. The recent economic transformation forced upon the Korwa of Central India provides an illustration. Traditionally, Korwa women collected roots, fruits, and other forest products, while men procured game. Open access to plentiful resources sustained gender and social egalitarianism. People did not try to accumulate more than they needed. They considered themselves well off. Abundance and autonomy characterized their existence and worldview as long as they lived in the forest (Gaur and Patnaik 2011).

In the 1970s, forced settlement and exclusion from the forest ecosystem pushed the Korwa into poverty. People felt deprived and disempowered once they found themselves in an unequal socioeconomic system in which they occupied the bottom position. With no knowledge of farming and with small, low-quality allotments of land, they could not make a living. They sold firewood, sought work in quarries and on construction sites, and took loans they could not pay back – which lost them their land.

Korwa marriage customs prescribe bridewealth as part of a system of gift-giving that includes regular food offerings to ancestors and spirits. In the past, on the rare occasions in which a couple eloped, they and their families were obliged to hold a "punitive" feast for everyone in the community, which restored their good standing. Now, many couples are constrained to elope because their families do not have anything to give, and the same lack of resources precludes holding a punitive feast later on. This leaves the entire family symbolically outside the community, lacking social support. Members of all 12 of the families that did not hold a punitive feast after an elopement reported illness due to fever, fatigue, weakness, and aches and pains. In contrast, while these common symptoms occurred among the remaining 13 socially integrated families, they were not considered severe enough to constitute illness.

The changes have led to increased gender inequality and mistreatment of women. Men are preferentially hired in the wage economy, leaving more women than men deprived of an economic role. Access to alcohol contributes to men's abandonment of and violence against their wives. Women without a husband are seen as liminal, ambiguous people and consequently suspected of being dangerous, which opens the door to witchcraft accusations. These women report constant physical suffering. Their marginalization weakens the social fabric.

In a similar manner, the intrusion of the Soviet state into its northernmost regions over the 20th century led to increased strife and lower wellbeing among Eveny reindeer herder-hunters (Vitebsky 2005). Their nomadic life following wild herds across an expansive, stark landscape is built on a cultural system emphasizing restraint and reserve between people and a quiet reverence for spirits and nature. The ideal person is steady, observant, and able to survive any situation through a combination of flexibility and perseverance. In deference to the spirits inhabiting the landscape, people should not sing while walking. If they come across a grave, they should not look back when they walk away, just as they do not look back when saying goodbye in general. Being too attached to any one place is inappropriate for the living, for only the dead may settle.

The Eveny share reindeer and hunted meat such as mountain sheep with all their relatives, no matter how distant. Animals killed for consumption are treated with humility and gratitude, for they have allowed humans to take their lives and will do so again after reincarnation if shown respect. These beliefs preclude overharvesting, for people must take only what they need of the soul-force in the landscape. In fact, too much luck in hunting is feared as a sign of imminent death – a sudden disbursement of the hunter's remaining fair share of animals all at once.

In the mid-20th century, the Soviet state redefined herding as an economic activity, not a way of life. The state virtually eliminated nomadism and delegated herds to a small number of men instead of extended families. The landscape was drained of women, who no longer traversed a vast territory. They worked in education and government services, although a few continued to join the herds with their children over summer breaks from school. The powerful and prestigious village positions went to men, often outsiders. Unless involved in herding, military service, or trade, men also were confined to the village. Social class and gender disparities emerged in place of interdependence and complementarity. Women displayed class distinctions by wearing mass-produced long coats, symbolic of their detachment from the land. Social tensions flared as people were enclosed in villages, like reindeer in a corral. Then, in the 1980s and 1990s, the politico-economic collapse of the Soviet Union cut off the flow of capital, goods, and personnel that had allowed for the creation of villages in the first place. Impoverishment and inequality intensified, bringing an increase in fighting, suicide, and alcohol abuse.

These cases show that egalitarianism and interdependence require effort and vigilance, whereas the seeds of social stratification take root and flourish with minimal encouragement. Yet, some societies manage to avert the damage from increased stratification. For example, a comparison of 13 villages of Tsimane' forager-horticulturalists in Bolivia indicates that, in their case, the degree of inequality is not related to self-reported health, and only minimally related to the number of self-reported sick days – which is slightly higher among low-ranking individuals (Undurraga et al. 2011). The apparent reason is that even villages which are highly integrated into the market economy continue to maintain traditional kinship ties through cross-cousin marriage (spouses chosen from among the children of one's mother's brother or father's sister). The resulting family networks generate interwoven reciprocal exchanges and obligations which counteract psychosocial stress and isolation. However, over time, increasing market integration could compromise the system through marriages with people from farther afield, which can be expected to fragment the social support system and turn households inward.

The religious cargo system in Mexico and Central America offers another illustration of institutions that counteract the tendency for inequality and invidious status comparisons to intensify and spread. The system seems to have originated with the official roles Spanish priests would assign to Maya and other indigenous men as the Church extended its control through the countryside.[9] Men cycle through year-long religious/civil offices, or cargos, arranged on a series of levels of increasing rank. The lowest-level tasks include delivering messages, keeping streets and buildings clean, and police functions. The highest-level commissions are the ones with the most religious and ritual significance. As a man moves up the levels, he takes on increasing financial responsibilities, to the point of spending huge sums on feasts, masses, and festivals in honor of saints. Men raise the money through extra wage labor or increased production on farms and ranches. Eventually they retire and join other older men who together hold significant authority in the community and appoint younger men to cargo assignments.

Participation brings men power and prestige, for which they willingly take on cargos that channel their effort and assets to the community rather than themselves and their relatives. In fact, if a family happens to remain wealthy for a second generation, it customarily accepts greater financial responsibility for religious observances. The cargo system demonstrates how even an elaborately ranked society need not generate self-interest and social atomization. To the contrary, it brings the community together through offices that obligate men to participate in collective life and give up their personal wealth. In short, the system both maintains social differentiation and works against inequality.

Modern nations also redistribute wealth and put brakes on inequality through transfer payments, estate taxes, government ownership of infrastructure and utilities, and caps on executive pay. Paradoxically, these measures are often opposed by voters and politicians for interfering with individual economic freedom, but they protect the autonomy of individuals by dampening the tendency for wealth and power to concentrate in the hands of the few. In the process, they reduce the harmful effects of inequality on health and social cohesion.

. . . . .

This chapter has shown that, while conflict may arise in any group of people, small, face-to-face societies discourage interpersonal violence. Shared decision-making and fluid group boundaries make it difficult and unacceptable for people to dominate one another. Interdependence, open access to resources, and the lack of transportable wealth narrows the range of reasons to fight. In contrast, stratification in large agricultural and industrial societies interferes with social connectedness and chronically activates the stress response. Even among wealthy nations, greater inequality is associated with reduced wellbeing and higher rates of one-on-one violence.

Cross-cultural evidence contradicts the presumption that evolution favored competitive, hierarchical relationships within and between groups. Ancestral humans did not need to be suspicious of strangers or avoid encountering other groups for fear of violent conflict over land and valuables. In short, patterns of violence point to social, ecological, and demographic factors, not all-out homicide and warfare as humankind's evolved default setting.

Notes

1 On capital punishment in face-to-face societies, see Fry (2006).
2 On non-aggression and interpersonal violence in band societies, see Kelly (2003); Turnbull (1978).
3 On the interpretation of specimens thought to indicate violence, see Fry (2006); Hart and Sussman (2005).
4 On criticisms of this idea by anthropologists, biologists, and primatologists, see Travis (2003).
5 For an analysis of wartime rape in Croatia and Bosnia-Herzegovina, see Olujic (1998).
6 On hunting rules, see Clastres (1972); Shepard et al. (2012); Tracer (2003); Wiessner (2002).
7 For a schematic illustrating this relationship across seven societies, see Kelly (2003).

8 For the examples of reciprocity in this section, see Mauss (1970).
9 On the religious cargo system, see Cancian (1965).

References cited

Cancian F. 1965. *Economics and prestige in a Maya community: the religious cargo system in Zinacantan.* Stanford: Stanford University Press.

Cashdan EA. 1980. Egalitarianism among hunters and gatherers. *American Anthropologist* 82(1):116–120.

Chang J, Berg CJ, Saltzman LE, Herndon J. 2005. Homicide: a leading cause of injury deaths among pregnant and postpartum women in the United States, 1991–1999. *American Journal of Public Health* 95(3):471–477.

Clastres P. 1972. The Guayaki. In Bicchieri MG, editor. *Hunters and gatherers today: a socio-economic study of eleven such cultures in the twentieth century.* New York: Holt, Rinehart, and Winston. p. 138–174.

d'Errico F, Backwell L, Villa P, Degano I, Lucejko JJ, Bamford MK, Higham TF, Colombini MP, Beaumont PB. 2012. Early evidence of San material culture represented by organic artifacts from Border Cave, South Africa. *Proceedings of the National Academy of Sciences* 109(33):13214–13219.

Drybread K. 2014. Murder and the making of man-subjects in a Brazilian juvenile prison. *American Anthropologist* 116(4):752-764.

Dunbar R. 2003. The social brain: mind, language, and society in evolutionary perspective. *Annual Review of Anthropology* 32:163–181.

Fiske ST. 2011. *Envy up, scorn down: how status divides us.* New York: Russell Sage Foundation.

Fry DP. 2006. *The human potential for peace: an anthropological challenge to assumptions about war and violence.* New York: Oxford University Press.

Gaur M, Patnaik SM. 2011. "Who is healthy among the Korwa?" Liminality in the experiential health of the displaced Korwa of Central India. *Medical Anthropology Quarterly* 25(1):85–102.

Gelfand MJ, Raver JL, Nishii L, Leslie LM, Lun J, Lim BC, Duan L, Almaliach A, Ang S, Arnadottir J, et al. 2011. Differences between tight and loose cultures: a 33-nation study. *Science* 332(6033):1100–1104.

Grossman D. 2009[1995]. *On killing: the psychological cost of learning to kill in war and society.* New York: Back Bay Books.

Gutmann MC. 1996. *The meanings of macho: being a man in Mexico City.* Berkeley: University of California Press.

Handwerker W. 1998. Why violence? A test of hypotheses representing three discourses on the roots of domestic violence. *Human Organization* 57(2):200–208.

Hart D, Sussman RW. 2005. *Man the hunted: primates, predators, and human evolution.* New York: Basic Books.

Heise LL. 1997. Violence, sexuality, and women's lives. In Lancaster RN, di Leonardo M, editors. *The gender/sexuality reader.* New York: Routledge. p. 411–433.

Kelly RC. 2003. *Warless societies and the origin of war.* Ann Arbor: University of Michigan Press.

Lee RB. 1969. Eating Christmas in the Kalahari. *Natural History* 78(14):i6.

Lee RB. 1979. *The !Kung San: men, women, and work in a foraging community.* New York: Cambridge University Press.

Mauss M. 1970[1924–1925]. *The gift: forms and functions of exchange in archaic societies.* Cunnison I, translator. London: Cohen and West.

McAnany PA, Yoffee N, editors. 2010. *Questioning collapse: human resilience, ecological vulnerability, and the aftermath of empire.* Cambridge, UK: Cambridge University Press.

Olujic MB. 1998. Embodiment of terror: gendered violence in peacetime and wartime in Croatia and Bosnia-Herzegovina. *Medical Anthropology Quarterly* 12(1):31–50.

Rogers DS, Deshpande O, Feldman MW. 2011. The spread of inequality. *PLoS One* 6(9):e24683.

Sahlins M. 1999. What is anthropological enlightenment? Some lessons of the twentieth century. *Annual Review of Anthropology* 28:i–xxiii.

Service ER. 1962. *Primitive social organization: an evolutionary perspective.* New York: Random House.

Shepard GH Jr, Levi T, Neves EG, Peres CA, Yu DW. 2012. Hunting in ancient and modern Amazonia: rethinking sustainability. *American Anthropologist* 114(4):652–667.

Tracer DP. 2003. Selfishness and fairness in economic and evolutionary perspective: an experimental economic study in Papua New Guinea. *Current Anthropology* 44(3):432–438.

Travis CB, editor. 2003. *Evolution, gender, and rape.* Cambridge, MA: MIT Press.

Turnbull CM. 1965. *Wayward servants: the two worlds of the African Pygmies.* Garden City, NY: Natural History Press.

Turnbull CM. 1978. The politics of non-aggression. In Montagu A, editor. *Learning non-aggression: the experience of non-literate societies.* New York: Oxford University Press. p. 161–221.

Undurraga EA, Nyberg C, Eisenberg DT, Magvanjav O, Reyes García V, Huanca T, Leonard WR, McDade TW, Tanner S, Vadez V, Godoy R. 2011. Individual wealth rank, community wealth inequality, and self-reported adult poor health: a test of hypotheses with panel data (2002–2006) from Native Amazonians, Bolivia. *Medical Anthropology Quarterly* 24(4):522–548.

United Nations Office on Drugs and Crime. 2006. International homicide statistics. http://www.unodc.org/documents/data-and-analysis/IHS-rates-05012009.pdf.

Vitebsky P. 2005. *The reindeer people: living with animals and spirits in Siberia.* Boston: Houghton Mifflin Company.

Wiessner P. 2002. Hunting, healing, and Hxaro exchange: a long-term perspective on !Kung (Ju/'hoansi) large-game hunting. *Evolution and Human Behavior* 23(6):407–436.

Zimbardo PG. 2007. *The Lucifer effect: understanding how good people turn evil.* New York: Random House.

12

PEACE AND WAR

Patterns and prevention of violent intergroup conflict

The warring-tribes version of human evolution suggests that irrepressible impulses drive violent behavior, and that humankind is helpless to stop homicide and warfare without the great civilizing efforts of modern states. It casts humans as naturally fearful of and violent towards strangers due to inborn us-them thinking, and aggression and greed as natural and intractable traits that render peaceful coexistence fortuitous and fragile. Accordingly, all that can be done is to penalize violence and deter it through the threat of punishment. Yet, as we have seen, envy and power do not universally define human relationships. Police and military forces are not needed in nomadic foraging societies as well as many contemporary societies throughout the world today. The distribution of violence varies with factors such as demographic pressure and socioeconomic inequality, which affect the context in which people interact and create material motives for conflict.

All societies have developed means of avoiding, mediating, and resolving disputes, many of which are transferable to other contexts. It is not possible for a crowded world to split up into small, autonomous face-to-face societies, but there are ways to reduce the likelihood of violent confrontations between individuals and countries. Even large nation-states could expand upon existing techniques of conflict prevention and resolution, and borrow new ones. They could emulate cultures which discourage physical aggression. All of this is more probable if misconceptions about the inevitability of warfare are replaced by appreciation of its non-random geographical and historical distribution.

. . . . .

The Neolithic Revolution brought an increase in the frequency of interpersonal violence and led to the emergence of warfare beginning around 10,000 years ago, but especially 6,000–5,000 BP. This historical trajectory indicates that war is an outgrowth of material and social forces, not inborn panhuman traits.

There is no unequivocal evidence of warfare among pre-Neolithic foragers. While some viewers see "warlike" behavior in certain rock paintings in southern Africa (Konner 2006), Paleolithic art does not contain images of warfare. Skeletal remains likewise do not suggest intergroup violence before 10,000 years ago.

The earliest evidence of intergroup violence remains equivocal, as it does not clearly point to organized warfare. At Nataruk in the Lake Turkana region of Kenya, 10 skeletons showing definite signs of violence have been dated to 10,000 BP, leading to the assertion that foragers engaged in warfare (Lahr et al. 2016). The site also contains two skeletons without signs of violence and the partial remains of 15 or more other individuals. However, there is no accompanying evidence of fortified settlements, artistic representations of war, or specialized weapons (the bone damage suggests clubs, arrows, and stone blades, all of which serve other purposes), suggesting a spontaneous battle or internal conflict rather than planned massacre. Moreover, these humans are likely to have stored food and remained settled or partially settled around the lake, which was much larger at the time, as indicated by evidence of pottery and the richness of the environment. As in the case of foragers in the Sudan who left evidence of lethal violence somewhat earlier, they were not representative of nomadic foragers, casting doubt on claims about the ordinariness of hunter-gatherer warfare. Similarly, the scarcity of adolescent skeletons at the site has led to the speculation that the invaders were after captives, but many other explanations are possible. The youths could have been away on a social visit or out collecting food or firewood.

In any event, with the transition to agriculture intergroup violence became more frequent but nonetheless remained uncommon. Endemic warfare appeared about 6,000 or at most 7,000 years ago with state societies. From that period of time on, archeological sites contain evidence of military installations, fortified cities, and the destruction and repopulation of conquered settlements. This pattern appears first in the Near East and subsequently in other locations in the Old and New Worlds. Sites dated between 6,000–4,000 BP indicate an accelerated spread of warfare through alterations of the built environment, weapons for hand-to-hand combat, and increased proportions of skeletons damaged by projectile points. In addition, a decline in male skeletons in local cemeteries suggests that a portion of the men died away from home (Fry 2006).[1]

Along the Northwest Coast of North America, human bones from 5,000 BP indicate blows as from club wounds sustained during nonlethal violence. Later, beginning about 2,000 years ago, skeletal remains show signs of lethal violence. This shift occurred alongside a change in settlement pattern that resulted in larger villages built in defensive positions. Unmistakable signs of violence also have been found on 10 male skeletons out of a total of about 440 recovered from several sites in Tennessee, dated from 4,500–2,750 years ago. There were stab wounds and projectile points lodged in the bones; some limbs had been cut and heads scalped. Ancient Maya and Zapotec buildings and art indicate that warfare was well-known to these societies as well.

The fact that warfare is rare among nomadic bands but common among complex foragers indicates that subsistence base *per se* is less determinative of organized aggression than settlement and stratification, which lead to the establishment of military classes and chiefly rulers. Ingrained stratification amongst settled foragers was a monumental change in human social organization, and one shared with early agricultural societies, along with more intergroup conflict. Over time, warfare has spread far and wide, giving rise to the idea that it is ubiquitous and unstoppable.

The existence of societies with no history of warfare, which tend also to have low levels of internal violence, indicates that human groups are not in fact biologically destined to attempt to eliminate each other. Douglas Fry (2006) has compiled a conservative list of 74 nonwarring societies throughout the world, including Europe (Saami/Lapp), North America (Shoshone, Southern Paiute, Greenland Inuit), South America (Siriono, Panare, Warao), Asia (Batak Agta, Semai, Sherpa), Africa and the Middle East (Mbuti, Ju/'hoansi, Hadza), and Oceania (Australian Aborigines, Tiwi, Ifaluk).

Comparative analyses of warfare tend to exclude or de-emphasize these warless societies, given that their focus is on violence rather than peace.[2] Moreover, as Fry demonstrates, definitions and categorizations can amplify the number and symbolic significance of warlike societies. Carol and Melvin Ember define warfare as fighting between politico-territorial entities, yet they count feuding and revenge killings in their quantitative analyses of warfare. These kinds of violence involve inter-family or inter-individual fighting for honor rather than political objectives, and encompass ambush killings of one or two people at a time. Their inclusion makes warfare appear far more common than it otherwise would.

For instance, Fry notes that the Embers classify the Andaman Islanders as a society continuously involved in warfare. However, all of the violence in ethnographic accounts from the last century consisted of fighting, murder, and revenge killings between individuals, sometimes with the help of family or friends. Reviewing the evidence, Fry finds that people who conducted research among the Andaman Islanders, such as Alfred Radcliffe-Brown and Elman Service, stated that the population did not ever practice warfare although there was some fighting and feuding. The violence against unfamiliar traders and travelers seems to have been a defensive reaction owing to past experience of slave raids by men arriving on ships from Burma and Malaysia.[3]

In separate comparative study, Carol Ember focuses on 31 hunter-gatherer societies in order to argue that foraging societies are not peaceful.[4] She maintains that around two-thirds of the societies engaged in external conflicts at least once every 2 years. However, this proportion concerns 16 simple nomadic bands pooled together with 15 complex foraging societies and equestrian foragers. In addition, Ember counts feuds and revenge killings, even against a single person, as instances of warfare. As a result, the extent of warfare appears much greater than it would under a more restrictive definition of warfare. The recent origin of equestrian societies and the sociopolitical changes they underwent upon contact with Europeans – especially loss of land and a rise in conflict – render them especially inappropriate societies to include in a study of foraging bands.

Fry points out that even analyses which use the broadest criteria to generate the highest frequencies of warfare in indigenous societies nonetheless turn up a large number of societies in which war is absent or very rare. Of the 186 predominantly non-industrialized societies in Murdock's Standard Cross-Cultural Sample analyzed by the Embers, 28% practiced warfare rarely (less than once in a decade) or never. In another study, Charlotte and Keith Otterbein looked at a sample of 50 societies, having rejected 61 others as candidates for analysis. For 24 of the 61 not included in the analysis, there was no mention of warfare in the ethnographic sources. Of the 50 the researchers selected, four never practiced internal or external warfare and one more did so infrequently – which together add up to 10% of the societies. Another 15 infrequently attacked other societies, for a total of 40% on the peaceful end of the spectrum. A separate analysis by Harold Driver indicates that most Native American societies from northern Mexico to the northern reaches of North America lacked warfare until the Europeans came, although some societies participated in feuding. In all geographical areas, including ones with warring tribes, there were societies in which violence of all sorts – interpersonal violence, feuding, raiding – was very uncommon.

In the 1940s, international law scholar Quincy Wright sought to determine the proportions of peaceful and warring societies based on data concerning 590 societies of all types compiled during the first decades of the 20th century. Wright found no evidence of warfare such as weapons or military buildings in 30 societies, or 5% of the total. More than half of the societies were not warlike or practiced only mild warfare: 346, or 59%. The remaining societies made war for economic reasons or, much less frequently, political ones.

Since Wright's study was published, some of the warring societies have been re-classified. In addition, Wright included feuding, revenge raiding, one-on-one duels, and small-scale raiding in the category of mild warfare. The study therefore overstates the extent of warfare in both the mild and warring categories, but even without correcting for these problems it shows that the majority of societies do not regularly engage in genuine warfare.

. . . . .

As in contemporary wars, resource scarcity was a principal factor in early warfare. For instance, divergent environmental conditions explain why a warlike Polynesian source population from 2,500 years ago gave rise to one society in which the warrior tradition became stylized and ritualized, and another in which it developed into endemic violence (Kirch 2010). On the lush Hawai'ian islands, divine kings and a chiefly class oversaw a productive agricultural economy. On the southern Cook Islands, the paucity of irrigable land led to constant competitive struggles between warlords for supremacy over each other and a population kept down through draconian tactics, including the threat of cannibalism.

In addition to resource constraints, social and demographic factors explain some of the variability in violent conflict across societies and historical periods, as shown by dozens of pre-contact Polynesian societies with shared ancestry but different geographical, demographic, and political circumstances (Younger 2008).

These societies ranged in size from a few hundred people to tens of thousands, and from ones with no weapons to ones with endemic warfare. Stratified societies had more of both internal, one-on-one violence, and external, group-against-group violence than egalitarian ones. The more peaceful societies had weak chiefs of the big man type rather than strong chiefs with formal authority as are found in more highly stratified societies. Especially on large, socially stratified islands, war was a main pathway to status and social advancement. Significantly, internal violence did not drive external violence. On the contrary, participation in warfare conditioned people towards violence inside the group as well as against other groups. External violence drove internal violence.

In addition, increased population size was associated with increased violence, whereas increased population density was associated with reduced violence. The most peaceful societies were those with fewer than 1,000 people. Among these small societies, the most peaceful were those most isolated from neighboring societies (more than 100 kilometers away). At the same time, less densely populated islands had a higher tendency toward violence than more densely populated ones. This seemed to be related to the stronger development of social mechanisms of cooperation, interdependence, and egalitarianism in more concentrated populations, and points to the importance of social and cultural institutions with regard to the control of warfare.

Social disruption due to contact is another frequent cause of increased violent conflict. For thousands of years leading up to the early 1000s, warfare among indigenous tribes of North and Central America was very rare. For a variety of reasons, hostilities between some but not all tribes became more common in the centuries before the arrival of the Europeans, as seen in a rise in traumatic injuries – broken bones, arrow points or bullets lodged in bone, and, preponderantly, damage to the skull. About 17% of thousands of skeletons from after contact were affected, compared to 11% before, for an increase of over 50%. This is a conservative estimate, since gun wounds may leave no mark on the bones (Steckel et al. 2002).

The proliferation of violence once Europeans were present in the Americas extended to tribes that were not in direct contact with the outsiders. Most of the injuries were inflicted by Native Americans upon each other during intertribal conflicts. There was much to fight about: access to the fur trade; territory and resources needed to obtain trade goods; and attribution of blame for European diseases. Some of the additional warfare was due to European incitement to internal battle and imperial conquests, as well as increased population pressure associated with the settlement of nomadic tribes.

In highland Papua New Guinea, contact with Europeans in the second half of the 20th century brought easy access to goods such as salt and steel axes. In Simbu Province, complex trade relationships involving fur, feathers, pigs, and seashells, broke down. Contact between villages declined in the 1970s and 1980s, leading to a drop in intertribal marriages compared to the 1960s. Since marriage brought lifelong mutual obligations between families involving visits and gifts of food, the changes undermined an important institutionalized mechanism of social integration, and the level of violence increased dramatically (Podolefsky 1984).

Papua New Guinea has gained a reputation for warfare, in part through publicity from popular authorities such as Jared Diamond. In an article in *The New Yorker*, Diamond (2008) names people, locations, and motives for warfare in New Guinea that indicate severe endemic violence. However, Diamond's evidence has been challenged in court by his source, driver and translator Daniel Wemp, together with Henep Isum Mandingo, a man Diamond credits with dozens of other men's deaths. Scholars working in the region support the two men's efforts to correct the sensationalistic portrait of indigenous men as bloodthirsty warriors bent on revenge by providing thorough descriptions of traditional and state systems for maintaining order. Indeed, the highlands area offers concrete examples of methods for maintaining peace in the absence of centralized government (Sillitoe and Kuwimb 2010).

In the highland province of Enga, wars became more deadly in the 1990s with the arrival of weapons such as shotguns and semi-automatic rifles. Before this time, some firearms were available but fighting was done with bows and arrows (Wiessner and Pupu 2012). The rate of violent death – combining homicide and warfare – rose to 103 per 100,000 inhabitants in 1990 and 100 a decade later. Thereafter, the people grew weary of violence and strengthened local institutions for conflict resolution. The rate of violent death fell to 32 in 2011.

With guns, battles between groups could bring dozens or even hundreds of deaths instead of one or two. The number of deaths per war rose by about five times, from under 4 during the first half of the 20th century to 18 or 19 in the period from 1990–2005. Then, from 2005–2011, the rate of deaths per war fell again to 5 or fewer. Moreover, the decline in warfare brought an increased likelihood that the fighting would stop after only a few fatalities: the proportion of wars which ended after 1–5 deaths increased from under one-fourth in 1991–1995 to three-fourths in 2006–2010. Finally, the number of wars dropped from 100–150 for every 3-year increment of the first decade of the 21st century, to 28 during the period 2010–2011.

An estimated 400,000–500,000 Enga horticulturalists are divided into clans numbering 350–1,000 individuals. As is typical in Papua New Guinea, clans are connected through marriage ties thanks to exogamous marriage (spouses chosen from outside the clan). Clans traditionally were also linked through formal exchange networks. Relationships would be destabilized periodically by conflict but reaffirmed through warfare and subsequent ritualized peacemaking involving the exchange of pigs and the sharing of a ceremonial beverage. This system grew between 1650–1950, an era of increased conflict due to the arrival of the sweet potato and consequent demographic expansion. It effectively kept warfare from displacing groups since they could make peace by paying compensation and reaffirming trade relationships. Then, Australia's colonial administration began pacification efforts in the 1930s, which reached Enga in the 1950s and 1960s. The suppression of warfare by armed agents of the state was accompanied by a rapid decline in traditional practices of many kinds. People increasingly relied on the formal court system as a result.

When the country became independent in 1975, responsibility for pacification was transferred to the new state, but the highlands were relatively ungovernable due to geographic isolation. Warfare increased again in the 1970s as the court system of a weak state proved unable to resolve disputes in a satisfactory way. Judicial procedures resulted in decisions that failed to respect traditional values of shared responsibility and the mutual resolution of conflicts. Young men began to turn firearms against people, not just animals, beginning in the 1990s, leading to the escalation of interpersonal violence and lethal warfare over the ensuing years. At the same time, demographic changes had generated an overabundance of young men and a reversal of the traditional age-based political system. Gangs of warriors flouted the clan system and pursued their own interests under a novel system of rules and values. There was a rapid rise in armed conflict and property damage. The police withdrew as the situation became intolerably dangerous.

Beginning around 2005, the Enga people began to take steps to curb the violence in spite of high tensions related to a couple of elections. Wiessner facilitated the establishment of a cultural center which contains a museum as well as conference rooms where tribal leaders can meet in neutral territory. Recourse to the informal court system has swelled. Local leaders oversee the mediation of disputes that can be taken to the state-sponsored village court if immediate resolution is not possible. Traveling judges organize public hearings in which anyone can voice an opinion. Combined with cultural and demographic changes, these courts have contributed to a precipitous decline in warfare in the last few years.

The local and village courts are effective because they are not constrained by formal legal procedure and because they practice restorative rather than punitive justice. Virtually all cases are resolved through compensation. The victim or victim's family receives material assistance and recognition of the crime endured, while the offender acknowledges fault. Pigs and money are paid by one set of relatives and clan members to another, which spreads responsibility and restores honor through compensation offered in the proper spirit of respect and contrition. In contrast, the state-run district court rarely succeeds in resolving cases. Only 10% of cases end with a jail sentence or fine; the rest are terminated for procedural reasons or withdrawn to be heard in village courts.

As noted below, judicial processes that facilitate reconciliation tend to bring a more satisfactory resolution to victims than incarceration of the guilty party. However, Wiessner and Pupu point out that contemporary social changes related to migration and consumerism may erode cultural codes and clan ties, and weaken commitment to collective responsibility. In addition, economic changes due to foreign aid and natural resource extraction could provide new reasons for fighting.

The Enga case shows that levels of warfare are highly sensitive to circumstances and may move in both directions. It is likely that other tribal societies have experienced a rise in warfare during phases of integration into states, contrary to the usual assumption that social complexity and formal systems of justice bring a reduction in violence. By working among the Enga since the 1980s, Wiessner has been able to observe how culture change and local initiatives may be more effective than police or formal legal institutions in bringing about a reduction in violence.

West of the Enga territory in New Guinea, the Dugum Dani inhabit the Grand Valley of the Middle Baliem in the central highlands. The Dugum Dani are known for a ritualized form of warfare conducted through the middle part of the 20th century in which opposing sides would line up across from each other, separated by a wide swampy area, and shoot bows and arrows or throw spears. They would take breaks for lunch and yell jokes and insults to the other side, sometimes calling people by name. They also took time away to tend to their crops. The winning side of a battle did not pursue their opponents but instead allowed them to return home unmolested. The rates of injury and death were minimal. This type of fighting is the subject of Robert Gardner's film, *Dead Birds* (Film Study Center 1964).

Dugum Dani warfare has long been considered an example of restraint: that is, a system which allowed neighboring groups to practice their battle techniques, dress up and prove themselves as individuals, and enjoy the thrill of danger without risk of serious injury. Anthropologists visiting the area in the 1960s found that no one remembered any case in which the Dugum Dani or their neighbors massacred each other or appropriated property. While confederations of tribes within large alliances sometimes fought each other or fought confederations from other alliances in earnest rather than in a sportive or theatrical way, the Dugum Dani seem not to have been interested in causing mortal harm to their immediate neighbors.

Recently it has been suggested that Dugum Dani warfare was restrained in appearance only; that if it were not for the terrain the warriors would have ambushed each other and carried out more efficient, deadly battles (Roscoe 2011). This assertion is based on an analysis of the topography as an obstacle to effective intergroup fighting, along with comments by a few older men about wanting to kill their enemies back in the day. However, the demonstration that better terrain would have favored bloodier battles is not sufficient to argue that the Dugum Dani would have massacred each other if given the chance. Moreover, fighting words are not the same as acts, any more than the taunts and jeers of modern-day sports teams and their fans are equivalent to a true desire to kill. In sum, speculations about what might have happened cannot alter the fact that the warfare observed in the 1960s was stylized, rule-based, and mostly harmless. Dugum Dani battles demonstrate the ability of human groups to coexist in close proximity without the benefit of state institutions, even in areas of the world with recurrent warfare.

Across Southeast Asia 80 million people live in societies that remain beyond the reach of states, as highland peoples have done for many centuries. Although they often have been forced to flee and disperse in response to the demands of valley people for labor, taxes, and military service, the hill people nevertheless maintain their own internal social structures organized by marriage and family relationships. These stateless societies are a reminder that order may be maintained, and internal and external violence repressed, in the absence of modern governmental systems. In other words, complex civilization is not necessary for groups of people to inhabit adjoining territory without trying to eliminate each other.[5]

. . . . .

The examples above indicate that humankind's alleged primeval murderousness is more accurately pinned on proximate environmental causes than timeless psychological traits. Cross-cultural analysis confirms that resource scarcity or fear of unpredictability is closely correlated with the likelihood of frequent warfare (Ember and Ember 1992). Other factors include intensive agriculture, socioeconomic inequality, male-oriented kinship organization, and the marginalization of women from production.

Comparing across socioeconomic categories, there is a clear pattern of increasing warfare from nomadic foraging societies to complex foragers, simple horticulturalists, advanced horticulturalists, and, finally, agriculturalists. There is no evidence of warfare for 13 of the nomadic and semi-nomadic band societies in the Standard Cross Cultural Sample, but ethnographic evidence suggests warfare for the other eight. In contrast, there is evidence of warfare for all of the nine complex and five equestrian societies (Fry 2006).

Not only is little or no warfare much more common than constant warfare among foraging societies, but ethnographic accounts of warfare among band societies do not suggest anything like prolonged, organized warfare. The evidence consists of reports of past warfare based on what informants have said about it, or stories of warfare that on closer examination turn out to be revenge killings, feuds, or defensive reactions to outsiders that include fleeing from aggression.

Population density among foragers is so low that warfare is virtually unfeasible. Today, population density among foragers is about 10 times higher than it was 25,000 years ago. As we have seen, foraging societies tend to define territories loosely and to make use of land and resources without conflict. Warfare among nomadic foragers is exceedingly rare in spite of the restriction of territory that has occurred as a result of the rise of states. It is hard to imagine that Paleolithic groups would have had *more* reason to fight than contemporary ones given the much lower pressure on resources and the greater need for interdependent relationships as a buffer against climatic and environmental variability. Moreover, ancestral humans inhabited a world in which foraging bands were the only kind of society. Foraging societies ever since the Neolithic Revolution have had to contend with sedentary societies which require permanent access to ever-increasing amounts of land.

Endemic warfare does not exist in any of the foraging societies in a sample compiled by George Peter Murdock (Nolan and Lenski 2011). About one-fourth of the societies, or 6 out of 22, periodically engage in warfare. In the remaining 16 societies, warfare is rare or absent. By contrast, the majority of horticultural societies in the sample practice warfare commonly or perpetually, although simple horticultural societies are much less warlike than complex ones. Among 22 simple horticultural societies, warfare is continuous in only 1 (5%), common in

12 (55%), and rare or absent in 9 (41%). In contrast, warfare is perpetual in 10 of 29 advanced horticultural societies (34%), common in 14 (48%), and rare or absent in only 5 (17%).

Based on a subset containing 115 of the 186 preindustrial societies in Murdock's Standard Cross Cultural Sample analyzed by Ember and Ember, Patrick Nolan (2003) reports that warfare is rare or absent in 39% of 23 foraging societies, 30% of 27 simple horticultural societies, and 14% of 35 advanced horticultural societies. The proportion of 30 agricultural societies in which warfare is rare or absent is similar to advanced horticultural societies, at 17%. In the remainder, warfare is present either regularly or unceasingly. These proportions confirm that increased agricultural intensity is associated with increased warfare.

Population density also is related to warfare, although not uniformly. Nolan (2003) reports a population density rate per square mile of 0.6 for 27 foraging societies, 13.8 for 35 simple horticultural societies, 42.7 for 38 advanced horticultural societies, and over 100 for 27 agricultural societies. In other words, population density rises precipitously in step with the intensification of food production. Advanced horticultural and agricultural societies have both the most warfare and the highest population density.

Nolan finds that, across categories, increasing population density is associated with an almost perfectly stepwise increase in the likelihood of regular warfare (at least once a year). The largest jumps in population densities and rates of warfare occur between nomadic versus settled foragers and between simple horticultural societies versus advanced horticultural and agrarian societies. Using an either/or criterion (warfare either rare or absent, or present), Nolan finds that about one-half of the foraging societies with population densities under one person per square mile never or rarely engage in warfare. In contrast, none of the foraging societies with densities above this level meet the criterion of never or rarely conducting warfare.

Among simple horticultural societies, the proportions do not vary between those with more or fewer than 25 persons per square mile. Notably, for advanced horticulturalists increased population density brings a higher likelihood of peacefulness. That is, warfare is rare or absent in 8% of societies with 100 or fewer people per square mile, compared to 27% of societies with more than 100 persons per square mile. In contrast, among agrarian societies population density correlates with lower likelihood of peacefulness. Warfare is rare or absent in 31% of those with fewer than 100 persons per square mile, but only 6% of those with more than 100.

Although the numbers of societies in Nolan's analysis are small, they are congruent with the finding that among foraging societies increased population density is related to settlement and consequently to warfare. They also dovetail with cases showing that increased population density tends to be associated with more violence but can be offset by institutions that prevent conflict. The connection between reduced warfare and increased population density at the higher levels among horticultural societies is consistent with the increase in interrelationships and political integration between tribes. In contrast, increased warfare is linked to higher population density among agricultural societies due to the resource needs and political systems of populations which practice intensive agriculture.

In addition to the factors enumerated above, the marginalization of women from production in agricultural societies and some horticultural societies is associated with a higher probability of warfare. As noted in Chapter 8, women are primarily or equally responsible for food production in three-fourths or more of horticultural societies, but well under one-half of agricultural societies. Among both horticultural and agricultural societies, those with a lower rate of participation of women in production are more likely to regularly conduct warfare, as are societies in which men avoid women (and children) by eating and sleeping in separate areas (Whiting and Whiting 1975).

Higher degrees of gender stratification bring an elevated likelihood of external violence in several ways. For instance, the aggregation of men apart from women is associated with cultural practices that emphasize the training of boys for warfare. Patrilineal kinship systems and patrilocal residence cluster male relatives together, whereas matrilineal systems disperse them and thereby prevent the convergence of interests that is associated with increased violence. As seen in Chapter 8, matrilineal societies are rare among agricultural societies but common among horticultural ones.

The information presented above indicates that settlement is a necessary precondition for endemic warfare. Bands of nomadic preagricultural humans had friends and relatives in neighboring bands, used resources cooperatively, and avoided intergroup conflict. In contrast, Neolithic agriculturalists experienced increased competition and social and gender inequality, which brought a higher frequency of warfare. This latter scenario is congruent with the picture of human societies as naturally fearful of and hostile to each other, avaricious, and quick to fight over resources, but inconsistent with the long view of human evolution.

. . . . .

The foregoing has indicated that many societies persist over time without becoming warlike, and that the level of warfare conducted by any given society may rise or fall with changing circumstances. These observations conflict with commonsense ideas and scholarly theories about natural human bellicosity. For instance, historian Francis Fukuyama (2011) asserts that warfare has been the driving force behind political evolution from the time of humanity's earliest origins to the French Revolution. Fukuyama argues that warfare is adaptive in a biological sense because it brings reproductive and resource benefits that allow some societies to outcompete others. Complex governmental forms such as centralized states therefore emerged from rudimentary tribal warfare. In other words, endemic warfare was the motor for the historical process of political integration.

Cross-cultural evidence contradicts the idea of a uniform politico-military progression valid for all times and places. While warfare may have been a main reason for centralization in some times and places, many societies have been locked in warfare for years or generations without generating the political order associated with states – for example, tribes in Africa, New Guinea, and South America.

Alternatively, some states consolidated for other reasons such as colonial extraction, as in the case of 18th century England. Moreover, not all societies have chronically waged war. Very few nomadic foraging societies or simple horticultural societies have done so. Under certain conditions, horticultural populations fight their neighbors or join with them to fight other federations, but they also *stop* fighting if conditions change. Warring tendencies are reversible, not progressive.

Most fatally to the thesis, the evidence does not support the assumption that foraging bands were formed around a core of male relatives motivated by shared genes to fight other groups of men for their land and women. These groups' entanglement in continuous violent scuffling is the alleged seed from which tribes grew in order to better organize for warfare. As we have seen, foraging bands are not made up of close relatives, and it is rare for adult male relatives to live together. There is no kinship foundation on which to build a theory of warfare as an evolved trait.

Unquestioned assumptions about biology and evolution have a widespread effect on theorizing about armed conflict today, such as the proposal that providing women hormonal contraception would allow them to resist their husbands' pressure for more children and thereby prevent warfare through reduced resource depletion, environmental degradation, and competition for territory (Potts and Hayden 2008). This idea obscures the structural reasons for women's unequal social position and construes social institutions as spontaneous and neutral. As we have seen, greater population density does not necessarily correlate with either homicide rates or warfare. Earlier chapters showed that people have long restricted family size without women being "empowered" by modern technology. If the problem is men's desire for many children, then the solution should address the social and economic features of societies in which it is in people's interests to have large families or keep trying until they obtain at least one son. Genuine female empowerment would indeed reduce the likelihood of warfare, but would require changes to social systems that privilege males, deny economic autonomy to women, and limit women's agency with respect to sexual relationships and reproductive choices.

Theories of warfare as an automatic outgrowth of material forces that engender competition fail to account for the role of suitable ideological conditions. As modern wars plainly demonstrate, ideological incompatibility with the enemy is a key ingredient in the mobilization of people and resources for fighting. Warfare is not just about control over land or other valuable goods, for there are less costly ways of settling disputes than bloodshed. Warfare erupts where societies come into conflict over deeply-held beliefs about the nature of things.

Elaine Scarry (1987) argues that warfare is undertaken to prove the validity of foundational cultural beliefs through the production of evidence in the form of maimed and dead bodies. Bodies are not metaphors or ideas, although they may be thought of as such: they are real and concrete. Engaging in collective violence that risks lives and has the aim of killing enemies is a struggle to establish the supremacy of a way of thinking. Wounded and dead bodies are irrefutable facts; evidence that reality is non-negotiable. By producing these facts, warfare serves to validate the derivation of a belief system from transcendent truths of natural or divine law; truths which are not open to debate or change. Consequently, any challenge to ideology, whether from the inside or outside, constitutes a threat. This suggests that warfare would not occur if no worldview were more sacred than another.

For those called upon to fight, prosocial attitudes such as empathy must be channeled into compliance with fundamentally antisocial designs. As shown in previous chapters, humans have a strong need to feel socially integrated and appreciated. The flip side is an equally strong need not to experience disapproval. Dread of censure and exclusion underlies the widespread human susceptibility to charismatic figures and zealous groups, who provide a refuge from fear and responsibility and a source of meaning and certainty in the face of ambiguity and doubt. The threat posed by an enemy provides a unifying identity to the group. In cults as in war, leaders maximize the gulf between us and them, for contact between groups calls presumed dissimilarities into question and weakens allegiance to the cause.

As long as all societies were foraging societies, the demographic and ecological conditions for warfare were lacking along with the ideological backdrop. As societies differentiated historically in terms of socioeconomic organization and cosmological or religious beliefs, it became more likely that they would clash on ideological grounds, both internally and with other societies. Disputes over land or any other contested resource could become a pretext for warfare, if combined with threats to established ideology.

In sum, warfare can be expected where societies uphold inflexible, incompatible worldviews. The maintenance of cultural barriers and moral/philosophical isolation render warfare especially likely. Conversely, cross-cultural exchanges and face-to-face interactions between societies – analogous to recurrent intergroup contact in both foraging and horticultural societies – help to prevent warfare.

. . . . .

Acts of humanity and inhumanity are equally natural to the human race. The foregoing discussion has identified circumstances that favor violent behavior. The remainder of the chapter concerns circumstances that promote harmonious relationships and nonviolence between individuals and between societies, as well as specific techniques of conflict avoidance and remediation.

Tribes in Central Brazil's Upper Xingu River Basin exemplify some of the characteristics and practices of nonwarring societies. Fry (2006) explains that the area's 1,200 people are organized into tribes including the Mehinaku, Kuikuru, Kamayura, and several others, and speak languages from four different language families (Carib, Arawak, Tupian, Trumaí). The tribes have been analyzed by anthropologists for four generations and have been known to Westerners since at least the time of the German explorer Karl von den Steinen's visit in the 1880s. Observations over this entire period indicate a complete absence of warfare, although there have been occasional defensive reactions to aggression from tribes outside the river basin. In addition, witchcraft accusations and associated killings have occurred between tribes.

The tribes all make a living by slash-and-burn horticulture supplemented by fishing and some hunting. Crops including the staples of manioc and maize require the work of both sexes: women work the land after men clear it. Husbands and wives may have numerous lovers, as shown by a study among the Mehinaku which found that the 20 men had 1–10 lovers each, while the 17 women had 3–14, except for 3 women who had none. There is a certain amount of bickering and physical aggression – such as women pulling their rivals' hair, or men beating their wives and verbally assaulting their wives' suitors in public. However, as for any other cause, while physical aggression can happen it is very rare, especially among older people, and it is considered shameful given the value placed on a peaceable demeanor.

Around one-fifth of the men are considered "chiefs," but, like big men elsewhere, they do not have institutional backing. They give speeches that bring the community together and gain authority through wisdom and conduct that earns them respect. Chiefs lead by example, demonstrating peacefulness, self-control, generosity, respect for cultural rules, and a placid, unruffled demeanor. Peace is a moral virtue whereas conflict and violence are considered immoral.

All of the villages that share a language participate in a network of trade relationships, ceremonial functions, and marriage exchanges. There is a division of labor between villages that is based on social convention rather than differences in skills or access to resources. Different groups specialize in the production of particular goods such as shell necklaces, salt extracted from water hyacinths, pottery, and bows. People are cognizant of the social dimensions of trade and respect its boundaries. They compliment their trading partners on the quality of the products, and value the personal relationships cultivated through exchange.

When couples marry, usually the wife goes to her husband's village, but sometimes the reverse happens. In about one-third of cases, spouses come from different tribes and speak different languages. Some tribes are strictly exogamous, marrying outside their own tribe as a rule. Consequently people have relatives dispersed among other tribes, and are exposed to other cultures through marriage partners brought into their own. As in the examples from New Guinea above, trade, marriage, and ceremonial relationships work against conflict between groups.

In addition to smaller ceremonies that involve a few villages, ceremonies for inaugurating chiefs and commemorating their deaths are attended by all the tribes in the river valley. People trade, wrestle, and sing and dance. A Yawari custom involves the ritualized performance of a "battle" between different tribes that ends with demonstrations of friendship and goodwill.

In sum, tribes of the Upper Xingu avoid external violence through economic and cultural exchanges, gender and social egalitarianism, and shared beliefs about appropriate behavior which render aggressiveness dishonoring.

. . . . .

While the Upper Xingu example points to ways to prevent conflict, other cultural practices illustrate how it is possible to avert violence in the event of a quarrel. For instance, the informal dispute resolution system used by the Enga in

Papua New Guinea, discussed earlier, shows that where people have a chance to back down and set things right within a socially supported context, they are less likely to resort to violence or allow a conflict to escalate. Similar collective discussions and institutionalized mediation systems have been reported with respect to many societies around the world, including the Semai, the Buid in the Philippines, and native Hawai'ians and Fijians (Fry 2006).

Like other African societies, the Kpelle people in Central Liberia maintain local methods of resolving conflict alongside the formal judicial system. The latter comprises the state judiciary as well as the network of paramount chiefs who hear civil cases and impose punishments such as brief jail sentences or payments to the aggrieved party. The informal yet ordered, procedural, and binding system which James Gibbs (1963) describes as a "moot" involves Sunday hearings in which everyone present is permitted to talk about the many sides of the issue. The person making a complaint hosts the meeting. All the relatives of both parties come, but there is no set seating arrangement or division between them. After a blessing, a lively discussion ensues as people question the disputants and offer testimony. The crowd comments and interrupts throughout. Eventually, the entire group reaches a decision by consensus, without a leader. The losing party pays a penalty in the form of rum or beer shared by all, as well as gifts to the winner. The amount of compensation is high enough to matter, but low enough not to generate resentment, anger, and new hostilities. The losing party makes a ritualized apology in which he or she acknowledges fault and agrees to the group's decision. His or her supporters share the blame.

The system prevents disputants from being isolated in a stressful situation. It gives everyone a chance to freely express their opinions and feelings in a safe setting. Bad behavior is not resented or returned; everyone understands that it is part of the process. The gifts and acknowledgment of fault bring reconciliation and return the losing party to grace.

The moot provides a structured, predictable context in which to socially re-integrate the disputing parties and change their thinking about the issues at hand. It forces them to recognize their shared responsibility for the conflict, in contrast to the tendencies of an impersonal, punitive legal system. To illustrate, a formal court process can do little but seal a divorce between disputing spouses. In a moot, the two can air their differences and possibly settle them with the help and obligation implicit in their relatives' collective decision and support. The first approach depends on coercion, the second on collaboration.

Mediation, interventions in the case of drug or alcohol addiction, and community and school hearings represent similar informal ways of resolving conflicts. Like the practices described above, they tend to involve a larger group of people than merely the protagonists of the situation. In contrast, the formal court systems of mass societies have opposite effects. They individualize conflicts and isolate the disputants rather than involve them in a socially supportive process. In face-to-face societies, violence is curbed not just by the greater social control that exists where everyone knows each other's business, but also the communal type of dispute resolution available when conflicts erupt.

The same principles apply to conflict between societies. Many existing international institutions provide a context for collective decision-making and mediation. These include multi-country and regional association meetings and negotiations surrounding trade, governance, environmental regulation, human rights, disease control, and other domains of potential conflict.

A second social practice for managing disagreements and hostilities involves ritualized singing and other forms of verbal dueling.[6] In societies throughout the world, adolescents and adults, women and men, engage in formal verbal scuffles. In addition to providing a forum for creative expression, social bonding, and venting emotions from infatuation to grief, these traditions allow individuals to reconcile interpersonal conflicts. Well-known examples of verbal dueling come from Inuit populations of northern Canada, the Tiv of Nigeria, Fiji Indians, and teenage boys in Turkey. There are similar traditions in highland Bolivia, China, Sumatra, Lebanon, Palestine, Italy, Malta, and North India, among many other locations. The European heroic narrative tradition suggests that verbal competition and performance have existed for a very long time.

Elizabeth Mathias's (1976) analysis of Sardinian shepherds' songs illustrates how these cultural practices provide men a way to express anger, conflict, desire, and power. The improvised but structured songs follow a standard format of five or, more often, eight lines, and respect a rhyme scheme of 12 beats per line. They are always sung in the local dialect for a group of listeners, whether in the sheepfolds in the countryside or on a stage in town. The singer addresses either one man or the whole group through plays on words, metaphors, and direct insults. Through song, men communicate about and resolve conflicts over grazing, relationships involving their female relatives, the quantity and price of milk and cheese produced, and dealings with owners of sheep and land. They express male values surrounding women's chastity, men's honor, and gender roles. They assert their strength, manliness, and virility in a way that allows them to articulate feelings such as fear and doubt without appearing emotional or weak.

The Netsilik of the Central Canadian Arctic used song duels to diffuse tensions between men who might otherwise attack each other physically, as observed by visitors in the 1950s and 1960s. Fry (2006) explains that the culturally acceptable practice of female infanticide created a gender imbalance that led to tensions and fighting over contested women. Some marriages were polyandrous, with one woman married to two or more brothers, a situation that often led to high emotions and competition. However, killing another man was unwise because it set in motion a series of revenge killings and, in addition, was considered disgraceful. Through song, a wronged man could challenge his opponent about small to major grudges and arguments involving hunting and sharing, unmanly behavior, adultery, and disputes over a woman. The two men would sing insulting songs to each other, and the audience would decide the winner. If a song duel failed to diffuse the tension between two men, they could fight physically, but only under strict rules. The two would hit each other, starting with the challenger taking the first blow.

They would strike each other in turns on the shoulder or forehead until one gave up. Afterwards the dispute was forgotten.

Sports serve similar expressive functions, even if they are not played for the explicit purpose of expressing emotions and insecurities or dealing with interpersonal conflicts. Nonetheless they often provide a context for doing so, along with a safe forum for spectators to vent feelings and hostilities by singing, yelling, and gesturing – although occasionally violence erupts. Sports events for ex-combatants may help neighbors reconcile after civil war through the positive dynamics of teamwork and play. In contrast, the experience of 100 communities in Sierra Leone indicates that formal truth and reconciliation meetings for victims and perpetrators bring increased depression, anxiety, and post-traumatic stress that counteracts the benefits in terms of social cohesion and participation (Cilliers et al. 2016). One reason suggested by the discussion above is that the hearings facilitate forgiveness but do not permit restorative payments.

For a third example, citizen exchanges for the purpose of improving cross-cultural understanding help to prevent conflict, similarly to the cross-cutting relationships typical of foraging and horticultural societies discussed above. Historically, political leaders sent their children or other citizens to live in distant territories as a sign of goodwill and trust. For instance, General Xenophon's sons went from Athens to Sparta as *trophimoi*, foreign students classified as foster sons in Sparta. Similar exchanges occur in a variety of ethnographic settings throughout the world. Horticultural tribes in Papua New Guinea send boys to live in other villages. Parents throughout the world send their children to the United World Colleges, an international consortium of lower and upper schools that serve international student bodies on campuses in multiple countries including India, Norway, and Singapore. The US government sponsors international exchanges of students, scholars, journalists, artists, and others through the Fulbright program. Individual schools and universities send and receive students and faculty through programs and individual initiatives with matching institutions around the world. These and other citizen exchanges involve hundreds of countries and create meaningful relationships between individuals and between institutions. The evidence reviewed in the last few chapters suggests that they help to avert violent confrontations both through social networks and by weakening ideological boundaries.

Anthropological analysis suggests that citizen exchanges are more effective than foreign aid with respect to promoting peace. Like gifts in general, foreign aid highlights power differences between parties and imposes obligations for return gifts that the other party may be unable to meet (Cronk 1988). In the potlatch described in Chapter 11, recipients of great feasts are humbled by the excess poured upon them, and unable to restore their prestige until they can provide a lavish celebration in turn. In contrast to the cycle by which tribes alternate between giving and receiving, in the case of impoverished countries there is no hope of returning the gift. Foreign aid leaves the wealthier country in the gatekeeper position discussed earlier, which actually increases the likelihood of violence and exploitation. The evidence suggests that the surest way to decrease warfare would be to dismantle the structural inequalities between countries.

. . . . .

The last three chapters have shown that violence varies in frequency across societies and time, and that its patterning and scale are not random. Consequently, biological explanations explain only some aspects of violence, most notably the sex difference in physical aggressiveness. Across cultures, men commit the lion's share of homicides. Weapons tend to be made by men, and warriors tend to be men. Reasons for men's greater tendency to violent behavior include androgen-influenced brain development in fetal life, genetic variants that affect males more frequently than females, and hormone levels in men who do not experience intimate partnership or participate directly in parenting. However, even in men with predisposing conditions, the violent expression of frustration, rage, and anger depends on life experiences and the sociocultural setting.

From an evolutionary point of view, the sex difference in violence is due to greater mate competition among males than females. Yet, competition for reproductive opportunities is not the same as a natural drive to eliminate competitors. In other words, evolution explains male aggressiveness but not homicide or warfare. Violent behavior does not increase men's reproductive success – even without considering that it increases the odds that their lives will be cut short. The purported evidence for such a link is based on a miscalculation concerning Yanomami horticultural tribes which, besides, are not representative of ancestral human society. Moreover, other primate males do not habitually form violent male coalitions that attack other groups to steal their females. Instances of collective chimpanzee violence have arisen in anomalous situations such as a highly unusual number of young males, and involved attacks on single individuals rather than entire groups. Our other closest primate relatives, bonobos, do not attack strangers.

It does not follow from the mistreatment of women in historical and modern wars that the evolutionary purpose of warfare is to supply men with more female bodies in order to increase their own reproductive success. This idea expresses the uncritical projection of current cultural beliefs about men's natural superiority and rights over women onto other societies and times. It glorifies war as an entirely masculine enterprise and demonstration of male potency and heroism. In reality, armed conflicts demand the work of entire populations and may harm civilians more than combatants through malnutrition, disease, displacement, persecution, excessive and dangerous labor, bombings, and direct violence. During the Second World War, these causes accounted for 40 million lives lost in Europe. The double tendency to naturalize warfare and disregard the contributions and losses of noncombatants remains a significant obstacle to the comprehension and prevention of violent conflicts.

Warfare and other forms of violence emerge through particular social contexts, not out of a uniform male psychology fatally driven towards primal raiding. The characteristics of foraging societies suggest that ancestral societies were not plagued by intergroup conflict and did not encourage violent conflict resolution between individuals. The nomadic lifestyle necessarily exists only where population density is low. Interdependence and the impossibility of accumulation favors egalitarianism and disfavors arrogance and aggression. Bilateral kinship averts the conglomeration of male relatives that occurs in patrilineal societies. Men are not distanced from family life and child care. Valued traits such as humility and generosity protect personal autonomy and prevent people from gaining authority over others. Self-effacing behavior is expected of even the most gifted or lucky people. Foragers resolve conflict face to face and make decisions collectively, by consensus. There is no formal leadership or coercive power. Nomadic bands of foragers regularly meet up with others to visit friends and relatives, not to fight.

Some interpersonal conflicts undoubtedly arose in Paleolithic foraging bands, as they do in contemporary ones. The conflicts may have escalated into hostilities between members of different bands, but ethnographic and archeological data suggest that it did not lead to anything like warfare. In sum, the evidence points to the conclusion that over most of human evolution our ancestors avoided domination, inequality, conflict within groups, and warfare. They developed social institutions favoring nonviolence through cultural means, not selfish genes. Their way of life depended upon traits such as empathy, cooperativeness, and attention to fairness. These traits are already in place in us at birth, and reliably manifest themselves in situations that model the kind of face-to-face, long-term relationships typical of foraging societies.

That more recent human societies became warlike is not surprising given the social changes, resource competition, population increase, and ideological divergence that came with food production and permanent settlement. Settled populations depend on access to natural resources including land, water, and minerals which vary in quality and proximity. There is much to fight over, but at the same time little scope for individuals or groups to shift alliances and residence. Socioeconomic and gender stratification arose all over the ancient world as civilizations grew and became more permanent and internally specialized, increasing the likelihood of homicide, domestic violence, and warfare. These conditions, not ancestral foraging, promote the greed, self-aggrandizement, hierarchy, and endemic violence reputedly dictated by human nature.

There is no society in which killing is considered normal or tolerable, although some make exceptions for warfare and capital punishment. The existence of peaceful societies, including some contemporary industrialized nations, points to the role of not only social-structural factors but also cultural beliefs about human interaction and what constitutes appropriate behavior. Where respect, restraint, and reserve are valued, physical aggression is not a legitimate way to deal with emotions or achieve personal objectives. In contrast, where the ideal individual is self-oriented, assertive, confrontational, and domineering, the expected reaction to being wronged is to seek redress and recompense, if not to get revenge. These attitudes are congruent with Western society's emphasis on individual self-determination, which emerged in earlier times of opportunity and abundance.

They do not harmonize with present circumstances of economic stagnation, socio-economic inequality, and an increasingly evident lack of social mobility.

Belief systems which glorify or simply facilitate violence may appear to have something to do with human nature, but they are no more natural than other worldviews that emphasize social sensitivity and self-effacement. In addition, they do not match the on-the-ground reality that cordiality or at least avoidance is a more characteristic behavior than violent confrontation. Family members, room-mates, coworkers, and strangers on the street are far more likely to hold back, even when angry, than to strike out. People regularly behave generously toward strangers and even show concern for anonymous others in far-flung corners of the world. Together with evidence of the health consequences of prosocial versus agonistic behavior, this frequency difference between violent and nonviolent interactions indicates that humans are not inevitably driven to hierarchy and hostility.

Physical violence is a possible behavior and a statistically rare one compared to nonviolent human interaction. Like reading or riding bicycles, homicide and warfare are common behaviors across the globe, but prevalence does not constitute evolutionary significance. The reasons for violence can be found in proximate factors of the kind explored in the last three chapters, without recourse to "deep" killer impulses in a remote primate ancestor or mythical society of prehistoric warriors. As we have seen, positive interactions based on cooperation and mutual respect are common, ordinary, and responsive to encouragement through institutions and cultural practices that prevent conflict and provide effective mechanisms for resolving disputes. Far from being "in our genes," warfare occurs under particular social circumstances which can change in favor of either more or less conflict and physical violence.

The evidence considered in this book suggests that it is impossible to know whether, left to their own devices, people would act or be a certain way, for people are nowhere left to their own devices. Behavioral variability is meaningful, not a corruption of a deep biological essence unsullied by culture. If human beings do things in multiple ways, the species evidently is not confined to one. This is not to say that there is no such thing as humanness or that it cannot be grasped. Rather, it is to point out that the masculinist, confrontational, winner-take-all perspective that pervades popular and scientific thought gets in the way of thoroughgoing analysis by proposing *itself* as human nature. Such a complex, dynamic, multi-layered subject as the human condition demands a more flexible, adaptable approach to framing questions and interpreting empirical data.

Notes

1 On prehistoric warfare, see Fry (2006).
2 This section is based on Fry (2006).
3 Regarding violence against foreigners in the Andaman Islands, see Kelly (2003).
4 For the original study, see Ember (1978).
5 On stateless societies, see Scott (2009).
6 On verbal dueling, see Pagliai (2009).

References cited

Cilliers J, Dube O, Siddiqi B. 2016. Reconciling after civil conflict increases social capital but decreases individual well-being. *Science* 352(6287):787–794.

Cronk L. 1988. Strings attached. *The Sciences* 29(3):2–4.

Diamond J. 2008 21 April. Vengeance is ours: what can tribal societies tell us about our need to get even. *The New Yorker.*

Ember CR. 1978. Myths about hunter-gatherers. *Ethnology* 17(4):439–448.

Ember CR, Ember M. 1992. Resource unpredictability, mistrust, and war: a cross-cultural study. *Journal of Conflict Resolution* 36(2):242–262.

Film Study Center. 1964. *Dead Birds.* Gardner R, director. Peabody Museum, Harvard University.

Fry DP. 2006. *The human potential for peace: an anthropological challenge to assumptions about war and violence.* New York: Oxford University Press.

Fukuyama F. 2011. *The origins of political order: from prehuman times to the French Revolution.* New York: Farrar, Strauss, and Giroux.

Gibbs JL. 1963. The Kpelle moot: a therapeutic model for the informal settlement of disputes. *Africa* 33(1):1–11.

Kelly RC. 2003. *Warless societies and the origin of war.* Ann Arbor: University of Michigan Press.

Kirch PV. 2010. Controlled comparison and Polynesian cultural evolution. In Diamond J, Robinson JA, editors. *Natural experiments in history.* Cambridge, MA: Harvard University Press. p. 15–52.

Konner M. 2006. Human nature, ethnic violence, and war. In Fitzduff M, Stout CE, editors. *The psychology of resolving global conflicts.* Volume 1. Westport, CT: Praeger Security International. p. 1–39.

Lahr MM, Rivera F, Power RK, Mounier A, Copsey B, Crivellaro F, Edung JE, Fernandez JM, Kiarie C, Lawrence J, et al. 2016. Inter-group violence among early Holocene hunter-gatherers of West Turkana, Kenya. *Nature* 529(7586):394–398.

Mathias E. 1976. La gara poetica: Sardinian shepherds' verbal dueling and the expression of male values in an agro-pastoral society. *Ethos* 4(4):483–507.

Nolan PD. 2003. Toward an ecological-evolutionary theory of the incidence of warfare in preindustrial societies. *Sociological Theory* 21(1):18–30.

Nolan PD, Lenski G. 2011. *Human societies: an introduction to macrosociology.* 11th ed. Boulder, CO: Paradigm Publishers.

Pagliai V. 2009. The art of dueling with words: toward a new understanding of verbal duels across the world. *Oral Tradition* 24(1):61–88.

Podolefsky A. 1984. Contemporary warfare in the New Guinea highlands. *Ethnology* 23(2):73–87.

Potts M, Hayden T. 2008. *Sex and war: how biology explains warfare and terrorism and offers a path to a safer world.* Dallas: BenBella.

Roscoe R. 2011. Dead birds: the "theater" of war among the Dugum Dani. *American Anthropologist* 113(1):56–70.

Scarry E. 1987. *The body in pain: the making and unmaking of the world.* New York: Oxford University Press.

Scott JC. 2009. *The art of not being governed: an anarchist history of upland Southeast Asia.* New Haven: Yale University Press.

Sillitoe P, Kuwimb MJ. 2010 28 August. Rebutting Jared Diamond's savage portrait. iMediaEthics. www.imediaethics.org/News/170/Rebutting_jared_diamonds_savage_portrait_.php. Accessed 24 May 2016.

Steckel RH, Rose JC, Larsen CS, Walker PL. 2002. Skeletal health in the western hemisphere from 4000 BC to the present. *Evolutionary Anthropology* 11(4):142–155.

Whiting B, Whiting J. 1975. *Children of six cultures: a psychocultural analysis.* Cambridge, MA: Harvard University Press.

Wiessner P, Pupu N. 2012. Toward peace: foreign arms and indigenous institutions in a Papua New Guinea society. *Science* 337(6102):1651–1654.

Younger SM. 2008. Conditions and mechanisms for peace in precontact Polynesia. *Current Anthropology* 49(5):927–934.

APPENDIX

Life expectancy rate calculations

The following pages provide a quantitative demonstration of the points made earlier in this book concerning the difference between life span and life expectancy, and the preponderant effect of infant mortality rates on life expectancy rates. These issues will be analyzed through a series of demographic scenarios. The discussion includes instructions for the calculation of life expectancy rates either from age-specific death rates current in a population at a single point in time, or knowledge of the age at death of every individual in a cohort of people born the same year.

The first step is a consideration of the average age at death, which is roughly equivalent to life expectancy at birth. The former takes account of all the people who die in a population either in a particular interval of time, such as one year, or over more than a century in the case of a cohort of people born at the same time and followed until each has died. Life expectancy, by contrast, is a projection from age-specific death rates at a given point in time. It shows how many years of life a hypothetical group of people has left on average at the beginning of each age interval, assuming that, as they move through time, the age-specific death rates stay the same. The number of years remaining may be calculated at any age, not just at birth.

Life expectancy rates at different ages are interesting to life insurance companies, because the numbers provide an estimate of the benefits the companies are likely to have to pay over time. For scholars and policy makers, life expectancy rates are helpful for comparing health conditions in different times and places. Since infant mortality rates have such a strong impact on life expectancy at birth, the following discussion emphasizes the connection between the two.

To show that the average age at death is close to the average life expectancy at birth for a given population, we will analyze a hypothetical population of 850 people born the same year somewhere in Western Europe. Although it is not a workable premise for real-life populations, we will assume that complete and accurate information exists for every person, and that no one migrated into or out of the cohort. Three sets of data will be considered, each one pertaining to a different mortality-rate scenario (moderate, high, low).

We start by grouping the individuals into 5-year intervals based on the age at death, with three exceptions: the first two and the last age groups. The reason is that mortality in the youngest and oldest age intervals is unlike mortality in other age groups. For 0–1-year-olds the average age will be set at 0.1 year or around one month, given that most deaths of babies occur soon after birth. For the 1–5 interval, the age is set at 2.5, somewhat below the midpoint since deaths in this age group cluster more toward the low than the high end of the age range. For the 100+ interval, the age is given as 102, since more deaths occur closer to 100 than 105 or older. For all other age groups, the average age will be the midpoint, indicating that deaths are spread out evenly over the age interval.

The number of person-years for each interval is the product of the number of individuals in the category and the average age at which they died. It represents the total number of years lived by the subgroup. To determine the average age at death, all the totals are combined and divided by the total number of individuals.

In the first scenario in Table A.1, living conditions are moderately good. The infant mortality rate is 5%, or 50 deaths in the first year per 1,000 live births, and the average age at death is around 54.8 years. In the second case, conditions have worsened considerably. The infant mortality rate is 27%, or 270 deaths per 1,000 live births. The average age at death is around 36.3 years. In the last scenario, mortality rates are very low. Infant mortality is under 1% (0.6% in this table), as it is in the US and other developed countries now. The average age at death increases to 77.7. These scenarios are presented in Chapter 3 as corresponding to a prehistoric foraging society with moderately low infant mortality, a preindustrial agricultural society with high infant mortality, and a typical wealthy industrialized society today with very low infant mortality rates.

In all three cases, the population includes people who died in their 70s, 80s, 90s, and beyond. That is, it is possible to have very old people in a population where the average age at death is 36.3 years. The table below shows the dampening effect of low infant survival values on a population average.

Now it is time to discuss average life expectancy rates. The tables look more complicated than Table A.1, but are likewise derived from basic mathematical operations – addition, subtraction, multiplication, and division. Often, life tables concern either males or females, but for simplicity's sake they are combined here. While some life tables present intervals of 1 year, involving more than 100 rows, others, such as the ones below, have 5-year intervals with the same three exceptions as in Table A.1 (0–1, 1–5, 100+).

Life tables express what has happened, or project what would happen, to a group of people followed for more than a century. "True" or "cohort" tables track a group of people from birth to death, as in the sample populations below. More

TABLE A.1 Average age at death of three cohorts under different mortality-rate scenarios

		Cohort A: moderate infant mortality		*Cohort B: high infant mortality*		*Cohort C: low infant mortality*	
Interval	*Average age*	n *deaths*	*Person-years*	n *deaths*	*Person-years*	n *deaths*	*Person-years*
0–1y	0.1	42	4.2	230	23	5	0.5
1–5y	2.5	8	20	36	90	0	0
5–10y	7.5	4	30	17	127.5	1	7.5
10–15y	12.5	8	100	18	225	1	12.5
15–20y	17.5	15	262.5	22	385	2	35
20–25y	22.5	27	607.5	25	562.5	3	67.5
25–30y	27.5	29	797.5	26	715	3	82.5
30–35y	32.5	45	1462.5	30	975	4	130
35–40y	37.5	48	1800	36	1350	6	225
40–45y	42.5	56	2380	41	1742.5	9	382.5
45–50y	47.5	58	2755	45	2137.5	13	617.5
50–55y	52.5	64	3360	47	2467.5	18	945
55–60y	57.5	66	3795	48	2760	28	1610
60–65y	62.5	68	4250	48	3000	44	2750
65–70y	67.5	62	4185	40	2700	64	4320
70–75y	72.5	50	3625	34	2465	85	6162.5
75–80y	77.5	48	3720	28	2170	116	8990
80–85y	82.5	51	4207.5	29	2392.5	142	11715
85–90y	87.5	49	4287.5	26	2275	140	12250
90–95y	92.5	33	3052.5	16	1480	101	9342.5
95–100y	97.5	14	1365	6	585	48	4680
100+	102	5	510	2	204	17	1734
Total		**850**	**46576.7**	**850**	**30832**	**850**	**66059.5**
Average			**54.8**		**36.3**		**77.7**

commonly it is necessary to construct "period" or "current" tables, which are based on death rates taken at one point in time. This means that, unless they are based on real cohorts of people, life expectancy rates are projections. With a period table, rather than using actual numbers of real people, we follow an imaginary cohort of 100,000 people all born at the same time. We filter the cohort through each age-specific death rate to see how many are left at the end of each interval. The result is carried into the next line, until the entire group has died.

Ideally, death rates are calculated from census data on the number of people of each age who were alive at the beginning of a period of time and the number alive at the end, but where reliable data are not available death rates must be estimated in other ways. Even with good reporting systems, there are always problems of data quality due to migration, error, uncertainty about identities or dates, and other causes. For real people, current death rates may no longer be the same when they reach older ages, due to changes in living conditions, infectious diseases, medical therapies, and other factors. A life expectancy rate calculated for 30-year-olds today may not be congruent with the same cohort's life expectancy rate 20 years from now. These topics are covered in all demography textbooks. Actual life tables and life expectancy rates may be found through sources such as the National Center for Health Statistics (www.cdc.gov/nchs/) and the World Health Organization (www.who.int/gho/en).

Once the life table has the number of people alive at the beginning and end of each interval, based either on the age-specific death rate in a period table or the recorded years of every individual life in a cohort table, the aggregate number of person-years is calculated. This number represents the total number of years lived by the group in each interval, combining the full amount lived by the survivors and the partial interval lived by the people who died. When the bottom row is reached and all the people have died, the person-years are added up, cumulatively, from the bottom of the table to the top. The last step is to divide these numbers by the number of people alive at the beginning of each interval. The result is the average life expectancy at the beginning of each interval – whether it is birth or 25 or 60.

To begin, we will confirm that the average age at death is about the same as life expectancy at birth, starting with the moderate-infant-mortality population. We will calculate life expectancy rates for the cohort since we know the age at death for each individual. This allows us to estimate life expectancy at ages other than birth, in contrast to the single value that results from calculating the average age at death.

The first step is to enter the total population 850, at the top. From this number, the number of deaths in each interval is subtracted, step by step, and the balance entered on the following line. The last line is for the 100-and-over interval, where the mortality rate is 100%.

To calculate the person-years, first we work down, then up. For all but the 0–1, 1–5, and 100+ intervals, we will take the average of the number alive at the beginning and the number alive at the end of the interval, and multiply it by 5, which is the number of years in the interval. For instance, for the 25–30 year age group, we add 746 and 717, divide the total by 2 to obtain 732, and multiply by 5 to yield 3,658. Alternatively, we can add 746 and 717, then multiply by 2.5 to obtain the same result of 732. This result is the combined number of years the group lived during the 5-year interval, including those who lived the entire interval and those who lived part of the interval. We can take the average of the two because in reality deaths are scattered throughout the interval in most age groups except for the three exceptions, explained further forthwith.

In the 0–1 interval, if we use the average of the number alive at the beginning and at the end of the interval, the result will be too large, given that most infant deaths occur in the early days or weeks. As in Table A.1, we will assume an average age at death of about one month, or 0.1 of a year. To calculate person-years for the 0–1 interval, we will add the total at the end of the interval times 1, since those people all lived through the whole year, plus the number of deaths times 0.1. This latter number sums up the partial years lived by all those who died in the interval. Similarly, for the 1–5 age group, we will calculate person-years by adding the number of individuals alive at the end of the interval times 4 years, to the number who died times 1.5. The latter indicates that the average age at death of children who died in this age group is about 2.5 years, the same as in the table concerning the three populations above. Finally, for the 100+ interval, we will multiply the number alive at the beginning of the interval by 2, in accordance with an average age at death for people in this age group of 102 years. In all of the scenarios below

TABLE A.2 Cohort table for Population A with moderate infant mortality rate

Age interval	*n at beginning of interval*	*n deaths in interval*	*Person-years in interval*	*Cumulative person- years*	*Life expectancy*	*Proportion deceased*
0–1y	850	42	812	46584	**54.8**	0.04941
1–5y	808	8	3220	45772	56.6	0.00990
5–10y	800	4	3990	42552	53.2	0.00500
10–15y	796	8	3960	38562	48.4	0.01005
15–20y	788	15	3902	34602	43.9	0.01904
20–25y	773	27	3798	30700	39.7	0.03493
25–30y	746	29	3658	26902	36.1	0.03887
30–35y	717	45	3472	23244	32.4	0.06276
35–40y	672	48	3240	19772	29.4	0.07143
40–45y	624	56	2980	16532	26.5	0.08974
45–50y	568	58	2695	13552	23.9	0.10211
50–55y	510	64	2390	10857	21.3	0.12549
55–60y	446	66	2065	8467	19.0	0.14798
60–65y	380	68	1730	6402	16.8	0.17895
65–70y	312	62	1405	4672	15.0	0.19872
70–75y	250	50	1125	3267	13.1	0.20000
75–80y	200	48	880	2142	10.7	0.24000
80–85y	152	51	632	1262	8.3	0.33553
85–90y	101	49	382	630	6.2	0.48515
90–95y	52	33	178	248	4.8	0.63462
95–100y	19	14	60	70	3.7	0.73684
100+	5	5	10	10	2.0	1.00000
Total		**850**				

we will use the same rules for calculating person-years, even though in reality the exact distribution of deaths in an interval varies from one population to another.

Once the person-years have been calculated, we add them from the bottom up, cumulatively (10 + 60 = 70; 70 + 178 = 248, and so on). For the "life expectancy" column, starting at the top, we divide the cumulative person-years by the number alive at the *beginning* of the interval. That gives us the average life expectancy at each interval. In this case it is 54.8 years at birth, as in Table A.1. The new column on the far right shows the proportion of the age cohort that died in each interval; that is, the number who died in the interval divided by the number alive at the beginning of the interval.

Now for the high-infant-mortality population. As shown in Table A.3, following the same procedures we end up with an average life expectancy at birth of 36.3 years, the same as the average age at death found in Table A.1.

TABLE A.3 Cohort table for Population B with high infant mortality rate

Age interval	n *at beginning of interval*	n *deaths in interval*	*Person-years in interval*	*Cumulative person- years*	*Life expectancy*	*Proportion deceased*
0–1y	850	230	643	30867	**36.3**	0.27059
1–5y	620	36	2426	30224	48.7	0.05806
5–10y	584	17	2878	27798	47.6	0.02911
10–15y	567	18	2790	24920	44.0	0.03175
15–20y	549	22	2690	22130	40.3	0.04007
20–25y	527	25	2572	19440	36.9	0.04744
25–30y	502	26	2445	16868	33.6	0.05179
30–35y	476	30	2305	14423	30.3	0.06303
35–40y	446	36	2140	12118	27.2	0.08072
40–45y	410	41	1948	9978	24.3	0.10000
45–50y	369	45	1732	8030	21.8	0.12195
50–55y	324	47	1502	6298	19.4	0.14506
55–60y	277	48	1265	4796	17.3	0.17329
60–65y	229	48	1025	3531	15.4	0.20961
65–70y	181	40	805	2506	13.8	0.22099
70–75y	141	34	620	1701	12.1	0.24113
75–80y	107	28	465	1081	10.1	0.26168
80–85y	79	29	322	616	7.8	0.36709
85–90y	50	26	185	294	5.9	0.52000
90–95y	24	16	80	109	4.5	0.66667
95–100y	8	6	25	29	3.6	0.75000
100+	2	2	4	4	2.0	1.00000
Total		**850**				

TABLE A.4 Cohort table for Population C with low infant mortality rate

Age interval	*n at beginning of interval*	*n deaths in interval*	*Person-years in interval*	*Cumulative person-years*	*Life expectancy*	*Proportion deceased*
0–1y	850	5	846	66036	**77.7**	0.00588
1–5y	845	1	3378	65190	77.1	0.00118
5–10y	844	0	4200	61812	73.2	0.00000
10–15y	844	1	4218	57612	68.2	0.00118
15–20y	843	2	4210	53394	63.3	0.00237
20–25y	841	3	4198	49184	58.5	0.00357
25–30y	838	3	4182	44986	53.7	0.00358
30–35y	835	4	4165	40804	48.9	0.00479
35–40y	831	6	4140	36639	44.1	0.00722
40–45y	825	9	4102	32499	39.4	0.01091
45–50y	816	13	4048	28397	34.8	0.01593
50–55y	803	18	3970	24349	30.3	0.02242
55–60y	785	28	3855	20379	26.0	0.03567
60–65y	757	44	3675	16524	21.8	0.05812
65–70y	713	64	3405	12849	18.0	0.08976
70–75y	649	85	3032	9444	14.6	0.13097
75–80y	564	116	2530	6412	11.4	0.20567
80–85y	448	142	1885	3882	8.7	0.31696
85–90y	306	140	1180	1997	6.5	0.45752
90–95y	166	101	578	817	4.9	0.60843
95–100y	65	48	205	239	3.7	0.73846
100+	17	17	34	34	2	1.00000
Total		**850**				

Table A.4 provides life expectancy rates for the low-infant-mortality population. It shows that life expectancy at birth for this group is 77.7, the same as the average age at death, and a rate similar to current life expectancy at birth in the US. Tables A.2, A.3, and A.4 confirm that the average age at death and the life expectancy at birth calculated from cohort data are the same.

We will now construct a period table based on the same death rates that were used to construct Table A.2. These rates of loss appear in the second column of Table A.5, and are the basis of the entire table. The results are the same for the hypothetical population of 100,000 as the cohort of 850 individuals: 54.8 years for a population with a moderate infant mortality rate.

To see how the table is constructed, imagine it blank except for columns 1 and 2. First, we enter 100,000 in the third column of the first row (0–1 year). We

TABLE A.5 Period table under moderate-infant-mortality scenario*

Age interval	*Proportion deceased*	n *at beginning of interval*	n *deaths in interval*	*Person-years in interval*	*Cumulative person- years*	*Life expectancy*
0–1y	0.04941	100000	4941	95553	5480565	**54.8**
1–5y	0.00990	95059	941	378824	5385012	56.6
5–10y	0.00500	94118	471	469412	5006188	53.2
10–15y	0.01005	93647	941	465882	4536776	48.4
15–20y	0.01904	92706	1765	459118	4070894	43.9
20–25y	0.03493	90941	3177	446762	3611776	39.7
25–30y	0.03887	87764	3411	430292	3165014	36.1
30–35y	0.06276	84353	5294	408530	2734722	32.4
35–40y	0.07143	79059	5647	381178	2326192	29.4
40–45y	0.08974	73412	6588	350590	1945014	26.5
45–50y	0.10211	66824	6823	317062	1594424	23.9
50–55y	0.12549	60001	7529	281180	1277362	21.3
55–60y	0.14798	52471	7765	242942	996182	19.0
60–65y	0.17895	44706	8000	203530	753240	16.8
65–70y	0.19872	36706	7294	165295	549710	15.0
70–75y	0.20000	29412	5882	132355	384415	13.1
75–80y	0.24000	23530	5647	103530	252060	10.7
80–85y	0.33553	17882	6000	74412	148530	8.3
85–90y	0.48515	11883	5765	45002	74118	6.2
90–95y	0.63462	6118	3882	20882	29116	4.8
95–100y	0.73684	2235	1647	7508	8234	3.7
100+	1.00000	588	588	1176	1176	2.0
Total		**0**	**100000**			

*Age-specific death rates are taken from Table A.2.

multiply 100,000 by the 0–1 rate to yield the number who died in the first year and enter the result in the next column. We then calculate the number of survivors by subtracting the number of deaths from the number of individuals alive at the beginning of the interval, and enter it in the next row concerning the 1–5 interval. This number multiplied by the corresponding death rate yields the number of deaths in the 1–5 age interval, from which we repeat the process again and again until reaching the oldest age group.

The information in the third and fourth columns provides the basis on which to calculate the number of person-years in each interval. Working downward in the fifth column, for all intervals except 0–1, 1–5, and 100+, we take the average of the number of people at the beginning and at the end of the interval and multiply by 5 (or, alternatively, the sum of the two numbers multiplied by 2.5). For 0–1, we take the number of survivors and add the number of deaths times 0.1; for 1–5 we combine the survivors times 4 and the number of deaths times 1.5; for 100+ we multiply the total (all deaths) by 2.

Once the person-years for all age groups have been inserted into the table, we work from the bottom up. We start by putting the same number for the 100+ year-olds representing the person-years lived in that interval at the bottom of the sixth column. Then, we add the 95–100 interval's person-years from the fifth column to that and enter the total in the sixth column, and so on up the column until calculating the cumulative total at the top, for the 0–1 interval.

The last step is to complete the final column, which contains the average remaining years of life at each interval. This is the number from the sixth column, divided by the number of people alive at the beginning of the interval, in the third column.

Now we will switch to an exercise involving the more common scenario in which larger populations are studied over shorter time periods. We will calculate life expectancy rates for an imaginary city of 300,000 people divided into the same age groups above. Assuming we have perfect data on the number of deaths in each age range, we determine the current death rates for each age interval and then construct a life table.

As is typical of developed countries today, the city has crude birth rates and crude death rates of around 10 per 1,000 per year. As a result, there are about 3,000 births and 3,000 deaths per year. This means that over 5 years, about 15,000 people are subtracted from the population. Table A.6 begins with a typical age distribution for a population with low mortality and fertility. It provides a count of all the people at the beginning of each age interval one day, and the number remaining 5 years later (with the exceptions of 0–1, 1–5, and 100+). The mortality rates for each age interval including infants are close to those obtained for the low-infant-mortality population of 850 discussed above.

Table A.6 shows the link between population data from a census and a life table that moves 100,000 individuals through the same rates of loss at each age interval. The result is an average life expectancy at birth of 77.7 years. The age-specific death rates that yield the life expectancy rates in the table are similar to those pertaining to the US and other developed countries today. They are intermediate between the currently lower death rates for women and higher death rates for men. As noted in Chapter 3, sex differences in life expectancy rates narrow in the older-age intervals, and vary across social and historical contexts.

There is one more point to make. As we have seen, reducing the infant mortality rate has an enormous impact on average life expectancy at birth, an effect that dwarfs improvements at other age intervals. To further illustrate this relationship, we will compare the moderate-infant-mortality population to one in which improvements are made in other age groups than 0–1, whose death rate we will hold constant at 5%. For the age groups until 50 years, death rates are reduced by 25 to 50%. For older age groups, death rates are lower but closer to those of the sample population with a moderate infant mortality rate.

TABLE A.6 Period table for a city of 300,000 with a low infant mortality rate

Age interval	n *at beginning*	n *deaths*	*Proportion deceased*	n *at beginning of interval*	n *deaths in interval*	*Person-years in interval*	*Cumulative person-years*	*Life expectancy*
0–1y	3000	18	0.00600	100000	600	99460	7767419	77.7
1–5y	12000	14	0.00117	99400	116	397426	7667959	77.1
5–10y	15000	11	0.00073	99284	72	496238	7270533	73.2
10–15y	17000	20	0.00118	99211	117	495762	6774295	68.3
15–20y	18000	40	0.00222	99094	220	494920	6278533	63.4
20–25y	22000	78	0.00355	98874	351	493492	5783613	58.5
25–30y	21000	75	0.00357	98523	352	491735	5290121	53.7
30–35y	20000	96	0.00480	98171	471	489678	4798386	48.9
35–40y	21000	152	0.00724	97700	707	486732	4308708	44.1
40–45y	22000	240	0.01091	96993	1058	482320	3821976	39.4
45–50y	23000	368	0.01600	95935	1535	475838	3339656	34.8
50–55y	25000	560	0.02240	94400	2115	466712	2863818	30.3
55–60y	22000	780	0.03545	92285	3272	453248	2397106	26.0
60–65y	16000	930	0.05812	89014	5173	432135	1943858	21.8
65–70y	11000	990	0.09000	83840	7546	400338	1511723	18.0
70–75y	9000	1170	0.13000	76295	9918	356678	1111385	14.6
75–80y	7000	1440	0.20571	66376	13654	297745	754707	11.4
80–85y	6000	1900	0.31667	52722	16695	221872	456962	8.7
85–90y	4000	1830	0.45750	36027	16482	138928	235090	6.5
90–95y	3000	1825	0.60833	19544	11889	67998	96162	4.9
95–100y	2000	1476	0.73800	7655	5649	24152	28164	3.7
100+	1000	1000	1	2006	2006	4012	4012	2.0
Total	**300000**	**15013**		**0**	**100000**			

TABLE A.7 Cohort table for moderate-infant-mortality population with improvements at intervals other than 0–1 years

Age interval	n *at beginning of interval*	n *deaths*	*Age*	*Person-years*	*Proportion deceased*	n *at beginning of interval*	n *deaths in interval*	*Person-years in interval*	*Cumulative person-years*	*Life expectancy*
0–1y	850	42	0.1	4.2	0.04941	100000	4941			**77.7**
1–5y	808	6	2.5	15	0.00743	95059	706			
5–10y	802	2	7.5	15	0.00249	94353				
10–15y	800	4	12.5	50	0.00500					
15–20y	796	12	17.5	210	0.01508					
20–25y	784	20	22.5	450	0.02551					
25–30y	764	22	27.5	605	0.02880					
30–35y	742	34	32.5	1105	0.04582					
35–40y	708	38	37.5	1425	0.05367					
40–45y	670	42	42.5	1785	0.06269					
45–50y	628	52	47.5	2470	0.08280					
50–55y	576	62	52.5	3255	0.10764					
55–60y	514	73	57.5	4197.5	0.14202					
60–65y	441	77	62.5	4812.5	0.17460					
65–70y	364	70	67.5	4725	0.19231					
70–75y	294	58	72.5	4205	0.19728					
75–80y	236	56	77.5	4340	0.23729					
80–85y	180	60	82.5	4950	0.33333					
85–90y	120	58	87.5	5075	0.48333					
90–95y	62	39	92.5	3607.5	0.62903					
95–100y	23	17	97.5	1657.5	0.73913					
100+	6	6	102	612	1.00000					
Total	**0**	**850**		**49571.2**						
Average age at death				**58.3**						

Table A.7 shows that, with improvements in death rates after age 1, the increase in average age at death (in other words, life expectancy at birth) is less than 4 years, from 54.8 to 58.3. The columns on the right for person-years and average life expectancy have been left blank, in case readers would like to calculate them on their own. The result for life expectancy at birth is 58.3 years.

In all the scenarios above, there is a range of ages in the population. Higher average life expectancy does not mean that people will live longer, but rather that a larger proportion of people reaches old age. Low life expectancy rates do not express a situation in which everyone drops dead before they turn 30 or 40. Rather, infant mortality rates are high, which indicates poorer living conditions. If the infant mortality rate is high, then the person-years lived in all subsequent intervals is much lower, since the base population declines rapidly at the beginning. If the infant mortality rate is lower, more of the initial cohort of 100,000 is still alive in subsequent intervals. The average remaining lifetime at birth therefore is much higher since all those numbers add up to a larger total.

Table A.7 above shows that changing the mortality rates at older ages raises life expectancy at birth relatively little compared to changing infant mortality rates. In other words, rates of life expectancy at birth are affected far less by eliminating causes of death that affect people in older age than ones which affect infants and children, such as nutritional stress, accidents, and infectious diseases. As noted in Chapter 3, death rates at older ages are less sensitive to environmental, behavioral, and medical conditions compared to death rates at younger ages.

Table A.8 compares the age-specific death rates in each scenario described above. It shows that death rates increase with each age interval after 5–10 years,

TABLE A.8 Comparison of death rates of four cohorts and one city population

Age interval	*Cohort A: moderate mortality*	*Cohort A: with improved mortality rates after age 1*	*Cohort B: high mortality*	*Cohort C: low mortality*	*City: low mortality*
0–1y	0.04941	0.04941	0.27059	0.00588	0.00600
1–5y	0.00990	0.00743	0.05806	0.00118	0.00117
5–10y	0.00500	0.00249	0.02911	0.00000	0.00073
10–15y	0.01005	0.00500	0.03175	0.00118	0.00118
15–20y	0.01904	0.01508	0.04007	0.00237	0.00222
20–25y	0.03493	0.02551	0.04744	0.00357	0.00355
25–30y	0.03887	0.02880	0.05179	0.00358	0.00357
30–35y	0.06276	0.04582	0.06303	0.00479	0.00480
35–40y	0.07143	0.05367	0.08072	0.00722	0.00724
40–45y	0.08974	0.06269	0.10000	0.01091	0.01091
45–50y	0.10211	0.08280	0.12195	0.01593	0.01600
50–55y	0.12549	0.10764	0.14506	0.02242	0.02240

(Continued)

TABLE A.8 (Continued)

Age interval	*Cohort A: moderate mortality*	*Cohort A: with improved mortality rates after age 1*	*Cohort B: high mortality*	*Cohort C: low mortality*	*City: low mortality*
55–60y	0.14798	0.14202	0.17329	0.03567	0.03545
60–65y	0.17895	0.17460	0.20961	0.05812	0.05812
65–70y	0.19872	0.19231	0.22099	0.08976	0.09000
70–75y	0.20000	0.19728	0.24113	0.13097	0.13000
75–80y	0.24000	0.23729	0.26168	0.20567	0.20571
80–85y	0.33553	0.33333	0.36709	0.31696	0.31667
85–90y	0.48515	0.48333	0.52000	0.45752	0.45750
90–95y	0.63462	0.62903	0.66667	0.60843	0.60833
95–100y	0.73684	0.73913	0.75000	0.73846	0.73800
100+	1.00000	1.00000	1.00000	1.00000	1

which is what actually happens in real populations. In addition, death rates across the board are lower in a population with low infant mortality rates than one with moderate or high infant mortality rates. Finally, at older ages the rates converge, whereas in the younger age categories the rates vary more widely.

INDEX

ABO blood groups 110, 128
addiction 143, 144n12, 278
Adler, S. 119
Afar Depression 32
African Americans 88, 129, 144n4, 177
aggression 26, 42, 111, 142–3, 151, 157, 206, 219, 226, 228, 249–50, 264, 266, 272, 276; male-male 153; non- 261n2; physical 235–6, 243, 245, 264, 277, 282; sexual 186
Agta 26–7, 179, 195, 243, 266
Ahima, R. S. 121
alcohol 68, 87, 90, 106, 120, 143, 233, 259, 260, 278
allergies 85, 88–9, 97n7, 119
alloparenting 41–2
Alzheimer's disease 36, 91, 93, 102, 115, 117–18, 137
American Heart Association 109
anatomy 137; behavior shapes 33; brain 131–2, 194, 197, 213; cerebral 203; predator 26; reproductive 144
Andaman Islands 253, 266
Andeans 82–3, 162, 173
androgen insensitivity syndromes 138
androgens 140–1, 157–8, 281
anemia, iron-deficiency 55, 57, 79, 81, 91, 191
anemia, sickle cell *see* sickle cell anemia
animal tissues 26, 32, 37, 40
anthropophagy 220–1, 223, 238n1–2, 245, 267
Arapesh 151–2
asexual reproduction 137–8
Ashraf, Q. 9
asthma 78, 88–9, 113
australopithecines 26, 29, 31–2, 40, 42, 49, 153, 168, 245
Australopithecus afarensis 32, 35, 153

baboons 154, 166, 226, 228
Bacon, F. 15
bacteria 53, 75, 87, 92, 111, 166; anaerobic 54; *Bifidobacterium longum biovar infantis* 89–90; *Clostridium difficile* 68; commensal 89; gut 89; *Escherichia coli* 91; *Helicobacter* 89; mycobacteria 84, 89; *Pseudomonas aeruginosa* 91; salmonella 56, 84; *Shigella* 91; staphylococcus 54, 57, 68, 90–1; streptococcus 57, 68, 91; *Streptococcus pneumonia* 91; streptomyces 56, 64; treponemes 55, 57
Barí 174
Batak Agta 243, 266
bejel 55, 57
Betsileo 178, 187
BiDil 130
bilateral kinship 152, 251, 282
birth rates 41, 47, 59, 61–7, 294
blood pressure 37, 85, 102, 105, 113, 118, 129, 231, 233; anxiety 208; high 19, 104–5, 110, 129, 234
Blumenbach, J. 129
Boas, F. 126, 131, 175
body odor 165

body size 32, 213 brain, human 35–6; female 153; gorillas 155; primates 169
bonobo 9, 31, 42, 106, 154–5, 160, 226–8, 238, 281; sexual and social behavior 169n4
brain 8–10, 15, 18, 38–9, 94, 131–2, 150, 160, 194–5, 199, 213, 220–1, 254; activity 208; ape 35; archaic *Homo sapiens* 33, 35; *Australopithecus sediba* 32; cholesterol 111; cortisol 208; cultural environment 201–2; development 125, 132, 134–7, 140, 142, 197, 203, 281; dopamine 142–3; food 105; gender 126, 134, 197; genetics 82; glucose 110; *Homo erectus* 35; *Homo habilis* 35; hominid 26, 33, 35; hormones 158; humans 36, 40–1, 51, 125, 132; infectious diseases 134; intelligence 134; large 33, 35, 37, 42–3; left- 203; love 165; mental disorders 134; motivation-and-reward system 159; mutations 131; Neandertal 36–7; neurotransmitters 142; non-human primates 36; plasticity 203; pleasure centers 208, 233; primates 35; proteins 95; remodeling 132; sex and violence processing 248; sex differences 197; size 29, 32, 35–7, 40–2, 44n4, 126, 132–5, 144n7; social hierarchies 250–1; Sudden Unexplained Nocturnal Death Syndrome 119; testosterone 157–8; -to-behavior causal relationships 195; use 133, 135; visual attractions 165
breastfeeding 41–2, 56, 59, 101–2, 121n1, 164, 222
breasts and waists 165, 169n6
brideprice/bridewealth 177
Brøgger, J. 187
Buss, D. 158–9, 163, 209

Cahokia 58
Campbell, J. K. 184
cannibalism *see* anthropophagy
capital punishment 244, 246, 257, 261n1
carbohydrates 8, 37, 90, 102, 105, 107–11, 113–14, 121n6
Cassell, J. 150–2
Çatalhöyük 53
cave paintings 39
Cenozoic Era 31
cephalic index 126
Chagas disease 93
Chagnon, N. 9, 223–4
child abuse 190, 248
childbirth 40, 44n6, 56, 65, 82, 88, 158, 167, 173, 178
child selection 14
chimpanzees 31–2, 35, 37–8, 41–2, 154–6, 166, 226–9; diet 106–7; digestive problems 106; testes volume 169n2; violence 9, 225, 281
cholesterol 111–15, 140
chronic diseases 8, 47, 55, 61, 64, 68, 93, 102–5, 107, 109, 115, 117, 121
CIA 13
climatic shift 35
Clinton, B. 5
Clovis 34
College Board 211
Collier, J. 188
color preferences 16, 230
competitiveness 182, 210
Conant, Abbie 18
congenital adrenal hyperplasia 138, 141
cooking 8, 37, 110, 244
cooling system 28, 32
cooperative parenting 41, 172
Cordain, L. 121n6

dairying/herding 55, 76, 78, 90, 107, 110–12
Davis, L. J. 128
Dawkins, R. 4
dementia 114, 118, 137
Denisovans 34, 84
diabetes 78, 100–1, 118, 233; drugs 70n12; mellitus 102; Type I 89; Type II 102
Diamond, J. 51, 70n3, 269
Dickson's Mounds 56, 58
dietary intakes 90, 114, 121n4
diffusion tensor imaging 136
dirt, consumption of 88–9, 97n7
divination 120, 167, 201
DNA 4–5, 7, 11–13, 34, 75, 84, 93–6, 107, 116, 119, 228, 234; mitochondrial 95, 130–1, 137
dopamine 142–3, 208, 228, 233, 248; -mediated pathway 105, 158
dowry 177, 184, 222
Driver, H. 267
Duffy antigen 84
Dugum Dani 271

economic inequality 69
economic transitions since Neolithic Revolution 47–69
egalitarianism 8, 24, 51, 179–80, 236, 238, 247, 253, 257–8, 260, 268, 277, 282; gender 29, 180, 183–4
Einstein, A. 134
Eleanor of Aquitaine 49
El-Hemmeh 52
Eliot, L. 202–4
Ember, C. R. 266–7, 273

Ember, M. 266–7, 273
emotional expression 204–5, 231
empathy 157, 206, 219–39, 276, 282
Enga 269–70, 277–8
epigenetic marks 75, 95–6, 97n10, 130, 144
evolution 3–20, 27, 29, 42, 104, 109–10, 114, 128, 131–2, 134, 137, 149, 153, 155, 157, 159, 161–3, 165–8, 173, 175, 194–6, 220, 223, 226, 229, 233, 248, 261, 275, 281, 283; childbirth 44; grandparenthood 44n9; hominid 35, 43n3; lactose tolerance 78; political 274; *see also* co-evolution of human anatomy and sociality; human evolution
Ewald, P. W. 92–3

fat, dietary 110–11, 113–14
fathers 43, 157–8, 166, 174–6, 179, 184, 186, 190, 196, 198, 223, 249
fiber, dietary 89, 102, 108, 110, 112, 136
firearms 52, 141, 269–70
fire 33, 37, 52, 253; campfires 37; statuettes 167
firewood 103, 196, 259, 265
First World War 16, 66, 133
5-alpha-reductase deficiency syndrome 138
food production 36–7, 63, 100, 151, 172, 174, 176, 181–2, 184–5, 221, 242, 254, 257, 273–4, 282
Food and Nutrition Board of the Institute of Medicine 109
foragers 24, 26–9, 35, 39, 43, 57–8, 100–3, 106, 251; Aché 51; Agta 26–7, 179, 195, 243, 266; Ainu 181; Aka 27, 173, 179; Au and Gnau 232, 252; birth and death rates 61; Central African forests 85; complex 265, 272; conflict resolution 282; contemporary 103, 108, 166–7, 196; contemporary nomadic 56; Efe 42; equestrian 256, 266; exercise 103; fat eaten 107; fiber intake 108; Gana 253–4; infectious diseases 54; inland 108; Inuit 113, 181, 243, 266, 279; Ju/'hoansi 87, 108, 252–3; #Kade San 108; Mbuti 28, 177, 179, 195, 243–4, 247; Neolithic 55; Netsilik 244, 279; nomadic 59, 223, 251, 265, 272–3, 282; Paleolithic 53, 109; population density 272; preagricultural 53–4; prehistoric 103, 166; pre-Neolithic 265; serum cholesterol levels 111–2; settled 26, 251, 266; Sudan 265; Upper Paleolithic 252
Fore 152, 220
Frederick II 49
French Revolution 274
Friedl, E. 179–81
fructose 110–11
Fry, D. P. 224, 236, 243, 249–50, 266–7, 276, 279, 283n2
Fukuyama, F. 274
Fulani 76, 84

Gajdusek, D. C. 220
Gal, D. 159
Galor, O. 9
Gates, H. L. 8
Geertz, C. 237
Geller, P. L. 167–8
gender and sexuality 194–213
gender differences 16, 134–6, 150, 159, 162–4, 194–6, 203–5, 207–10, 257
gender egalitarianism 29, 180, 183–4
gender inequality/stratification 19, 161–2, 166, 172–3, 177, 179, 181–2, 187, 206, 209–11, 224, 247–8, 253–4, 259, 274, 282
Gene by Gene 12
generosity 282
genetic determinism 6–7, 12–14
genetic essentialism 4–5, 11
genetic manipulation 20n4, 228
Genetics and Public Policy Center 13
genetic testing 13, 115, 117
gene variant 5–6, 8–9, 83, 117, 127, 131
genome sequencing 4–5
ghrelin 89, 114
Gibbs, J. 278
Gilmore, D. 187
glucose 104, 110–11
Goodall, J. 225
gorillas 31, 41–2, 106, 154, 226–7; testes 155, 169n2
Gould, S. J. 133
grandmothers 43
grandparents 42, 44n9, 49
greed 10, 253, 264, 282
growth 14, 33, 82, 85–6, 102, 110, 209; growth (physical) 14, 55, 57–8, 78, 85–6, 96, 97n6, 101–2, 106, 115, 134, 140, 153, 157–8, 174, 191, 202–3; growth factors/hormones 102, 110, 113; growth standards 86; stature 14, 33, 55, 58, 82, 85–86, 97n6, 102–3, 113, 133–5, 153–5, 209, 212–3
G-6-PD deficiency 81, 127
Gutmann, M. C. 188, 250

Hadza 28, 108, 180, 266
Hallan Çemi 52
Hammurabi 49
Han Chinese 82
Handwerker, W. P. 248–9
Hansen's disease (leprosy) 57–8, 84, 89
harassment, sexual 212

Hardin Village 58
Hart, D. 26, 43n3, 261n3
Hawthorne Effect 231
health transitions since Neolithic Revolution 47–69
Heise, L. 247–8
herding 24, 52, 56, 175, 183–4, 247, 260
Hibbing, J. R. 6
Hidatsa 175, 195
hierarchy 9, 19, 23, 150, 154, 219–20, 224, 227–9, 233, 235, 238, 242, 250, 253, 283; political 181
high altitude 82–3, 96n3
high blood glucose 102
high blood pressure 19, 104–5, 110, 129, 234
high-density lipoprotein particles (HDL) 111–13; very- 111
hijras 201
Hittites 186
Hmong 119
Hoebel, E. A. 181
Holocaust 11
Holocene 31
homicides 141, 224, 229, 243–7, 261, 264, 269, 275, 281–2
Homo 26, 29, 32–3, 40–2, 153; *antecessor* 33; *erectus* 31, 33–8, 42, 83, 245; *denisova* 34; *ergaster* 33; *floresiensis* 34; *habilis* 33, 35; *heidelbergensis* 33, 38; *mauritanicus* 33; *naledi* 32; *neanderthalensis* 31, 43; *pylori* 89; *rudolfensis* 33; *sapiens* 33–6, 38–9, 43, 83; *soloensis* 33
honor and shame ideology 185–9, 249
Hopi 195, 221
Hrdy, S. B. 41
human evolution 23, 26–7, 43, 105, 126, 164, 169n6, 219, 264, 274, 282; blood and milk 75–96
human genome 5, 11, 75, 94
Human Genome Project 4
human leukocyte antigens (HLAs) 84
human variation 125, 127–9, 131, 144n1
hunting 8, 10, 16, 24, 26–9, 41, 52, 108, 149, 163, 166–7, 173–4, 179–81, 183, 191, 194–7, 225, 244, 252, 259, 277, 279; large-game 26, 43, 172; Neolithic 29; rules 261n6
hypothalamus 105, 140, 142, 158

Ice Age 29, 51, 108; Great 31
Idols of the Mind 15
Igbo 177
imaging technologies 9, 116; computed tomography (CT) 116; diffusion tensor imaging 136; magnetic resonance imaging 116, 135
immunization 84, 233
Indian Knoll 58
indigenous peoples 23, 54, 102, 106, 113, 127, 132, 162, 167, 173–5, 178, 224, 244, 256; Andeans 173; Baffin Island 197; homicide 246; Siberians 83–4; South American 182; Tahitians 247; warfare 268–9
individualism 4, 163
Industrial Revolution 59, 63, 92, 127
inequality 8, 12, 68, 100, 183, 204, 211, 219, 236, 242, 258, 260–1; economic 69; gender 19, 161–2, 166, 172, 177, 179, 181, 187, 206, 209–11, 248, 253–4, 259, 274; social 93, 130, 179, 235, 238; socioeconomic 56, 68, 184, 235, 264, 283; stress 234
infanticide 65, 67, 181, 222–3, 279
infectious diseases 47, 54–9, 62, 64–5, 68, 78, 84–5, 90, 92–3, 96n5, 100, 106, 134, 138, 153, 198, 257
intelligence testing 133, 144n6
intergroup conflict 266, 274, 281
interpersonal conflict 152, 243–4, 253, 258, 279–80, 282
interpersonal violence 43, 47, 242, 247, 261, 261n2, 264, 270
intersex conditions 139, 199–201, 213n2
Inuit 113, 181, 243, 266, 279
Iron Age 31
irritable bowel syndrome 120

Jackson, D. 18
Jeffries, L. 8
Joel, D. 135–6
Jolly, A. 169n2
Ju/'hoansi 28, 51, 87, 108, 180, 243–4, 246–7, 252–3, 266

#Kade San 108
Kahn, G. 12
Kamayur 276
Klinefelter syndrome 138–9
Konyak Nagas 182
Korwa 258–9
Kottak, C.P. 187
Kuhnen, C. 9–10
Kuikuru 243, 276
Kwakiutl 175, 256

lactose tolerance/intolerance 76, 78
Lahn, B. 8
language 5, 15–16, 37–8, 43, 53, 64, 120, 129, 132, 149–50, 152, 204, 229, 231,

237–8, 252, 276, 277; color perception 20n5; gendered nouns 17
Lazar, M. A. 121
LDL *see* low-density lipoproteins
Lee, R. 244–6, 252–3
Lévi-Strauss, C. 182
Lewontin, R. 128
life expectancy 7, 29, 47–51, 54, 58, 61, 65, 68–9, 100, 235–6
life span 7, 23, 42–3, 44n8, 47, 49, 69
Lindenbaum, S. 220
lipoprotein 93 *see also* high-density lipoproteins and low-density lipoproteins
Lock, M. 120
Lombroso, C. 126
Lombrosianism 11
Lovedu 176–7
low-density lipoproteins (LDL) 111–13; very- 111
Lowie, R. H. 175
Lynn, R. 10

major histocompatibility complex (MHC) 84, 165
malaria 54–5, 68, 70n6, 75, 79, 81, 84, 91–2, 96n2, 127, 129
male-male competition 42, 153–4, 229
male provisioning 165, 167–8, 172, 177, 179, 185
Mandino, H. I. 269
Mapuche 85, 155
Marmot, M. G. 234
marriage 48, 65–8, 151, 153, 162, 175–7, 179, 184–6, 188–9, 190, 222, 244, 255, 271, 277, 279; age 161; alliances 187; arranged 161, 200; cross-cousin 180, 260; endogamous 127; exogamous 269; "ghost" 174; intermarriage 252; intertribal 268; Korwa 259; plural 29, 177–8, 180
Martin, E. 190
Martin, M. K. 191n2
Masai 195, 205
Mathias, E. 279
matrilineal kinship 176, 183
Mayans 85, 87
Mbuti 28, 177, 179, 195, 243–4, 247
Mead, M. 151–2
Mehinaku 276–7
melanin 8, 85
menopause 86–7, 101
menstruation 86–7, 101, 158, 173, 180, 186
Mesolithic age 31
metabolic syndrome 105, 109
metalworking 31
MHC *see* major histocompatibility complex
Middle Stone Age *see* Mesolithic age
Mischel, W. 236–7
mitochondrial DNA 95, 130–1, 137
molds 55, 89
Money, J. 199
Montagu, A. 133
Morgan, L. H. 175
mortality: agriculturalists 58, 191; bicycling 105; "breadwinner effect" 191; breast cancer 117; child 58, 191, 257; China 67; decline 64, 66–7; drinkers 106; employment grade 234; England and Wales 64; Europe 59; females 137; infant 49–51, 56, 58–9, 67, 161, 191, 248–9, 257; living conditions 238; long-term relationships 233; lower classes 258; males 64–5, 137, 181; maternal 56, 59, 61, 65; physical activity 104, 114; rates 42, 44n8, 47, 49–51, 59, 63–9, 100, 104; rise 69; second transition 64; sex differences 144n8; social integration 233; socioeconomic inequality 235; stress 234
Mosuo/Musuo/Na 176
Mother Goddess 53
mothers 16, 40–3, 55–6, 88, 101, 105, 126, 158, 190, 198, 223; Andes 83; bonding 222; bonobos 227; Brazil 222; chimpanzees 154, 226; clan 12; foraging 166, 184; hunting 173; love 238n3; matrifocal societies 177; multiple 174, 178–9; non-working 191; nursing 103; stress 96, 234; Tibetan 83; wealthy 222; *see also* breastfeeding; childbirth
Mueller, J. 18
multiple parentage (multiple paternity, multiple maternity) 174
Mundugumor 151
Mundy, L. 10
Munich Philharmonic Orchestra 18
Murdock, G. P. 109, 272–3
Muslims 175–6

Native Americans 12, 28, 68, 127, 180, 195, 200–1, 267–8
Nayar/nair 178
Neolithic Revolution 31, 47–69, 107, 264, 272
Nesse, R. 235
net hunting 28, 179, 244
Netsilik 244, 279
Ngogo 225–6
NIDDM *see* non-insulin-dependent diabetes mellitus
Nolan, P. D. 273

nonhuman primates 15, 26, 32, 36, 40–1, 49, 79; comparison with human 31–43, 126
non-insulin-dependent diabetes mellitus (NIDDM) 101–3, 105–6, 110
Nootka 175
Nuer 174, 177
Nuremberg Code 11
nutritional deficiency diseases (including pellagra, scurvy, protein-energy malnutrition) 55, 57 58

Old Stone era *see* Paleolithic era
Old World Monkeys 31
oppositions 19, 174, 187; symbolic 20n6
Organization for Economic Development 210
Otterbein, C. 267
Otterbein, K. 267
overdiagnosis 116–17, 121, 121n7
overweight/obesity 8, 68, 85, 89–90, 97n7, 101, 103–5, 107, 110–11, 114–15, 117, 212, 233–5
oxidation (oxidants, antioxidants) 81, 107
oxytocin 140, 158, 230

Paleolithic era 29, 51, 53, 103, 109, 167, 265, 272, 282
Paleolithic lifestyle 8
Paranthropus 32, 35
parenting 149, 157–8, 168, 173, 176, 213, 228–9, 248; alloparenting 41–2; collaborative 138; cooperative 41, 172
paternal care 9, 40–2, 154, 158
patrilineal kinship 12, 152, 169, 172–3, 175–7, 183–6, 190–1, 223, 248, 254, 257, 274, 282
Pawnee 195
peaceful societies 243–5, 268, 282
penis 140–1, 199
"Personalized" medicine 130
Plasmodium 90–2; *falciparum* 79, 84, 92; *malariae* 55; *vivax* 54, 84, 92
Pleistocene Epoch 31
plow-based agriculture 174–5, 184–5, 190
polyandry 154, 178, 279
polygyny 176–8, 180–1, 254
polyunsaturated fatty acids (PUFAs) 112–13
Presidential Commission for the Study of Bioethical Issues 20n3
Polynesians 258, 267
pregnancy 27, 82–3, 86, 88, 96, 101–2, 141, 156, 160, 165, 174, 188, 191, 222, 234, 236, 247–8
preventive health 100–21
Programme for International Student Assessment (PISA) 210–11
prolactin 42, 140, 158
protein 55–6, 89, 93–5, 102, 105, 107–10, 112, 114, 116, 121n6, 253; animal 27, 36–7, 166, 181; excessive 26; high- 37; milk 78; regulatory 84; serum 128
PUFAs *see* polyunsaturated fatty acids
Pupu, N. 270
Pygmalion Effect 231

Quaternary (Fourth) Period of Cenozoic Era 31
Quechua people 82

racial ideologies 125–6
rape 186, 229, 236, 248; wartime 261n5
reciprocity 24, 183, 219, 230, 242, 252, 255, 262n8
Reimer, D. 199
reindeer 183, 259–60
religious beliefs 184–5, 192n4, 276
religious cargo system 260–1, 262n9
reproduction 6, 13–14, 47, 66, 106, 137–8, 149, 153, 160–1, 167–8, 229
reproductive senescence 43, 66
Retzius, A. 126
Richard III 4
rock carvings 39
Roman Empire 7, 48, 256
Rosenthal Effect 231
roulette study 9, 159–60
Rubin, J. Z. 197–8
Rushton, J. P. 10

Sahlins, M. 20n1, 51, 256
Saint Anthony's Fire 55
Salish 175, 256
Sarakatsani 184
"savage races" 126
Scarry, E. 275
Schell, H. 159
Scheper-Hughes, N. 222
Schneider, J. 66, 186
Schneider, P. 66
Second World War 11, 61, 281
sedentary lifestyle 100–1
self-effacement 134, 206, 237, 282–3
self-knowledge 13, 131
self-objectification 206, 213n4
Semai 182, 236, 243, 246–7, 266, 278
sense of touch 18
sex and gender 167, 194–213

sexual activity 65, 140, 157–8, 160–1
sexual differentiation 18, 42, 125, 134–8, 140–1, 143, 144nn8–9, 144n11, 149–51, 155, 197, 199, 213, 281; biological 205; visual ability 169n7
sexual harassment 212
sickle cell anemia 79, 117, 119, 127
skin color 126, 129
sleep 37, 41, 101, 104, 143, 154, 157, 274; REM 119
social inequality 93, 130, 179, 235, 238
sociality 36–7, 195, 202
socioeconomic inequality 56, 68, 184, 235, 264, 283
Soffer, O. 28
sperm competition 155, 169
Standard Cross-Cultural Sample 267, 272
stateless societies 271–2, 283n5
stereotypes 18–19, 163, 195, 198, 202, 206–8, 213; gender 17, 136, 197, 205, 210–12
Sudden Infant Death Syndrome 101
Sudden Unexplained Nocturnal Death Syndrome 119
Sussman, R. 26, 43n3, 261n3
sweat glands 32, 39, 83
Swyer syndrome 138
syphilis 55, 64, 129

Tchambuli 151
teeth 26, 29, 32, 36, 39, 54, 57, 102, 113, 116; dental conditions and diseases (human) 26, 29, 32–3, 36–7, 39, 220, 231; dental conditions and diseases 54, 57–8, 102, 113
Tell Sabi Abyad 76
telomeres 115, 234
testosterone 42, 134, 137, 139–42, 156–8, 202
thalassemias 81, 127
Theodora 49
Theodoric 49
Tibetans 82–3, 178
Tierney, P. 224
Tiwi 26, 177, 180, 266
Tlingit 175
Tolai 155
triglycerides 105, 107, 111–13
Trobriand Islands 162, 174, 255
Tsimane' 232, 260
Tsimishian 175
tuberculosis 54–5, 57–8, 64, 68, 78, 84, 89
Turner syndrome 138
two-spirit 200–1

Upper Paleolithic 28, 31, 39, 252
US Food and Drug Administration 129–30

vasopressin 5–6, 142, 158, 228
Venus figurines 167
verbal dueling 187, 279, 283n6
verbal skills 135, 205
Vienna Philharmonic Orchestra 17–18
virginity 153, 162, 186, 188, 200
viruses 54, 68, 84, 89, 91, 93
vision 102, 121n1, 135, 194, 203–5
visuo-spatial skills *see* vision
Vlachs 184
von den Steinen, K. 276

war: and peace 264–83; *see also* First World War; Second World War
Ward, M. C. 182
weaving 28, 168
Wemp, D. 269
Whiting, B. B. 204
Whiting, J. W. 204
WHO *see* World Health Organization
Wiessner, P. 270–1
Wilson, E. O. 229
Women's Health Initiative 137
World Health Organization (WHO) 86, 121n2
Wright, Q. 267
Wu (emperor) 49

X chromosome 81, 95, 137, 139–40, 142

Yanomami 9, 223–4, 281
Yawari 277
Y chromosome 131, 137, 139, 197
Yerkes, R. 133
Young, A. 200

zadruga 175–6
Zen meditation 132
Zimbardo, P. G. 251
Zwane, A. P. 10